THE FABULOUS LIFE OF
DIEGO RIVERA

THE FABULOUS LIFE OF

Also by Bertram D. Wolfe

A Life in Two Centuries, 1979
An Ideology in Power, 1969
The Bridge and the Abyss: The Troubled Friendship of Maxim Gorky and V.I. Lenin, 1967
Lenin and the Origins of Totalitarianism, 1966
Strange Communists I have Known, 1965
Marxism: One Hundred Years in the Life of a Doctrine, 1964
The Fabulous Life of Diego Rivera, 1963
Rosa Luxemburg and the Russian Revolution, 1961
Communist Totalitarianism, 1961
Six Keys to the Soviet System, 1956
Khruschev and Stalin's Ghost, 1956
Three Who Made a Revolution, 1948
Mundo sin Muerte, 1942
Diego Rivera: His Life and Times, 1939
Keep America Out of War, 1939 (with Norman M. Thomas)
Civil War in Spain, 1937 (with Norman M. Thomas)
Portrait of Mexico, 1937
Portrait of America, 1934 (with Diego Rivera)
El Romance Tradicional en Mexico, 1925 (with Diego Rivera)

DIEGO RIVERA

by BERTRAM D. WOLFE

Scarborough House/*Publishers*

Scarborough House
Lanham, MD 20706

FIRST SCARBOROUGH HOUSE PAPERBACK EDITION 1990
Second printing 1992

The Fabulous Life of Diego Rivera was originally published in paperback by Stein and Day/*Publishers* in 1969.

Text designed by David Miller

Library of Congress Cataloging-in-Publication Data

Wolfe, Bertram David, 1896-1977.
The fabulous life of Diego Rivera / by Bertram D. Wolfe. -- 1st Scarborough House pbk. ed.
p. cm.
Reprint. Originally published: New York : Stein and Day, 1963.
Includes bibliographical references.
ISBN 0-8128-1259-X :
1. Rivera, Diego, 1886-1957. 2. Painters--Mexico--Biography.
I. Title.
ND259.R5W56 1990
759.972--dc20
[B] 90-8256
CIP

to E. G. W.
companion of my Mexican journeys

TABLE OF CONTENTS

NOTES ON ILLUSTRATIONS

Following Page 42

1. Diego's Parents on Their Wedding Day.
   Photo V. Contreras, Guanajuato.
2. Diego at the Age of Three.
   Photo V. Contreras.
3. The Little Engineer. 1890.
   Photo V. Contreras.
4. As an Art Student in Madrid. 1909.
5. Landscape by José M. Velasco. 1898.
   Oil on canvas. Collection Salo Hale, Mexico. Photo Kahlo, Mexico.
6. Citlapetl (Peak of Orizaba). 1906.
   Oil on canvas, 10 x 18 in. Frida Kahlo Memorial Museum.

7, 8. The End of the World.
   Engraved on zinc cuts by Jose Guadalupe Posada to illustrate a popular broadsheet ballad (corrido).

9. Portrait of Rivera by Leopold Gottlieb. Probably 1918.
   Collection of Dr. Troche, Paris.
10. Portrait of Rivera by Modigliani. Probably 1914.
    Oil on canvas, 100 x 81 cm. Museum of Art, Saõ Paolo, Brazil. Photo Marc Vaux, Paris.
11. Bust of Rivera by Adam Fischer. 1918.
    Stone, height 80 cm.
12. Self Portrait. 1918.
    Pencil. Collection Carl Zigrosser, Philadelphia. Photo Soichi Sunami, New York.
13. The House over the Bridge. 1908. (?)
    Oil on canvas, 1.08 x 1.45 m. Museo Nacional de Arte Moderno, Mexico.
14. Streets of Avila. 1908.
    Oil on canvas, 1.40 x 1.28 m. Museo Nacional de Arte Moderno, Mexico.
15. Portrait of a Spaniard. 1912.
    Oil on canvas.
16. Paisaje Zapatista. 1915.
    Oil on canvas, 1.44 x 1.23 m. Collection Marte R. Gómez, Mexico.
17. Portrait of Angelina. 1917.
    Oil on canvas. Collection Leonce Rosenberg, Paris.
18. Portrait of Angelina ("The Woman in Green"). 1917.
    Oil on canvas, 1.29 x .89 m. Collection Alvar Carillo Gil, Mexico.
19. Portrait of Angelina. 1918 (?).
    Oil on canvas. From a poor photograph.
20. Portrait of Angelina and the Child Diego ("Maternity"). 1917.
    Oil on canvas, 1.30 x .81 m. Collection Alvar Carrillo Gil, Mexico.
21. Adoration of the Shepherds. 1912-13.
    Wax on canvas. Collection, Guadalupe Marín, Mexico.

22. Two Women. 1914.
    Oil on canvas. Photo Peter A. Juley. Courtesy Museum of Modern Art, New York.
23. The Alarm Clock. 1914.
    Oil on canvas, 63 x 145 cm. Frida Kahlo Memorial Museum.
24. Landscape, Majorca. 1914.
    Oil on canvas, 1.09 x .898 m. Collection Guadalupe Marín, Mexico.
25. Man with Cigarette (Portrait of the Sculptor, Elie Indenbaum). 1913.
    Oil on canvas, 82 x 72 cm. Collection Salomón Hale, Mexico.
26. The Architect (Portrait of Jesús Acevedo). 1915.
    Oil on canvas, 1.43 x 1.13 m. Museo Nacional de Artes Plásticas, Mexico.
27. Portrait of Martín Luís Guzmán. 1915.
    Oil on canvas, 71 x 58 cm. Collection Martín Luís Guzmán, Mexico.
28. Portrait of Ramón Gómez de la Serna. 1915.
    Oil on canvas. Collection Ramón Gómez de la Serna, Buenos Aires.
29. Still Life. 1916.
    Oil on canvas, 55 x 46 cm. Private Collection.
30. Still Life. 1917.
    Oil on canvas, 1.15 x .89 m. Collection Weyhe Gallery, New York.
31. Eiffel Tower. 1916.
    Oil on canvas, 1.15 x .89 m. Weyhe Gallery, New York.
32. The Telegraph Pole. 1917 (?).
    Oil on canvas, 1 x .80 m. Courtesy Leonce Rosenberg, Paris.
33. Portrait of Maximilien Volochine. 1917.
    Oil on canvas, 1.10 x .90 m. Courtesy Leonce Rosenberg.

34. The Painter in Repose. 1916.
    Oil on canvas, 1.27 x .96 m. Courtesy Leonce Rosenberg.
35. Still Life. 1916.
    Oil on canvas.
36. Still Life. 1916.
    Oil on canvas.
37. Marika at Seventeen.
    Photograph supplied by Rivera as "a picture of my daughter, Marika."
38. Diego and his Mexican Daughters. 1929.
39. Edge of the Forest, Piquey. 1918.
    Oil on canvas, 65 x 82 cm. Collection, Salomón Hale, Mexico.
40. The Aqueduct. 1918.
    Oil on canvas, 65 x 54 cm. Collection Weyhe Gallery. Photo Soichi Sunami.

Following Page 106

41. Still Life. 1918.
    Pencil, 17 x 13 in. Private Collection. Photo Juley, courtesy Museum of Modern Art, New York.
42. Horse's Head. 1923.
    Pencil, 13⅛ x 8½ in. Private Collection, New York. Photo Juley, courtesy Museum of Modern Art, New York.
43. Portrait of Elie Faure. 1918.
    Oil on canvas, 48 x 35 in. Private collection, Paris. Photo Juley, courtesy Museum of Modern Art.
44. The Operation. 1920.
    Oil on canvas, 18 x 24 in. Collection, Dr. Jesús Marín, Mexico.
45. The Operation. 1925.
    Fresco, monochrome pseudo-relief. Secretariat of Education, Mexico.

46. Standing Figure. 1920.
Pencil, 12 x 8¾ in. Frida Kahlo Memorial Museum, Coyoacán. Photo Juley, courtesy Museum of Modern Art, New York.
47. Italian Girl. 1921.
Pencil, 23 x 18 in. Collection Paul J. Sachs, Cambridge, Mass.
48. Creation. 1922.
Encaustic. 109.64 square meters. National Preparatory School, Mexico. Photo Alvarez Bravo, Mexico.
49. Head. 1922.
Sanguine. Study for "Music" in the Preparatory Mural. Photo Juley, courtesy Museum of Modern Art, New York.
50. Head. 1922.
Sanguine. Study for "Faith." Photo Lupercio, courtesy Museum of Modern Art.
51. "Woman." 1922.
Detail, Preparatory Mural. Photo Alvarez Bravo, Mexico.
52. View of Frescoes and Architecture, Section of the Court of Labor, Secretariat of Education, Mexico.* Photo Tina Modotti.
53. Top Floor, Court of the Fiestas, Education Building.
Frescoes in ballad series shown in relation to architecture. Photo Tina Modotti.
54. El Trapiche (The Sugar Mill). 1923.
Fresco. Court of Labor. Education Building. Photo Lupercio.
55. The Embrace. 1923.
Fresco. Court of Labor. Photo Lupercio.
56. Weaving. 1923.
Fresco. Court of Labor. Photo Lupercio.

* The total surface covered by Rivera's fresco paintings in the Secretariat of Education consists of 1,585.14 square meters or 17,062.43 square feet.

57. Care for a National Treasure. Secretariat of Education during the period when Rivera's work was threatened with destruction. Photo Tina Modotti.
58. Awaiting the Harvest. 1923.
    Fresco. Court of Labor, Secretariat of Education. Photo Lupercio.
59. Foundry. 1923.
    Fresco. Court of Labor. Photo Lupercio.
60. Industry Serves the Peasant. 1926.
    Fresco from the "Ballad of the Bourgeois Revolution" Series. Top floor, Secretariat of Education.

61 to 64. Guadalupe Marín. Photos by Edward Weston.

65. Reclining Nude. 1925.
    Charcoal study, 19 x 24½ in., for Chapingo. Model Guadalupe Marín. Collection Museum of Modern Art. Photo Juley.
66. The Fecund Earth. 1926.*
    Fresco, front wall of Chapingo Agricultural School Chapel, showing part of ceiling and side walls and nature of architecture. Surrounding the Earth are figures representing Air, Fire, Water, Electricity and Chemistry at the service of man.

Following Page 170

67. Portrait of Guadalupe Marín. 1926.
    Wax on canvas, 65 x 20 cm. Collection Jackson Cole Phillips, New York. Photo Tina Modotti.
68. Sketch on Canvas for Portrait of Guadalupe. 1938.
69. Portrait of Guadalupe Marín. 1938.
    Oil on canvas, 1.212 x 1.61 m. Collection Guadalupe Marín, Mexico.
70. Guadalupe and Ruth in the Rivera Home. 1926.
    Photograph, Foto Mantel, Mexico.

* The total painted surface of the Chapingo frescoes is 708.52 square meters.

71. Guadalupe Marín Carrying the Head of Jorge Cuesta. 1937.
    Drawing for Cover of Guadalupe's Novel, *La Unica.*
72. Portrait of Ruth Rivera. 1949.
    Oil on Canvas, 1.99 x 1.05 m. Collection Ruth Rivera Marín, Mexico.
73. Germination. 1925.
    Detail from Chapingo Chapel, Right Wall. Photo Tina Modotti.
74. The Earth Oppressed. 1925.
    Detail, Chapingo.
75. Distribution of the Land. 1926.
    Detail above Stairway, Chapingo.
76. Bad Government. 1926.
    Detail, Chapingo.
77. Night of the Rich. 1926.
    Ballad Series, Top Floor, Secretariat of Education. Detail showing the Head of Rockefeller.
78. Night of the Poor. 1926.
    Ballad Series, Top Floor, Secretariat of Education.
79. Hands. 1926.
    Detail from Fresco, "Taking over the Factory," Ballad Series, Education Building.
80. The Architect. Self Portrait. 1926.
    Detail from Head of Stairway, Education Building.
81. Red Cavalry. 1928.
    Watercolor. This and the next three plates are reproductions of water color sketches from a notebook of 45 sketches made on May Day in Moscow. The photos are by Tina Modotti. Collection Museum of Modern Art, New York, donated by Mrs. John D. Rockefeller, Jr.
82. Red Horsemen. 1928.
83. Red Army Formation. 1928.
84. Red Army Truck. 1928.

85. May Day in Moscow. 1928.
    Oil on canvas. Collection Moisés Sainz, Mexico.
86. Children Playing in Snow. 1927.
    Oil on canvas (Moscow, Winter 1927).
87. Sawing Rails. 1927.
    Pencil, Moscow. Photo Schneider and Boehm, Munich, courtesy Museum of Modern Art, New York.
88. Communards. 1928.
    Color cartoon in tempera for cover of *Krasnaya Niva*. Collection Dr. Hubert Herring, New York. Photo Tina Modotti.
89. Frida at Thirteen.
    Photo Kahlo.
90. Frida and the Author's Wife.
    Photo Lucienne Bloch.
91. Frida in 1939.
    Photo Nikolas Muray, New York.
92. Frida and Diego. 1931.
93. Frida Distributes Arms. 1927.
    Ballad of the Proletarian Revolution, Top Floor, Secretariat of Education.
94. Frida and Cristina. 1935.
    National Palace Mural.
95. Frida Kahlo. Self-Portrait. 1939.
    Oil on Gesso. Photo Nikolas Muray, New York.
96. Knowledge. 1928.
    Fresco in Health Building.*
97. Continence. 1928.
    Fresco in Health Building.
98. Frida and Guadalupe. 1934.
    Photo Lucienne Bloch.
99. Portrait of Guadalupe Marín by Frida Kahlo. 1932.
    Oil on canvas.

* The total painted surface in the Health Building is 111.53 square meters. In addition, Rivera did four stained glass windows.

* The National Palace Stairway and Corridors were painted with interruptions during the years 1929 to 1945. The total painted surface is 362.38 square meters.

** The total painted surface of the Cuernavaca frescoes is 146.60 square meters.

114. Diego Painting in Detroit. 1933.
115. The Belt Conveyor. 1933.*
    Fresco in Detroit Institute of Fine Arts Patio, showing architectural detail.
116. Vaccination ("The Holy Family"). Detroit. 1933.
117. Turbine.
    Detail, West Wall, Detroit.
118. Portrait of Edsel Ford. 1932.
    Oil on canvas. Background a blueprint of a then unissued new Ford model. Collection Edsel Ford.

Following Page 298

119. Diego at Work in Detroit (after losing over 100 pounds, cf. Plate 114).
120. Lucienne Bloch and Steve Dmitroff, Assistants to Rivera in Detroit and New York.
121. Portrait of the Author. Radio City, 1933 (Subsequently destroyed).
122. Sketch of the Author. 1933.
    On rough coat at New Workers School.
123. Resurrected Radio City Mural in Palace of Fine Arts, Mexico City. Detail, Center of Fresco.**
124. Imperialism. 1933.
    Wall Sketch, New Workers School. Plates 124-128, Photo Peter A. Juley, New York.***
125. Imperialism. 1933.
    Fresco panel, New Workers School.
126. Civil War (In foreground John Brown and J. P. Morgan the elder). 1933.
    Fresco panel, New Workers School.

* The total painted surface in the Courtyard of the Detroit Institute of Fine Arts is 433.68 square meters.

** The total painted surface of the resurrected mural is 55.53 square meters. That of the original fresco in Radio City was 99.5 square meters.

*** Total painted surface, 28.64 square meters.

127. The First International. 1933.
Fresco panel, New Workers School.
128. Communist Unity (Showing "Stalin the Executioner of the Revolution," Marx, Lenin, Engels, Trotsky and other Communist Leaders). 1933.
Fresco panel, New Workers School.
129. The Bandit Hero. 1936.
Detail, Carnival Series, Hotel Reforma. (One of four fresco panels, the painted surface of each being 6.19 square meters, the total of the four, 24.76 square meters.)
130. General Porkbarrel Dancing with Miss Mexico. 1936.
Detail, Carnival Series, Hotel Reforma.
131. Loading Burro. 1936.
Chinese ink, Collection Edward G. Robinson, Hollywood, California.
132. Woman with Bowl. 1936.
Chinese ink.
133. Burden bearer. 1936.
Chinese ink.
134. Basket Vendors, Amecameca. 1934.
Watercolor. Collection Mr. and Mrs. Karl A. Wittfogel, New York.
135. Mother and Children. 1934.
Watercolor on canvas, 48 x 622 cm. Collection, Oscar Atkinson, Los Gatos, California.
136. Dawn. Illustration for *Popol Vuh*. 1931.
Watercolor. Collection John Dunbar, New York.
137. Pineapple Man. Design for costume for Ballet, *H P.* 1931.
Private Collection, New York.
138. Banana Man. Same. 1931.
139. Portrait of Roberto Rosales. 1930.
Wax on canvas. Collection Edward Warburg, New York.

140. Girl in Checked Dress. 1930.
Oil on canvas. Private Collection, New York.

141. Sleep. 1936.
Watercolor on canvas.

142. Landscape near Taxco. 1937.
Oil on canvas. Collection Edward G. Robinson, Hollywood, California.

143. Vegetable Vendor. 1935.
Watercolor on canvas. Collection Marc Khinoy, Philadelphia.

144. The Assassination of Altamirano. 1936.
Tempera on masonite. Collection Edward G. Robinson, Hollywood, California.

145. The Burning of Judas. 1937.
Chinese ink.

146. Landscape, Sonora. 1931.
Wax on canvas.

147. Sketch for a Landscape. 1944.
Pencil, 38 x 26.5 cm. Frida Kahlo Memorial Museum.

Following Page 362

148. Day of the Dead. 1934.
Oil on masonite. Collection Museo Nacional de Arte Moderno.

149. The Indian City (Mexico City before the Conquest), 1945.
Fresco detail, National Palace Corridor, Courtesy Visual Arts Section, Pan American Union.

150. El Comalero. 1947.
Oil on canvas. Courtesy Mrs. Florence Arquin, Chicago, Illinois.

151. Portrait of Dolores del Rio. 1938.
Oil on canvas 1 x .65 m. Collection Dolores del Rio, New York.

THE FABULOUS LIFE OF
DIEGO RIVERA

INTRODUCTION

This is my second attempt to put Diego Rivera into a book. My first life of the painter was completed in 1939 when he was at the height of his powers. My second is being published a quarter of a century later and six years after his death.

I met Diego in 1922. He had just returned from a decade and a half in Europe to a Mexico plowed up by twelve turbulent years of formless uprisings. In 1922, as in 1910, it could be said only that "the Revolution was promises."

Diego returned with a predisposition to believe in the Revolution and its promises. He brought back an undigested mixture of Spanish anarchism, Russian terrorism, Soviet Marxism, Mexican agrarianism, and Paris studio revolutions. He also brought back with him a highly sophisticated technique and sensibility, memories of a thousand great works he had seen in the cathedrals, palaces, and galleries of Europe, love for his native land, a determination to build his art on a fusion of his Paris sophistication with the plastic heritage of his people, and to paint for them on public walls. When I got to know him, he was beginning the first of those walls.

In this book I have tried to keep a distance from the man

with whom I had so long an intimacy, in order to get a fresh perspective on the legendary figure and on the artist who has made so large an impact upon the painting of his time. I have tried to keep in their proper proportions absurdity and seriousness, weakness and strength, *farsante* and genius. At the outset, however, I should put the reader on notice that I owe Diego a great debt, for it was through his eyes that I first learned to see the visible world somewhat as artists see it, and to perceive Mexico's landscapes, people, and history as a succession of "Riveras." Through his eyes and from his lips I got my first view of the painting of others, the art of distant times and places, the isms of the Paris he had just left, the wonders he had seen in wanderings through Italy, Spain, and the Low Countries, the painters he had known, the esthetic theories which had formed the subject of so many controversies. It was in his company that I first met his fellow artists. It was a spark from his sensibility that gave me fresh delight in the folk arts of Mexico, which I already knew and loved, and in the stirring but hitherto inscrutable pre-Conquest sculpture. Though in time I learned to see independently and often to differ with his esthetic judgments, not to mention his judgments in other fields, it was a priceless gift to have had my vision and sensibility enriched by the contagion of his enthusiasms.

Our association lasted over three decades, during which I made more than one attempt to set down on paper aspects of his work and views. In 1923 I wrote what was probably the first article on the Mexican artistic awakening to be published north of the Rio Grande. Rivera occupied the central place. In 1934 I did a book with him on his paintings in the United States, entitled *Portrait of America.* Today I do not think too well of the *Portrait,* for which I gave him much of the iconographic material and "intellectual" briefing. In any case, he knew his own country better and more deeply than ours, and did much better work on the walls of public buildings in Mexico than any he did in the United States.

In 1936 I did a second book with Diego, dealing with his own country: *Portrait of Mexico.* His vision was truer, and for my part, I had learned, I think, something more of the arts of writing and historiography. Moreover, for better or worse, I had become more independent of Diego's overpowering mind and his way of seeing his country and the world. Both of us were more pleased with our second book than with the first.

In 1939 I wrote a biography entitled *Diego Rivera: His Life and Times.* It was an "authorized" biography, in the sense that Diego opened his files and papers to me, answered all questions (often leaving me more bewildered on hearing the answer), and gave me the addresses of his sister, relatives, and friends, and innumerable photographs of his work. He did not see a word of it, however, until it was in print. Then it both infuriated and pleased him. Thereafter he referred to me in interviews as "my biographer," continuing to make available to me, directly or through his wife Frida, accounts of new adventures, photographs of new paintings, clippings, and other materials. I saved what I received, but as a writer I thought I was through with Rivera. Three books with and about him were enough; this giant of a man would surely outlive me and go on painting and adventuring into old age; moreover, I had become increasingly engrossed in Russian historiography, a subject too large for any man.

In 1947 I wrote a monograph on Diego Rivera at the request of the Pan-American Union. In 1954, when he rejoined the Communist Party after years of guerrilla war, I did his political profile in an article entitled "The Strange Case of Diego Rivera." Through mutual friends he continued to send me messages, clippings, and photographs. When he was dictating material for his intended autobiography to Gladys March (published posthumously without his final revison), he still referred to me as "my biographer," drew freely on passages from my book of 1939, pointing out only one secondary disagreement with what I had written.

A number of things have combined to impel me to write this second life of Diego Rivera. First is the fact that several publishers had suggested I consider reprinting the 1939 life, long unavailable. I took a fresh look at the book I had written more than two decades earlier and was not pleased with the style of the man who had written it, nor with his judgments on art, politics, Mexico, and Rivera's painting.

In 1939, moreover, when I completed his life, the painter had before him eighteen more years of amazing productivity and no less amazing adventures, political, artistic, and personal. In 1957 he died, so that the tale of his life was told.

Even in 1939, when I was looking at my biography's newly printed pages, I had the uneasy feeling that in some ways Diego had escaped me. His words were there, his theories on art and politics, his deeds, a goodly number of reproductions of his work, the factual scaffold, and some of the color of his life. But one dimension in particular I felt I had communicated only inadequately: the dimension which finds expression in the title of this second life, in the word *fabulous*.

Diego's person and bulk were fabulous. His life was fabulous, his accounts of his life more fabulous still. His fecundity as an artist was fabulous, too. His talk, theories, anecdotes, adventures, and his successive retellings of them, were an endless labyrinth of fables. His paintings on the walls of public buildings in Mexico are one long, beguiling fable concerning his world, his time, his country, its past, present, and future.

The tall tales for which Diego was famous, improvised effortlessly as a spider spins his web, their pattern changing with each retelling, were fables wrapped in fables, woven so skillfully out of truth and fantasy that one thread could not be distinguished from the other, told with such artistry that they compelled the momentary suspension of disbelief. If Diego Rivera had never touched brush on wall or canvas, merely talked and had his talk set down, Baron Münchausen would have to look to his reputation.

To be sure, this was hard on his would-be biographers, hard, too, on the young woman who tried to take it all down as "autobiography," especially since he made a number of novel alterations in his accounts calculated to offend and shock her young womanhood. But this is no different from his usual procedure: he seemed always to be probing the cherished beliefs and point of tolerance of his listener. If it was a congress of archaeologists, he was ready to give an incredible account of the pre-Conquest sculptures and ceramics he had collected, calculated to offend their sense of the seriousness of their science. When Leon Trotsky was his honored guest, he drove the old man into such a towering rage by outrageous inventions of "facts" and doctrines in the field of politics that the argument ended with Trotsky and his wife packing their bags and leaving their goods on the sidewalk until they could find a new refuge. Those who sought to discuss matters with him seriously, or question him in order to write about him, were likely to end up speechless with wrath, stalking off offended in their inmost being because he seemed to take neither them nor truth seriously.

If I managed to enjoy a friendship with him for over three decades, it was not because I did not take truth seriously, but because I took Rivera seriously as a creative artist, regarding his wild fantasy and fertile invention as an essential, if sometimes upsetting, aspect of his overflowing creativity and character as artist and man. His life as he recounted it was by no means the least interesting of his works of art, though it had greater formlessness than his more carefully composed images on canvas and wall.

If Diego rarely told the simple truth, he did not tell simple lies either. His tall tales could be outrageous, but they were never told merely to deceive or gain advantage. They were art for art's sake, not for profit or self-serving.

No matter how impassive I would keep my face, Diego must have seen unbelief in my eyes. Indeed, it was hard to say whether or how long he himself believed what he was saying.

But he was always bent on telling his tale with such skill, with such a show of frankness and taken-for-granted assent, with a knowing wraith of a smile and snorts of certitude, with such elaborate underpinning of supporting detail, that one found it hard not to become an accomplice, hard not to act as though both speaker and listener believed.

Diego counted on his listener's politeness as much as his credulity. Who could be so discourteous, who so foolish and dully matter-of-fact, as to disbelieve such attractive, exciting, baroquely designed, richly detailed, marvelously verisimilar yet preposterous stories, told while the painter smiled and snorted, his bulging eyes fastened directly upon one's own? Was it not clear that the teller had no practical purpose nor mean calculation? What he got out of it was what he got out of painting: the shock and wonder of the beholder, the joy of making things live, the sense of mastery which comes from creating a world of his own where such things could be.

The pleasure of creation, he seemed to feel, should evoke the pleasure of appreciation . . . or at least momentary suspension of doubt. Like Frida Kahlo, the being who was closest to him, I learned to marvel at and enjoy this side of his artistry, to listen with inward laughter, sharing the smothered amusement in Frida's eyes if we happened to be listening together. Though I tried hard to put this on paper in the life I did in 1939, I knew I had not altogether succeeded. In trying again, I have begun with the very title.

There was much in my earlier life of Diego which was satisfactory, and I have done my best to plagiarize what I could from the biographer of that remoter day. But alas, I had used too many adjectives for my present taste. Too many of the things I thought I knew, weren't so. In the end I found it necessary to modify every sentence, except those containing quotations from others, then to rewrite one section after another, alter judgments, revise appraisals, re-examine old controversies, make good injustices, do what I hope is a better and a fairer book. And, of course, I had now to examine the works and deeds of Diego's life from 1939 to 1957. Seventeen years had elapsed from the day I met Diego to the day I published the first life. Eighteen more elapsed between the day I ended the first biography and the day death wrote *finis* to Diego's fabulous career.

As a typical example of a re-examined controversy, there is the "Battle of Rockefeller Center." When I wrote that chapter, I was too close to the battle, in which I had been a combatant on Rivera's side, and in which my own portrait was one of the casualties when the painting was ground off Radio City's walls. Now the dust of the destroyed mural has subsided. I have reviewed the record afresh, pondered a discussion between Diego's assistant, Lucienne Bloch, and the former Mrs. Nelson Rockefeller, re-examined the letters exchanged between Diego Rivera, Frances Flynn Paine, Raymond Hood, and Nelson Rockefeller, looked again at the various preliminary sketches and verbal description submitted by the painter to the patron and his architect. Neither painter nor patron comes out now completely unscathed, but the new account, I am sure, is closer to the truth.

Or to take a more personal episode: when Diego married Frida, I asked him about his divorce from Lupe. "I was never married to Lupe," he answered. When I interviewed Lupe, she told me: "We were wed in church." Perhaps because he thought a religious wedding unworthy of a Communist painter, Diego's comment was: "I did not go to church with Lupe. She took somebody as a proxy." Since it did not occur to me to doubt this, it was thus that I set it down, whereupon Guadalupe Marín was deeply aggrieved. On this and other matters she brought suit for libel. She did not fare well in the suit, yet in its course I began to think that I had been taken in by Diego's proxy story. Research for the present volume showed me that Diego Rivera, in June 1922, personally entered the Church of San Miguel in Lupe's native city of Guadalajara and signed the marriage register in his own unmistakable hand. I regret that Lupe's feelings were hurt and here correct the error. Whereupon I ask myself: Are there other such errors in this book? Surely there must be. Hence, here, in the introduction, I post the notice: *Caveat lector!* For those who skip introductions, I have posted the same notice on an early page of the opening chapter.

It is impossible to record here by name all those to whom I owe a debt of gratitude for photographs, anecdotes, information, insights, criticisms of my earlier work. Rivera usually sent me photographs of his new paintings without any notation of the photographer's name. All the museums which contain work of the painter, all the art libraries, from that of the Museum of Modern Art in New York to those of the University of California in Berkeley and Davis, and the Department of Plastic Arts of the Institute of Fine Arts of Mexico, have been most generous with reproductions and other help, as have many individual collectors who have taken the trouble to have photographs made of works hanging on their walls.

I have a special debt to acknowledge to José Gómez Sicre, who is Director of the Division of Visual Arts of the Pan-American Union, to Concha Romero James of the Hispanic Foundation of the Library of Congress, to Dr. William Valentiner and Dr. Edgar P. Richardson of the Detroit Institute of Arts, to Carl Zigrosser, to the Weyhe Gallery, and to Alberto Mizrachi, of the Central Art Galleries of Mexico City.

I am grateful to Jean Charlot for a reassuring letter, unsolicited, to the effect that I have dealt fairly and justly with him and with the other painters who were Diego's associates and sometime rivals and competitors. I am indebted for information to Juan O'Gorman, the painter-architect; to Lucienne Bloch and Stephen Dimitroff, his former assistants, who are today fresco painters in their own right; to the late Walter Pach, who gave unfailing help and advice.

Rivera's four wives, Angelina Beloff, Guadalupe Marín, Frida

Kahlo, and Emma Hurtado, were generous with information, answers to questions, photographs of works in their possession. To the late Frida Kahlo my debt is immeasurable, for she understood Diego and his art as no one else did, and for many years she was unstinting in her efforts to communicate to me that understanding.

I derived some insights into the subject matter of modern painting from Meyer Schapiro, whose course of lectures I attended while working on the earlier version of this book. I owe an especially deep debt to the French critic Elie Faure, author of *Spirit of the Forms*. Already bedridden by a bad heart when I visited him in Paris in the thirties, Dr. Faure spent long hours propped up on his pillow day after day, discussing matters of esthetics, art movements prior to 1914, and Rivera's Paris days and paintings. Others who contributed material on Diego's life in Europe include André Lhote, André Salmon, René Huyghe, Charles Peguin, Mme. Elie Faure, Mme. René Paresce, the art dealer Léonce Rosenberg, the late Miguel Covarrubias, and Germán Cueto. Florence Arquin, who is herself doing a book on Rivera, was kind enough to send me photographs of some of his paintings from her personal collection. To all these and many more I owe a debt. But of course none of them can be held responsible for anything said in *The Fabulous Life of Diego Rivera.* Even Diego, except for the direct quotations, must be exonerated from any responsibility for such defects as this book may contain.

Bertram D. Wolfe

1. SILVER AND DREAMS

Guanajuato is flooded with light. The sun beats down with brilliant intensity upon its flat-roofed houses, fills with purple darkness their windows and doorways, gives bulk to solid forms, draws clean the line that separates surrounding hills from light-drenched sky. The valley in which the city dozes is seven thousand feet above the sea. Narrow cobblestone streets circle through the old center, then begin to climb into the hills. At the outskirts trees become discouraged; ridges rise bare and brown into a sky deep, remote, free from haze, standing out sharp against the light-filled emptiness of space.

He whose eyes have been nourished on these clear forms, solid volumes, and light-filled space will never be altogether at home in the pale yellow sunlight and soft outlines of Paris treetops and towers, where the light is diffused by haze that forever hints of rain. A boy born here may get lost for a while in the Paris fashions of his day and experiment inadequately with fugitive flecks of light and blurring washes of haze in which outlines waver, planes merge, and objects lose their volume; but he can never really find himself as a painter until he has rediscovered the strongly defined forms, pure colors, clear atmosphere, and omnipresent flood of light that gives solidity to all the objects it illumines without seeming itself to appear upon the scene at all.

The mother veins of silver that made Mexico the treasure house of the world run almost uniformly from northeast to southwest. Nowhere do they run thicker or deeper than here, where tunnels sink often to depths of over a thousand feet. Today the city which once supported the magnificence of the house of Count Rul has grown sad and sleepy. No new house of consequence has been built here for over fifty years. Yet there is enough silver in the adobe of the abandoned dwellings baked from the waste mud of a richer day to suggest the re-mining of the dwelling walls. There is silver in the granite bowels of the hills, silver in the soil, silver in the walls, silver in the dreams of the inhabitants.

Saturday night, October 7, 1882. Saturday nights are a little gayer than other nights, with singing of ballads in dim-lighted *pulquerías* to the sweeping of fingers over mournful strings. Señor Diego Rivera, handsome, huge-bodied, black-bearded bachelor school teacher, thirty-four, was to be married that night to María del Pilar Barrientos, little more than half his size and twelve years his junior, daughter of Juan B. Barrientos, telegrapher and mine-operator of Spanish extraction, deceased, and of Nemesia Rodríguez de Barrientos, his widow, native of Salamanca, Guanajuato, of mixed Spanish and Indian blood.* (See PLATE 1).

---

* In 1952 Rivera said to an audience in Mexico City that his ancestry was "Spanish, Dutch, Portuguese, Italian, Russian and—I am proud to say—Jewish." That same year he told a Jewish reporter that he was "three-eighths Jewish," his paternal grandfather being Anastasio de la Rivera Sforza, son of an Italian Jew born in Petrograd, and his great-grandmother on that side Chinese. He told another audience of having witnessed an experiment in which a "distinguished Soviet scientist . . . produced a pure white from the

The pair was regarded as well matched, both of respected but now fatherless families whose fortunes had declined. The groom had known poverty since his father, Anastasio Rivera, had died, overwhelmed with debts from a struggle with a caved-in mine. Born in Spain, the latter was successively a merchant in Cuba, mine owner, soldier, and revolutionist in Guanajuato. A man of amazing vigor, at fifty he had married seventeen-year-old Ynez Acosta, Mexican of Portuguese-Jewish descent, and at sixty-two had joined Benito Juárez in his *Guerra de la Reforma,* against the combined forces of the landowner-clerical reaction and the French army under Archduke Maximilian of Austria, Emperor of Mexico. Don Anastasio never returned from the field of war to finish his battle with the caved-in mine. To his young widow he left his debts and the bringing up of their children. She had managed to give Diego senior sufficient education to qualify him as *profesor de primeras letras,* corresponding to primary-school teacher in the United States. Now, after twenty years of widowhood, she rejoiced to see her son marrying the daughter of her friend, the widow Nemesia Rodríguez de Barrientos, pious woman of like age with herself, owner of a little *dulces* shop opened after the death of her husband, to support herself and two daughters in honorable poverty.

The discrepancy in the age of groom and bride did not bother the bride's mother, nor the poverty of her son-in-law, who was a man of talent and ambition. If she worried on this joyous occasion, it was because of a strain of liberalism in her son-in-law's blood. His father had been a Masonic official whose death had been a wicked one, fighting with Juárez against the Holy Mother Church. The young school teacher was a

---

ninth generation of crossings between Negroes and Mongols" (*The Compass,* New York, March 9, 1952, Magazine Section p. 10). For each would-be biographer he rattled the dice of his ancestry afresh, ending by telling his "autobiographer," that his mother "passed on to me the traits of three races: white, red, and black" (*My Art, My Life* [New York, Citadel Press, 1960], p. 18). I have followed the parental marriage license in which none of these interesting permutations shows up.

Mason too. He consorted with freethinkers and atheists, having the "Jacobin" druggist Leal and the "positivist" engineer Lozano as witnesses at the wedding! She suppressed her fears as she thought on her widow's estate and her other daughter, Cesaría, withering into elderly virginity.

Wednesday night, December 8, 1886. The city of Guanajuato was celebrating the festival of the Conception. The Church of San Diego on the Plaza was crowded with black-veiled kneeling women. The lesser church, where Nuestra Señora de Guanajuato is housed, was aglow with tapers lighted by the faithful, where the sterile mingled the prescribed prayers with beseechings that they might conceive. Don Diego's elderly, virginal sister-in-law, Doña Cesaría, was not praying for the unsealing of her womb, but invoking the Virgin's blessing on her sister María, pregnant for the fourth time in as many years, that she might have better luck than on the preceding occasions.

All day Doña Cesaría fluttered around the vicinity of the Plaza. From her sister's home at 80 Pocitos Street to the apothecary's for gauze, cotton batting, disinfectants; to the doctor's to say María's pains had begun; to the churches she passed on her errands—it took just a moment to light an extra taper, invoke another saint, run through another prayer. Then back to the little house on Pocitos Street where her sister lay, and the bearded school teacher Don Diego, a municipal councilor now, paced restlessly up and down, pausing to converse in whispers with his friend the doctor, or gently teasing his wife in the intervals between her pains about buying her another doll since she seemed incapable of giving birth to a live baby. Three such toy children he had bought her, partly because she seemed but a child, partly to tease and console her for three stillbirths, chiefly to make her feel that he himself did not hold against her his continued childlessness.

The past four years had not been unfruitful in other respects. He had got the Liberal nomination for city councilor under conditions assuring his election. The Governor had made him a rural school inspector. His head was full of schemes for the "redemption" of the Indian peons by rural education, which was to bring nourishment to body and spirit.

That very year he had purchased some mining rights; not with money, but with notes that were to weigh with a lengthening chain for years to come. On his desk was an unpaid bill from Ponciano Aguilar, mining engineer, dated July 5, 1886, for the survey and assay of ores in Los Locos, La Trinidad, and Mina de Jesús y María—the Madmen, the Trinity, and the Mine of Jesus and Mary. If the Madmen or the Trinity should begin to pay now . . . if his rural school plan should be adopted . . . if the Liberal program should be converted from promissory notes to achievements . . . if he should rise in political life to a place where he could really expedite social reform . . . if he should get the money to start the liberal paper of which he dreamed . . . if María would give birth to a living son—silver, social reform, a career, a son—bright dreams blended with the thoughts of his wife on her bed of labor.

A hush in the house; he had heard it three times before. Was that a baby's wail? Cesaría stood in the doorway, her face wreathed in radiance.

"Is it alive?"

"They're both alive."

"Both?" That meant mother and child! "A boy?"

"Two! Two boys, two *hombres,* two sons, both, both alive. Two little baby boys!"

"Which came first?" asked Don Diego. "He shall be called Diego after me."

"I promised the Virgin," said his wife weakly, "that I would name it after her. Today is her day and María de la Concepción is their saint. *Both* of them should bear her name."

Eleven days later the twins were recorded in the civil register as Diego María Rivera and Carlos María Rivera. But their mother and their aunt Cesaría, aided by a great-aunt Vicenta and a pious wet nurse Antonia, bore the children afterwards to Our Lady of Guanajuato. There the elder was baptized Diego María de la Concepción Juan Nepomuceno Estanislao de la Rivera y Barrientos Acosta y Rodriguez.* The younger, Carlos, was to die in his second year. The elder was to become a world-famous painter, signing his canvases and murals, not with all the names his mother had showered upon him, but "Diego María Rivera" until his father's death, thereafter simply "Diego Rivera."

* I have not seen the baptism certificate, but the name was thus given to me by the painter. Throughout this work, where no other source is given, the source is usually Rivera. Whether we take his accounts literally or not, they always represent some image of himself and some reworking of liberal fact by his boundless creative fantasy. In any case, all I can say is, "*Caveat lector!*"

2. THE LITTLE ATHEIST

In his third year Diego became Guanajuato's "wonder child." Photographs reveal him as an erect little lad in skirts, with a forehead too wide and high for his face, a sturdy body, tiny feet, unexpectedly prominent and expressive-looking hands (PLATE 2). He began to walk earlier than most and to talk in ample paragraphs, arguing parental commands, telling tall tales, causing his pious mother and surrounding aunts to lament and his father to admire.

Almost before he learned to walk or to talk he began to draw. Nothing could keep him from clambering over the furniture to the high-top desk where papers and pencils lay; scrawls and likenesses of the things around him were on bills and letters, in account books, on walls. "The earliest memory I have," he once wrote, "is that I was drawing." As his inches increased, the wall disfigurements rose higher, until his father gave him a room of his own, with walls covered with blackboard as high as he could reach and unlimited crayons, pencils, chalks.

There Diego did his first murals. He spent long hours lying on the floor, surrounded by his drawings: trains, soldiers, animals, mechanical toys, which were his passion, and imagined beings with whom he held converse, for his imagination was preternaturally vivid. The world of his dreams was as real as the world around him. This is a trait that must persist into adulthood if one is to be a creative artist: in every artist, no matter how mature and sophisticated, there remains something always of the unaging child, still marveling at the daily discovery of the wonder and beauty of the world, still eager, as children are, to communicate each discovery.

But it was not his passion for drawing that made little Diego Guanajuato's wonder child, but his precocious "Jacobinism." In his fourth year, according to his sister María, who had the story from his Aunt Vicenta, in his third according to him, the future artist and revolutionist launched upon his career as an atheist.

Diego's father was away on one of his periodic journeys on horseback to distant villages. It was some holy day—there are so many in Mexico—his great-aunt Vicenta took the boy walking past the shrines that knew her footsteps so well. It occurred to her to initiate him into the mysteries of Holy Mother Church.

"Look, Dieguito, kneel to Our Lady and pray that she bring your father safely home, guard your mother's health, and lead you on the path of righteousness."

"What for, Totota?" ("Totota" was his pet name for her.) "Don't you see that this Lady is like the saints we have at home? Made of wood, Totota. How can they hear what I say? They haven't even holes in their ears."

The good woman was not moved to admiration by the powers of observation which were to be so important to the lad. But she had learned her catechism well, and some echo of the Nicene Creed must have come to her aid: *For the honor which is paid to the image passes to that which the image represents. . . .*

"This Virgin," she said, "is an image of the one in heaven. What you ask of her image, she herself will hear and grant to you."

"That's nonsense. If I take my father's picture and pray to it for a steam engine, do you think it will give me one? He is far away now. Will he hear?"

Worshipers crowded around the pair; Vicenta fled in shame and confusion, dragging the little boy after her.* Clacking tongues spread the tale until it reached the ears of Diego's father and his cronies. Thereafter the youthful Jacobin was admitted into their circle and could sit each evening till bedtime in front of the druggist's or on the favorite park bench of Guanajuato's freethinkers. The youngest Jacobin was a proud recruit as he gravely answered their questions concerning his views, teased the locomotive engineers into promising him rides in their cabs, listened with child mind filled with confusion at the big thoughts and long words that circled in the tobacco smoke above his head. Till the family left Guanajuato for Mexico City when Diego had attained the age of six, something close to sixty was the average age of his closest associates.

Diego's father dedicated "the little engineer" to Science and Rationalism; he was obviously cut out to be a thinker, inventor, and constructor. But his mother and reinforcements of virginal aunts were beginning to fear that the boy's dedication was to the devil. The impression that there was something monstrous in the bulging-eyed little infant was deepened by an incident attending the birth of his sister María. He was five then, and obsessed by the passion to take things apart, to find out what

* In a late account he told Gladys March that he had climbed up on the steps of the altar and delivered an atheist harangue to the astonished worshipers. It is a better story than he told me. (*My Art, My Life* [New York, Citadel Press, 1960], pp. 23-29).

they were made of and what caused them to function. The news that a baby was coming aroused his curiosity to a fever pitch.

On the day of birth, one of his aunts took him walking through the park to get him out of the way. Feeling that she should be at her sister's bed, "Look, Diego," she told him, "a little brother is coming for you today. I must go home because your mother isn't well. You go to the station to wait for him."

The lad went to the station. He spent hours there, forlorn, forgotten. Few cars laden with ore passed these days; the solitary passenger train was not due till nightfall. He became hungry, ill humored. The sun was setting when the station agent appeared to open up for the evening train. What had happened? the boy demanded. Where was his brother? Why was the train so late on which they were shipping him?

The station agent, a family friend, already had the news. "*Ay, hombre,* I forgot to tell you, your little sister has come. We sent her home some time ago in a beautiful little box."

Mystified by the arrival without visible conveyance and the inexplicable change of sex, the boy set out for home. They took him to his mother's bed where the new-born girl child lay. "How ugly!" said Diego. And then: "Where is the box in which the station agent brought her?"

Anxious aunts ransacked the house. All they could find was a dust-covered shoe box. Diego became thoughtful.

"You have told me many lies," he said. "Now I know that my little sister did not come in a train or in a box. They gave mother an egg, and she warmed it in bed."

The merriment which greeted his *omnes ab ovo* theory caused him to march off to bed in a fury though he had gone without food since morning. A few days later his mother caught him trying to cut open the belly of a living mouse with a kitchen knife, "to find out," he explained, "where little mice come from and how they are made." The shock was too much for her; she was convinced that she had brought a monster into the world.

But his father limited himself to asking whether his desire to understand the mechanism of the animal had been so strong as to make the boy forget the pain caused by cutting it up alive.

"At my father's question," Diego wrote later, "I had a feeling that a dark, indefinite void had opened up in front of me. I felt myself dominated by a deeply perverse but fully inescapable force."*

His father supplied him now with information on sex and birth and showed him books containing anatomical reproductions. Now the boy added drawings of animals and the human figure to his endless pictures of toys and trains. He drew wrecks and collisions, with broken and wounded bodies strewn about the wrecked car. Thus early in life he felt reluctant to draw things the inner structure of which he did not understand. For years, he once told me, he felt unequal to drawing a mountain, until he had mastered the details of geological formation. When he came to the United States to paint murals expressive of American industry and science, he spent many hours in machine shops and laboratories, peering through microscopes and telescopes, studying cells, bacteria, tissue sections, observing the spin of nebulae, watching the movement of machines until he knew the design and function of their mechanism, before he would begin even tentative sketches for the works he did in Detroit and at Rockefeller Center. His youthful investigations into the anatomy of a mouse were the forerunners of a lifelong interest in observation, dissection, and analysis for the sake of his syntheses in paint.

Now something made the father change his mind as to the boy's future. "I was eight when my father found a number of papers I had hidden. I had drawn battle plans on them and notations on planned campaigns. I had cut out five thousand

* *Das Werk Diego Riveras* (Berlin, Neuer Deutsche Verlag, 1928). With a brief autobiographical note by the painter.

soldiers of cardboard* and urged my playmates to acquire similar armies. I organized wars and was able to make powder and simple grenades. The joy of my father when he discovered my new passion was enormous." †

The military career was the great highroad in Mexico, the father mused. His father and grandfather had won honor on the field of battle. He took Diego to military friends: they were as delighted with his military attainments as the Guanajuato Liberals had been with his precocious Jacobinism. General Pedro Hinojoso, an old family friend now Minister of War, promised that he would be admitted to the National Military Academy at thirteen instead of eighteen. Alas for paternal dreams of glory! When Diego entered a military preparatory school in Mexico City at the age of ten, his ardor cooled; his pursuit of a soldier's career lasted about a week. Drill, mechanical discipline—he was never one to take orders—every aspect of life in a military academy he found intolerable. He came home crying, "I won't go back. I hate it! I beg you not to send me back."

This was one of the rare occasions on which he appealed to his mother against his father: the alliance was victorious. Diego's military career ended before it had begun. Only to one still unformulated interest had he not been fickle: whichever "career" he adopted for the moment, his devotion to it had found expression in piles of drawings.

In the interval between dedication to surgery and dedication to military science, the family moved to Mexico City. For the Riveras the change represented defeat. The mines had proved greater consumers of treasure than producers. Their fate was symbolic of the local silver industry: its lode had been worked for four centuries, and shafts had to be sunk deeper and deeper;

* In his posthumously published autobiography they were "Russian soldiers."

† *Das Werk Diego Riveras*, op. cit.

new regions extracted the ore at lower cost. Defeat settled on the treasure city, with growing exacerbation of the social relationships of its people. The Liberalism of the head of the Rivera household became more unpopular with the authorities as it became more popular in its implications. His weekly, *El Democrata,* founded to propagate the cause of "social redemption" through educational reform, called more and more upon Liberals to concern themselves with such illiberal things as the living conditions of the poor. Those who might have been awakened to enthusiastic support by his new views were illiterate; while most "decent folk," as they liked to call themselves, read the modest proposals for reform with distaste. Don Diego waged the unequal battle till newspaper, silver mines, and political hopes crashed about his ears. His wife's health suffered as she worried at his unpopularity with the authorities, his growing radicalism, his increasing ill temper. She pleaded with him to surrender, then took the law into her own hands. When he returned from one of his periodic absences, Don Diego discovered that his wife had sold whatever of his furniture had not previously found its way to the local *monte de piedad* (pawnshop), and set off with her six-year-old son and one-year-old daughter for a "visit" to relatives in Mexico City. Suddenly the city of Mexico began to seem full of promise. Thousands like him were drifting from provincial capitals to the "City of Palaces," which Díaz's centralized rule was soon to build into a city of a million inhabitants. But the boy Diego was for a long time unconsolable.

Mexico City is 7,500 feet above the sea. Its climate, its infertile surrounding mountains, and circumambient light differ little from those of Guanajuato. But the hills are farther away, less friendly and accessible. Streets are in no hurry to climb. Diego missed the locomotives he had ridden on, the mines and miners, his cronies of the Jacobin Club. There were no plants, no animals, no trains to watch and draw. Their new home was smaller, with no place for his "studio." He became ill tempered, quarrelsome. For a year he almost stopped drawing altogether. He was taken seriously ill, first with scarlet fever, then typhoid.

During his illnesses Diego was drawn to his great-aunt Vicenta. She nursed him, told him stories, read to him while he was convalescing. Excited by the new world books opened to him, he requested from Aunt Totota instruction in reading and writing. He began a marvelous journey through his father's library: travel, adventure, social reform, history, biology, chemistry, literary classics. In the history books were wars and battles, and the boy began to draw again, plans, battle scenes, soldier cutouts, with the energy and passion he dedicated to anything that aroused his enthusiasm. It was his father's discovery of these activities which had set him upon the road to becoming a Mexican general.

Aunt Totota offered another attraction: her collection of keepsakes. These were objects of Mexican popular art, of little cost and, to most "decent folk," of less value. But Vicenta possessed a taste which extended beyond the prevailing limitations. The boy spent happy hours playing with handwrought silver jewels, embroideries, ceramic sculptures, tiny wood carvings, little wares of clay and lacquer. He accompanied her to neighborhood churches, where he stood lost in contemplation before votive offerings painted on tin by men of the people to give thanks for some miracle of saintly intervention in the donor's life. His awakening senses stirred to the naïve and expressive paintings of these *retablos,* while Aunt Totota knelt before the gaudy image at the altar and hoped that his rapt expression betokened the beginning of conversion. She had given up attempts to impose her thoughts upon him, while he in turn had lost his hostility to her and was closer to her now than to his mother. As for Aunt Cesaría, that the boy was possessed of a demon had become her settled conviction. She drew in the skirts of her soul as he approached, while fingers twitched with an incipient sign of the cross. After his other relatives had reconciled themselves to a mystified pride in their famous painter, she held the fortress alone, refused to ask for or accept his aid or hospitality, nor would she go to live with his sister. "He is possessed," she told me. "The devil is in him and no good can ever come of him. His sister, too, is excommunicated"—to Aunt Cesaría this was a state of the soul rather than an act of the Church—"for she never goes to Mass and makes money by 'throwing cards' to tell fortunes!"

In 1894 Diego, being then eight, declared that he wanted to go to school. His father had been waiting for that moment, warding off attempts to force him until he should ask. The request settled one controversy, but opened another. The mother favored a school run by the clergy; the father, a secular school and training for the military; the boy wanted to learn "everything," be an engineer, a general, and a painter.

His age worked against the possibility of art or military science, so his mother won out; he went to a school run by the clergy. In 1894 he spent three months in the Colegio del Padre Antonio. A report card for August 1895 shows him a bright pupil in the Colegio Católico Carpantier, "perfect effort and proficiency," several latenesses under "attendance," condemnation with faint praise under the heading of "cleanliness." The habits of coming late, bathing not too frequently or zealously, and dressing carelessly were to remain with him all his life.

A report card, dated December 1896, shows him a pupil in the Liceo Católico Hispano-Mexicano, under the "advocacy" of the Sacred Hearts of Jesus and Mary, where he won first prize in the examinations of the third year. At the end of 1898, less than four years after he first entered school, we find him passing with honors examinations for the completion of his elementary schooling. These examinations were serious, with juries of three Christian fathers examining in each subject. Thereafter he was eligible to enter the National Preparatory School.

To these years belongs a letter (undated) which he wrote to his mother on her birthday, internal evidence suggesting that it was dictated by an aunt or a teacher. Decorated with doves and Spencerian curlecues, or their more elaborate Mexican equivalents, it gave little notion of the unconventional spirit in the process of formation. As his first "literary" effort, and as a key to the "education" to which he was being subjected, it is worth reprinting:

Dear Mamma:

Receive in these badly fashioned lines the affectionate congratulations of your son and the fervent prayers I raise to the Divine Providence that you should be happy and live many years, so that, like the nautical star of the sailors, you may guide me, as well as my sister, on the path of virtue, to escape the stormy shoals of youth and reach the port of true felicity, which is honesty.

Your son, who loves you infinitely,

Diego María Rivera

If it appears from the letter that the boy had lost his precocious "Jacobinism," an anecdote from the same period gives a contrary impression.

Upon entering the first of the Catholic schools, Diego was put into the class in Christian doctrine to prepare for his First Communion. According to his sister, two priests disputed the privilege of instructing this promising youngster in the sacred science. But the successful disputant, one Padre Enrique, soon repented his victory. The pupil was swift to learn; however, each dogmatic declaration of the catechism stirred inquiry. The good father, versed in apologetics, at first enjoyed the childish tests of his skill. But when, on hearing of the sacred mystery of the Immaculate Conception, Diego demanded, "How did the child Jesus leave her body, she being and remaining a virgin?" the Father preferred to conduct the class without the boy who asked such embarrassing questions. Padre Enrique came in person to Diego's mother to tell her to give him religious training at home, where he could not disturb the faith of less tough-textured minds. So ended Diego's instruction in Christian doctrine.

From his sister I derive the following macabre tale. When he was eight and she three, a little brother was born and christened Alfonso. The child was sickly; on the eighth day it died. The body was put in a tiny coffin lined with white satin, surrounded with gardenias and lighted candles, atop the piano, where Diego was accustomed to sit for hours at a time drawing and painting. There Diego found it while the adults were in another room. He and his sister proceeded to "play house" with the waxlike corpse. Their games, beginning in mutual joy, always ended in open warfare. In a few moments María was screaming at the top of her lungs. The sound brought the grown ups into the room to find brother and sister tugging at the dead child! The scandal is still a shuddering memory in the family; to Aunt Cesaría, gruesome confirmation of her hypothesis that "Diego was a devil in the form of a man"—and María not much better.

Years afterward—forty-two, to be exact—when Deputy Altamirano was shot down before our eyes as Diego and I were sitting in the Café Tacuba, I was to observe the same matter-of-factness on Rivera's part in the presence of death. His first impulse had been to draw his pistol and intervene, but I thrust him backward from the line of possible cross fire. When it became clear that the body slumped against the wall had suffered immediate death, Diego became calm, except for eager protruding eyes, drinking in, memorizing, fixing forever each detail. Two days later I found him in his studio, completing a painting of the assassination (PLATE 144). If to take death thus is a sign of possession by the devil, the demon that Aunt Cesaría so early uncovered was with the painter to the end.

3. THE EDUCATION OF AN ARTIST

When Diego fled from military glory, he knew at last what he wanted. Soldiering interfered with drawing. Marching and countermarching were wasted motion in a world where painting alone seemed important. He had sketched and painted since he could hold a pencil in his fist or direct the movements of a brush's tip. He had done it naturally as children leap or play. He did not change from game to game and toy to toy, but from drawing trains to drawing animals, from animals to anatomy, from anatomy to soldiers and battle scenes. Now he knew that his interest in mechanics, surgery, war, had been phases of an interest in the forms and motions and appearances of the visible world. Whatever he might experience in the future—be it love or sorrow or struggle—as artist he would approach it, as artist serve it and make it serve him. He was not renouncing hope of fame and glory nor a hero's life, but would seek them with brush instead of sword. He was to justify the expectations of his boyish dreams: the painter's life was to prove a not unheroic one; it was to have its unequal struggles, its lonely vigils, its unending drill, its dedication to dreams of betterment such as he had already absorbed from his father's word and deed.

As a boy of ten, standing red-faced, embarrassed, and angry before a family council of father, mother, and aunts, inarticulately demanding to be sent to art school to learn to paint and draw, much of this was yet obscure. But he knew with a settled conviction that painting was to be his work. His father disliked coercion, his mother thought the word "artist" had a not unrespectable sound, the boy was obviously determined—in the end he won. Señora Rivera even reconciled her tender conscience with stretching of his brief number of years, to get him admitted to the San Carlos Academy of Fine Arts before he had reached eleven. His oversized body helped give verisimilitude to her declaration.

The capacity for hard work which he had displayed from infancy stood him in good stead now: San Carlos at night, general schooling by day, and, between times, hours and hours of sketching. From 1896 to 1898 the double schooling continued; yet he completed his elementary education with honors and attracted sufficient notice at the Academy to win second prize in drawing. He selected as his prize a little box of oils, soon used up in a new passion: painting landscapes from nature. Next year he won a scholarship, thirty pesos (fifteen dollars) a month, which enabled him to transfer to day school.

The education of an artist is one of the most chaotic branches of formal education. In the medieval world, where artists were simply the best of the craftsmen in the arts, apprenticeship and training were settled matters. But as the artist became isolated from society, and taste in patron and people suffered a decline, art became more esoteric, less workmanlike, bound more by arbitrary formulas, while art education became a monopoly of the schools. There was no longer a winnowing system of apprenticeship; it became ever more of an accident who would "study art" and more of a wonder that creative personality should sometimes escape destruction in the genteel and deadening routine.

The turn of the century was a particularly infertile time. Davidian classicism, its force long since spent, still held sway in academic halls. The future cubists and post-impressionists, then hopeful students, would "find themselves" only after long periods of wandering in wastelands followed by blind revolt against their training, in which revolt they all too often threw out the positive values of classical painting along with the routine of its academic systematization.

Rivera, too, was to know the heartaches of disorientation and get lost for years in a wilderness of jangling creeds and isms. The lad who had started to paint so young, and so early attained technical competence, would not develop his characteristic style until after he reached his thirty-sixth year!

Yet Mexico was not the worst place in which to study art in the last decade of the nineteenth century. The country's academic product was feeble enough, derivative, lagging a quarter-century or so behind Paris and Madrid. The renegade Liberal Díaz had organized his dictatorship in a narrow granite mold—a French boulevard or two, an Italian opera house in the worst nineteenth-century style, an Italian post office in the best Renaissance taste, palaces furnished in faded Versailles grandeur, overstuffed with bibelots as ugly as those which adorned the Czar's Winter Palace in St. Petersburg—such were the artistic symbols of the Díaz regime.

Nevertheless, subterranean forces were at work: antagonisms soon to break out in violent upheaval. In the folk a still living plastic sense found daily expression in toys and pottery, blankets and baskets, *pulquería* murals and church *retablos,* folk festival and *corrido* illustrations, the arrangement of foods and wares in the market place. These things could not help influencing a boy with talent and sensibility. "Polite society" might seek to cure him of his taste for what it regarded as "vulgarity"; the school might overlay it with a thick crust of academic doctrine; it might get buried so deep as to seem to be lost; but when life should plow up the depths of the artist's soul, it would come to the surface at long last to fertilize his spirit.

Within the limitations of the Academy Diego had luck. The old Convent of San Carlos, which housed the School of Fine Arts, had several unusual teachers at the moment. There was Felix Parra, incurable academic, but redeemed by what his colleagues regarded as a harmless aberration, a fanatical enthusiasm for pre-Spanish Aztec sculpture, which he communicated to the young student. There was José M. Velasco, an excellent landscapist (as PLATE 5 shows) and an excellent teacher of the laws of perspective. There was old Rebull, Mexican painter of Catalonian origin, pupil of Ingres, who recognized an unusual talent and gave the encouragement so helpful at a certain stage in an adolescent's development.

Rebull was seventy-five or so and Diego but thirteen or fourteen. One day the instructor paused to watch the fat little lad at his drawing. "It's easy to see that you're not accustomed to drawing nudes from the living model," he said at last, "and you've attacked your drawing from the wrong end." Then he proved his verdict to the blushing youngster while the class of fifty looked up to observe, then mock at the unusual colloquy. "But what you are doing interests me, son," the master said. "Tomorrow morning early, come up to my studio and we'll have a talk."

Diego appeared at an early hour at the studio which it was said no one had been invited to enter for many years. The painter showed him treasured pictures, and spoke to him of the laws of proportion and harmony, which he asserted ruled the construction of masterpieces in all ages. Diego drank it in as the first real instruction he had known. The words that sank deepest were those spoken to comfort him when he told the master how his fellows had jeered at him the preceding night. "Let them, my child," he said. "The only important thing is that movement and the life of things interest you. In our craft everything runs parallel with this common life that binds us. These things which we call pictures and sketches are nothing but attempts to put onto a flat surface whatever is the essential in the movement of life. The picture should contain the possibility of perpetual movement. It should be a kind of solar system enclosed in a frame. My son, I do not know whether you will ever amount to anything. But you look carefully, and you have something in your head. If you do, it will be because you have learned to comprehend that."

Diego re-examined pictures he had loved, regarding them with a new interest and understanding, tracing their proportions and equilibriums with a stirring sense of wonder. A haze seemed to lift before him; he got his first glimpse of the wondrous organization in nature and the work of man. The veil was to close down again presently. From that height he was to stumble and wander in the depth of uncomprehending imitation of painters and styles for many years. Yet he carried the memory of that momentary vision and struggled to attain it again. From Rebull, too, he learned, if only at second hand, something of Ingres's mastery of the flowing line, which was to make him a master draftsman.

The greatest of Diego's "instructors" was not on the faculty: his real master, he was to claim later, was the popular engraver of illustrations for broadsheet ballads, José Guadalupe Posada. His little shop was near the art school, at Number 5 Santa Inez, now Calle de la Moneda, in the carriage entrance just off the Church of Saint Inez. Each afternoon the boy stood, nose flattened against the dirty pane, gazing at naïve, dynamic engravings hanging in the window. They appealed to something in his spirit, for Posada was a great artist of the people, the greatest that Mexico has produced—indeed one of the greatest folk artists in the world. Only two or three times in his life was Diego to feel the same intense sensation: before a window in Paris where he saw his first Cézanne; before a crumbling wall in Italy where his heart filled with the resolve to become a muralist, painting in public places.

Posada did his engravings on metal plates, tacked onto wooden blocks and locked up, along with spotty type, in a little frame on a rickety old printing press. From 1887, when he came to Mexico City, until his death in 1913 Posada was to do over fifteen thousand of these to illustrate the songs, jests, prayers of the Mexican folk (see PLATES 7 and 8). Crudely printed on red, yellow, blue, green, and purple tissue, these engravings, with rude texts composed by nameless bards, traveled with roving singers over the Mexican land. Millions gathered at crossroads and market places to hear the singers strum guitars and chant hoarse, melancholy tales of the latest train wreck or political event or some beloved bandit's heroic life and death. In a land where most were illiterate and the cost of a daily newspaper represented a fifth of a day's earnings, these broadsheet ballads were the living journalism and literature of the folk. They learned the ballad by ear, and bought the text so that some lettered villager could help them with forgotten lines. They gave the precious centavo willingly because the minstrel was worthy of his hire, then gazed exultantly upon the engraving with which Posada had made yet more vivid the tale.

The awakening artist and the imaginative Mexican lad reinforced each other as Diego gazed into the window of the little shop to see the latest drawing there, alongside one unchanging picture, an engraving of Michelangelo's *Last Judgment*. In the boy's eyes there was no incongruity. One day Posada took notice and called him in.

"Do you like those pictures?"

"Indeed. I like them all."

"How is that possible?" asked the engraver. "One is by Michelangelo, and the rest by your humble servant."

"They are alike precious," said the boy. "They are different, yet the same."

"Now will you please tell me where you see any similarity between Michelangelo and this?"

"Movement," said Diego, who had learned his master's lesson. "Can't you see, *señor*, in one as in the other the figures move? They move about together and they astonish one because they seem more alive than people passing in the street."

"Imagine, little boy," said Posada, flattered, "no one else in all the world but you and me knows this thing!" And a friendship sprang up between them.

Every afternoon thereafter the fat little boy could be seen standing at the elbow of the fat little man, watching him work, listening to humble aesthetic wisdom or political criticism of the apostate Liberal, Díaz, and his regime. For Posada, in addition to his folk-ballad illustrations, drew caricatures for obscure papers which were preparing the popular mind for stormy years to come.

In 1929 Diego Rivera, then an artist of world renown, was to acknowledge his country's debt and his own to the greatest of his Mexican masters by painting Posada on the walls of the National Palace and by preparing, in collaboration with Paul O'Higgins and Frances Toor, a monument in print for this great artist of the people who had died nameless as he had lived. They reproduced all that could be recovered of Posada's massive work: in the introduction Rivera compared him to Goya and Callot and pronounced him as great as they. To those whose judgment requires support from the accumulated mass of the printed and respectable word, the comparison may seem far-fetched. But if the reader will get the pictures and let them talk in their own never-faltering tongue, he will concede the right of José Guadalupe Posada to an honored place among the immortals of art.*

* In 1948, in his enchanting "Dream of a Sunday Afternoon in the Central Alameda," Diego painted himself as a fat little boy holding by the hand Death tricked out in her Sunday best. Death's other arm is held by Posada, an allusion to the latter's striking *Calaveras*, illustrated verses for the Day of the Dead (Plate 154).

Parra, the academician who admired Aztec art; Velasco, the landscapist who was a master of the laws of perspective; Rebull, the pupil of Ingres who loved movement and mathematical harmony in structure, line, and color; Posada, the engraver who expressed in his naïve-powerful draftsmanship the soul and struggles of his people—these were no mean faculty to direct the training of a future artist. In a Mexico imitative and trivial in cultural life, beset by meretricious elegance and bad taste, it was the boy's fortune to begin his study of painting under the hand of tradition as expressed by these men. This schooling confused and disoriented his spirit, curbed and subjected his nascent personality, made him submit, as it did all art students of his day, to the outmoded academic traditions against which he would have to rebel before he could find his own mode of expression and relation with his own times. Yet to this solid training he owes the ability to survive the eclectic confusions and rebel isms of his days abroad, to develop in the end the individual style which stamped itself upon all his riper work.

Not to this alone, to be sure, or all his fellow students would have ripened with him. To sound training must be added innate capacity, the biological inheritance of eye and hand and mind, the high potential of artistic and spiritual energy which cannot be dammed up, and the circumstances of his experiences with the men and movements of his times. These are just as surely incalculables as the laws of artistic training which have been elaborated with a fine disregard for their very existence.

It must not be imagined that all Diego's schooling was as stimulating as these masters. Most of his teachers were mediocre, pedantic, dictatorial. He would snort with rage when they tried to break him of the very characteristics which were the germs of his future personal style. How he chafed at copying from plaster casts and the yet more stupid copying from engraved replicas of such casts. Still, judging from the specimens of his student work, he did the hated exercises with competence. The competence underscores the dullness and boredom of the performance. In after years he tried to protect the children of Mexico from this "imbecile practice of copying engravings of fragments of plaster sculpture without any conception of space. Stupidity and barbarism, which the plastic and imaginative powers of the human child were almost never able to survive."* When he became a force in the art training of his native land he scourged the disciples of the plaster cast out of the schools.

In 1902 the cup of bitterness ran over: Rebull retired and a new "up-to-date" Catalan painter of Moors and musketeers, Antonio Fabrés, was appointed director of San Carlos to "modernize" the school. He introduced the "latest" techniques of the European art schools, rooted in a Spanish academicism, senile at birth, which had not grown younger since.

The Díaz regime, too, was growing old. The dictator was rounding out his third decade, his cronies growing old along with him. The student youth, excluded from a career by the league of old men, grew restless. The wave of revolt did not yet reach to the dictator's feet, but subordinates began to feel in their faces the spray of coming storm. The student body of the university entered into a demonstration directed against a priest accused of sexual corruption, and through him, against the dictator's complaisance at the violation of the anticlerical clauses which Juárez had written into the constitution. Diego and his comrades joined the "riots," adding the new art-school director to the list of grievances. Before the end of his fifteenth year Diego, along with a number of others, was expelled. The storm blew over, the students were reinstated, but Rivera was sick of the school. Having attained the ripe age of sixteen, at which, strictly speaking, he became eligible to enter the academy, Diego left San Carlos; he was not to return until almost three decades later, as its director.

Armed with brush and pencil and high resolve, the sixteen-year-old lad went out into the world to seek his fortune. Four

* Diego Rivera: "Children's Drawings in Present Day Mexico," *Mexican Folkways* (Vol. II, No. 5 [December-January 1926-27]).

years he ranged the countryside, painting: houses, streets, churches, Indians, volcanoes, the picturesque and dramatic Mexican land. The impress of Velasco was on his style: his work was not unworthy of his master, though it lacked the latter's gentle clarity. He made one attempt at portraiture in 1903, his mother. When she saw it, she burst into tears, crying that it was ugly and common and that her son did not love her. The picture did not survive, but I imagine it was nearer to the Rivera of today than the painting of *Citlapetl*—the Indian name for the peak of Orizaba—which did (PLATE 6).

The young painter was happy catching on canvas the splendors of the Mexican landscape. The people around him, including older artists, acclaimed him as one of them—and he tried to believe them. Yet he knew better. The more he painted, the more dissatisfied he grew. He became preoccupied with questions of color: the pure colors on his palette began to seem dirty. He grew sick of oils; they seemed black and sour to him; certain colors set up a revulsion of feeling: burnt sienna produced a feeling of nausea. He abandoned oils and experimented with pastels. Then questions of form began to torture him: his outlines were not sharp enough; something was lost between pencil sketch and painting (this last would often be true of Rivera's work, all his life); Mexico's solid granite mountains lost their solidity on canvas, and he didn't know why. Form became an obsession: he thought of dropping painting for carving wood and stone with steel.

Dissatisfaction made him ill; a touch of hypochondria, which characterized him always, made him believe that he was going blind. He neglected painting to sit nightly in the front row of a music hall, gazing at a popular actress with whom he was in love. When she was attracted at last by the prospect of an affair with this strange young lad and granted to him casually such favors as she had granted to many older and wiser and, above all, wealthier admirers, he suffered a revulsion.

He drank a great deal to show his manhood and keep up

with friends. His father watched without comment, then presented his son, on the latter's birthday, with a case of wine. Diego drank too much and got deathly sick. Still no rebuke. His father's only comment: "I guess you're not as good a drinker as you thought." Thereafter Diego drank always in moderation.

He drove himself, starting to paint at dawn and straining to complete his pictures in the fading evening light, for an idea was taking shape that required a great accumulation of pictures: he was beginning to dream of Europe!

Surely there was more to the painter's craft than he had thus far mastered. In Europe there were teachers and schools and the treasures of the old masters. Spain and France and Italy would answer the questions that tortured him. But how to get there? His paintings were beginning to sell; perhaps, if he did a great number, he might raise money for his passage. But how to live? Aid would be forthcoming from his family if he could convince his father. Diego, Senior, did not object—all Mexicans who could afford it went to Spain, some to France, to "complete their education." Yet, as he demonstrated to his son, the family fortunes, though ascendant once more, were insufficient.

Don Diego was now an inspector in the National Department of Public Health, his duties carrying him to many parts of the Republic. On his next trip to his native state he took samples of his son's work, petitioning the Governor of Guanajuato for a scholarship for young Diego. The Governor was not interested in art.

Yellow fever broke out in the lowlands of Vera Cruz. Assigned to cope with the disease, Señor Rivera took his son along, leaving him in the higher, healthier ground at Jalapa, the state capital. Diego was enchanted with the warm fruitfulness of Jalapa, its soft nights, brilliant, green-tinted days, the grace of its semitropical foliage, the magnificent background of Orizaba's snow-capped cone rising seventeen thousand feet into the sky. Refreshed by the change, he sketched and painted in

Jalapa's lovely streets. Cannily, the father, on an official visit to report to the Governor concerning his work, brought samples of the boy's sketches.

Don Teodoro A. Dehesa, Governor of Vera Cruz since 1892, was a cultured gentleman of the old school. Years before he had saved General Díaz, then a colonel, from the firing squad. Don Porfirio as President knew how to be grateful: Governor Dehesa remained at his post. There were those who thought he took undue advantage of the President's gratitude, for he opposed the clique of *Cientificos,* under the leadership of Treasury Minister Limantour, who formed the aged dictator's latter-day court. He even ventured to run against Ramón Corral, Don Porfirio's hand-picked vice-presidential running mate and rumored successor. He didn't get far, for Díaz ran the election and "counted" the vote. Yet Don Porfirio remembered his debt of gratitude and did not act against him.

Within the state he ruled, Governor Dehesa dedicated himself, like the good nineteenth-century positivist and Liberal he was, to the reform of humanity through education. He invested fourteen million pesos of a meager budget in new schools. He scoured his domain for young men and women of promise to send abroad that they might return to be teachers and leaders in culture and education. He was a lover of the arts; he knew ability when he saw it, and was struck with wonder at Diego's youthful talent.

"Why do you not go abroad to study, my son?" he asked. "You have within you the making of a very great painter."

Diego was too confused to do more than mumble thanks. His father spoke for him. "He needs assistance, Don Teodoro, and I cannot give it."

"Why does he not apply to the Governor of his state?"

"Our Governor has no use for artists—says they become drones and loafers and return home only to show off their Paris airs."

Don Teodoro's eyes clouded. "We will show your Governor,"

he exploded, "that we *Veracruzanos* know how to appreciate art and the luster it reflects on our fatherland. From today on, young man, you will receive a pension for European study. It will continue as long as you send me evidence that you are benefiting. I am sure you will use it well and become a glory of the state that adopts you this day as one of its sons."

Back in Mexico City, the youth hastily arranged an exhibit, aided by an older schoolmate from the Academy, Gerardo Murillo (better known as Doctor Atl), then directing the Museum. There were fourteen or fifteen landscapes in oil, in crayon, and a few portraits. Diego sold them all, though the prices were not sensational, and thus secured his passage. Dehesa had a monthly pension equivalent to three hundred French francs waiting for him, and Diego Rivera, now twenty-one, cash in pocket and high hopes in his heart, was off on a ship bound for "Mother Spain"!

4. A COLONIAL IN EUROPE

A few months before his departure, while Diego was painting at the foot of the great volcano that dominates Vera Cruz, he witnessed a significant strike in the history of Mexican labor. The experience left a mark upon his mind and determined in some measure the impressions he was to absorb from Europe.

It was the winter of 1906-07. The peasants who had come from the mountains to the textile factories dotting the foothills around Orizaba's peak were showing signs of losing their patience, hitherto regarded as inexhaustible. Humbly they had accepted the tutelage of foreman, priest, and *jefe político*. They had not grumbled because their poor wage, paid in tokens redeemable only in the company store, bound them by a chain of continuous debt to their employers—were they not used to debt peonage on the ranch? But that lean winter when fresh wage cuts were decreed, they balked, as overloaded burros balk. Without previous organization, they walked out of the mills.

The *Gran Círculo de Obreros Libres*—whose greatness had

1. Diego's Parents.

2. At the age of three.

3. The Little Engineer.

4. As an Art Student in Madrid.

5. Landscape by Rivera's teacher,
José M. Velasco. Oil. 1898

6. Citlapetl (Peak of Orizaba). Oil. 1906

7,8. The End of the World. Corrido illustrations by Posada.

9. Portrait of Rivera
by Leopold Gottlieb. 1918 (?)

10. Portrait of Rivera
by Modigliani. 1918 (?)

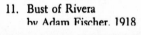

11. Bust of Rivera
by Adam Fischer. 1918

12. Self-Portrait. Pencil. 1918

13. The House over the Bridge. Oil. 1908-09

14. Streets of Avila. Oil. 1908

15. Portrait of a Spaniard. Oil. 1912

16. Paisaje Zapatista. Oil. 1915

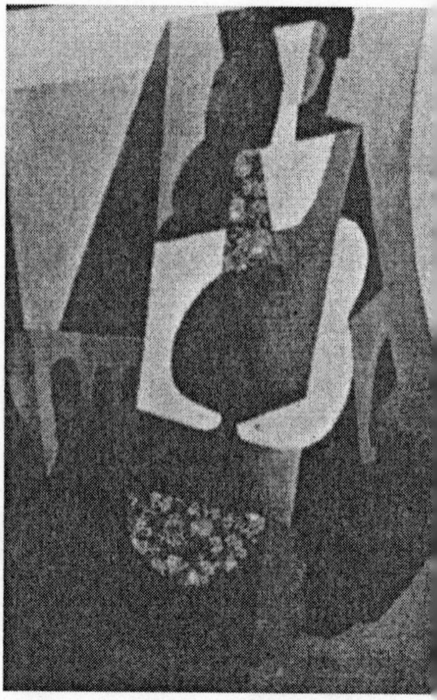

17. Portrait of Angelina. Oil. 1917

18. Angelina Pregnant. Oil. 1917

19. Portrait of Angelina. Oil. 1918 (?)

20. Angelina and the child Diego. Oil. 1917

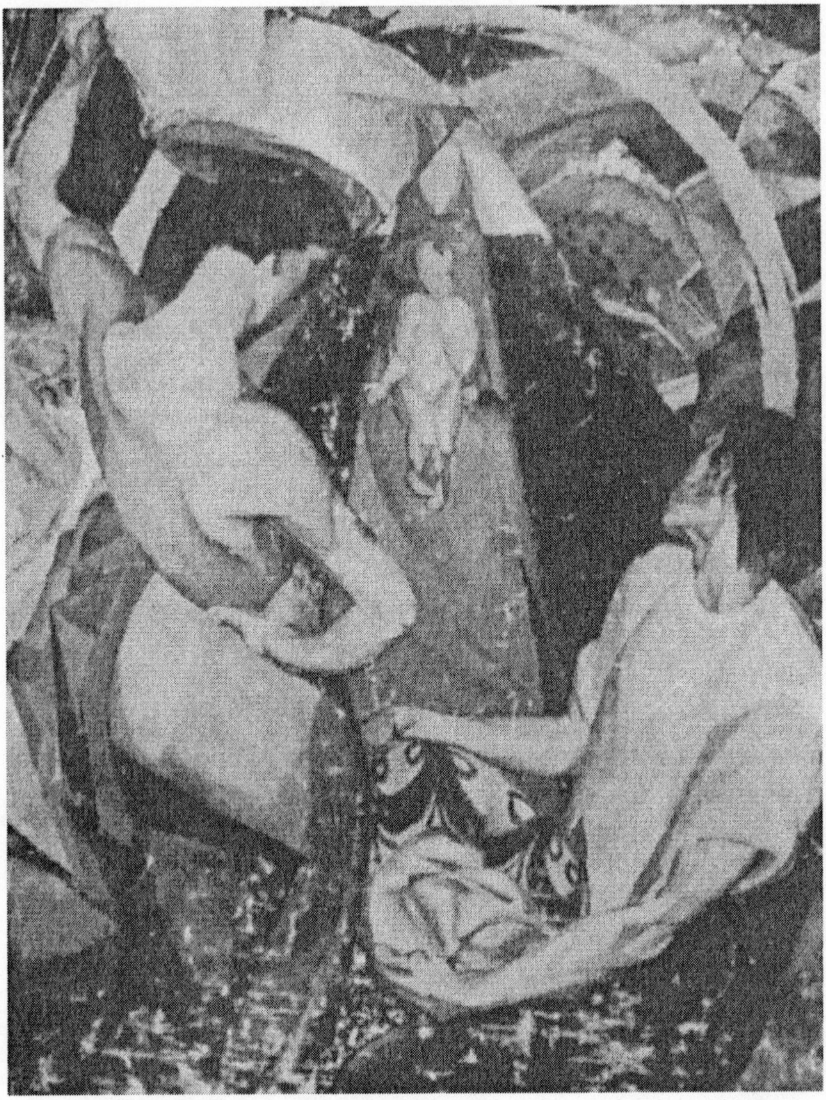

21. Adoration of the Shepherds. Wax on canvas. 1912-13

22. Two Women. Oil. 1914

23. The Alarm Clock. Oil. 1914

24. Landscape. Majorca. Oil. 1914

25. The Man with the Cigarette. Oil. 1913

26. The Architect. Oil. 1915

27. Portrait of Martín Luís Guzmán. Oil. 1915

28. Portrait of Ramón Gómez de la Serna. Oil. 1915

29. Still Life. Oil. 1916

30. Still Life. Oil. 1917

31. Eiffel Tower. Oil. 1916

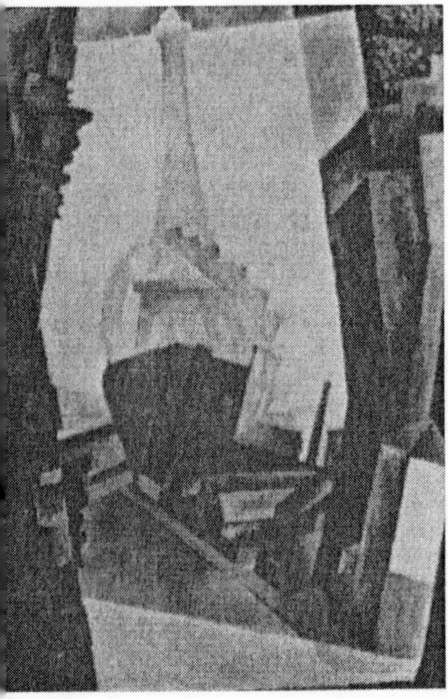

32. The Telegraph Pole. 1917 (?)

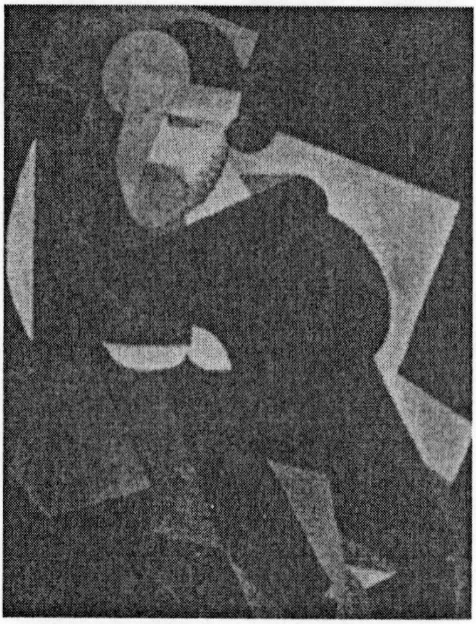

33. Portrait of M. Volochine.
Oil. 1917

34. The Painter in Repose. Oil. 1916

36. Still Life. Oil. 1916

35. Still Life. Oil. 1916

37. Marika at Seventeen.

38. Diego and his Mexican Daughters. 1929

39. Edge of the Forest, Piquey. Oil. 1918

40. The Aqueduct. Oil. 1918

been limited to its aspirations—suddenly found itself swollen to a size justifying its name. It had been formed by anarchist workingmen from Cuba and Spain and emissaries of the Flores Magón brothers, who, from their exile in California, had been smuggling revolutionary journals into the country for so long that their names had become as legendary as those of bandit heroes.

During the strike Diego ceased painting. The cavalry charge and point-blank fire upon closely massed men, women, and children, the melting away of the panic-stricken crowd, the silent figures lying motionless on blood-stained cobblestones, were burned into his memory. For days afterward he could not resume his painting. It did not occur to him to paint those scenes; yet they shut out everything else.*

But what, after all, had a young painter to do with such as these? It did not come into his mind then, nor for many years, that his painter's skill might be of service to these peons. There was nothing in the teachings of the Academy, in the practice of his fellow artists, nor, so far as he knew, in the traditions of his profession, to suggest it. Twenty years later, when he had thought it all through for himself, he was to paint the Flores Magóns, Lucrezia Toriz, woman leader of that strike, and Rafael Moreno, who died that day when the troops of Díaz fired upon unarmed men and women, on the central wall of the National Palace, where Dictator Díaz once held sway.

The sons of Mexico's "better families" go to Paris for initiation into the elegant vices, to New York to learn "business and

* Whether these cavalry charge scenes were real or only vivid "memories" of the analogous 1905 "Bloody Sunday" in Russia, Diego was convinced that he had witnessed them. In *My Art, My Life* (New York, Citadel Press, 1960), this became a story of personal participation in the clash with the police and a stay in prison, "where the stale prison bread was the most wonderful food I have ever tasted" (pp. 50-51). Be that as it may the long textile strike of 1906-07 stirred the Mexico of the aging Díaz and left its imprint on Diego's spirit.

confor" (something far more unctuous and sybaritic than American or British "comfort"), and to Spain for traditional culture. They spend years in Havana, New York, Madrid, Rome, Paris, acquiring in the course of the *grand tour* an easy polish, an encyclopedic knowledge, and casual skill, in all the varieties of vice, a graceful mastery of the art of killing time, and a detachment from the humbler and more essential processes of living. The sons of the lesser bureaucracy, to which Diego belonged, are not so likely to get to Europe unless they show exceptional talents or their families possess influence. In that case they may go abroad on "pensions"—scholarships, we would call them—to Spain, Italy, or France, to study medicine, music, painting, architecture, letters. Thereafter, unlike their "betters," they are likely to engage in some useful occupation, a desultory—or serious—practice of their respective arts, or teaching, politics, or diplomacy.

Anybody could see by looking at Diego that he fitted ill into this traditional system. Even in Spain, with its chiseled, seamed, and weathered faces and regional types, everyone ceased playing cards or dominoes, drinking, talking, when Diego entered a café. Despite his twenty years he was more than six feet tall and weighed three hundred pounds. His bulk would fill the café doorway, then the room itself with his presence. As people looked up, they saw a great broad-brimmed hat, an unkempt curly beard surrounding an attractively ugly face with good-natured froglike features, and protruding dark eyes that seemed to look all around without their owner having to turn his head. His clothes, thick in substance as a board, were wrinkled, paint-stained, ill-fitting, bursting with the effort of containing the colossal body.

Spain was not the best place for a young Mexican artist only half conscious of the need of freeing himself from "colonial" and academic limitations. The Mexican Academy was an enfeebled reflection of the Spanish; that, an enfeebled reflection of the French, dimmed by the dust from Spain's own past. Not that Spain's past is lacking in glorious models; its great hours produced an El Greco and a Velázquez, capable of teaching not only Spanish artists but those of all the Western world. Yet for centuries the land had been going through a slow, inglorious decay: in economy, social life, culture, the arts. The nineteenth century had dawned with sudden brilliance, the great popular effort to shake off Napoleonic vassalage finding its artistic expression in the colossal figure of Goya. But Ferdinand succeeded the *Junta* of Cadiz, bringing back with him the Jesuits, the Inquisition, the latifundian lords, all the sad train of reaction and decay; while the great Goya had no successors except beyond the frontier.

Where reaction holds sway a people is not taught to admire the best in its past and despise the worst, but to revere it *en bloc* merely because it is its own, until standards of selection and discrimination are destroyed. Thus Spanish art was not only a cultural "colony" of the French schools (and not the best of them); it was at the same time enslaved to its own past. And Diego had come to Old Spain to escape the derivativeness of the New!

Diego reached Spain on January 6, 1907. He brought a letter from Gerardo Murillo, Mexican painter of volcanoes (Doctor Atl), who had previously studied in Spain. Murillo's letter was directed to the Spanish painter Chicharro, under whom he urged Diego to study. The choice was not a bad one, though it guaranteed that for several years Diego would see "modernism" through the eyes of Zuloaga and Sorolla.

Eduardo Chicharro y Agüera was still fairly young, only thirteen years older than his pupil. A native of Madrid, he studied in the Academy of Fine Arts there, then apprenticed himself in turn to Domínguez and Sorolla. Honors had been heaped upon him: medals and honorable mentions in Madrid, Barcelona, Saragossa, Valencia, Liége, Munich, Buenos Aires. Generally regarded as the leader of the younger generation of

Spanish painters—"younger" meaning younger than Sorolla and Zuloaga, for in the twentieth century an art "generation" is closer to a half-decade than to the traditional quarter of a century—Chicharro represented a transitional figure between these two painters and the coming postimpressionists. As is the fate of transitional figures, he was to be less regarded than his masters, then eclipsed by his successors. The artistic expression of his land was to be represented by Picasso and Gris—who were to make Paris their home. The young Mexican pupil whom he accepted and taught in 1907 and 1908 was also destined to eclipse him in accomplishments and fame.

Diego worked hard under his new master. His letters home are full of the paintings he has done, modest yet confident appraisals of their technical attainments, newspaper clippings praising his work. If he was assailed by doubts, no inkling appeared in his letters. To his sister he sent affectionate postcards, which he adorned with pen-and-ink sketches of the Spanish landscape. To his father he sent reports of progress. To Governor Dehesa and his secretary, Espinoza, he sent pictures from time to time to indicate the work he was doing and to justify his scholarship. The paintings delighted the old Governor. Dehesa was convinced that his judgment had been sound and the outlay of three hundred francs a month would bring honor to his country and his name. The reputation of the boy from Guanajuato began to spread in Vera Cruz and Mexico City. Years after, when Diego was doing murals in Mexico, there were older men and women who shook their heads and sighed for a return of the talented young man who had sent such "nice pictures" from Spain (PLATES 13, 14, 15).

Within a few months of Diego's arrival in Madrid his mother conceived the idea of coming with his sister María to look after her boy. The idea threw him into a panic lest the visit should interfere with his search for he knew not what mystery of the painter's art. He wrote, as he thought, with tact, urging her to delay till the following year, when she might leave with him for a trip to Paris and Rome, "which I think will be better for her," he explained to his father, "than to come to Europe and not know more than Spain, a nation which, though it possesses treasures of art which make it inexhaustibly interesting and agreeable to me, for her will cease to possess novelty and enchantment in two or three months."

Tactful—but his mother, not his father, answered the letter:

> Your father, his mother, and my aunt reciprocate your affection and so does your unhappy mother, whom you will never have the displeasure to see again.

In a long explanation to his father (dated June 24, 1907) he anxiously analyzed his motives—how little time he would be able to spend with her, how bored she would be in Spain, how much more he could be with her while on his travels, how much more she would see.

"I can say without exaggeration: I study and paint from the time I get up until I go to bed. And this ought to continue still for some eight months before I can stop working so hard." He did not seem to realize that he would never have time for the social amenities; even when he reached fifty and sixty, something would still be driving him to work to the limit of his powers.

Light on Diego's work is shed by the report Chicharro wrote after he had been studying six months in Spain:

> He has, from the time he arrived to the present, done numerous landscape works in Madrid and Toledo, and in those and in the works he has completed in my workshop of nudes and compositions, has made much progress, which I do not hesitate to qualify as astonishing. And therefore I am pleased to state that Señor Rivera, my pupil, shows that he has magnificent qualities for the art in which he is engaged, and united with them, as shown by the great number of works executed in that time, the qualities of a tireless worker.

Diego sent this to the Governor and a copy to his father, with a comment, stilted and bashful in its affection:

Receive these words as first fruits until I can send you something better, for you see that I am trying to "honor my father and mother," the only commandment in my divine law.

His letters describe the works with which he hoped to "honor his father and mother," and his own name. On January 6, 1908 he sent Governor Dehesa three pictures:

. . . a "grandmother" cleaning utensils of various metals on a little table, half figure, natural size, as a sample of what I have learned of my *métier* . . . moreover, the picture is agreeable and "accessible."

To Dehesa's secretary he sent a picture he had shown in Madrid—"a street of a Biscayan village with a figure of an old woman who, with a prayer book and rosary in her hands, is on her way to prayer."

And as "official shipment" I am sending my picture *Old Stone and New Flowers*—an old Gothic church whose filigrees and bricks time has blackened and gilded, in shadow, showing its portico and part of the elevation of its bell tower, . . . forms the background of the picture. Then a street in whose stony age no traffic has left its trace, and in the foreground, above the wall of an orchard with bushes of white roses, rises straight, strong, and graceful a rosebay tree, which on the background of the ancient church exhibits the opulent overflow of its red flowers bathed in sun.

Other pictures done at the time include *Banks of the Tagus* (1907); *Fishing Ships* (Biscay, 1908); *Interior of a Church at Ávila* (1909). The last mentioned is a study of the dimmed interior of a church lit by shafts of slanting light filtered through stained glass, the dusky interior contrasting with the glowing colors of the sun-illuminated windows. The first of these was purchased by Señora Díaz, wife of the Mexican President, at Diego's Mexican exposition of 1910. The second was a gift to Espinoza; the third, to Dehesa. All of them, after suffering various fates, in Mexican museums and collections, came to rest in the museumlike home of Salo Hale in Mexico City, a businessman and art patron of Polish-Jewish extraction, the leading Mexican collector of early Riveras, and for years one of the country's most generous and discriminating private Maecenases. The other paintings of this period, and there are an enormous number, are scattered through Europe, the United States, and Mexico; Rivera had long lost track of them, and I have not been able to locate many either.

Several Spanish paintings of 1911 to 1914 (when Diego was living in Paris, yet was tormented by the feeling that he had not mastered Spain, which impelled him to return there again and again) have been easier to trace because they were in the Paris expositions of the Autumn Salons or the Society of Independents, or because they were purchased by that sensitive American collector, swift to recognize developing talent, the late John Quinn.

When Quinn died in 1925, he owned over two thousand works, ranging from El Greco to the ultramoderns, mostly contemporary. He had purchased them on the basis of his own taste, often, as in the case of his Riveras, well in advance of critical acclaim. In the auction which liquidated his estate, there were six Riveras, all done between 1912 and 1915. Five are cubist works and do not belong in this part of our discussion.

Item 127 in the sale was chosen for reproduction in the catalogue. Entitled *The Samaritan,* it is described thus:

> In a simplified landscape setting a peasant girl in purple and shaded yellow and an old wrinkled and pallid-faced Samaritan, wearing a flowing brown robe, proffering help with the heavy water jar she is about to carry; under a vast somber sky. Signed at lower right, Diego M. Rivera, and dated Toledo, 1912. Height, 6 feet, 6 inches; width, 5 feet, 4 inches.

It was sold to E. Weyhe and resold to Mrs. James Murphy of New York. It was in the Rivera one-man show at the Museum of Modern Art in 1931, so that the reader can find a reproduction in the catalogue under its better-known title, *The Crock.* Other Riveras at the auction went to Morris Hillquit, the Socialist lawyer, F. Howald, and the dealers Weyhe and Dudensing.

The Samaritan reveals the plight that Rivera had got into as a painter. He had come to Spain in search of himself and had lost what little self he had had in Mexico. Technically it is more skillful than his Mexican work, but in theme, composition, color, spirit, almost pure Zuloaga! The tall cloaked figure, the picturesque "type," the great cloudy sky, all tell the same story. Even the enormous size—perhaps a painter's trick to attract notice in the maze of pictures in the Autumn Salon—was in keeping with Zuloaga. Yet there is a geometrical solidity in the houses climbing the hill in the background, and in the female figure, that indicates an independent personality struggling to be free.

The same spell is on his *Portrait of a Spaniard*, illustrated here (PLATE 15), exhibited at the Autumn Salon of 1912. It attracted notice in the Paris press, standing out—among many thousands—sufficiently to be one of twenty reproduced in the annual article of Fernand Roches, director of *L'Art décoratif*, on the Salon. The tall figure that dwarfs the melancholy Castilian tableland and stands out against a lowering sky is Zuloaga—with one important reservation: Zuloaga rarely attains this tenderness and simplicity of drawing that are a hallmark of Rivera's draftsmanship.

Moreover, Rivera's "hero" is a humbler figure than those dominating Zuloaga's vasty landscapes, not an aristocrat, nor a peasant, but an intellectual. The umbrella shows that; the brow shows it, shining with thought. He does not belong in this unurban landscape at all. The battered hat and baggy clothing are as far removed from Zuloaga's gentlemen and ladies as are the tenderness of expression and depth of thought. On closer inspection, even the structure of the painting has in it much of Rivera's own: the clouds sweep upward and outward to expand the canvas beyond the limits of its frame. *Ancha es Castilla*—"Broad is Castile"—the Mexican says far more intensely than the Castilian who has so often wrestled with the problem in his mountain backgrounds. The tripartite division of sky, middle ground, and darker foreground, reflected in the divisions of the figure, the face, the lines of hat and brow and tie and sensitive hands, hint at a mastery of structure subtler, richer, and deeper than the showier work of the man under whose spell it was painted.

The same struggle for self is in Diego's *Toledo* (1912). He has taken the scene El Greco made known throughout the Western world. One can feel by looking at it how El Greco must have tormented the young Mexican painter; yet he could not penetrate the secret of the master's power. The painting is Toledo, not as Rivera saw it, but as El Greco might have seen it if his vision had been dimmed by a reluctant apprenticeship to Zuloaga and Sorolla. If the reader will examine Sorolla's *Castillo de San Serrando, Toledo,* and Zuloaga's, El Greco's, and Rivera's versions of the scene, he will feel how hard the painter must have wrestled with the task—three times abandoned and started afresh, still unsatisfactory when completed. He tried again and again without success, until in the end he settled accounts with El Greco in a tall tale, in which, some forty years later, he told his "autobiographer" that he had forged three Goyas and an El Greco in 1907 or 1908 which now hang in genuine collections of those two masters, having escaped detection.*

Diego's letters strove to keep up an optimism he no longer felt. He drove himself furiously to accomplish something, but was exasperated to the point of frenzy because he did not himself know what it was. He was gaining in technical skill, in feeling for the texture of materials and surfaces, in mastery of the rich neo-impressionist Spanish palette, in clarity and sureness of line. But he had left Mexico feeling that there was something missing which technical growth alone could not supply. Painting was somehow capable of achievements beyond the

* *My Art, My Life* (New York, Citadel Press, 1960), pp. 52-53.

range of competence and skill. In Europe he hoped to find a key to unlock he knew not what magic door. He had been in the Old World for several years and worked hard, yet his quest continued. He had not even found out what he was looking for!

His canvases pleased him while he was working on them, for the act of painting provided a sheer animal joy. Yet he possessed a tardy objective faculty for self-criticism that mocked and tormented him after he had finished his picture and had pronounced it good. He approved of each because he did well, indeed better and better, what he attempted. Later he would fly into a rage that he had not attempted more. He would beat his head against the walls of his studio, then flee to some café to give vent to his despair in boastful, ill-humored, fantastic talk with Mexican and Spanish painters and writers.

Diego became sick with uncomprehending overwork. A glandular trouble, which probably explains his bulging eyes, was reinforced by anxiety and hypochondria. He was plagued by a succession of disorders, part real, part imaginary. He entered upon the first of his notable courses of diet that alternately inflated and deflated his enormous body. He fed himself on prodigious quantities of fruits and vegetables, excluding cereals and meats. He inundated his liver with seas of mineral water. He worked himself to exhaustion on this insufficiently energizing diet, then marveled to find himself exhausted. He blamed his solitary life and began to seek casual sexual encounters with models and women of the half-world surrounding the world of art. Previously they had sought him out because of his attractive ugliness and bulk and the exotic strain of "Mexican savage" which they perceived in him. Now he was so irascible and full of fury that they avoided him.

Ever more frequently, he fled his studio, which meant fleeing from himself. The indolent habit of café conversation which possesses so many Spanish writers and artists took hold of him. The heated arguments, the tall stories with which he showed contempt for his auditors and still more for himself, excited him without giving him pleasure or solace. More soothing were long walks, excursions through the various quarters of Madrid and the Castilian countryside, talks with workingmen and peasant folk. When with them, he listened much and talked little, observed, sketched, thought. The sketches were more truly Rivera than the formal paintings into which they later dissolved.

Diego was exactly of an age with Alfonso, King of Spain. A year before Diego arrived in Madrid, a bomb was thrown at the carriage in which Alfonso was riding with Victoria, his English bride, from their wedding. The carriage was wrecked, twenty-four persons killed, but the bridal pair unhurt. Before the painter had been abroad many months, King Carlos of Portugal was assassinated in the streets of Lisbon. The heir apparent was killed with him. His successor, Dom Manuel, was driven from the throne before three years were up. The peninsula was seething with revolt; older politicians and intellectuals talked republic, younger intellectuals and the masses talked anarchy; everyone was confident that Alfonso would never finish out his reign.

In 1909, the third year of Diego's stay in Spain, this "emperor" of a nonexistent empire tried to carve out an overseas dominion in North Africa to justify his title. His troops met reverse after reverse, being completely wiped out by Moroccan tribesmen at the battle of Melilla. To redeem the "honor of Spain's glorious army," the country was denuded of troops; whereupon the workers or Barcelona, under anarchist leadership, proclaimed a general strike. It spread to the industrial centers of Catalonia and Valencia, forcing Alfonso to recall his "glorious army" from North Africa for war with his own people. Thus came about the attack and insurrection known as Barcelona's "Bloody Week." Executions followed, then months of secret assassination of labor leaders by government *pistoleros*, culminating at last in the judicial murder of the gentle anarchist educator, Francisco Ferrer.

Fresh strikes; renewed government terror; mutiny on the battleship *Numancia;* resignation of the Prime Minister responsible for Ferrer's execution; death of the new Prime Minister by an avenging anarchist bullet; his successor fired at three times in a single year. Such was the Spain which Diego now discovered; it was to fructify his art more than instruction by the best master might have done.

He purchased quantities of anarchist tracts and brochures of "popular culture," consuming them with the appetite of a Gargantua. The books, too, drove him into a fury, with their large-promising titles followed by undeceiving thinness and lack of a core of solid thought. Hungering for answers to unformulated questions, he waded through the whole of Sempere's popular library—paper-backed volumes at a peseta each containing selections from Reclus, Huxley, Haeckel, Darwin, Bakunin, Kropotkin, Sorel, Fabbri, Leone, Malatesta, Taine, Buckle, Draper, Moleschott, Renan, Loria, Labriola, Büchner, Nietzsche, Schopenhauer, Pío Baroja, Voltaire, Zola, the Russian novelists, and countless others.

Here, in a fantastically bad translation and selection, he made his first acquaintance with the work of Marx, an exiguous one-peseta volume which did not scruple to dignify its leanness with the stout name of *El Capital.** He browsed in many books, but finished few, for his swift, prehensile, opulent mind permitted him to develop the merest hint into an elaborate structure of thought of his own. Then he would lose patience with the slower pace and feebler imagination of the author (who had developed his "hint" to other, less satisfying conclusions).

He painted less and less. Neither books nor wine nor talk nor sex nor friends could satisfy his secret hunger. He fled classes, studios and systematic work to wander with other painters through Spain and Portugal, sketching, visiting museums and churches, seeking out masterpieces, studying the life of the folk.

* It is sufficient to note that this "edition" translated *commodity* as *comodidad* in place of *mercancía!*

Next he took a long tour of France, Belgium, Holland, England, seeking the solution of a problem whose terms he had not been able to define. In London he made his first contact with an industrial civilization, observing with fascinated revulsion the spectacle of poverty in the heart of the then workshop of the world. He sketched and wandered down by the docks, in the squalid quarters of the East End, in the industrial sections. He spent days and nights watching the London poor, at work, at rest, crossing London Bridge at night to sleep on the Embankment of the Thames. What shocked him most was the careful way in which his landlady kept "edible" food apart from other rubbish, that it might be picked up by the poor, and the respectful and acquiescing misery and terrible patience shown by human debris cast out untimely on the industrial scrap heap after they had given their best years to productive labor. He meditated confusedly on the disorder in the social organism, the inadequacies of sporadic and individual protest such as Spanish and Latin American anarchism had caused to seem natural. He was puzzled at the timorous respectability of the powerful British trade unions. For the first time he wondered whether Marx and not Bakunin might not be the better social guide, and resolved to study Marx's *Capital.* Actually he could not drive himself to read it. "I felt," he said later, "the power of human organization—above all, the power of organization in the negative sense." * Of pictures in London he remembers little—only Hogarth and Blake, with whom he was enchanted, and Turner, who interested but did not completely satisfy, and a sense of amazement that, aside from these, England seemed to be without artists or plastic sensibility.

In Brussels he felt the impact of Breughel; if he could find the secret that made Hogarth, Breughel, and Goya draw and paint the way they did, he would be satisfied.

In Bruges he began painting again. There, he and his friends

* Organization, be it remembered, is at the heart not of Marxism but of Leninism. These words were written when Rivera fancied himself a Leninist. But his conversations with me never revealed more than a few clichés from either of them.

ran into some women painters they knew from Spain. Among them was María Gutiérrez Blanchard, better known as María Blanchard, with whom he had already formed an intimate friendship in Madrid. A little hunchbacked girl, half Spanish, half French, with large glowing dark eyes and a gentle yet shrewd and penetrating wit, María formed a striking contrast to the huge Mexican painter. Her painting was personal, tender, feminine, yet solid, suffused with a wistful and haunting quality that must have clung to her personality as well. I never met her, and she is dead now, but to her I am indebted for many gay tales about Diego which she told to her cousin, the Spanish-born Mexican artist Germán Cueto, who told them to me. She knew Diego in Spain, traveled with him and others on some of his journeys, later shared a workshop with him in Paris. Through her, in Bruges, Diego met her Russian friend, Angelina. But the story of Diego and Angelina belongs to a subsequent chapter. . . .

The high light of Diego's wanderings was his stay in Paris. Already he had been drawn thither by glimpses of paintings in art magazines. Then he was excited by a letter Luis de la Rocha showed him. Written in doubtful Spanish by a young American painter, Walter Pach, who had left Spain for France, it communicated the excitement its writer felt at wonderful things doing in Paris. Rivera and Walter Pach did not meet until much later; when they did, Diego reminded Pach of the letter Pach had long forgotten, expressing his gratitude as if he himself had been the original recipient.

From the Paris railway station Rivera and his friends went to the shop of Clovis Sagot in the rue Lafitte. It was showing works by Fauves and stranger and newer painters, beginning to call themselves *Cubistes*. In the window there was a large harlequin by Picasso and still lifes by Derain and Braque. Now Diego was sure that he wanted to make Paris his home. Next day he went to the Galerie Vollard.

In the window was a painting by Cézanne, the landscape

with the old man and his pipe. All morning Diego stood there, walking up and down, looking, looking, excited as he had never been before. At noon, M. Vollard went out to luncheon, and noted without favor the young admirer. When he came back, Rivera was still there. Somewhat annoyed, the proprietor removed the picture and replaced it with another—also a Cézanne. And so the afternoon went, with changing pictures. The excited loiterer was interested in all of them. This was more nearly a revelation in painting than any he had ever experienced. At the end of that long, exciting day, Diego told me, he "developed a high fever which a doctor diagnosed as caused by nervous shock." *

A minor reputation preceded Diego to Paris; his teacher, Chicharro, had been there, bringing some of Diego's work and singing his pupil's praises. We can glean some notion of the ease of his entrée into Paris art circles by a letter home, dated April 24, 1909. He was homesick, though he would not confess it, and had received permission from Dehesa to return to Mexico to exhibit in connection with the coming centennial celebration of Mexico's independence, scheduled for the autumn of 1910. He would start for home as soon as he could get back some pictures he was showing in the Autumn Salon and with the Independents. The Salon had accepted

> An oil landscape [something from Bruges], entitled *La maison sur le pont,* 1 meter 84 cm. by 1.25—not very big, to be sure, but that doesn't prevent its representing two months of work, of which a great number of days were spent on the scene and a still greater number here in Paris with the studies made in Bruges. . . .†

> . . . the fact that they admitted it has no importance for me in itself except for what the Salon represents . . . for no one better than I knows the little I know of my art *consciously known,* and the vast

* In Diego's latest account the fever of 104° continued for three days, and in his delirium a succession of Cézannes passed before his eyes, including "exquisite Cézannes which Cézanne had never painted." (*My Art, My Life,* op. cit., p. 66).

† Fig. 13. It was sold in 1910 to the Mexican Government for 1,000 pesos.

amount which is lacking for me to arrive to capacity. [The old sureness is gone from the letters—no more does he feel that all he needs is eight months of hard work!]

But as I told Mother, I value the fact [of the Salon acceptance] in respect to the government and the persons to whom I owe the subsidy which enables me to study. For, being young, without knowledge, "name," money, and other potentialities, it is not easy to get into that exhibit universally desired, considered, discussed . . . accepted by virtue, after all, of its antiquity, official character, and *réclame*.

He was showing also with the Independents, where there was no difficulty about being "accepted." In that vast, bizarre circus, the thing was to get "noticed." He found there "much that is average, more that is stupid [*mulo* is the word he used], some that stands out for its virtue or exceptional badness." He found this a good opportunity for the comparative study of his own things, since "all possible tendencies rub elbows here with 6,000 canvases. . . . On such a stormy sea it is good to launch one's own bark and see clearly on which side it is loaded. Among 2,000 authors of pictures in active disconcert, it is really difficult to be noticed . . . as you can imagine, and, above all, for the first time. . . .

"In two critical reviews of the exhibit they have cited me favorably. In one unfavorably. Press debut in a sardine can, but at least not discordant."

He encloses the press clippings, with the comment: "generally here, for a line or a mere single word of favorable publicity, one must open one's purse or bend one's spine in two. As for me, the few words didn't cost me more than five centimes for the copy of the paper I bought."

5.
THE FALL OF DON PORFIRIO

Then began for me a series of misty days. The disappearance of the qualities of my childhood sketches, sad and banal works. One museum after the other, one book after the other, I swallowed. So it went till 1910, the year in which I saw many pictures of Cézanne, the first pictures of modern painting which gave me real satisfaction. Then came pictures of Picasso, the only one for whom I felt a kind of organic sympathy. Then all the pictures of Henri Rousseau, the only one of the moderns whose works stirred each and every fiber of my being. The dregs which bad painting had left in the poor American student when he still faced Europe so shyly were washed away.*

So Rivera summarized the three and a half years he spent in Europe prior to settling in Paris. Cézanne, Picasso, and Rousseau became mentors for the next decade—the discerning eye can still trace their influence upon him. But before he could settle down to working under these new masters, he made a trip home.

* *Das Werk Diego Riveras* (Berlin, Neuer Deutscher Verlag, 1928), p. 5.

Mexico in 1910 was at a turning point. The country was in gala array to celebrate thirty years of rule by Porfirio Díaz and the hundredth anniversary of Father Hidalgo's insurrection. The aged dictator, as full of medals and honors as of years, presided over the ceremonies. Diego returned to take part and to exhibit the fruits of four years abroad.

The exhibition was a success—social and financial. Carmen Romero Rubio de Díaz, wife of the President, inaugurated the art show, and purchased six of forty paintings Diego entered in it.* The Academy of Fine Arts bought a number. There they remained for years, as Diego complained in his fresco days, *sólo para fastidiarme*—"just to annoy me." Aged connoisseurs still hold these works up against the later Riveras and shake their heads over his "uglyistic" degeneration—he was once a lad of such promise!

By ordinary standards, the young painter, now twenty-four, had arrived. Orders for portraits in abundance, a ready sale for landscapes, an instructorship in fine arts, a minor bureaucratic or diplomatic post with regular income, and no duties save those of enhancing the repute of his country by more paintings —all these were his for the taking. Yet in his heart Diego was sick of those paintings as soon as the exhibition enabled him to see them all hanging together—a backward look at the road which he had been traveling. He had seen Paris; sensed vaguely what Cézanne had been after; been excited and moved by his glimpses of the experiments of Picasso and the cubists; exulted at the work of Rousseau. His heart was not in the success he was having; his heart was in Paris among the newest painters. He was pleased by the compliments and the ready sale; but a reluctant honesty with himself prevented him from calling good the works that had caused such travail. His past struggles, crystal-

* In his last dictated "autobiography," Diego claimed that he had been planning to assassinate Porfirio Díaz at the opening of the exhibition, but was foiled when the President sent his wife (Luis Suárez, *Confesiones de Diego Rivera* [Mexico, 1962], p. 111).

lized into forty paintings—not bad, any of them, many even good—yet in them he read the signs of his defeat. They were not what he had dreamed. They were but means of getting funds to go to Paris and renew the battle.

Don Porfirio was eighty, two of his cabinet older still, fifty-five the age of the only "youngster" in the official family. A contemporary writer characterized the Senate as "an asylum for gouty decrepits," the House of Representatives as "a host of veterans, relieved by a group of patriarchs." Of twenty state governors, two were past eighty, six past seventy, seventeen past sixty. A pro-government newspaper (no other kind was permitted) referred to the bureaucracy as "the pyramids of Egypt joined to the pyramids of Teotihuacán."

What career was open to young intellectuals in this mummifying government? Or outside of official employment either, when the country's industries were in foreign hands and run with imported technicians? Young men were restive. Bandwagon politicians speculated on the Old Man's successor. Foreign capital speculated too—how long could Don Porfirio continue to serve? Would his successor lean towards British capital or American? Already he had angered American interests by giving sweeping drilling rights for the newly discovered petroleum to Pearson and Son. When a million barrels came in during 1907, the oil was sufficient to raise Pearson to the peerage as Viscount Cowdray, and to arouse the envy of American companies. The ground was becoming slippery under the aged dictator's feet.

But the real forces of upheaval were subterranean: Indians whose communal lands had been taken from them by subtle "reform laws" to make up great *latifundios;* debt-chained peons hungry for land and liberty; peasants herded into mines and factories controlled by foreign capital, forbidden to strike or organize, stirred by strange words like anarchism, socialism, syndicalism, solidarity, revolution.

The week Diego's exhibition opened, Francisco Madero declared that Díaz had stolen the recent presidential elections, and, from the United States, launched a call for revolt. The movement gathered headway slowly, for the Liberal politicians were inept and cowardly. Then peasant bands rose under Pascual Orozco, Pancho Villa, Emiliano Zapata, believing that the call was to take the land and restore to themselves their ancient heritage. The uprising assumed the aspect of a tidal wave: in less than five months it swept Díaz out of the presidential palace and made Madero the leader of the nation.

Diego lost interest in his exhibit when the insurrection began. Bursting with excitement, he watched the swift flow of events from close by in the State of Morelos. He forgot to paint, even to make sketches; but everything he saw, heard, and imagined was etched in his memory, destined to serve as a notebook for his future frescoes. Though he never was to admit or become fully aware of it, the admiration conceived for Zapata was to become the core of his revolutionary philosophy for the rest of his life.

The victory came too easily: a swift landslide, a rush of bandwagon politicians, a compromise peace which changed nothing —in five months it was over. The masses who had furnished the driving force had not begotten their own leadership and organization, nor their own program. Before they could ripen in struggle—if indeed they could at all—before they had time to test and reject inadequate leaders, before the settled crust of the old order could be plowed up by the plow of revolution, it was over. It was confined to the narrow limits of a change of administration and democratic electoral reform—a reform which solved nothing and could not itself be realized without a prior social and cultural transformation.

"At the end of the first Revolution," John Reed reports a soldier's having said to him, "that great man, Father Madero, invited his soldiers to the Capital. He gave us clothes, and food, and bullfights. We returned to our homes and found the greedy in power once more."

Diego felt as cheated as the expectant peasants when the revolution was called off before it had well begun. Feeling his excitement die, he thought again of painting. By the end of 1911 he was back in Paris—this time to stay in Europe for a decade.

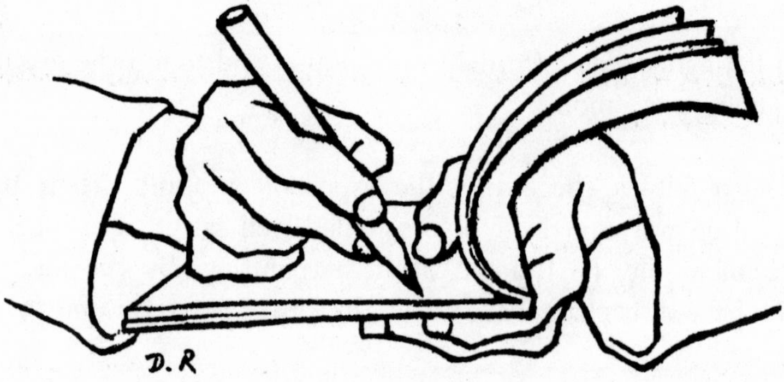

6. PAINTER'S PARIS

From the far corners of the earth men and women come to Paris to paint. They paint some hundred thousand works a year, a figure not to be explained by the city's needs—or, as the market goes, the world's. They stay for years, some all their days, remaining ever alien to its workaday life. Rivera will spend ten years here, arguing, studying, painting, fighting, feasting, starving—learn much, do much, and leave in despair, as un-French as if he had never lived here at all.

"I suppose you will take advantage of your trip to Russia to renew your acquaintance with Paris," Walter Pach said to Diego in 1927.

"The last place in the world I want to go to," was his answer. "I hate the town, and everything it stands for." Yet he regarded cubism as the most important experience in the formation of his art—and cubism spells Paris and his stay in it. When Rivera thinks of the French metropolis, gratitude and hatred mingle—as if the city were a wayward mistress who had treated him shabbily while teaching him the art of love.

To call a random roll of his Paris companions is to give some notion of the cosmopolitan brotherhood of art that exists as a world apart in the heart of the capital of France: Picasso, Gris, Picabia, Zarraga, Ortiz de Zarate, the half Spanish María Blanchard, and a whole galaxy of Latin Americans with whom Diego could debate art issues in his native tongue; Modigliani, Severini, and the futurist tribe; Gottlieb, Kisling, Marcoussis among the Poles; Jacobsen, Fischer, and other Danes; a dozen Englishmen and Americans whose names he never quite got straight; Foujita and Kavashima from Japan; and a host of French painters and writers, including André Salmon, Guillaume Apollinaire, Max Jacob, Cendrars, Jean Cocteau, and Elie Faure. Many sought him out in his studio or in the Rotonde to listen to his pronouncements on painting and his tall stories, to argue, provoke, tease, and learn from this Mexican who could talk and spin theories as easily as he painted. Great were the battles with the futurists, who insisted that the mechanism and speed of the age could be put on canvas by multiple simultaneous images, and Diego, who insisted that the movement in a picture was a function of its composition, the moving equilibrium inherent in a living design.

But most of all, or so he remembered it, his friends in Paris were Russians, Poles, Lithuanians, and Jews from Eastern Europe, from the empire of the czar. It was Angelina who first brought him into the circle of her Russian friends. A subsequent affair with Marievna Vorobiev, whose education and friendships were largely Russian, further enlarged the circle of his friends from the East. These included Ilya Ehrenburg, whom he inspired to write his fantastic novel, *Julio Jurenito* (born like Diego in Guanajuato, and a disciple of the Devil); Sternberg, who later, as a Soviet official, invited him to Russia; Lipschitz, Archipenko, and Zadkine, Larionov, Gontcharova, Bakst, Diaghilev; Boris Savinkov, the terrorist-revolutionist whom Diego knew first as an exile from the autocracy of the czar and later from the dictatorship of Lenin, and many Russians of lesser renown. With Angelina, he would visit them or meet them in the café. At first he could but listen in silence, for after a brief exchange of courtesies in the language of Paris, they would warm up to discussion in their native tongue. By dint of sheer persistence and constant exposure—he was never one to open a grammar—Diego claimed to have absorbed the intricacies of Slavic speech sufficiently to expound his views on their favorite theme: the coming revolution and its relation to the coming art. When his Russian failed him, he would force the discussion back into French. Expounding, arguing, improvising, he gradually clarified his opinions on this subject destined to be so important for his future work. Angelina, for her part, being a more orderly soul, studied grammars and literature to master Spanish against the day when she would go with her lover to his native land.

Throughout his stay in Paris, regardless of other affairs, Angelina was the center of his household. Only one other woman in Paris played an important role in his life, Marievna Vorobiev-Stebelska. She was a painter of modest talents who had been educated in Tiflis and the art school in Moscow and then had come, like so many others, to Paris to paint. Her father was a Pole who served as a Russian official; her mother, whom she never knew, a Jewish actress. "My nature," she said, "was very wayward . . . one minute I would be as shy as a small girl, the next, play the rowdy before God himself if I had the chance." Her life with Diego was stormy, for the art colony took Angelina's side, regarding Marievna as mistress and Angelina as wife.

In 1919, Marievna gave birth to a daughter, Marika, whose paternity Diego never legally acknowledged, though he did provide intermittent financial help for many years while the lone woman abandoned painting to work at more gainful tasks to give her daughter a decent home, an education, training in dancing and for the stage. Marievna has written of these hard years quite without bitterness, even acknowledging, as many have, a debt to Diego as artist. ("Under Rivera's influence, I learned to see nature and objects differently; my love for art became deeper and more complete.")

Marievna was six years younger than Diego, Angelina, six years his senior. It was the latter who kept his household for him, shared his hardships, mothered him, and by all but legal or sacramental standards, was his wife. Angelina was a product of the prewar Russian intelligentsia. Born in St. Petersburg in one of those middle-class families that were the source of Russia's liberalism and radicalism, early attracted to the arts, she was obliged by her parents to follow the fashion for "advanced women" in her day, namely to prepare for a profession. But in her last year at the university, she began to study painting and drawing at night. She won a scholarship to the St. Petersburg Academy of Fine Arts, where, after expulsion for joining a student strike and readmission, she completed a course for a license as teacher of drawing. The death of her parents leaving her with a modest income, Angelina went to Paris to pursue her girlhood dream. When Diego came, this slender, blue-eyed, blonde-haired Russian girl became a part of his life in the French metropolis. "A kind, sensitive, almost unbelievably decent person," he wrote of her in *My Art, My Life,* who "much to her misfortune became my common-law wife."

I met Angelina only after she and Diego had been separated well over a decade. Though she talked freely about him, over the old wound of their parting the scar tissue was sensitive still. Their love on both sides appears to have been "at first sight." Understanding came easily and naturally, without bell, book, vows, without dowry, support agreement, settlement, or marriage contract—institutions so highly developed among the French. Without words of wooing or attempt to discuss duration or conditions, they took to living and facing life together.

Angelina was a sweet and winsome creature. Her lightness,

gentleness, infinite patience—"she was well named when they called her Angelina," Diego said to me twenty years later—contrasted vividly with his physical bulk and "Mexican savagery." She was six years older and much calmer; in her attitude towards him there was a touch of the maternal. She bore Diego's excesses of anger and savage gaiety with angelic patience. "He will always be a child," she said to me, summing up his character. "His painting was all he ever lived for, and though he loved me for a few years and then other women, his painting was all he ever truly and deeply loved."

Blue eyes, light sky-blue. Blue jersey or smock, blue suit of trim, resolute lines, covered a slender, not unfeminine figure. Gómez de la Serna fancied that he detected an enveloping blueness all around her. Birdlike in her movements and lightness, in the poise of her head slightly tilted to one side when she was lost in contemplation, in the delicately aquiline profile, in the lips always pursed into the shadow of a meditative smile, birdlike in the thin, reedy, chirping note of her high monotoned voice, "to which the fumes of the acid with which she worked the etching plates gave a wounded tone"—Angelina was nicknamed "bluebird" by Gómez de la Serna. Thirty years later when I met her, though time had worked its changes, the sobriquet still fitted.

Diego paid court to her as to everything else in life which attracted him, through his brush. No sooner seen than he wanted to catch her on canvas. Before me I have a portrait of her (PLATE 19); unfortunately, the photograph is poor, with all the firmness of body and chair lost in darkness—but the face serves to give some notion of Angelina when she first came to his studio. The painter's love for his model is visible in the tenderness of the painting: a birdlike tilt to the head, brows arched, forehead broadened upward and outward to express what the painter felt in her of sensitiveness and intelligence, eyes that suggest the facing of life with a touch of wonder, a wistful mouth drawn ever so slightly and musingly together.

Later the painter made a cubist record of a phase of their life together: the birth of Diego, Junior. During the course of the year 1917 he painted three Angelinas—before, during, and after. The first, at the year's beginning (PLATE 17), suggests the birdlike head on slender neck, the slightly pouting lips, and the rounded curves of her body.

The second portrays an advanced state of pregnancy (PLATE 18). The heavy belly is the center of the picture, framed and emphasized. To relieve the severity, and underscore it by contrast, we have two patches of the flowered print of her garment. The tracery gives unwonted richness to the severe painting.

The third (PLATE 20) "deflates" the model; slender arms, angular neck and shoulders, angles of chair, shadows and geometric background, the downward line from the stylized eye, all converge towards the center of the painting: "Diego, Junior." The model's spirit no longer goes outward from the canvas towards the painter (and the spectator) but inward towards the child.

Throughout Diego's stay in Paris he lived in Montparnasse as part of that Bohemia which is in Paris but not of it. Art colonies are a modern phenomenon, not a sign of social and esthetic health but of illness and fragmentation. When art and life were more closely joined, artists tended to congregate together and there were centers of artistic production, but not art colonies as we know them.

Though Diego was to form part of this fraternity for a decade and enter with gusto into its extravagant escapades and experiments, he never altogether accepted it nor it him.

He began to meditate over the days when the artist formed part of the community and art was an essential aspect of life. As he studied the works of the Renaissance, he was fired by the vision of the artist beautifying his city, with the whole community looking on, celebrating and inspiring the work. The further back he followed European painting the more beautiful it seemed to him, and the closer its connection with communal life. Obscurely he grasped what the relation of artist and tribe must have been in the hieratic-magical life of pre-Conquest Mexico.

Art was no luxury for early man, he told himself, but a necessity of life, like bread and labor and love. The artist was no alien being, but a craftsman among craftsmen, a man among men. He worked directly for a society of which he formed a part, and which, appreciating his labor as directly social, worked in turn for him. The communal artist had not employed a private and esoteric language such as the Paris *Quartier*, himself along with the rest, was now so proud to flaunt in the Philistine's face. In those days the artist-craftsman had employed a language common to all men—not a degraded language either, Diego assured himself as he remembered the ancient Mexican masterpieces. Daily intercourse of the whole community with beautiful and prideful public structures, and daily employment of objects of sacred or common use that had been elaborated with loving care, had served to feed the warming flame of communal appreciation.

As Diego visited one by one Europe's great medieval cathedrals and called to mind the ancient Mexican temples, he began to comprehend that architecture, the most public of the plastic arts, had once been the central axis of them all. Sculpture and painting, stone-cutting and plastering, roofing and wood-carving, had rubbed comradely elbows with each other. The resulting works were truly monumental, enduring and worthy to endure. Their greatness lay in an expression of a common humanity and sociality that seemed no longer to exist.

It was not mere coincidence that the same moment of history which had witnessed the individual's separation from the social whole had seen the miniature leave the pages of the illuminated manuscript, the stone carving step out from its niche to become the statue, the figure of the wealthy patron detach itself from the group scene to become an individual portrait, the artist get separated from craftsman and community to become an outcast, a Bohemian, dwelling somewhere on the fringes of society, misunderstood, defiant, pridefully incomprehensible, suspect—worst of all, ignored.

In common with most of his comrades, Diego was keenly aware of the dilemma of the artist in modern society. He shared with them a common nostalgia for that earlier day when the patron had been a proud and closely linked community, or a clergy and nobility that could boast of taste and an important social role. Together with the rest of the denizens of Montparnasse he mulled over this problem and engaged in all the brave and silly and complicated gestures with which they signified their defiance of the bourgeois. But his growing interest in anarchism and socialism, and especially his deepening understanding of the folk art and ancient masterpieces of his native land, were to give a different direction from theirs to his efforts to break out of the closed circle.

At no time in history was art so isolated from life as at the moment when Diego came to Europe. Folk arts and communal feeling for art had perished in the great centers of modern industry. Poverty could provide no patronage, degraded taste no sustenance nor inspiration. The public building and the public statue no longer had any connection with art. The bourgeois had no use for painting and sculpture; the plutocrat, if he took a flyer in esthetics, could not trust his own taste, preferring to invest in dead beauty of assured value rather than risk sums on living artists. The methods of accumulation of great fortunes were such that only by accident and rare exception was the potential patron likely to be a man of aesthetic sensitivity.

> The history of art in the nineteenth century [writes Roger Fry], is the history of a band of heroic Ishmaelites, with no secure place in the social system, with nothing to support them in the unequal struggle but a dim sense of a new idea, the idea of the freedom of art from all trammels and tyrannies. . . . It is impossible that the artist should

work for the plutocrat; he must work for himself, because it is only by doing so that he can perform the function for which he exists; it is only by working for himself that he can work for mankind.

That was the secret of the forced gaiety of the Bohemia in Montparnasse which Diego had entered. It drank too much—when it had the price; wore "daring" clothes; engaged in freakish pranks; moved restlessly from ism to ism; thought up elaborate ways of showing its contempt for the "Philistine"; painted defiantly for itself because it did not know for whom else to paint. These were but brave and pitiful devices with which the artist protected his spirit's inviolability. The bourgeois world had no use for him; he answered by inscribing "*Epater le bourgeois*" on the banner of his defiance. Powerless to alter his surroundings, he cast about for ways and means of vanquishing them in the realm of fantasy.

There was no uniformity as to clothes or conduct in the *Quartier*, except not to dress—or act—like a "bourgeois." Foujita and Kavashima wore "Grecian" robes of materials they themselves had woven, fashioned their own sandals, wore their hair in fringes down on the forehead with bands of ribbon around their heads—two Japanese "Athenians" following Raymond Duncan in cultivating the graces of what they deemed an artistic life in this slightly daft world of art. Diego once painted them in full regalia, and must have enjoyed himself hugely in the doing of it.

Nina Hamnet, English sculptress who got to know Diego in Paris, has written memoirs of these times. They are full of gay drinking parties (not so gay in retrospect, for always the symbolic figure of Modigliani is there, drinking himself to death). She tells of stripping to prove that her breasts are firm and her body lithe, dancing nude before a friendly applauding crowd; nudity in the *Quartier* was something different from nudity in respectable England from whence she came. Perhaps exaggerating to enhance the picture, she tells of affairs with men whose names she did not bother to learn, whom she brought home to her studio because she took a fancy to them or because they had no place to sleep. She recounts escapades for which Montparnasse was noted—pranks whimsical or full-blooded, complicated intellectual contrivances, artistic stunts, *blagues,** practical jokes, frivolities, parodies, solemn frauds, meant to upset the pompous, advertise the "cause," alarm the Philistine—devices enriched by all the humors of this international *camaraderie,* from so many lands, and with a special sauce of Gallic wit. Occasionally they were half serious, or became so in their consequences. Mostly they were taken as lightly as dress and drink and sex and money—as lightly as all things except only art and ideas about art. These were serious: indeed in them all truth, honor, beauty and devotion lodged, for they were the *raison d'être* of Bohemia.

Prodigious were the disputes the painters had about art. The jangle of conflicting creeds and doctrines, intensified by the diversity of strongly individualized temperaments, led to epic battles in which no mercy was shown nor quarter given, no victories won nor defeats conceded, truce coming only as a result of the combatants' exhaustion. One of these mighty quarrels as it appeared to an outsider, is described by Ramón Gómez de la Serna, writing on *Riverismo* (in his book on *Ismos*):

> There in Paris everyone was afraid of him. I saw him once quarrel with Modigliani, who was drunk; quarrel while he trembled with twisted spasms of laughter.
>
> Some coach-drivers listened to the discussion without ceasing to stir the sugar in their coffee.
>
> Modigliani wanted to excite Diego. . . . The young blonde of

* Perhaps Diego's tall stories are but the monstrous hypertrophy and Mexicanization of Paris *blague*. But the monstrousness and prodigiousness are not so much Mexican as Dieguesque.

Pre-Raphaelite type who accompanied Modigliani had her hair combed in *tortillons* on her temples like two sunflowers or earpieces, the better to hear the discussion.

Picasso had the attitude of a gentleman waiting for a train, his beret jammed down to the shoulders, resting on his stick as if he were a fisherman patiently hoping for a bite. . . .

The reader need not take the combat any more seriously than the disputants did; actually Modigliani and Rivera were friends. During the war they roomed for some time together; Diego, whose pension had ceased with the overthrow of Madero but who earned enough by his indefatigable industry, helped out the often hungry and ever thirsty Italian—as he did many another starving artist—whenever he and Angelina did not happen to be starving themselves.

Modigliani was strongly impressed by his tremendous Mexican friend—and who in the artist's quarter could fail to be? Leopold Gottlieb painted him, huge, massive, monumental, eyes full of tender sentiment; there was such a Rivera, but few have seen that side of him (PLATE 9). Adam Fischer, the Danish sculptor, carved him, slumbrous, sphinxlike, in stone (PLATE 11.) A Russian woman painter's version of Rivera, which I have not been able to locate, is described by Gómez de la Serna thus:

They told fantastic tales about him: that he had the ability to suckle young at his Buddhic breasts . . . that he was all covered with hair, which must have been true because on the wall of his study, by a Russian woman artist, Marionne [probably Marievna Vorobiev], who painted in his studio, in a man's suit with the boots of a tiger-tamer and a lion's skin, was his portrait, nude, with legs crossed and armored in kinky hair. What serious obscenity in that drawing. . . .

But the best of the Rivera portraits are three attempts by Modigliani, wrestling with the problem of getting into his sketches something of the savagery, smoldering sensuous fire, fantastic imagination and mighty irony for which Diego was famous. His Rivera is large and heavy, savage and overflowing, mocking and bombastic. How strong must have been the impact of Diego's personality so to alter Modigliani's usually simple, lyrical line! One of these portraits, a pen and ink drawing in the collection of T. E. Hanley of Bradford, Pennsylvania, incorporates Rivera's name into the picture as an integral part of the design. Another was owned by Elie Faure. A third (PLATE 10) was offered for sale by Henri Pierre Roché in 1929 for 150,000 francs—a bargain price for a lesser work by a man whom society had permitted to die a decade earlier of starvation and neglect! While living, he had traded many a sketch for five or ten francs, the price of a meal, a bit of hashish or cocaine, or a bottle or two of strong drink. No wonder Bohemia drank hard, engaged in brave, foolish, defiant gestures, acted a little mad!

7. THE ISMS IN ART

Even after Diego settled in Paris he returned each year to Spain. The year 1911 found him in Barcelona, painting in neo-impressionist pointillism; part of 1913 and 1914 he spent wrestling with the Toledo landscape, to drag the secret of cubism out of the modeled hollows and writhing outlines of El Greco. His earliest cubist landscape deals with Toledo, too.

His visits to Paris were mainly for the purpose of exhibiting his work and seeing how it fared in the sea of painting at each Autumn Salon. From Mexico he had brought two large landscapes which he exhibited in 1911. They attracted no attention. In 1912 he showed *Portrait of a Spaniard* (PLATE 15), noticed to the extent of being reproduced by Fernand Roches in his annual review in *L'Art décoratif*.

That year the painter Lampué, dean of the Municipal Council of Paris, honored the show by writing to Minister Bérard:

> You will ask yourself (if you visit the exhibition): Have I the right to lend a public monument to a band of malefactors who conduct

themselves in the world of art as *apachés* in ordinary life? You will ask yourself on leaving, *Monsieur le Ministre,* if nature and the human form have ever suffered such outrages. . . .

An interpellation on "the scandal of the *Salon d'Automne*" was made in the Chamber; the *Revue Hebdomadaire* demanded that the state close its schools and the Academy in Rome or put an end to the "anarchy" of the salon. The storm blew over, but the annual exhibition still stands as one of France's proudest adornments. The bitter campaign, by no means without precedent in the history of modern French art criticism, gave Diego some notion of the hospitality he and his fellows might expect from bourgeois and academic Paris. Though his part in the affray was insignificant, it taught him faithfulness to his own vision and contempt for Philistinism.

In the Independents' show of 1913 Diego exhibited *La jeune fille aux artichauts* and *La jeune fille à l'éventail* (*Girl with Artichokes* and *Girl with Fan*). They attracted a certain amount of notice. In 1920, when Gustave Coquiot wrote his history of the Society of Independents, he selected Diego Rivera as one of the more promising of the cubists and *Girl with Artichokes* as one of the few cubist works to reproduce. It must be borne in mind, however, that M. Coquiot lost little love on cubism. Here is his comment:

> Rivera—Two paintings by M. Diego Rivera: *La Jeune Fille aux artichauts* and *La Jeune Fille à l'éventail.* . . . These two pictures, in a grey, rose, and green harmony, possess a beautiful decorative feeling. They resemble two frescoes [an interesting observation concerning such early work] and have all the austerity and attraction of frescoes.

Of more interest in his personal development than *Girl with Artichokes* is his *Adoration of the Shepherds* (PLATE 21). Few canvases cost him such effort. He began struggling with the theme in Toledo early in 1912, abandoned it, dragged the canvas to Paris and back, reworked it several times to give it greater solidity and dynamism, finally completing it, in Toledo once more, in the spring of 1913. He had lost his old facility because he was going through an internal struggle; his steps were hesitant on the new path; he did not know himself where it would lead.

The canvas (when last I heard of it, in the possession of Guadalupe Marín and much the worse for wear) is worth examining. In the foreground a shepherd with a loaf of bread and a peasant girl bearing a basket on her head are adoring an image of the Madonna and Child. Their figures, slightly cut up into geometric patterns—without, however, breaking the outline—represent a connecting link between the female figure in *The Samaritan* and the three *Angelinas* mentioned previously. The landscape (Toledo once more) shows the river and bridge that El Greco painted, to the girl's left, climbing to the orchard and farm near the top, and receding mountains beyond. The bridge, the lines of the hills, repeat and widen the lines of the pyramidal Madonna, the whole being cut up into geometrical shapes that almost merge with the figures; the receding planes, flattened, uptilted, turn on an invisible axis, bending towards the foreground. The artist is engaged in an effort to distort the natural forms according to the plan of his plastic vision—he is trying to find his way to the solution of the problems that were even then preoccupying the cubists in Paris. The influence of Cézanne is manifest in the angular construction, in the flattened planes that merge distance with foreground; the influence of Delaunay is in the curved planes; the influence of El Greco in the choice of landscape, even the religious theme, so unusual for Rivera. Yet there is nothing of Cézanne or Delaunay and less than nothing of El Greco in the painting. We are in the presence of visible signs—too visible—of an artist's wrestling with his problem.

Girl with Artichokes and *Adoration of the Shepherds* mark the transition of Diego Rivera to cubism. They reveal him joining not as a servile follower but, like a Mexican guerrilla fighter, alone and on his own, and always ill at ease when enlisted in a regular army. He could truthfully say, "I came to cubism fighting." And three years later, still fighting, he left it.

In the spring of 1914 Rivera assembled all his Spanish works and a few early efforts in the new style for his first one-man show, at the Galerie B. Weill, 26 rue Victor-Massé. It contained twenty-five recent pictures, including most of those we have discussed. The critics greeted the show with silence. But more disillusioning than their silence was the dealer's loquacity and obvious indifference to the wares she was offering. The catalogue mispelled the artist's name as Riviera, and gave him the middle initial H. The dealer herself wrote the introduction, in which she succeeded in saying nothing at all about the painter or his work. It showed only too clearly what every painter has had to learn, that to many gallery owners the painter's ardent work is exalted merchandise and mystery. Here is the text of Rivera's first full-length introduction to the world of gallery frequenters:

> We present here to the *Amateurs des "Jeunes"* the Mexican Diego H. Riviera, whom the researches of cubism have tempted.
>
> We do not want to run the risk of making a panegyric of this young artist; let us permit him to develop, and some critic or well-intentioned Barnum, breaker into open doors, will find himself just on time some day to discover him. Of the danger of burning incense too soon before artists we have a thousand proofs. Such a one, showing some talents, is pushed, encouraged; a run of luck attains him a little notoriety; *crac!* he bourgeoisifies; he wants to earn "a lot" of money; he becomes very "*talon rouge*"; after the manner of such and such a Maecenas of elegant fashion, he believes himself of the line of Louis the Great; his genius has no equal but that of . . . the Bastille; his work, actually? he delivers himself more and more mightily of a mouse; often, forgetful of his lineage, he lingers in the antechambers, but wall tapestries have found an . . . innovator; hurrah! . . .
>
> Come and see the young, free, independent, and you will find in their works, amidst awkwardnesses without limit, the springtime charm of youth; no search for the desire to please, which will please you!

His period of hesitation over, Diego delivered himself to cubism. A whirlpool of aesthetic theories swept him off his feet. The old standards—those of yesterday, those of a century ago, and those of a millennium—were being called in question. Art had become a search for new truth. Each day's discovery was elevated by systematizers into the revelation of eternal laws—next day forgotten for the morrow's innovation.

There are lands and times in which the basic features of a traditional style have continued with little change for centuries; now each "style" scarcely outlasted the drying of the ink on the manifesto proclaiming it eternal. Change was in the air in those dizzying years that began the twentieth century's second decade; the rapid dance of isms kept pace with the speed of locomotion, the stir of ideas, the race between armor plate and armor-piercers, the nervous rhythm of a world rushing compulsively, blindly, towards the precipice of total war.

Even as the painter watched, firm outlines began to waver, certainties became uncertain, all axioms were challenged at once. The very universe dissolved into transmuting elements, whirling emptinesses, mathematical formulas; space was losing its vacancy, matter its solidity, time its uniformity; matter and motion were converting into each other; the solid, dependable, three-dimensional world, the stable universe of Newton, the clear geometry of Euclid, the gradualism of Darwin, were all being undermined. How could one keep one's two feet on the ground when the earth itself was melting away into formulas?

The Ishmaelite artist, recruited from the middle class and tied indissolubly to it by his battle against its outlook, felt all this more keenly than the ordinary citizen. The workingman, engrossed in wages and hours, seeking a little more diversion and creature comfort, paid no attention to the intellectual hubbub. The burgher was made vaguely uneasy and a little angry. The rebel artist was stirred with excitement, his fantasy kindled, his loneliness replenished by an exhilarating sense of coming reinforcements in his unequal battle.

The dogma that denies us perishes, he told himself. The old order changes, the world turns upside down, art alone endures. To work then, at the designing of a brave new world. In the indescribable confusion, the artists thus banded together did not note that there were conflicting currents in the flood that threatened to sweep away the ambivalently loved and hated world: that individualist anarchism, neomedievalism, triumphant esthetic constructivism, and social revolution in the arts might all be ways of reacting against the bourgeois and his world, but differed fundamentally as to what should be put in its place.

Nor did these artists stop to ponder that the revolution of which the radical socialist spoke was something quite different from a revolution in the arts. Or that the terrible simplifiers might be more devoid of culture, more cocksure of their infallibility, less humble before the mysteries of art, and less tolerant of its waywardness than the hated bourgeois on whom artist and socialist were declaring their several wars.

For a brief instant all the attacking parties were united in a single onslaught on a common enemy, and not too cognizant of the esthetic or the social implications of their fight. All they knew was that they were rebels, nay, revolutionists in art, and they hailed each attack, as they did each succeeding ism, with a loud hurrah.

As we look back at these movements, we can begin to see cubism, futurism, suprematism, and all the other schools of abstraction and formal experiment in modern art as contrary eddies in a common current. Together they mark the culmination of a long process of growing isolation of art from society, the result of art's having been forced increasingly to turn in upon itself. If the painters could no longer paint for society, they could at least paint for each other, and increasingly they did. If their craft was no longer a means to public ends, they would make it an end in itself. Painting for such a specialized and sensitive and deeply interested audience as they themselves provided, they could experiment with color as pure color, with form as pure form, to their heart's content.

The enjoyment of many of these modern pictures, painted by the artist for his own special world, presupposes a refinement of esthetic perception almost as rare and specialized and difficult to develop as the creative faculty itself. True, painters cannot live by painting only for each other any more than the Chinese of the economic fable by taking in each other's washing. But at times like these, art begets its audience rather than vice versa; in the waste places left bare by the drying up of the springs of social appreciation, there had sprouted a rather delicate new growth: the *esthete*—that is, the specialist in esthetic sensibility. It was for the esthete—for the rare patron that was such, or followed the esthete's advice—for him and for his fellow painters that the "modernist" now began to paint.

Experimental work great artists had done in all ages, but now for the first time they offered the experiments themselves as finished works of art. Or they began to leave their works "unfinished," to exhibit technical aspects which previous generations of artists had wrestled with and mastered, but had then been at pains to assimilate into the structure of the completed picture. Working now for his fellow craftsmen and for the circle of specialists that had adopted his point of view, the artist could give free rein to a craftsman's interest in precisely those aspects of his workmanship. Hence the product became subordinate to the process. Much that is otherwise inexplicable in cubism and abstract and nonobjective art in general is made clear as soon as we realize to what extent this art is research, a report on an experiment, "painters' painting." Therein lies its subtlety, therein its service to the development of the painter's craft, therein, too, its limitations and the inevitable brevity of each ism's flourishing.

Those who dismiss the intense enthusiasm and creative excitement that inhered in the movement as mere desire to attract attention, to acquire an air of mystery, and to sell some worthless trash to gullible patrons expose thereby not cubism but their own insensitivity. Incompetents and poseurs there were among these men, as among all schools of artists, and there was more than a little desperate self-advertisement and nose-thumbing at a society which ignored and had outlawed the artist. But if in their work there was pose and fad and defiance, there was also artistic intuition, eager experiment, and quest for fresh sources of beauty—though the cubists were chary of using that much abused word.

Even the special subject-matter of cubist painting betrayed the growing isolation of the painter. The impressionists had sought "freedom" from the constraints of bourgeois society by going to the outdoors for their material: the flashing movement of the boulevard, the fleeting, evanescent personal impression, the portrayal of carefree scenes of recreation which extricated the "model" from the conventional ties which bound him to bourgeois society. From this it had been but a step to the painting of the outcast, the ostracized and rejected, the half world that existed at the margin of middle-class life. Beggars, floaters, prostitutes, charwomen, professional models, dancers, mountebanks, circus performers, occupied the canvases of the transition painters of the late impressionist and post-impressionist period. The pathos of these paintings lay in the perception of kinship on the part of the artist with this outcast world.

If you will observe the circus performers of Seurat, you will note that they are not only separated from society, but even from each other. They loom up out of the mist of dots and dashes like isolated solid towers, each surrounded by depopulated space. Surrounding forms repeat their form, but no answering eye catches their glance, no ear opens to their eager voice; none speaks, none listens, none sees or is seen. "We are at the outermost margins of society," each figure seems to proclaim, "and aside from the fact that we have each other to work with, each of us is utterly alone."

Daumier painted the downtrodden; his disciple Toulouse-Lautrec painted the rejected; and his disciple Picasso did harlequins, acrobats, jugglers, and, along with them, utterly dejected and broken starvelings and beggars—the progression is continuous. Are not these figures also "Ishmaelites"? And harlequin, juggler, ballet dancer, acrobat, are they not artists after their fashion? Do they not produce their beauty of form and movement out of their own person? Do they not stake all, risking life and limb, for beauty, for the entertainment of a spectator who may be fascinated by the spectacle but indifferent to the inner world of the performer? Is not the acrobat concerned with the subtle and perilous quest for balance and equilibrium, the slightest alteration in one part of the design he is making out of his body requiring a corresponding alteration in every one of its parts? Hence the attraction of these "anti-literary" painters for the "literary" pathos implicit in these figures.

The final step in the direction of a separate world of their own carried the artist from the external world of Bohemia to the internal world of his own studio. Cubist paintings are so often concerned with random studio objects, with wine and cognac bottles, glasses, musical instruments, newspapers, lay figures, plaster casts, tubes of paint, packs of cards, cigarettes and pipes. These are not the kitchen still lifes of Courbet, the living-room objects of Chardin, nor the parlor fruits of Cézanne. If there is a landscape in these paintings at all, it is usually the bit that can be seen by glancing from the studio window, or in some picture hanging on its wall.

Moreover, the objects depicted seem to have been seen not so much with the eyes as with the hand—as if the artist were in actual physical contact with the thing and painting it fragmentarily as he moved around it and it revealed itself in phases to his fingertips. Or as if the eye had got so close that it could only see a tiny fragment at a time, a segment that flattens out, becomes a mere jagged or angular or curved section of surface, loses its solidity, coherence, and relation to the larger whole. Strange that for these worshipers of solidity, of "volume in space," the actual world of objects should become mere broken-down bits of surface, random fragments, atomized tactile sensations and myopic close-ups!

But then—and here is where the greatest excitement came —the artist took all these casual fragments and, out of the depths of his own sense of form and structure, put them together into something new, a new pattern, a new solid, a new object— of his own creation. He had gotten close to things, had broken them up by "scientific analysis" into their components, had walked around them viewing them from all sides—from above, from below, from without, from within—touching and peering, analyzing and abstracting, till he had gotten into them and they into him. From the interior of the studio the last step could only be into the interior of the objects themselves and into the interior of the artist's own consciousness. Behold the ultimate in selection, distortion, and rearrangement, the ultimate in isolation from the conventional, the bourgeois, the Philistine, the oppressive social whole! Behold the ultimate in the sovereignty of the creative mind, the artist become architect, constructor, builder, creator of his own universe!

8.
HOW TO PRICE A PAINTING

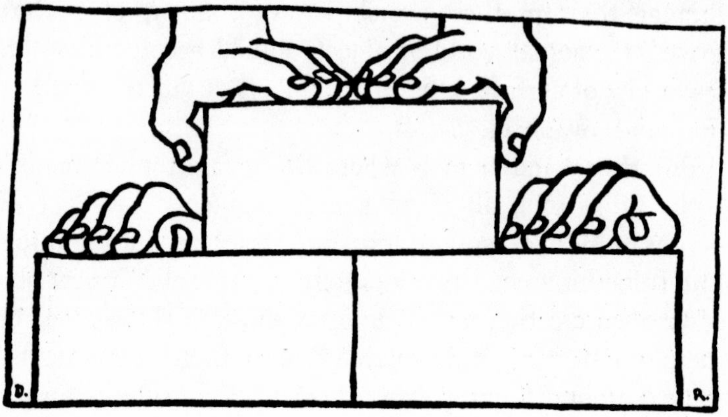

To follow a cubist in his evolutions is dizzying. All the more true is this of one who, like Diego, had started late and was bent on trying everything, imitating everybody, catching up with and outdistancing the cubist flock already in full and erratic flight; determined, also, to make his own original contribution.

How many cubist paintings Diego did between 1913 and 1917 no one knew, least of all himself. I succeeded in assembling in Paris, Mexico, and the United States some thirty photographs, and verbal descriptions of perhaps a dozen more, a mere fraction of the production of his indefatigable energy and zeal.

"Monsieur Rivera," the Parisian cubist art-dealer Léonce Rosenberg told me in 1936, "did about five major pictures a month for me, not counting sketches, pastels, water colors, etc. He was always one of my most prolific painters." This would imply several hundred "major works" in his cubist period. It was fortunate for Diego that he was so prolific, for his pension ceased at the beginning of 1914, with the downfall of Madero in Mexico. Angelina's remittances from Russia also ceased after war began. Diego was able to support the two of them—not without moments of hunger—and to help friends to meet the high living costs and scarcity of wartime Paris. Diego's paintings early attracted discriminating collectors and sold well. Today they are scattered all over the Western world.

The earliest cubist work of which I have been able to secure a reproduction (if we except transitional paintings such as *Girl with Artichokes* and *Adoration of the Shepherds*) is *Man with a Cigarette,* dated 1913 (PLATE 25). The model was Elie Indenbaum, the sculptor. The picture is influenced by Picasso—the Picasso of *The Poet* of 1911. Rivera has journeyed in the cubist manner around his model, seen fragments now from this angle, now from that, cut the fragments up into geometrical shapes that merge with the background, flattened the whole, reconstituting it into a physical and psychological portrait of the sitter. It is precisely this that made so many of Rivera's cubist pictures heretical to the stricter theologians of the school. In contradistinction to the work of his master Picasso, there seems to be more of an ornamentalizing and substantializing tendency. Rivera reconstituted the figure before he had completed the chopping up; the parts are distributed according to a pleasant ornamental all-over pattern rather than constituted into some new shape with mere conceptual reminiscences of the original "object." M. Elie Indenbaum is seen as if through the facets of some polyphase crystal; it has a jewellike effect without ceasing to be a human being and a recognizable portrait. The zealots raised their eyebrows at this new recruit. From the same period dates his *Bridge of Toledo,* his first cubist landscape, one more of his successive attempts to do the scene which the world will always see through El Greco's eyes. But Rivera's chief kinship, as in so many landscapes of his cubist period, is with Delaunay.

From 1914 date *The Alarm Clock* (PLATE 23), *Two Women on a Balcony* (PLATE 22), *Grandee of Spain,* and *Landscape, Majorca* (PLATE 24). *Grandee of Spain* is described in the Quinn catalogue as "an expressive cubistic work of conventionalized renaissance design; depicting an erect figure, wearing a coat of chainmail and full leg armor; a sabre and pistol girdled about his waist. Geometrical background of harmonizing colors with fine gradations of tone." It is six feet four inches high by four feet three inches in width, but, aside from size, of no special interest.

The *Two Women,* though their faces and parts of their bodies are seen both in profile and full face at once, also fail to break up. Clearly, form is firmly identified in Rivera's mind with flowing continuity. Involuntarily one thinks of the earlier Metzinger and Gleizes, their works and their dogmas.

The Alarm Clock represents an assemblage of a number of conventional cubist motifs. Angelina left her mark in the use of Russian instead of French lettering. Its imitativeness is betrayed by the musical instrument, the playing cards; Diego had little sensibility for music, never touched an instrument, detested cards; I doubt if he ever used an alarm clock; the fan, too, was alien. The concern with textures, conventional in the cubism of this time, seems more ornamental, with more subtle contrasts, brighter in color than in the other painters, the whole more monumental, and in some subtle sense Mexican. It makes one think of the elegant arrangements of objects in the Mexican secondhand markets (so different from the matter-of-factness of a heap of objects in the Parisian *Marché aux Puces*). It reminds one, too, of a Mexican *sarape* or hand-woven Indian blanket, which the reader can confirm by glancing at the bits of Mexican blanket shown in PLATES 16 and 27. To the sober chiaroscuro of cubism this heretic always insists on adding the intense bright and dark of the tropics.

Majorca is presumably the last of the four. Even if we did not know that he was there in the latter part of 1914, the signature would evidence it. *Man with a Cigarette* is signed at the top in cursive letters, "Diego Rivera 1913"; the next three, at the bottom in carelessly printed block letters—more formally and mechanically in the *Two Women;* but for the landscape, as for all the work of the following year, his fancy caught by the rigors of geometry, Rivera used a stencil, "D.M.R."

Cubist enthusiasm for geometry and mechanism did not end with signatures. The adepts developed a mathematical-mechanical formula for measuring a painting's value! The confraternity (which included the dealers who were young enough, or sufficiently courageous, to take their stand with the new school) concocted a code-book in which each painter was assigned a number indicating his "personal factorial value." This unit number, the personal element in the equation, differed from artist to artist; all the rest was as standardized as the multiplication table. Any given picture had only to be measured by square mensuration and classified as size so-and-so, then the personal-value unit was multiplied by the size factor to arrive automatically at the selling price! Léonce Rosenberg, to whom I am indebted for this information, determined thus both purchase and sale price, paying the painter so much money for so many square meters of painted canvas. Could quantitative estimate of humanity's subtlest products go further? It had the virtue of definiteness, and of eliminating much unpleasant haggling. If only we could find a reliable formula for the value exponent, we might recommend it to non-cubist painters as well!

M. Rosenberg remembers Rivera's pictures as generally size "60," for which he received between 250 and 280 francs. Among them the dealer indicated two of the cubist portraits of Angelina and a third portrait of a woman, more abstract and consistently cubist, as having been purchased by him as "size 60" (the dimensions of the latter portrait were 1 meter 27 centimeters by 97 centimeters) for about 250 francs each. He estimated their price in 1937 as about 2,000 francs each. The mark-up, however, is not so high in dollars as this would indicate, for the franc had depreciated to something less than one-third of its former value. It was only after Rivera's death that the price of his pictures really shot up. "Rivera was very enthusiastic, as I remember, for the mathematical value theory of picture prices," M. Rosenberg assured me. "The scheme still prevails among strictly orthodox cubists, and is not at all a bad idea."

A strange dry wine of mathematical theory for life and art that ranged from the treatment of a woman's curves to the stenciled signature and the price tag on a picture! Yet these were only externals of the passionate enthusiasm that was producing the flood of cubist works.

The latter half of 1914 and a good part of 1915 Rivera spent in Spain. He painted three interesting cubist portraits: of Jesus Acevedo, Martín Luís Guzmán and Ramón Gómez de la Serna (PLATES 26, 27 and 28): Acevedo was one of Diego's boyhood friends, had studied with him in art school, and was an architect in Madrid. He is portrayed surrounded by tools, materials, and diagrams, allusive to his profession. Martín Luís Guzmán is a friend of Diego's maturity, a novelist, Mexico's greatest, author of *The Eagle and the Serpent* and *The Shadow of the Caudillo*. For years he resided in Spain. This portrait is much better than that of the architect, I think, the novelist's Hispanism being playfully proclaimed by the headdress, his Mexicanism by the fragment of *sarape*. Rivera was no longer an imitator, nor the victim of the dogmas of the school; he had found his own equivalent for the spontaneous intellectual wit that characterizes most of the cubist work of his acknowledged master, Picasso, and was so often lacking in the men who made scholastic systems of Picasso's changing fantasies.

No less diverting is the portrait of Ramón Gómez de la Serna, at work in his studio, surrounded by the queer objects he loved to collect, with a view of Madrid at the upper right visible from his window. It is a psychological portrait of this somewhat precious modernist writer, with the quality and style of his works wittily suggested. Unfortunately, the picture as shown in PLATE 28 loses much because I have had to make it from a poorly printed plate which Gómez de la Serna used for the cover of his book *Ismos.* Don Ramón is portrayed writing, pen in one hand, pipe in the other, a revolver upside down on his desk. The surrounding objects give the picture a surrealist touch.

The "subject" has written a description of it worth giving for the light it throws on Diego's methods of work, and on certain aspects of cubism—at least as Rivera practiced it.

Every time I look at it I note that I resemble it more, and yet I look less and less like a mask they made of me right on my face, buried in plaster like a dead person during a quarter of an hour. . . .

Here is my complete anatomy. Here am I after the autopsy which one can suffer before dying or committing suicide, an autopsy marvelous and revealing . . . a true portrait, though it may not be a portrait with which to compete in beauty contests. . . .

When the great Mexican painted my eyes, he did not look at those chestnuts eyes of mine whose normal appearance is for "portraitists." . . . He understood the eyes he needed in the portrait, eyes which were complementary and clarifying to each other. In the round eye is synthesized the moment of luminous impression, and in the long shut eye, the moment of comprehension. . . .

I—how could it be otherwise?—am highly pleased with this portrait, which has the characteristic of being profile and front view at the same time . . . this palpable, ample, complete consideration of my humanness turning on its axis . . . and I have the pleasure of explaining it with a pointer, as if I were teaching geography, for we are genuine maps. . . .

In making this portrait of me Diego María Rivera did not subject me to the torture of immobility or a mystic stare into vacancy for more than a fortnight, as happens with other painters. . . . I was writing a novel while he was making my portrait, I smoked, leaned forward, leaned back, went out for a walk, and always the great painter went on painting my likeness; so much so that when I returned from the walk it looked much more like me than when I went out. . . .

When Diego finished it, it was placed in a store window centrally located, and so great were the crowds who came to see it, so menacing their attitude before the plate glass of the window, so disturbing that multitude to traffic on the street, that the Governor admonished the owner of the shop in writing to withdraw it from the window. . . .

It remains only to add that Diego kept to the end of his days the same habits of work, allowing the sitter the same freedom of motion and life, arguing with him, letting him go on with his work, seeing through and around him and into him, seeming hardly to look at him at all.

9. PARIS IN WARTIME

The summer of 1914 is remembered as exceptionally beautiful. Spring came early, full of sunshine, everyone dreamed of a trip to the country, a sea voyage to distant lands. Nature seemed bright and friendly, giving no hint of impending tragedy.

Diego, ever sensitive to currents of political rumor and swift to spin them into plausible pictures, kept assuring everyone that war was coming. But he had been doing that for so long! His friends egged him on to give more "secret details," called him "Mexican cowboy," implying thereby that war was for barbarous lands like his, not for civilized twentieth-century Europe. Whether or not Diego believed his own conjectures, he set out early that summer in the company of Angelina, María Blanchard, and other painters for a walking and sketching tour in Spain and the Balearic Islands. The outbreak of war caught them painting in Majorca.

The times seeming unpropitious for art shows in Paris, Diego and María Blanchard treated traditionalist Madrid to its cubist baptism, a two-man show. The two modernists cannot be said to have taken conservative Madrid by storm. Men like Gómez de la Serna, who wrote the introduction to the catalogue, rallied to their defense; Marie Laurencin, in Spain at the time, bought one of Diego's paintings; one of the portraits in a shop window blocked traffic in a Madrid street; but for the most part they were greeted with silence or scornful laughter.

The laughter extended from the paintings to the contrasting figures—huge, bulky Diego and diminutive, frail, hunchbacked María—as they walked together out of the showroom. The next time María came, a crowd followed her, jeering, through the town. Her spirit was bruised: "Spain is the only country," she said, "where a being like me is followed by people on the streets." She left the land of her father—her mother was French—never to return to it.

María had been Diego's friend and Angelina's before she introduced them to each other in Bruges. From Bruges the three traveled together. With them were Enrique Friedman, a Mexican, Benjamin Coria, a friend of Modigliani's, Dr. Freymann, later a publisher of scientific books in Belgium, and others. In Brussels, where the whole crowd shared a studio and sleeping-quarters, a fire broke out in the middle of the night. Diego valuing his canvases above his trousers, rushed out without pants but with his arms full of paintings. There he added to the entertainment of the crowd by accusing Friedman of starting the fire. "I saw you, I saw you with my own eyes," he kept insisting. Yet when calm was restored, they continued their journey together.

In London, Friedman boasted of being the only one who knew English, using his knowledge to such effect that the whole group spent their first night in a disorderly house. Thereafter they got along without Friedman's English.

Later, Angelina, María, and Diego shared a studio in Paris. Diego often rose at four of a winter's morning, and in the dimness and cold began to paint. He would paint all morning without tiring, often scrape off what he had done during the afternoon, while evening would find him still attacking the canvas.

When Angelina was away on a journey, there was war in the studio. Neither María nor Diego would cook, clean, wash a dish, clear away scraps after a meal. María told her cousin of a famous beefsteak which remained on a plate for twenty days; finally the concierge came and removed the offender after the neighbors began to scent it in the wind. Yet Diego could cook when he wanted to, and so could María. They vied with each other sometimes. María remembered fabulous feasts shared by Diego, María, Angelina, Guillaume Apollinaire, Modigliani, and others.

Diego at times acted "very queerly," and when questioned, claimed to be "wrestling with spirits." Again he would feel that the studio was too small to contain him, that he was filling the habitation and pressing against angles, walls, and corners, till he would throw open the window and feel himself spreading out all over Paris. There would seem to be something of the spirit of Marc Chagall in the episode. The memoirs of Ilya Ehrenburg and those of Marievna Vorobiev, published in 1962, both describe these "seizures," from which on occasion Ehrenburg fled in terror.

Cubist disputes were at the flood in Paris in 1914. The gabble was rising higher and higher, when it was stilled by the cannon's roar. All at once, M. Bourgeois recognized that M. Artiste might be useful after all: to draw recruiting posters; to use his power of accenting and distorting and concentrating reality to make war's horrors (as the enemy waged it, of course) more vivid and, if possible, more horrible; to use brush and paint and optics to make solid forms like trucks and cannon merge with their background; to camouflage the starkness and irrevocability of unnatural man-dealt death by adorning it with laurel leaves; at the very least, he might find a lowest common denominator with all able-bodied males of proper age and exchange brush for gun, thereby becoming, at last, a "useful" member of society. Art, in one form or another, enlisted or was drafted for the duration, and reintegrated into a disintegrating society.

When Diego returned to France in 1915, he attempted to enlist in the French army. He was not alone in this, many of the foreign artists in Paris having joined up in 1914, some because they had come to regard France as a second fatherland, some because they believed the French version of the origins of the war, some because they loved—or thought they loved—the "beauty of war," some because they were caught up in the general excitement and there no longer seemed any other way to live. How much these motives influenced Diego, and how much, as he claimed later, a mere desire to facilitate his return from Spain to Paris, I cannot say. Whether it was his huge bulk, his flat feet, or some other physical disability, or a record of connection with anarchists, he was rejected for the army but readmitted into France. He found Montparnasse deserted, art magazines in collapse, the nocturnal city darkened in anticipation of air raids, the cafés subject to curfew, queues beginning to form for the purchase of this or that, Paris feeling the pinch of wartime shortages and high prices.

He himself was penniless, his pension having stopped long ago. Angelina's income, too, had ceased. She cooked at home—that is to say, in their one-room studio-kitchen-bedroom—and did her best to meet the whims of Diego's hypochondriacal diet. Sometimes a few sous' worth of bones and vegetables would have to make a broth for several days; at others, when Diego had sold some pictures, they had bread, wine, real meat, and cheese; and, if he were in the mood for it, there were hungry and happy guests. Now that the Rotonde closed at ten-thirty or earlier, the artists and writers not in uniform fell to visiting each other. The fortunate one who had sold a picture or received a remittance would play host, and each would bring something—a bottle of wine, a cheese, a loaf. Most were foreigners now, or women: Picasso, Juan Gris, María Blanchard, Ortiz de Zarate, Angel Zarraga, Severini, Modigliani, Survage, Férat, Hayden, the sculptor Lipschitz, Angelina, and her Russian friends. These last increased in number as the war progressed.

The little group of artists were thrown closer together, like beleaguered folk in a hostile world that had no use for them and their activity. The war choked all forces that did not directly serve it. Artistic activity suffered most of all. During the early part of the war, cubist painting was dubbed *boche;* after the Russian Revolution the conservative journals fell to denouncing the modernists as Bolsheviks. (Later, the Bolsheviks would denounce them as bourgeois!) With great difficulty the poet André Salmon, aided by M. Barbazangeo, succeeded in securing the Galerie de l'Avenue d'Antin in 1916 for the only group exhibition of modern painting after the war began.

The artists painted, even more than before, for each other and the lonely, contracting world in which they lived. Their work became more esoteric still, their theories and discussions even more so. But the brutal fact of the war forced itself ever deeper into their consciousness and conversation. Diego, who had been derisively called a Mexican cowboy for predicting war, was derided now for talking of rumored mutinies in the French forces and coming international revolution. He spent more time than previously with Spaniards, Mexicans, Scandinavians, Italians, Russians and Poles and others from the empire of the czars. Not all of these were artists or even writers. Increasingly there were political refugees among them, and their talk became steadily more exciting to Diego. His Russian developed fluency as he listened and argued with them; when it broke down he spoke volubly in French. Art and Revolution, and Art and the Masses, were their predilect topics of discussion. The ideas formulated in these controversies were destined to have a momentous effect upon his future; for the time being, however, he continued to paint as if no new ferment were at work in his mind at all.

During 1915 and much of 1916 he carried his experiments with the technical resources of his craft even further, painting with wax instead of oil, on pressed cork instead of canvas, using plaster stucco on some of his canvases to give roughness and contrast of textures. He did still lifes of bottles and fruits, all rounded curves and circles of color, with just an angular table top as counterpoint. Human figures became more and more dehumanized and geometrical till all features disappear as in *Painter in Repose*, 1916. (PLATE 34); here the head suggests a wedge-shaped block of wood bounded by sharp straight lines like an inverted and dislocated pyramid. But suddenly, in 1915, he produced an exotic cubist painting of which the component parts were elements of the agrarian revolution going on in his homeland, the colors the warm, bright colors of Mexico and the background Mexico's mountains. He called it *Paisaje Zapatista*. More than he realized, it foreshadowed a turning point in his life and thought as man and painter (PLATE 16).

In ordinary times there are a thousand forms of use and wont, convention and subterfuge, that encase life and keep men from coming face to face with it and seeing even remotely its more terrible aspects. But this deceptive casing was shattered by war. Those whom its overwhelming presence did not stupefy, it quickened, intensifying intellect and passion and thirst for life. Mutinies at the front and orgies at the rear were but two diverse expressions of man's instinctive love of life, reasserting itself in death's kingdom. Men began to live with speed as if they felt they must crowd a lifetime into each hour. In Diego it took the form of a feverish desire to paint that drove him into injuring his health by working day and night, and led to increasing preoccupation with the idea that through his art he might aid in humanizing somewhat the antihuman world. Obscurely it motivated, too, Angelina's decision to have a child. Her pregnancy provoked terrible scenes because Diego feared an infant would interfere with his painting. His anger was maniacal. "If the child disturbs me I'll throw it out the window," he raged, as once he had threatened to commit suicide when he thought his mother might come to live with him.

The year 1917 was significant in Diego's life. It brought a new constitution in Mexico, the most advanced, at least on paper, that the world had so far known. The same year saw two successive revolutions in Russia. The conjunction of the Mexican and Russian revolutions or the superimposing of an interest in the Russian Revolution on his increasing absorption in the one already going on for seven years in his homeland was destined to transform Diego's mind and art. It was the year, too, of the first serious mutinies in the French army, to which he was closest. And it was the year of the birth of young Diego,

Portrait of the poet, José D. Frías
Ink, 1934

a seeming pledge to the future in the midst of the uncertainties of the present.

To José Frías, a bright, genial, and alcoholic Mexican poet, now deceased, I am indebted for a description of Diego's life in Paris at the time the child was born. Frías was a lifelong friend of Diego's and in later years a gay and entertaining comrade to his wife, Frida. He was a poet of polish, more brilliant as boon companion and conversationalist than as poet. In his last years he drank incessantly, carrying with him, when he could afford it or wheedle it out of a friend, a bottle of tequila or cognac. This did not slow up, rather warmed the flow of his wit. "I drink to drown my sorrows," he explained to Frida and me one day in 1936, glass in hand, "but the accursed things have learned how to swim!" He left Rivera's house that afternoon no drunker and no less kindly and good-natured than usual, but a stupid policeman cracked his skull in response to a witty or drunken remark, and a stupid hospital surgeon, attempting to operate without taking thought of the fatal effect of a combination of alcohol saturation with chloroform, finished him off. Diego grieved, and Frida wept bitterly.

Diego lived in the Montparnasse section in the rue du Départ [Frías told me]. When I first visited him, towards the end of 1917, he had moved there because of the birth of his son. He had a studio separated from the living room by a courtyard. It was cold, devilish cold, snowing outside, no heat within. I found Diego painting a French workingman, a M. Cornu. He greeted me in friendly fashion, chatted about art, Paris, the war, but never left off working. I was young and impressionable, and thought the cold flat, the snow, and the painting very romantic. "Just like *La Bohème*," I told myself. But when I tried to explain how I felt to Diego, he was unimpressed. For him painting was a serious business. He had already quarreled with Picasso, whose intimate friend he had been until then, and with most of the cubists, and was beginning an open break with the cubist school.

It was hard to see Diego often, because he begrudged every distraction from his work. Formerly he had gone to cafés, especially the Rotonde, but now he avoided them. When he did go, it was not so much to talk with the painters as with the Spanish and French anarchists and Russian refugees. He complained about his liver and kidneys, and followed a peculiar diet of his own in which no salt could be used.

Later I introduced him to Alberto Pani [engineer by profession and subsequent financier and politician of prominence in Mexican life]. Pani, an amateur of art, was swift to recognize that he was in the presence of an enormous talent. He urged Diego to return to Mexico to paint for the new regime; said it could be arranged by him. Diego answered that he was not ready, but he was plainly tempted.

During the hard winter of 1918, Diego and Angelina and their new-born son knew days of cold and hunger. Fuel was unobtainable, milk also, often food of any sort. Water froze in the pipes, the municipal pumping system broke down for lack of coal to run the engines. Diego and Angelina were able to stand it, but for the little boy it was too much; he died before the year was out, one of the innumerable, uncounted victims of the war. With his death, one of the ties that linked Diego to France (and to Angelina) was broken.

More than ever the war became an obsession. Lieutenant Georges Braque was decorated a Chevalier of the Legion of Honor. Diego's friend Guillaume Apollinaire was wounded in the head by shrapnel while writing poetry on a scrap of paper on the back of a cannon. His skull was trepanned. He died of pneumonia, complicated by the effects of his wound, on the eve of the armistice. So many young men full of creative promise whom Diego had admired, and quarreled with, marched forth to battle never to return. When the *Salon d'Automne* resumed in December 1919, it was on a somber note.

The *Comité de l'Entr-aide Artistique Française* [declared its catalogue], has just crowned its war work by organizing at the Grand Palais an exposition of the artists who died for the fatherland. An all too eloquent list of five hundred and sixty names permits us to measure the lives wiped out in the younger generation by the storm. Despite the efforts of the Committee, not all these valiant ones could be represented completely.

When Clive Bell, after the war, again met his old Paris friends and asked them about French painting, they talked only of their own work. "*Et les jeunes?*" he inquired. "*Les jeunes? Nous sommes les jeunes!*" The younger generation, the budding talents full of hope and promise, had been destroyed. That is one of the reasons for the decline of French art today, why the news is still of the work of the generation contemporary with Rivera.

To Diego it was inconceivable that mankind would further tolerate a system productive of such madness. His faith in man prevented his despairing; a break must come soon, he told himself, not realizing then how difficult it was to find or hack a path out of the jungle that had sprung up with the war and the crisis in European civilization which it signalized. "At that time," he wrote in the German autobiographical note from which I have already quoted, "I had discussions with my Russian colleagues, many of whom were revolutionary émigrés, on the role of painting in the future order of society to which the proletarian revolution would lead. In this revolution we all believed with burning certainty, and we awaited it as a necessary consequence of the Great War."

10.

QUEST FOR A UNIVERSAL LANGUAGE

For three years it seemed as if man had inured himself to the prospect of self-destruction; for three years all of life's manifestations were suppressed and crushed unless they served the ends of death; for three years the nations adopted the promotion of death as a way of life, intolerant of those who permitted themselves even to dream of any other. Then, of a sudden, the war structure began to crack and slip like a city in an earthquake.

Easter, 1916, was greeted by a revolution—unsuccessful—in Dublin. Christmas Day, at the year's end, witnessed a spontaneous mass fraternization of the soldiers of opposing sides in the trenches. Officers threatened to machine-gun no man's land before they could drive them back to their positions. All through early 1917 mutinies occurred and peasants deserted the armies *en masse*, stirred by thoughts of the spring planting. Pershing, arriving in Europe at this time, cabled Wilson urging that detachments of American troops be rushed before their training was completed, to impress the mutinous French soldiers. Even the entrance of America into the war did not fundamentally alter the drift towards peace, only its direction. It weakened the mutinous spirit in the Allied troops and revived a belief in the slogans of war till victory; and it strengthened the discontent in the ranks of the German armies. Recklessly, the German General Staff played with revolution in Russia while Wilson called for revolution in Germany. In February the Czar of All the Russias fell; in November came Lenin's seizure of power.

Easily the German war machine rolled over the prostrate and unresisting body of Russia; then the German and Austrian troops began to show signs of "Bolshevist contamination" and the infection of Wilson's propaganda. Returning to the western front, they carried the "contagion" with them. Rather than decisive military victory, it was war weariness and the arrival of an endless stream of fresh American troops that crumpled the Hindenburg line. Even in the late spring of 1918 the German army had been able to push forward; autumn found it intact in a military sense, and holding on French soil; the Hindenburg line collapsed from within, and was not broken. To that collapse, paradoxically, the exit of Russia from the war contributed as much as the entrance of America.

All at once bells were pealing, all Paris, France, Europe was dancing in the streets, stranger was hugging and kissing stranger, the world was engaging in a mad and unprecedented carnival. Life, triumphant over death, erupted into an orgy. Over the battle-scarred earth the Armistice bells evoked a revel, part thanksgiving, part witches' Sabbath.

Diego laughingly referred to a girl child born in 1919 to Marievna Vorobiev, as a "daughter of the Armistice." He often denied his paternity of Marika, but not the three-year affair with her mother. "Daughter of the Armistice" implies she might be anybody's daughter; once he told me that she was "the child of a Senegalese sharpshooter"! Yet her face (PLATE 37) shows signs of his share in her generation.* His sister, Marie, and his two Mexican daughters, Pico and Chapo (PLATE 38), bear a marked resemblance to their half sister, Marika. Diego sent money to her mother for the child's support, to meet emergencies like illness, to help with her schooling, and her studies in dancing. Elie Faure, Ilya Ehrenburg, and Adam Fischer, all intimates of Diego's in Paris, wrote him on more than one occasion of this or that need of his daughter. When he returned to Mexico he left money for the child with Adam Fischer, and later sent additional sums to Elie Faure for her. Diego saved various letters from his daughter, one including a painting she did when she was eleven. It is from Diego that I secured the photograph, taken when she was seventeen, on which I have based my conclusions as to her paternity. In his heart he acknowledged that paternity and made concessions to his responsibility for the child's existence. On Ehrenburg's last trip to Paris in the late 1950's, the Russian writer visited Marievna and her daughter. Marika was an actress and a dancer then, looked Mexican, and spoke French as her native tongue. She was married to an Englishman; speaking without bitterness or warmth of the father she had never known, she preferred to stress that she was "half Russian."

During the closing year of the war Diego made his break with cubism. He was not alone: many were questioning the dogma behind the new manner of painting or felt that they had exhausted its possibilities. One preached the "return to man," another "accessibility to the people," a third the "rights of the

* According to Angelina, "After our son was born, Diego had an adventure with Marievna . . . and went to live with her five months" (*My Art, My Life* [New York, Citadel Press, 1960], p. 295). Marievna herself has told the story in her autobiography, *Life in Two Worlds*, trans. by Benet Nash (London, Abelard-Schuman, 1962).

subject." Of all who strayed, Diego was most resolute, went furthest, and must have been among the first, for he was the subject of special recriminations. Perhaps they resented his action more because he had never really been a disciplined member of the school. Always the other cubists had charged him with deviation from the straight and narrow path, and with *exoticism.* This was intended to be a devastating epithet—yet in recognition of a personality that could not be compressed into a formula, it contained elements of a compliment. *Exoticism* in Rivera spelled Mexico!

With his first cubist paintings exhibited in the Salon of the Independents in 1914, Diego had received an official welcome from the pontiff who interpreted the mysteries of cubism to the public, Guillaume Apollinaire. In reviewing that Salon he had written: "*Rivera n'est pas du tout négligeable.*" That was the high point of appreciation Diego earned from official spokesmen! For other praise he had to depend upon semihostile forces like René Huyghe, Coquiot, Elie Faure. For some time Picasso defended him against attack and praised the work he was doing; in the end Diego quarreled with Picasso—over what, I could no longer find out from either of them. I doubt whether either remembered.

The school had its chiefs, but Rivera was not among them; it had its disciples, but Rivera refused to be one of them either. Like a Mexican *caudillo* he seemed bent on fighting independently, a lone outlaw. Since the madness and pride of experiment was upon them, it was a point of honor who was entitled to priority in what discovery. Picasso, arch experimenter and restless investigator of myriad phenomena in turn, viewed the controversy with amused indifference. He could afford to. Lesser men were annoyed at this latecomer who would not stay in line, but kept insisting, with and without reason, on his own originality. His love of a tall tale and a grand theory complicated matters, for they never knew when he was in earnest; their pendantry did not square with his wildness. They

41. Still Life. Pencil. 1918

42. Horse's Head. Pencil. 1923

43. Portrait of Elie Faure. Oil. 1918

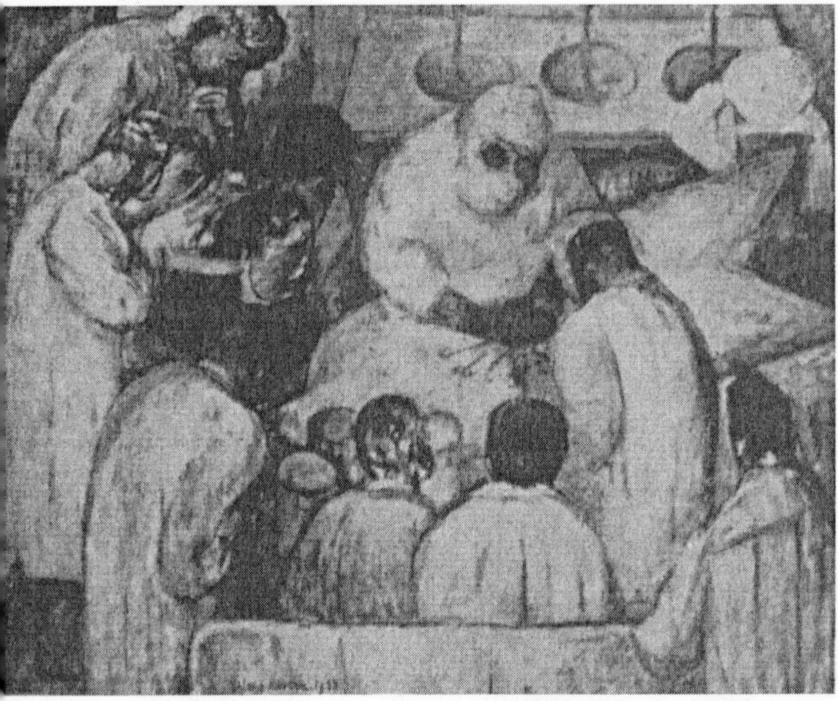

4. The Operation. Oil. 1920

45. The Operation. Fresco. Monochrome Pseudo-Relief. 1925

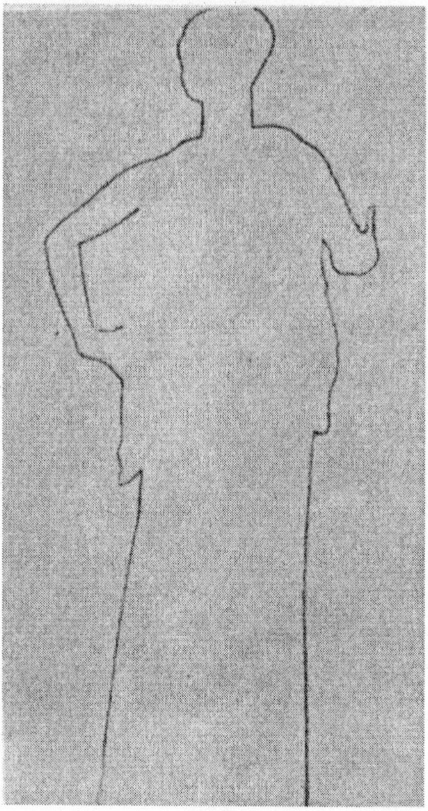

46. Standing Figure. Pencil. 1920

47. Italian Girl. Pencil. 1921

48. Creation. Encaustic. National Preparatory School. 1922

49. Head. Study for "Music" in Preparatory mural. 1922

50. Head. Study for "Faith." 1922

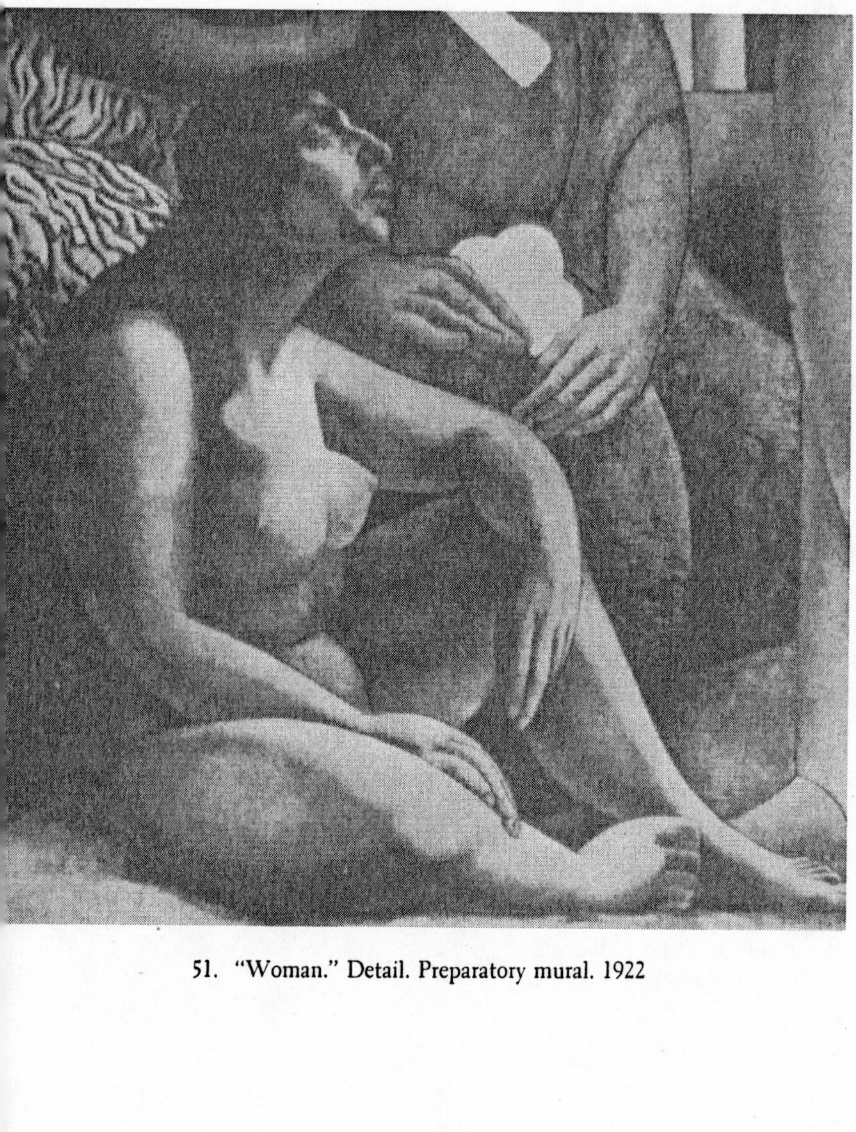

51. "Woman." Detail. Preparatory mural. 1922

52. View of section of the Court of Labor. Education Building.

53. Top floor. Court of the Fiestas. Education Building.

El Trapiche (The Sugar Mill).
Court of Labor.

55. The Embrace. Court of Labor.

56. Weaving. Court of Labor.

57. Care for a National Treasure. Secretariat of Education.

58. Awaiting the Harvest. Court of Labor.

59. Foundry. Court of Labor.

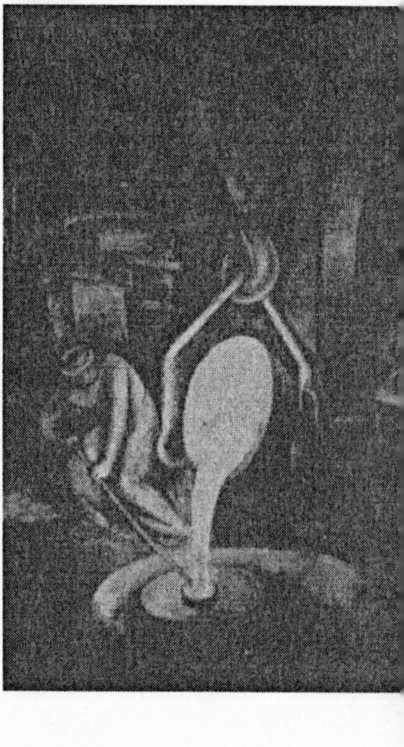

60. Industry Serves the Peasant. Ballad Series. Top Floor.

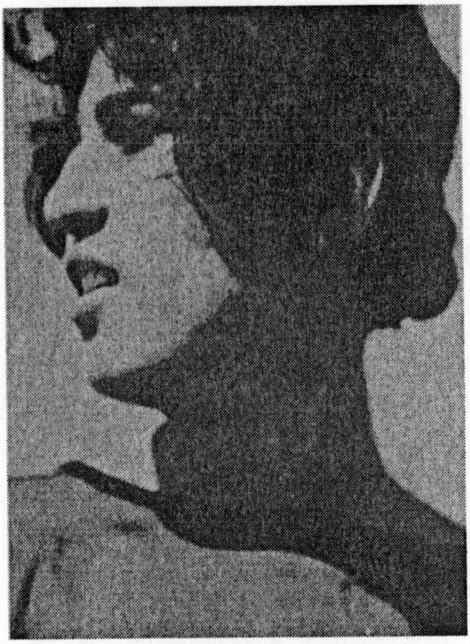

61,62,63,64. Photographs of Guadalupe Marín by Edward Weston.

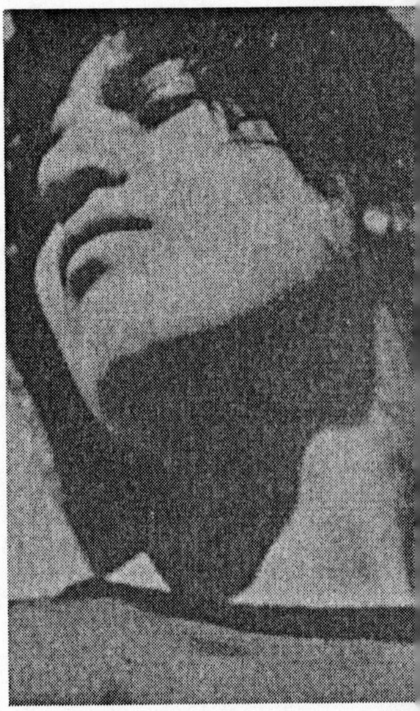

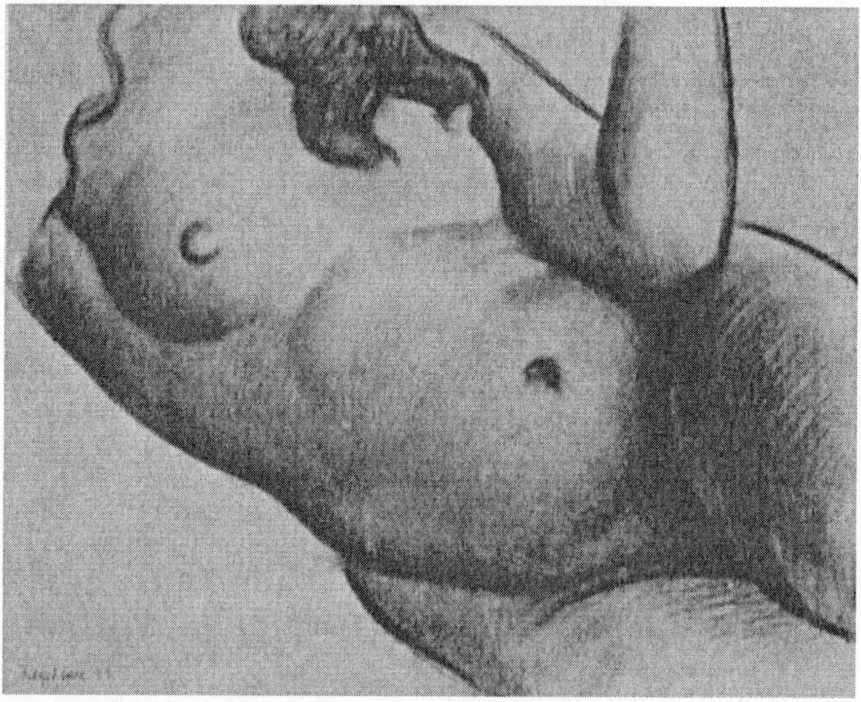

65. Reclining Nude. Study for Chapingo. Charcoal. 1925

66. The Fecund Earth. Chapingo. 1926

retaliated with the inevitable Parisian *blague*—a campaign of mockery, half jest, half rancor, that became a *cause célèbre* in the fugitive literature of the time as *l'affaire Rivera*. Neither from Diego nor his opponents was I able to reconstruct the *affaire*.

André Salmon, cubist poet and prophet, wrote mockingly of *l'affaire Rivera* in a book of 1920, *L'art vivant*. When I asked him about it in 1936, he said:

Each cubist claimed that his personal style was the only valid cubism. Rivera claimed to have found the secret of the fourth dimension. For convenience in demonstration he built a curious machine, a sort of articulated plane of gelatin. His French scientific vocabulary was modest. He called the apparatus *la chose*, which, in his Castilian-Mexican accent he pronounced *la soje*. This made his comrades mock, whereupon he would enter into comical furies. That is all I remember of *l'affaire Rivera*. He owes to his passage through cubism the validity of the great compositions which he has painted in Mexico. If he had remained among us, Rivera would have occupied an honorable place in the Paris School. We have not forgotten him.

Diego never denied his debt to cubism, nor did he hesitate to acknowledge his gratitude for what Picasso taught him. In 1949, he told a reporter, "I have never believed in God, but I believe in Picasso."

The war's end is a convenient point from which to take a backward glance at Rivera's own ten years of guerrilla fighting in the realm of art, with its tremendous skirmishes, its satisfying victories—and its over-all defeat. How many schools he had joined, or passed through, how many masters and manners he had studied and copied and assimilated as he rejected, how many styles he had painted in, now magnificently, now feebly, how many theories he had swallowed, or spun, how many Riveras there were, without there being one!

Concern with light and color and pointillism and vibration, concern with the clear outline of Ingres and David and Rebull and Matisse, with bulk and solidity and the architecture of painting, with the mathematics of the golden section, the analytic-synthetic geometry of cubism, the rigorous construction and vibrant color shaping form of Cézanne, a strong sense of the decorative derived, perhaps, from the Mexican popular arts, "exotic" themes and colors richer and more sensual than those of the other cubists—all these and many more styles and fashions and manners of painting he had tried to combine together as if he were seeking to master the entire range of the plastic language before using it as a way of himself expressing . . . what?

The armistice brought new friends—above all, Elie Faure. A doctor by profession, by vocation a poet, critic, lover of the arts and of ideas, Dr. Faure had lived through the war's nightmare, sawing bones and patching bodies in a base hospital. Diego met him on the day of his demobilization, painted him still in uniform: deep-set eyes that appear to look out upon the world, yet turn inward; eyes of a dreamer and poet such as could write a five-volume lyrical poem on the masterworks of men of all lands and ages and call it a "History" of Art; officer's uniform and Sam Browne belt denied by the negligent inclination of the body, the casual resting of one hand in pocket, the eyeglasses not put aside but held in the other, symbolizing the man of intellect and disconnecting the gaze from the outer world so that the myopic eyes may the better turn inward. A rude wooden table and staircase emphasize the man's simplicity; grapes on the table suggest grace of spirit and love of beauty; a dark tangled pattern of wallpaper as background to harmonize with the pattern of light and shade that helps demilitarize the uniform, and blends with the tangle of thoughts in the head of this poet-thinker; on body and surrounding objects no high lights save the illumination of the countenance—above all, the brow; on the face an expression of shining intelligence no uniform could militarize, expression of a man who has looked into life's depths and found it cruel and terrible and full of wonder. Those who have had the privilege of knowing Elie Faure will recognize this as magnificent psychological portraiture (PLATE 43).

To this period belong several other psychological portraits: one of Renato Paresce, Italian-Swiss painter (reproduced in *The Arts*, October 1923, p. 223), with background of books, palette, brushes, and studio objects; *Portrait of a Mathematician;* possibly the *Portrait of Angelina Beloff* which I have attributed to an earlier period. From Dr. Faure was derived the impetus for A *Surgical Operation* (1920, PLATE 44), worked out later, in monochrome fresco with the appearance of low relief, on the wall of the Secretariat of Education in Mexico City (PLATE 45). It was Faure who first took him to see an operation in a French hospital and pointed out the beauty of the functionally determined natural organic composition.

The portrait of Elie Faure marked the beginning of a lifelong friendship between these dissimilar beings, the most enduring relationship that Diego entered into in Paris.

The hours that these two great talkers spent together—as I, who have known the savor of each man's speech can testify—must have been rich beyond measure. Diego, for all his love of expounding a view and concocting a tale, did most of the listening, the older man most of the talking. From the lips of Elie Faure, Diego heard a poet's version of the theory that an artist is the product and expression of his time, his people, his geological surroundings, a sort of Marxism diluted with Taine, or perhaps more Taine tempered with a gentle poetic socialism.

"Art is the appeal to the instinct of communion in men," Faure told him. "We recognize one another by the echoes it awakens in us. . . .

"They have told you that the artist is sufficient unto himself. That is not true," he admonished. "The artist who believes it is not an artist. If he had not needed the most universal of our languages the creator would not have created it." *

From Elie Faure Diego derived confirmation of things he was already arriving at through his own reason and experience. "Do not be afraid of your intellect," this man of feeling told him. "That which kills is not learning; it is the failure to feel what one learns." Faure coupled his denunciation of the sterile rationalism that finds no higher room for passion and instinct with a denunciation of blighting antireason, which was even "now seizing upon rehabilitated intuition to enthrone it in a region outside of the intelligence, thereby condemning it to death. Intuition is only a flame," he said, "spurting forth at the point of contact with an infinity of previous analyses and of accumulated reasoning. . . .

"There is no hero of art who is not at the same time a hero of knowledge and a hero of the heart. When he feels living within him the earth and space, all that moves and all that lives, even all that seems dead—even to the very tissue of the stones—how could it be that he should not feel the life of the emotions, passions, sufferings of those who are made as he is? His art reveals to the men of today the solidarity of their effort."

Difficult and large were the tasks Faure assigned to art, and joyfully Diego agreed. Art could permit man to penetrate deeper than science into the structure of the universe and the nature of man. Through it man could define himself, know himself, leave the indelible mark of his spirit on unfeeling, inhuman matter. Art was the positive outcome of each generation's life on earth and alone gave each age a chance at a relative immortality—the might of the Pharoahs has perished but lo, the pyramids endure. Art could express "the multiple and infinitely complex relationships between the being in movement and the

* The talk of Elie Faure was so important to Diego's formation that I have ventured to try to reconstruct it. The conversation is a distillation of ideas Faure held at the time and continued to hold later, *expressed entirely in his own words* as set forth in his writings or in his letters to Diego or in his conversations with me when I visited him in 1936.

world in movement"; it alone could create "a harmony between sensuality and reason, between the most fleeting shudders of the moving surface of the forms and the most permanent laws of their inner structure; it is the most universal and the most veracious of the languages; into an immediate concrete form, living, existent, insistent, and having a reality of its own, it translates the abstractions and the relationships which reveal the solidarity of things among themselves and of these things with us." Whereupon it was Diego who added, "and of ourselves with each other." Faure readily agreed.

"You are right," he told Diego, "to refrain from listening to the professional philosopher, and especially to refrain from following him. But you are wrong to be afraid of passing for a philosopher."

He spoke of the unity that must be in each work of art. "Each fragment, because it is adapted to its end, must extend itself in silent echoes throughout the depth and breadth of the work. Let the work live, and in order to live, let it be one first of all! The work which is one . . . lives in the least of its fragments."

He urged Diego to become the voice of life itself: "The man who desires to create cannot express himself if he does not feel in his veins the flow of all the rivers, even those which carry along sand and putrefaction; he is not realizing his entire being if he does not see the light of all the constellations, even those which no longer shine, if the primeval fire, even when locked in beneath the crust of the earth, does not consume his nerves, if the hearts of all men, even the dead, even those still to be born, do not beat in his heart, if abstraction does not mount from his senses to his soul to raise it to the plane of the laws which cause men to act, the rivers to flow, the fire to burn, and the constellations to revolve."

After such conversations, whether they ended, as for the most part they did, in agreement or—less frequently—in quarrels, Diego would go home to lie wide-eyed for hours.

It was Elie Faure who aroused his enthusiasm for fresco.

"There is no monumental architecture without social cohesion," Faure told him. "If the reign of the individual ends by his returning to the multitude . . . architecture, the work of the anonymous crowds, will be reborn, and painting and sculpture will re-enter the monument. The whole of art today is obeying an obscure need of subordination to some collective task. . . ." *

That, Diego told himself, was what he had been seeking, what he saw in Italian frescoes and in pre-Conquest Mexican art. His work must become the conscious expression of that "obscure need."

Suddenly, it was obscure no longer. With brushes, paints, a few socks and things in a knapsack, he set off for Italy to see its walls. Seventeen months he spent tramping, drinking in Italy's treasures, making more than three hundred sketches, in Rome, Milan, Verona, Venice, Ravenna (the mosaics), Naples, Pompeii, the museums and archives with Etruscan ruins, Egyptian antiquities, Aztec codices—he found a continual feast for his bulging eyes. What he saw and sketched would leave traces on all his future work. The money for the trip came from the engineer, Alberto Pani, then Ambassador to France, who commissioned a portrait of himself and his wife, and purchased *The Mathematician.* Pani was to help him many times in the future, until their quarrel over the murals in the Hotel Reforma in 1936. It was Pani, too, who encouraged him, after the seventeen months in Italy, to return to Mexico for good.

Travel where he might, always he carried his land with him. As he wrestled with his sense of monumentality, so he resisted the strength of those mountains, the all-illuminating light, the clear forms, the lift of that uptilted land, the richness of the jungle verdure at its base, the color imbibed from native folk art, the strong and terrible figures of Aztec sculpture, the inspiration of Posada's engravings. The land which had formed

* When I spoke to Faure in 1936 he was anything but happy about the form which the "subordination of art to a collective task" was taking in Moscow. He had always assumed the voluntary subordination of art to a society whose collective aims were voluntarily undertaken—in short, he had taken for granted that most precious of the artist's needs: freedom.

his youth, given him his plastic sensibility and the raw material for his thoughts and feelings, showed itself in his work in despite of him. There was, for instance, the cubist painting later christened *Paisaje Zapatista,* a sombrero, a rifle, a sarape, volcanic peaks, broken up and put together in cubist fashion—pure Mexico. (FIG. 16). There was a forest landscape done in 1918 at Piquey on the coast of the Gulf of Arcachon (PLATE 39). He swore to me that he had painted faithfully what he saw there with his own eyes, modified merely by his sense of selection and formal organization, what any painter might have seen and painted. In the treatment of the background there are technical devices and ways of seeing learned from Cézanne, in the foreground a feeling derivable from Rousseau. But it turned out neither a Cézanne nor a Rousseau, but a Rivera, not a landscape of France, but of Mexico.

The truth is that Diego was becoming homesick, as artist even more than as man. The merest hints of Mexico, a softness in the air, a solitary century plant, were sufficient to set his nostalgic mood to work, determining the selection of details, the intensification of one thing and the playing down of another, the subtle and forceful factor of plastic organization that changes every note an artist does from nature into a product of his own being. He had carried his land with him as he had his personality; denied them, suppressed them, but never lost them. Given the impulse, they were there as ever.

For thirteen years he had struggled to be a European and had not succeeded. In Spain, despite ties of blood—if blood could tell, was he not more Spaniard than Mexican?—he had not become a Spaniard. Rather did he carry with him throughout life a deep resentment towards Spain. In Paris he had attempted to become a true citizen of the Republic of Montparnasse. But all he had to show for a decade of Frenchification was a softening and grammatical reshaping of the Gallic speech, a series of bitter quarrels and jests and defiant tales, a reputation for being a consummate liar and *farceur*—were they not all boasters and *blagueurs,* only lacking in his amplitude, as the Mexican tall tale is superior to the French, and the Mexican *vacilada* richer than the Paris *blague?*

Going on thirty-four now, Diego reviewed his work, his few laurels and fluent skill, and was not content. He was sure he had that within him which had not yet found expression: something, he dared tell himself, unique and significant to express. Within his brain a cosmos whirled, but from his skilled, obedient hand came only still lifes, portraits, and landscapes. Could not the cosmos itself be imprisoned in paint? Was his preoccupation with natural forces and social forces, with the entire world of nature and man, incapable of plastic expression? Was it forever to torment him with a hint of boundless possibilities only to rouse mocking laughter in others when he tried to tell of it, and blind fury in him when it could not be set down within any picture's limited frame?

The final impulse came from outside the world of art. It was the Russian Revolution, and the Mexican, that ultimately clarified his vision and enabled him clearly to set his future course. The whole of modern art, as we know it, is compressed between the limits of two world wars and two revolutions. It was born in the French Revolution and the Napoleonic Wars. Retrospective historians, I venture to predict, may say that it gave way to something new in the course of World War I and of the new "time of troubles" initiated by it.

The more Diego was fired with enthusiasm for the new Russia, full then of bright promise, and for the revolution which seemed then to be spreading to Hungary and Bavaria, striving to take possession of Germany and Italy, rolling up to the very gates of Warsaw and eastward to the Pacific, the more he thought of the Revolution in Mexico, of walls, of painting for the masses, of tying up his art with revolution. The more, too, he longed for contact with his own people, those he understood best, and the greater the significance he ascribed to the dreamlike tales of Mexican Revolution that his compatriots were bringing to Paris.

What was this Constitution of 1917, so attractive on paper? Who were these revolutionaries who followed Carranza, forced this constitution upon him, overthrew him for ignoring it, and were even then coming into power? What was this talk of a labor movement and "red legions," of folk heroes like Emiliano Zapata and Pancho Villa, of socialism spreading over the peninsula of Yucatán? When his old comrades, the Russian painters and refugees, who thought of themselves as now in power in the land of the Soviets, invited him to Russia to paint, he knew he must go to Mexico.

In Paris he had argued much with Russian futurists, cubists, and nonobjective abstractionists. He had stood quite alone. They tended to identify the bourgeois of the artists with the bourgeois of the Marxists, and the "revolutionary" painting of the modernists with revolution as such, hence with the proletarian revolution. Returning to Russia, they deluged the masses briefly with bewildering works of these esoteric schools —in poetry, in painting, in posters, in street displays—until the taste, or lack of taste, and the propaganda purposes of the new masters of Russia subjected art to dictatorship.

But Diego had held to a contrary theory. In the frescoes of the Italian painters, from the Byzantines to Michelangelo, he saw the answer to the needs of a popular art capable of nourishing the masses esthetically, reforming their taste, telling them a story as moving as that of the medieval church, giving birth to a social and monumental painting. That was what had sent him wandering down the Italian peninsula. He returned to Paris with 325 sketches and countless visual memories that would color all his future work. In Paris he found a telegram telling him his father was dying. He sold what pictures he had on hand, bade good-by to Angelina and to Marievna and his daughter, giving each woman to understand that when he could afford it he would send for her. He left several thousand francs with Adam Fischer for the support of his daughter Marika, and, scarcely stopping to bid good-by to the friends who meant most to him, he set out for Mexico.

11. THE WRETCHED AND

EXUBERANT LAND

As he watched the water fly past the vessel's side, Diego mused on his life in Europe and how it squared with the hopes of that youth who set sail in quest of the secret sources of art fourteen years before. He set up his easel on the deck—now as then, bent on catching the swirl of the water, the waves' pattern, the composition made by rigging, rail, and mast—but his brush was idle in his hands.

The warm Gulf winds blew into his face, carrying scents he had forgotten, memories that had tormented him even as he boasted himself the most European of Europeans, visions of a land that seemed made to provoke and replenish the painter's craft. Already his European stay was assuming the outlines of a dream. The feverish quest, humble copyings, exultation of achievement, succession of isms, the overloud self-assertion which had covered up a fear that perhaps he would never satisfy that undefined hunger and obscure conviction of destiny—all fit together as a prolonged apprenticeship. Almost thirty-five, yet, as so many times before, he felt as if he were making a new beginning. A long apprenticeship indeed.

The land, too, emerging from revolutions, trembled on the verge of new, unheard-of things. He was going home, he told himself. Not just back, but home! The talents gained in his long apprenticeship, the seeing eye, cunning hand, teeming brain he would put at the service of the building of a new land, a land that would fit in with his hopes for a new world.

"Unhappy Mexico!" he mused as he reviewed his country's barren history. A century old now, almost to the day; the entire century chaos, bloodshed, and unfulfilled hope. The Republic, conceived in idealism, had been born in treachery; betrayal had darkened every succeeding year. The executioners of the republican revolutionaries had proclaimed the Republic out of fear of contagion from the liberal movement suddenly begun in Spain! During the first half-century of independence the unhappy land had known over seventy changes of administration, almost all of them beginning with a trusted lieutenant's betrayal of one who had trusted him, and ending with the new chief's betrayal by one he had trusted. Each had sought to justify his bloody deed in the name of some sweeping plan, some noble constitution, some vast promise of redemption and transformation, but less than a handful of the seventy-odd successive heads of state had made any effort to convert promise into fulfillment.

Diego thought of the Mexico he had left in 1907, in relative peace but corroding under an aging dictator's rule, and of the flare-up of hope during his return in 1910, when Madero had led a short-lived movement for "redemption" through the process of democratic elections. Madero had fallen, too, assassinated by the general he had entrusted with command; then had come another decade of unceasing upheaval. Men, movements, and programs followed and succeeded and disputed one another like the changing patterns of a kaleidoscope: more than ten presidents and twice as many rebellious aspirants in ten bloody years!

Now it seemed to Diego, as he stood on the deck of the ship bearing him home, that the century of bloody, senseless turmoil was coming to an end in a deeper sense than the mere completion of its appointed tale of years. The new decade seemed to have some pattern, as if, despite the continued mutinies, assassinations and betrayals, a new Mexico were taking shape.

The government of General Obregón—the best military strategist then alive, yet more a civilian than a military man—had not yet defined its attitude in practice to the basic problems confronting it. It seemed to be the Revolution itself, organized as government. Its first pronouncements were bright with promise. Its first budget allowed as much for schools as for barracks. Its Minister of Education was a revolutionary student leader of the days of Diego's youth, José Vasconcelos, who believed, as Diego's father had, that education was the lever which might raise the country from the depths. Already Vasconcelos was at work planning publications, fomenting the popular arts, warring on illiteracy, teaching trades, building schools, opening libraries, *forjando patria*—forging a fatherland.

This was where he could fit in. He had left his native land fourteen years ago, a pensioner of the government; now he was returning, not to ask, but to offer. There would be building upon a mighty scale. The walls of schools and libraries and *Casas del Pueblo*—Houses of the People—would have to be covered with something, even if but a simple coat of plaster or cement, whitewash or paint. All he would ask was a workman's wage, such as any artisan who covers the wall might command. Here was the opportunity he had been looking for. Here at last art might re-enter the monument; become monumental; reconquer the right to speak to the people; put itself once more at their service; become again a significant part of life. A great age was beginning for painting, just as for Mexico and mankind. With his brush and his skill he would contribute to the building of the new worlds. Revolution had cleared away the evil rubbish of the old; now to build the new! As he gazed at the approaching horizon of his native land, it seemed resplendent.

The painter trembled with excitement as he caught his first sight of the pajama-clad, straw-sombreroed peons at Vera Cruz waiting to unload ship. What had the revolution done to them? He fancied he saw a new sense of dignity which enriched yet did not altogether destroy the gentle sweetness surviving from an earlier humility. His eyes bored through the bodies of the sweating, shirt-sleeved customs officials to wrest some secret from them: what were they like, the bureaucratic servants of the new regime? On the docks, in the street, at the railroad station, he asked innumerable questions, talked with everybody, tried to take in everything with those bulging, all-seeing eyes.

His mind worked furiously, making mental sketches of a million things so familiar, yet as if never seen before. His vision was suddenly unbearably acute, as if a new retina, unstaled by custom and use, were combining naïve innocence with years of refinement in learning how to see. It seemed as if he were seeing for the first time the delicate pastel tints and solid volume of the adobe houses, the intense shadows thrown by the flooding sun, the dark, ungainly vultures presiding as scavengers over the port, the clumped curves of the occasional foliage-laden tree, the sudden flame of tropical flowers, the dark faces against a luminous background, so unlike the pallid faces he had grown accustomed to in Europe, the faded blue and sunbleached white homespun garments, the magnificent lines of tension of peon bodies straining under loads depending from a forehead headband, the easy, unconscious grace of women walking erect and free with baskets on their heads. He was spellbound by the beauty and caught with a helpless feeling of sorrow at the poverty, beauty and poverty alike striking him as familiar things never really seen before.

The train rose slowly from sea level; climbed through long hours, strung end on end, into and out of the rich subtropical lands; circled in leisurely fashion through the midday sunlight around Orizaba's snow-capped eighteen-thousand-foot peak; puffed heavily up the arid, alternately parched and frozen, *maguey*-spotted *meseta* slopes; crept with hollow-voiced roar on bridges that hung over torrential canyon clefts whose walls were tumbling jungles of brush; halted for unexpectant waits in still villages and towns dominated by a soaring church's dome, a pulque-grower's baronial castle, and perhaps a castlelike textile mill; mounted over sierra saddles in which the train had to attain heights of more than twelve thousand feet, coming to rest at last in Mexico City's great mountain-rimmed valley floor seventy-five hundred feet above the level of the sea. The whole journey through the steeply uptilted land was a veritable orgy for Diego's eyes. Impression on impression until even his great capacity for seeing and recording could endure no more. Again and again he would whip out pencil and pad, only to leave the note half taken because already there was something else to see.

Fresco painters cannot paint from nature. They may take an occasional human model up on the scaffold with them, but not buildings, mountains, volcanoes, trees, formal relationships. Even sketches are perforce but fragmentary to the vast dimensions of a mural's master plan. The artist must feed his eyes ceaselessly on men and things, digest them in the juices of thought and imagination, assimilate their essence, meaning, relations with each other and with all things that exist, make them a part of his being. Then, when they are second nature, when they are he and he is they, they flow swiftly out of the brush's tip onto the resisting-yielding surface of the moist plaster that in a few short hours will be too dry to absorb another stroke. As the great frescoes later flowed from his hand, he would seem to paint as swiftly and with as much ease as if it were a mere act of improvising, but into each touch went the two decades and more of patient training, passionate apprenticeship, consuming observation, accumulated visual images, flashes of memories of other painters' solutions of kindred problems, and deep meditation on the world of nature and the world of men. This first journey of rediscovery and the six excited months of wandering up and down the land which followed were to be an inexhaustible notebook for his future frescoes. No quest for subjects now —they were all around him—the whole country cried to be painted. "On my arrival in Mexico," he wrote later, "I was struck by the inexpressible beauty of that rich and severe, wretched and exuberant land."

12. ANGELINA WAITS

"Since your departure," Elie Faure wrote Diego in Mexico, "it seems to me that the source of legends and of a supernatural world is drying up; that this new mythology of which the world has need is withering away; that poetry, fantasy, sensitive intelligence, and dynamism of spirit are dead. I have the blues—now you see—since your departure. . . ." (Letter of January 11, 1922.)

In the early 1930's Elie Faure undertook a tour of the world, in the course of it, visiting the fabulous Mexico which Diego had painted verbally for him in Paris.

> Some twelve years ago [he wrote in *Mon Périple*], on the day after the war, I met in Paris a man of an intelligence which was, so to speak, monstrous. Such, more or less, as I imagined the inventors of fables who abounded ten centuries before Homer on the slopes of the Pindus and in the isles of the Archipelago. About Mexico, where he was born, he told me extravagant things. *Mythologer*, I said to myself, *perhaps even mythomaniac!* Now look. [Here Faure gives an account of the fantastic,

incredible Mexican land and people as he found them, then continues:] . . . Diego Rivera, my mythomaniac become the most illustrious painter of the three Americas, was right!

It was not the only time that men who began by doubting utterly the unbelievable verbal pictures created by Diego's myth-making imagination were to end up by believing them.

"You ought to write from time to time to poor Angelina, whom I see sometimes, not as often as when you were here," continues the letter from which I quoted above. "She leads ever her valiant and solitary life, awaiting your return or a call from you."

Angelina had remained behind, in their studio. Diego was not sure how long he would stay in his native land, whether he could earn a living for one, much less two, by offering his services "to the people" through an impoverished and bankrupt government. If he should succeed, he had given Angelina to understand, and earn enough for the two of them, or find work for her, she might come to Mexico. If Mexico should reject his proposals, he would return to Europe. If he earned extra money and she, or his child, Marika, needed it, he would send some. If not, their comradeship implied obligations of mutual assistance, but none of one-sided dependence: she would have to earn her own living as best she could as she had always tried to. Angelina was completely devoted to her lover, kept his brushes in their place and his corner of their studio undisturbed, treasured every scrap of sketch and shred of memory of their turbulent and warm companionship, earned her meager living by etching and magazine illustration, kept up friendship with his friends, believed in the success of his venture, studied Spanish against the day of his sending for her.

In Diego's files I found letters from her, without date or definable order, a photograph, and on the back, in her rapidly improving Spanish:

> Your wife* sends you this with many kisses, dear Diego. Receive this photograph until we see each other. If it is not very good, yet in it and in the last one, you will have something of me. Be strong as you have been and pardon the weakness of your woman. I kiss you still. Quiela.†

Other letters express concern for the health of his father, send affectionate messages to his mother and sister—the family had long known of their life together and accepted her as belonging to Diego. She included greetings from his friends, put her own loneliness into telling how much they all missed him, rebuked him for failing to answer their letters and hers, and revealed between the lines a growing apprehension.

> It hurts me deeply to hear that Papa is so ill. After the letter he wrote me I feel even closer to him and I feel a real sorrow not to be able to see him—but of that I won't speak to you any more—the initiative would have to come from you, after all, and if not . . . useless to remember even that there are boats between France and Mexico.

She spent much time with the Mexican painters in Paris, she wrote him. They put her into a Mexican environment, "but not of the Mexico I used to know, of the Mexico young, a bit savage, but so full of life. . . . Will you succeed in gathering around you some of these elements, in shaking them, awakening them, freeing them from secular prejudices at least in the domain of art . . . ?

"You are the same as that Mexico, young but already formed, already strong, and long or short though your stay there may be, surely your coming will have stirred up many whirlpools in the current of ideas in many heads." She acknowledged the receipt of money and gave three hundred francs for his daughter, Marika, to the child's mother.

One fateful letter bears a date: July 22, 1922. It seems an eternity since she has written or heard from him. She does not

* As in French with the word *femme,* so in Spanish the word *mujer,* is used both to mean woman and wife.

† Pet name for Angelina.

write because it is difficult not to say certain things that she has in her heart and of which it seems useless to speak. She takes pen in hand only because she feels it is truly impolite not to thank him for the money he is sending her. She has failed to thank him for the last three remittances, of February 6, March 10, and the beginning of June with 260, 297, and 300 francs respectively. This, she realizes, makes four months in which she has not written, except to send him clippings of her engravings in the magazine *Floreal*.

It is very difficult for me, Diego, to write you [she explains]. Here it is a year since you left. I have not forgotten you, I have even forgotten you too little for that lapse of time. You left with intentions quite vague as regards me, or perhaps you had none at all and I lent them to you. Now, you see, I must know if you have any.

I can easily imagine that in your work, in your life in the country which stirs you, among the friends and enemies which surround you—all that kaleidoscope of faces, ideas and occupations, there remains little place for me. Perhaps none at all. I could accept it, I could admit it perhaps, but only as something already definitive. You will say to me that I ought to have guessed it long ago and not ask of you the painful task of putting it on paper in all its letters. What to do? I, you see, being woman, Russian, and sentimental, when you left still had illusions. It seemed to me that despite everything there still remained between us those very profound bonds which it is not worth while to break definitely, that still each of us might be useful to the other. . . . What hurts is to think that you no longer have any need of me at all—none at all. . . . Painful, yes, but indispensable to know. . . . Look, Diego, during so many years that we were together, my character, my habits—in short, all of me, was completely modified; I have become terribly "Mexicanized," I have become attached "*par procuration*" to your language, to your country, to a thousand little things, and it seems to me that I will feel considerably less foreign with you than in any other land whatsoever. The return to my own home is definitely impossible, not because of political events, but because I cannot find myself among my compatriots. On the other hand, I fit very well with your countrymen and feel myself more at ease with them.

They themselves have encouraged me to believe that I could earn my living in Mexico by giving lessons.

But, after all, those are secondary matters. The main thing is evidently that it is impossible for me to undertake anything in order to go to your land if you no longer have any feeling for me, if rather the idea of my presence is inconvenient to you. If not, as you know, I could even be useful to you, grind your colors, make your stencils, help as I did when we were in Spain together and in France all through the war. . . .

I want it set black on white. . . . You have had plenty of time to reflect and make up your mind at least unconsciously, if you have not had any occasion to formulate it. Well then, formulate it. . . . Otherwise we will come to useless suffering, useless and monotonous like a toothache, and with the same result. You see, you do not write me—you will write less and less if we let time run on; in a few years we will meet as strangers if we meet at all. As for me, I can say that the toothache will continue down till the root rots away to the bottom—well then, is it not better to pull out the tooth if you find nothing in you that draws you to me?

I often think, too, that perhaps the supposed difficulties and complications of a life *à deux* frighten you to a greater degree than the phantom of a certain imagined responsibility holds you back. I have thought of that often, but I believe that in your country, where we have never lived together, one might build a life for oneself in which more would not be given by one to the other than could be given readily. I imagine that with me earning my own living as much as possible (and consequently being quite occupied) and with you working as you work now, we would meet, with a little good will on both sides, on the ground which is still common to us, and only on that ground. Here in Paris the very poverty of life prevented that. . . .

She has lost her job as illustrator for *Floreal,* the letter continues, and has no income for the moment but what he sends, plus small sums derived from giving lessons to a child. She is looking hard for work, but her present desperate situation makes it necessary to decide the question of Mexico at once. She may have an opportunity to translate Ehrenburg's *Julio Jurenito,* inspired by Diego, from Russian into Spanish.

One might surrender, take a job as governess or stenographer, or anything else for eight hours a day, general *abrutissement,* play or movie on Saturday, promenade in Saint-Cloud or Robinson on Sunday. I don't want that. So I accept the tail of the line in application for the work I am seeking, poverty and worry if necessary, and your Mexican pesos.

More news follows in this letter that she finds so difficult to bring to a close, foreboding it may be her last, and all the news carries its overtones of loneliness and pain. Her best friend is ill, has broken her knee, will leave for Algiers to recuperate. The Siqueiroses are leaving for Mexico, and she will be more alone than ever. "I hold it against you, Diego, deeply, that you have refused to give me a child. That would be harder, but, my God, how much more sense my life would have!"

Again the letter returns to its melancholy budget of news: Jacobsen, his Danish painter friend who wants to go to Mexico, has sent him three cables in care of the National University, answer collect, but they remain unanswered. Elie Faure complains to her of Diego's silence. Everybody asks her for news of him, and she is embarrassed at having none. . . .

There! I see that I could write like this endlessly, but since you have little time to waste, this will perhaps be too long as it is. It is useless to tell you to write to me, but you ought to do it just the same. Above all, you must answer this letter, and answer in whatever way you will, but *en toutes lettres.* You need not give much explanation, *a few words will do so long as they are written.* And with that I embrace you warmly. . . .

Quiela

P.S. What do you think of my engravings?

His only answer was, not a letter making everything clear, but a cable bidding her come to Mexico, yet sending no money for the fare. Poor Angelina! Love cannot be compelled by pity. After years of intimate life with Diego, did she not know him well enough to perceive that all was over? Had he not refused to tie again the bond which had broken with the death of their boy? Had he not let her know that his passion had long yielded to a feeling akin to the fraternal? Had he not even brought to her, as to an unusually knowing friend and confidante, tales of his new passions for other women? His amour with Marievna Vorobiev he had begun without concealment, even without recrimination on her part, acknowledging to Angelina, if not to others, his paternity of Marievna's child. It was only then that Angelina became furiously jealous of Marievna.

His silences were eloquent. The cool spaces that lay between the lines of his dispatches of money should have told her. Did she not know him enough to understand how hard it would be for him to say directly, "I do not love you"? Perhaps the Russian way is for lovers to torture each other by lengthy analyses of their altered feelings, but the Latin hints more gracefully when he loves and with more subtlety when he has grown indifferent. In the Mexican middle class, to which this "proletarian" painter belonged, frankness in such matters is even more unwonted than it is in the pronouncements of Mexican politicians.

Doubtless he had contributed to the nourishing of forlorn hope by his conduct, so unusual in a Mexican *caballero*, of sending money to one mistress-comrade and money to the child of another. Angelina showed foreboding in every line she wrote, yet refused to know, as if by her admitting it some last thread would be broken. Her life was not centered in painting as his was, with all else subordinate. "For me painting and life are one," he had written to Renato Paresce in 1920. "It is my dominant passion . . . an organic function more than an activity of the spirit." For her, love and life were more nearly one, painting a mode of filling in the interstices. He was lover, comrade, son, and the prototype of hero painter. Gladly she had forsworn land and friends and language for his; she had built her life with him as its armature.

If she could have seen the paintings he was doing on Mexico's walls while she sat in their Paris room grieving, she would have known that he would never return. If she could have seen that rugged monumental nude, vast and solid-hewn (PLATE 45)—almost intimidating—voluptuously, overwhelmingly feminine, she would have known that he had found, not a new model merely, but a new mistress of his desires, an incarnation of what he had written of in that same letter to Paresce—*la beauté devenue femme*—someone he would cherish because she fitted into the core of his "dominant passion."

Even when Angelina knew of his Mexican love, her feelings did not turn against him, nor did she seek another love. She had talked bravely of pulling the aching tooth; now she hugged the pain and nourished the delusion that this love, too, would prove another Marievna, another passing fancy. Years later, Mexican friends found her in Paris, still solitary, still struggling with her unimportant painting, preserving in a corner of the studio Diego's brushes and effects as he had left them, still practicing the tongue that love had led her to, reading Mexican poets and Castilian classics, dreaming of the land that Diego had made seem to her, as to Elie Faure, a land of enchantment.

> You see, you do not write me—you will write less and less if we let time run on; in a few years we will meet as strangers.

Prophetic foreboding! In 1935, encouraged by Mexican painter friends, she went at last to the land of her longing. She did not seek Diego out—she did not want to molest him. When they met at a symphony concert, Diego passed without even recognizing her!

Germán Cueto took her to the Secretariat of Education to see Diego's frescoes. She went around that three-storied universe of paint, gazing long and silently at each panel. Only at the end did she speak, her eyes wet with unbidden tears: "I am glad that it was to do such great work that he left me!"

They had warned me that the "tooth" still ached when one touched it, and that she would not talk to me of Diego. But she received me graciously, talked freely, gaily, encouraged me to ask questions. Perhaps I am not cut out for biography, for I forbore to ask the questions I should have.

We became friends. She lent me photographs of the youthful Diego to copy, so that I have been able to reproduce them here. She did not seem to have his letters with her—or perhaps she did not care to show them. She talked of his boyishness, his wildness, his fantasy, his love of discussion for the sake of contradiction, but never a word did I hear in bitterness or unkindness. "Given my life to live over again," she said, "I would still choose to live those ten years, full of pain and happiness, over again with him."

"Good Angelina, she was aptly named," Diego said to me when we spoke of her afterward.

When last I heard of her, she was still living and working in Mexico City, painting and exhibiting there, teaching drawing to children in a government school, a faded, kind-visaged, gentle-souled slender woman—no wonder Diego did not recognize the companion of his youth. Yet she had the same pale-blue eyes, the same blueness about her, the same birdlike profile and wounded voice that had been noted by Gómez de la Serna.

In the summer of 1936 she thought of returning to her other home, not Moscow, but Paris. Needing money for the journey, she asked me if I would get Diego to sign the early sketches she had preserved, so that she might more easily sell them. So many people asked so many things of Diego that I had made it a rule never to ask for anything, for myself or for others. "You will find him all day long on the scaffold in the Hotel Reforma," I told her. "Go and look at his painting there and watch him at work. He doesn't mind, and I know it will interest you. If he is friendly, you can ask him yourself to sign the sketches."

That night I had dinner with Diego and Frida at their home in San Angel. He came home late as usual, on his face the expression of one who is tired and happy. After dinner we worked together on *Portrait of Mexico*. Running out of ink, I asked for his pen. "*Caracoles!*" he said with hand on breast pocket. "I forgot to give Angelina back her fountain pen." Thus I knew that he had signed her sketches.

13. A BYZANTINE DETOUR

The years of civil war had bled the country white. Its soil lay neglected, its cattle had been well-nigh wiped out by roving bands, its feeble economic machinery had broken down, its metallic reserves had fled or been reburied in the earth, its paper money was more cabbalistic symbol than medium of exchange. The land swarmed with fatherless children, war cripples, beggars, bandits, to whom turmoil had become a way of life. Everywhere was yearning for peace and expectation. Until now the Revolution was promises. Now the bright promises were to become reality in a new, marvelous, unpredictable world.

Above all, it was a time of plans. To lay down a mile of torn-up rail, to rebuild a single dynamited bridge over a mountain gorge, required capital, time, labor, prosaic attention to detail. But plans—they were another thing! All they required was an ardent imagination, a touch of poetry, and a heroic resolve. Plans hatched like mayflies on a summer day—and lived as long!!

The new President, corpulent and sanguine, candid, open-hearted, brilliant on the field of battle, shrewd in judgment of his fellows, fond of conversation and boon companionship and the ways of civil life, overflowing with genial wit, unassuming and democratic in his personal ways, was by no means immune to the idealism that was in the air. All the other great military chieftains having been killed off in battle or by assassination, he could be gentle, as befits confidence and strength. Time had not yet brought him face to face with the problem of the succession, the question of how to feather the nest of civilian retirement, or the most vexing question of all, that of recementing the broken-down relations with the United States. Meanwhile, one must reconstruct the ruined land, create oneself a place in history, accumulate the merits that would entitle one to illustrious renown.

Obregón was proud of his progress in stabilizing the currency, in pacifying or "eliminating" chieftains still in arms, proudest of all of the new Ministry of Education, hard at work rebuilding the culture of the land. The school system—never anything to boast of—had collapsed with the fall of Díaz; the federal Department of Education had been abolished by Carranza; the country was more than eighty-five per cent illiterate; culture, like the economy, was in ruins.

The new Minister of Education had been in arms, had suffered exile, had assimilated a hash of strange doctrine from Spain, the Church, India, had developed a blind faith in suffrage and literacy and civic honesty and valor as cures for Mexico's secular ills.

He surrounded himself with poets, painters, and visionary counselors of all descriptions, rode forth with this motley train on burro and horseback to all the corners of the land, warring on the illiteracy and rudeness of the times, laying foundations for schools, urging the preparation of the people for entrance into democratic political life.

As for Diego, he was an artist that Paris had delighted to

honor; hence, along with other artists, he was set to doing almost anything—except painting. One day he was made Director of Propaganda Trains. Propaganda for what? A question left brightly vague. Where to get the trains? Before a single railway car could be procured in a country denuded of its rolling stock, the appointment was forgotten and he received another: Art Adviser to the Department of Publications. This was closer to his craft; immediately Diego was a vast warm incubator hatching out plans—without even troubling to ask for eggs. Alas for the downy plans! The Department of Publications did not issue a book until months after Diego and the Department had forgotten each other. Along with Diego, they forgot his plans: why trouble to resuscitate them when any poet or painter who occupied the post brought with him a like fruitfulness and a new set of his own.

In November 1921 the Minister set out on one of his voyages of cultural exploration and propaganda to Yucatán, inviting several painters and poets, Rivera among them, to make part of his expedition. The voyage proved fruitful for Diego. He came back with sketches of the landscape, the huts, the *cenotes* (underground rivers), and the people which were afterward to figure in his murals and canvases. His mind was stirred by the great ruins at Uxmal and Chichén Itzá; and by the dimly comprehended spectacle of the uprising of the henequen peons, the *ligas de resistencia,* and the socialist governor, Felipe Carrillo Puerto, who ruled the State of Yucatán.* Him, Diego was to paint after his martyrdom, twice in the Secretariat of Education and again on the National Palace stairway. But most important of the results of his journey was that his ardent talk about murals and public buildings persuaded Minister Vasconcelos to offer him a wall!

* After Roberto Haberman, his American socialist adviser, quoted Marx to him several times, he said, "Where is this young fellow? Invite him to Yucatán."

It was indoors, in the auditorium of the National Preparatory School, part of the University of Mexico. The building was a sturdy baroque colonial structure completed in 1749 and used as a school by the Jesuit Fathers of an earlier day. Diego was given the front wall in the Anfiteatro Bolívar behind the platform, with a vague promise of side and rear walls later. It was solidly constructed, of flat masonry, bounded on the two sides by pillar supports for the ceiling arch, which described a wide flat curve. A smaller concave vault broke the wall surface to enclose a pipe organ.

The spell of Italy was still upon him, of the Ravenna mosaics, Byzantine and early Renaissance fresco painters, and Renaissance allegory. Since 1911 he had experimented from time to time with painting in wax colors. This was his first opportunity to get these accumulated tensions out of his system.

He calculated the dimensions and proportions of the wall, the curvature of the ceiling arch, the corresponding festooned curve that would result if a cord were hung in an opposed arc from invisible points at the top of the pillars supporting the vault (a curve later to be marked by the halos of the masculine virtues and feminine graces). He made sketches to scale, experimented with his theories of the golden section as ideal proportion for dynamic symmetry, made researches with blowpipe and spatula on each of the colors he wished to fuse upon the wall. In short, he brought all the resources of his technical training and accumulated lore to bear upon the work.

For a year he labored upon it. The result was imposing: almost a thousand square feet of wall* covered with huge superhuman allegorical figures over twelve feet high, with faces striking, forceful, insistent bodies marked out by deeply incised lines in severe and elegant geometric curves, a carefully calculated composition based upon the lines of the building, colors glowing like precious stones—deep greens, brick reds, ochers, violets, brilliant areas of

* How can a reproduction in a book communicate the impact of a fresco covering a thousand square feet of wall?

shining gold spilling over from a golden center where a semicircle of the deepest of blue skies studded with golden stars stands out against a shining background of the same bright gold. The design assimilates the pipe organ unto itself, compelling it to play a part in the decorative scheme (PLATES 48-51).

Yet, even before it was finished, Diego was dissatisfied with the work. It was not, he knew, what he had meant to do, what he should have done. The theme was too abstract and allegorical, the style too imitative; though the types chosen gave it special reference to the Mexican scene and Mexican racial mixtures, there was too much of Italy in its technique and symbolism, and nothing of the Mexican land and the great social upheaval which, even as he painted under the Italianate spell, was already filling his thoughts.

Later he attempted to apologize for the work and assimilate it to his subsequent philosophy by explaining the wall as an allegory of Pythagoreanism and Humanism, and maintaining that he had intended to complete the auditorium with side walls reflecting the entire history of Philosophy, culminating in Dialectical Materialism. However, these are afterthoughts.

His own explanatory notes, prepared shortly after he finished the mural, serve to show his intention and give the reader some idea of the banal allegory and richness of coloring and design:

> The theme chosen for the auditorium of the National Preparatory School is CREATION, with direct allusion to the Mexican race through representative types, from the pure autoothonous to the Spaniard, including the half-breed *criollos.*
>
> The painting of the scenarium wall is only the focus from which the partial compositions of the side wall and vaults will issue. The completed work is ONE SINGLE COMPOSITION, and the cycle of paintings, incorporating themselves in the building in its three dimensions and throughout all the aspects of its different parts, will create in the spirit of the spectator an additional dimension. This complete whole will constitute the work as the author has conceived it, if he is permitted to realize it.

On the central wall in the upper half and under the site of the keystone of the arch which limits the wall, there appears a semicircle of deep blue, outlined by the rainbow, in its center THE LIGHT-ONE or PRIMAL ENERGY, from which three light-rays issue in three directions, one vertically directly downward, two towards the two sides, rays which emerging from the rainbow objectify themselves into three hands; index and ring fingers point towards the earth, the other fingers remaining closed—a gesture which signifies FATHER-MOTHER. Between the rays are constellations, the one on the right including the form of a pentagram, the one at the left a hexagram—the masculine and feminine principles. The vertical hand leads to the point where MAN arises out of the Tree of Life, and the lateral ones to the two principles into which he is divided, male and female, MAN and WOMAN, represented by two nudes seated on the level of the Earth, partaking of its essence and quality in their form and structure.

The MALE is seated with his back to the spectator, his face turned towards a group of feminine figures with whom he is in colloquy, personages which represent emanations from his own spirit. They are seated on the ground in ascending pyramidal disposition.

Lowest, and to his left, in an attitude of explaining to the MAN, is KNOWLEDGE, yellow tunic, blue mantle with applications of gold, flesh of greenish tint. Next, facing him, with indigo mantle and cobalt cowl, diadem of gold, subtle, brown, macerated face, adding her necessary word to the explanations of the other, sits FABLE. Above to the left, eyes green as water, reddish-white skin, hair of gold scarcely shaded at all, dark ocher mantle, and somber gray-green tunic, hands hidden, is EROTIC POETRY. To her left the figure of an Indian working-woman with crimson skirt, *rebozo* of red earth, the hands in repose on her lap, TRADITION. And at the summit of the group, face covered with the mask of grief, TRAGEDY.

On an immediately higher level, disposed in an ample curve which follows the festooned curve whose invisible supports are in the intersection between the lateral walls and the ceiling of the hall, four figures standing, from the right side towards the center in the following order: PRUDENCE, tunic and mantle light green-blue, converses with JUSTICE, white robe, dark skin, pure Indian type. Clear light eyes looking into the distance, hands one upon the other supported on the edge of a shield and holding a broad dagger, stands STRENGTH; her shield is carmine red, bordered with vermilion, in its center a sun of gold. CONTINENCE closes the group, in greenish-gray tunic, veiled face, head and hands under a soft violet mantle.

Higher still, with her head almost touching the arch of the vault, seated on clouds near the central symbol, a figure of Aryan type, with head and glance inclined towards the figures below in possessive and persuasive gesture, yellow tunic, green-yellow mantle, is SCIENCE, which joins to the center the three hierarchies of the right panel.

To the left and seeking symmetry and equilibrium with the preceding by means of elements equivalent in weight and opposed in color: on the line of the Earth sits WOMAN, nude, with strong modeling of her breasts, arms, and legs, black hair which falls curling, face in profile looking towards the luminous center above. To her right, parallel with the edge of the panel, arms raised, white tunic with folds which suggest a slow involving movement accompanied by that of her hair in gold, DANCE—small forehead, great dark eyes, strong cheekbones, white skin, creole of Michoacán.

Close to the left edge, with black hair curling like the tendrils of grapevine branches, yellow ocher flesh, faunlike face, dressed in a goat-skin, MUSIC blows on a double flute of gold. Seated at her side is SONG, Jalisco creole type, tall of figure, dark of skin, with light eyes of lost glance, brick-red *rebozo*, dark violet skirt, holding on her lap her hands, between which she guards three Hesperian apples.

Above, standing, crowning the group and leaning towards the left, blue skirt, crimson bands, blouse embroidered in red, reddish chestnut *rebozo*, necklace of vermilion stones and earrings of the same color, hair combed in two braids, hands small, smiles COMEDY, figure of the most polished creole type of the mid-central plateau.

In the immediately superior level and in analogous disposition with that of the opposite side, THE THREE THEOLOGICAL VIRTUES, from left to right as follows: CHARITY, clad only in her reddish hair, her waist bound in silex, flesh greenish, the palm of her right hand open and the left over her breasts in a gesture of giving milk; near her HOPE, emerald-green tunic bound with a gold cord, mantle in tubular folds, yellow-green, hands joined over her breast, and with her face lifted in profile, looking directly at the Central Unity, her blonde hair in braids, Castilian type. At her side stands FAITH, purest Indian of the sierras which close the Valley of Mexico to the south, hands clasped on her breast in attitude of prayer, eyes shut, head right, *rebozo* falling vertically along her body.

In equivalent position to SCIENCE on the other side, on this side WISDOM unites the group to the central focus, tunic of cobalt blue, light-yellow mantle, vigorous figure of a southern Indian, looks down and shows through her two hands the gesture which signifies MICROCOSM AND MACROCOSM and INFINITY.

Within the little vault which is hollowed out in the middle of the wall (destined to contain the organ), under the vertical hand emanating from the source of light above, rises from the earth THE TREE. From it emerges, visible to the bottom of his chest, arms open in a cross in movement which corresponds to the principal directing lines of the composition, a figure of greater size than any of the others, following with his attitude the intention of the vault and manifesting foreshortening in relation to the general grouping in the different points of view, THE PANTOCRAT.

This work [the painter's notes conclude] has been executed in ENCAUSTIC, using the same pure elements and the same process employed in antiquity in Greece and Italy. This procedure, which the author restored by his own efforts, thanks to researches made during some ten years, is the most solid of the painting processes (in unalterability, resistance, and duration) except for fired enamel.

The amphitheater mural was not finished until the end of 1922, but long before its completion all Mexico was talking about it, taking sides for or against. Never had a work of art in Mexico occasioned such partisanship. Whatever its defects, its impact was so powerful that no one could ignore it. The press caricatured it. Comedians sang about it, made topical jokes about Rivera. It supplied material for whole evenings of well-bred conversation and violent café disputes. For the young artists it became a banner under which to go forth to battle.

I am able to record a typical evening's discussion in one of the more cultured homes of Mexico City, thanks to Elena Lombardo Toledano, sister of the then Director of the Preparatoria, Vicente Lombardo Toledano.

Time: Some evening late in 1922.

Place: The home of the Lombardo Toledanos in Mexico City.

Present: Elena; her brother Vicente, Director of the school; her father and mother; her sweetheart and some of her intimates; a number of university professors and intellectuals, including the Rector of the University, Antonio Caso, his brother Alfonso; and other family friends.

Someone: What do you think of Diego's painting?

My father: Two or three bad words, and silence.

My mother: Haven't seen it.

Pedro Henriquez Ureña: Without doubt one of the greatest painters of the modern world.

Antonio Caso: Stupendous!

Alfonso Caso: An excess of genius!

Brother Vicente: Mexico palpitates in his work.

Señora Caso and family (four old maids, ugly and devout): If we could, we would order the wall whitewashed.

Margarita Quijano: Could there be anything better in our painting?

Augustín Loera y Chávez: In time they will come to admire him as we admire the great painters of the Renaissance.

Rodríguez Lozano: He is a corruptor of art.

Augustín Neymet: How he paints is all right, but not what he paints. He is in love with ugliness.

My suitor: To understand it, one must be prepared, and I, frankly, am not. . . .

My brother-in-law: Maybe you mean to tell me, Elenita, that you like them? Now, don't lie to me. . . .

Professor Julio Torri: Genius doesn't create schools. Fortunately it's not contagious.

A. Gómez Arias (writer): He has the right to succeed by virtue of quantity, but certainly not by virtue of quality.

Laura Pintel (a friend): Each one paints as he is: Raphael painted beautifully because he was beautiful; Diego paints uglily because he is ugly. . . .

Josefina Zendejas: Whatever I know of painting he has taught me.

A visitor whose name I have forgotten: I would rather sweep the streets than paint like that. . . .

In March 1923 the much-discussed painting was officially inaugurated. On the occasion José Vasconcelos received an orange-colored broadside reading:

INVITATION

to the fiesta which the

Syndicate of Technical Workers, Painters and Sculptors
Will hold on Tuesday 20 of this month in honor of

DIEGO RIVERA

Beloved comrade and master of the shop

On the occasion of completing the work of decorating the Auditorium of the National Preparatory School, a work which resurrects monumental painting not only in Mexico, but in all the world, beginning thus in our country a new flowering which will be comparable to those of ancient times, and the great qualities of which: good craftmanship, wisdom in proportion and values, expressive clarity and emotional power (all within a purely organic Mexicanism free of unhealthy and fatal picturesqueness) mark the work as insuperable, and lovers of the profession of painting can obtain from it the science and experience here accumulated.
[And in honor of]

LICENCIADO DON JOSE VASCONCELOS

and

DON VICENTE LOMBARDO TOLEDANO

intelligent initiators and generous protectors of this work and of all the noble effort made toward the development of plastic art in Mexico.
[And of]

LUIS ESCOBAR, XAVIER GUERRERO,
CARLOS MERIDA, JUAN CHARLOT,
AMADO DE LA CUEVA

expert assistants of the maestro Rivera.

All this to give thanks to the Lord who kept them from terrible and horrible fall from the scaffold in nearly a year of most painful labor at the height of almost ten meters. 12:30, at Mixcalco 12, Tres Guerras Cooperative Shop of Painting and Sculpture. Five pesos without fail in the pocket.

Very important note: So that the honorees be not accused of sponging, they also will pay for their meal.*

Thus the painters united around Diego to begin their battle for a new art in Mexico. Diego was pleased with the role his painting had played. But he was not satisfied with the painting itself. He did not press for the other walls of the auditorium. The year's harvest he considered mostly negative. Already his heart was set on something else. The Preparatoria mural was a valiant but false start.

* Anita Brenner: *Idols Behind Altars* (New York, Harcourt, Brace & Company, 1929). The translation is Miss Brenner's.

14. A RED STAR RISES

Towards the close of the year 1922, the new movement got under way in earnest; by the end of 1923 Mexico found herself leading the world in mural painting.

Even before Diego had finished his encaustic, he was negotiating for frescoes in the Education Building, while the excited discussion caused by his first work had moved Vasconcelos to award other walls in the Preparatoria courtyards to Alfaro Siqueiros, just returned from Spain, to José Clemente Orozco, newly come from an unsuccessful invasion of the United States, Fermín Revueltas, and five men who had worked briefly as Rivera's assistants: Jean Charlot, Fernando Leal, Amado de la Cueva, Ramón Alva de la Canal, and Emilio Amero.

Within the next few years almost every painter in Mexico was to go on the payroll of the Education Department—with assignments as drawing instructors, art-school inspectors, "missionary" teachers, or whatnot, but actually to work for the government on canvas and wall. Young lads blossomed into painters overnight. Fermín Revueltas, only twenty, did an encaustic in the Preparatoria. Máximo Pacheco, Indian lad of fifteen, beginning as a peon spreading plaster and grinding colors for Diego, was soon painting intense and beautiful frescoes, a maestro in his own right before he reached twenty-one. From the first his art presented the rare spectacle of a painter in a state of grace whose work poured out with unthinking ease and freshness.

Such precious and highly refined painters as Roberto Montenegro and Adolfo Best-Maugard, whose views were not in the least revolutionary nor talents suited to monumental painting, were drawn into the current. Even Dr. Atl tried to enlarge his delicate landscape talents to the dimensions of a wall.

Word spread through the continent; painters from other lands presented themselves and received a chance at walls. Charlot from Paris, Mérida from Guatemala, Paul O'Higgins from California, later Grace and Marion Greenwood, and the Japanese-American sculptur Noguchi came to study and work and identify themselves for a time or completely with the Mexican art movement, each getting an opportunity to do a wall. Artists in the United States, in Latin America, even in Paris—so provincial when it comes to movements it does not itself originate—began to realize that something was occurring which for generations the artist had dreamed of, that the Mexican fresco revival, whatever its ultimate results, was already the most important development in murals since the Renaissance.

But why Mexico? Why precisely this impoverished and unhappy land? The racial heritage? Where had the "spirit of the race" been but yesterday? And what of the other American countries with similar racial admixtures? Was it the uptilted land, the volcanic contours, the brilliant sunshine, the folk arts? "Inca" Peru differs hardly at all from "Aztec" Mexico in these respects. Is it the mysterious accident of the birth of two or three great painters* and a half-dozen of at least moderate excellence on this spot of earth at this moment of time? The movement could not have occurred without them, yet why did Diego Rivera not mature until his thirty-seventh year, nor Orozco until his fortieth? What forces coincidently ripened this half-dozen or so of lesser talents at the same moment though their average age was about half Orozco's?

We can fix the decade, the year, almost the month of the awakening, and name the first public Maecenas, wherefore we can declare with certitude that the matrix of the modern art movement in Mexico was the 1910 Revolution.

But the relationship is not a simple one. Let no one deduce from it the "law" that if you want a great art movement all you need is a revolution! Of all the results of the decade of bloody and directionless strife between 1910 and 1920, this was the least predictable. Russia has had its revolution, too, much vaster in implication and scope. Yet how feeble, trivial, and banal is the plastic art of the new Soviet society! It is one of the sly anomalies of the historical process that the Revolution itself has so far found its aesthetic expression in the work of a Mexican painter. Even so did the French Revolution of 1789 and the British Industrial Revolution find their theoretic and philosophic expression, not in revolutionary France or industrial England, but in backward, petty-bourgeois, feudal Germany, which perhaps went so much further in its dreams because it was at that moment so limited in reality.

One of the great services of the Mexican Revolution to the painters was to break through the vicious circle of private patron-

* In this I do not take account of Rufino Tamayo, a gifted painter who ultimately, in the thirties, got a chance to do murals on public walls. He does not belong even remotely to this brotherhood or movement, his kinship, insofar as his strong sense of color and design can be said to belong to a "school" at all, links him with Braque, Klee, Chagall, several of the innumerable Picassos, and Gauguin, and with elements of the ancient Mexican and modern "studio" traditions not found in the general mural movement.

age. "I was sick of painting for the bourgeois," Diego told me in 1923. "The middle class has no taste, least of all the Mexican middle class. All any of them wanted was his portrait, or that of his wife or his mistress. Rare indeed was the sitter who would consent to my painting him as I saw him. If I painted him as *he* wanted, I produced shoddy counterfeits. If I painted him as *I* wanted, he refused to pay. From the standpoint of art, it was necessary to find some other patron."

The Revolution had promised so much: now the "Government of the Revolution" had to deliver something on account. The reforms it offered entailed a great building campaign: government buildings, schools, markets, recreation centers. Insignificant from the standpoint of the real needs of the masses and the lyrical promises of the politicos, it was more than sufficient to occupy all the artists whose social and plastic vision led them to paint frescoes, and even, as we have seen, some who were unsuited to it. In Paris, how many painters monumental in their talents and desires have sighed in vain for walls? Now poor Mexico had walls for all, even as the wealthy Italian cities of the Renaissance.

Though it had fallen on evil days, though its technical secrets had largely perished and its forms degenerated, fresco was still a living tradition in Mexico. The Indian had painted frescoes on the walls of his pyramids over a thousand years ago, before the Spaniard came. Catholicism had continued the tradition. To the idol of the Aztec was joined the idol of the Spaniard; the frescoes of Teotihuacán, Mitla, Monte Albán and Chichen Itzá were succeeded by those on thick-walled Romanesque churches of little window and great expanse of wall. It was Diego's hope that an illiterate people who had been told the stories of the saints through the painted image would respond to this new secular myth of the Revolution and its promises for man's life on earth. To be sure, the Church had lost some of its splendor and missionary fervor, and the Revolution was Jacobin and anticlerical. But that is a far different thing from the Hebraic deification of the abstract word, the Mohammedan detestation of the image, bare Puritanism's rejection of the senses, the festival, and the idol.

A temple of another sort had continued the mural tradition, a temple dedicated to a ragged and disreputable version of an ancient Dionysian god. On the walls of the *pulquerías* painters of the people were still producing joyous and ironical murals. There one could see portrayed bull-fighters and bandits, old crones, roguish cupids, and mischievous monkeys playing strange pranks. There one might gaze at the ravishing charms of the *Fair Jewess* and be comforted by the thought that just as she was innocent of baptismal water, so the *pulque* had never known water's adulterating touch. There were the *Men Wise Without Study*, the tavern dedicated to the *Memories of the Future*, and other festive and satirical visions which might delight a not-too-solemn follower of the surrealist school. Before he painted in the Preparatoria Orozco had already become a painter of significance in his mural work on the walls of his brother's café, with mocking caricatures drawing their themes from the world of drunkards and prostitutes.

The Revolution signified a new style and outlook more than new institutions. The new laws did little more than proclaim the promises that could not be fulfilled. Poverty, bad faith, and external pressure made fulfillment difficult. Plans and programs were entrusted to poets, painters, and orators, while the institutions remained in the hands of *caudillos* and generals. The new regime set up children's art schools; it could not even think of children's hospitals, orphanages, homes, child nutrition. It spread out magnificent frescoes before the gaze of a people to which it could not offer sufficient books or literacy, nor guarantee a wage sufficient for the purchase of a daily newspaper. In all this there was no conscious intention of irony for a people who, though never far from starvation, yet have always given freely of their meager substance for a bright succession of communal fiestas; a people who, lacking food, yet delighted in arranging their inadequate market store in patterns that rejoice the eye, carrying their pitiful purchases home in brightly woven bags and baskets, preparing and serving the food in fired clay vessels lovingly shaped and decorated. Bright raiment and poverty were no strangers to each other.

The effect of the stirrings of the revolutionary spirit upon Diego was overwhelming. We can follow it step by step in his painting and in his writing, for he hastened to proclaim each discovery to his fellow artists and the world. He wrote on *retablos* and ironically reminded the intellectual "that the peasant and urban folk produce not only grains and vegetables and industrial artifacts, but also beauty." He wrote on *pulquería* paintings that

> . . . the Mexican is eminently and above all a colorist. . . . If any designation can be justly given to the Mexican cuisine, it is that of a colorist cuisine. . . . I have looked into so many houses of adobe, so old and miserable that they seemed rather to be mole holes than human habitations, and in the depths of each of these holes I have always seen a few flowers, a few engravings and paintings, a few ornaments cut out of paper of vivid colors, all constituting a species of altar which gave testimony to the religion of color.

He wrote of children's drawings, of primitive Mexican portrait painters, of the folk arts and their products, and of the ancient Indian art. Gradually he turned to the political obstacles, politicians, classes, parties, foreign pressures, which seemed to him to prevent the realization of the possibilities in these people and this land.

These new discoveries quickly became partisan issues. The "decent folk," who formerly had ignored the popular arts, now came actively to detest them as savage and ugly, a heritage of backwardness, of a lack of culture and civilization. The bright "barbaric" color was an affront to their own discreet black garments, gray lives, neutral-toned and "dignified" surroundings. Aztec sculpture made them shudder.

Diego, for his part, began to idealize everything Aztec: daily life, ritual, cosmogony, way of waging war, even human sacrifice. Among his papers I found many unpublished fragments written in the early 1920's. Some deal with indigenous life before the Conquest, as Diego conceived it. From them I reproduce the following, altering it only by adding punctuation and division into a semblance of sentences, for Diego wrote as he talked and painted, in an opulent overflow of tumbling thoughts and images, with pauses only at the completion of some natural division because of exhaustion:

> This people [he wrote of the Aztecs], for whom everything, from the esoteric acts of the high priests to the most humble domestic activities, was so many rites of beauty; for whom rocks, clouds, birds, and flowers (*What is comparable to the enjoyment of flowers for their colors and aromas? Love is but a light thing beside it,* said the people in a hymn) were motives of delight and manifestations of the Great Material.
>
> For them what ingenuous missionaries and holy historians believed to be polytheism was only the marvelous plastification of natural forces, one in their unity and multiple in their infinity, beautiful always in their action favorable to man or unfavorable, positive or negative, always engenderers of life by birth—renovation, and death—transformation.
>
> And surely this highest sense of the universe made the Mexican see inevitable death as totally different from the impenetrable abyss which it was for the man of the Occident, who in his terror needed to create a paradise and an inferno where a spirit, element essential and distinct, would await resurrection of the flesh and eternal life. . . .
>
> Never will the poor contemporary man of letters of *criollo*—that is, Catholic—mind, comprehend the joy and the moral clarity of the Sacrifice, mystic culmination, from which anaesthesia eliminated pain, for pain would destroy the magic efficacy of the act. After a purifying preparation with beautiful living for two years, after having left in the bellies of two virgins, two new lives in exchange for his own, the victim converted himself into the sacred book of the revealing entrails of the Macrocosm, and his heart, like a splendid bleeding flower, was offered to the Father Sun, irradiating center of all possibility of life. Or to the

magnificent and beautiful Huitzilopochtli, of the beak and wings of a bird who, in the Flowery War, gave to men the possibility of being more beautiful than the tigers or the eagles. Or to Tlaloc, of the great round eyes, possessor of the secret waters generating life on the earth. All these were liberators from the end that comes by slow rotting, by the miserable condition of dissolving illness, or consumption by age, or slow reduction to total impotence—the highest good to which the mortal can attain who is incapable of preferring to these THE RITE OF SACRIFICE.

In writings such as these one can see the fantasy of the painter at work, making use of real facts of archaeological discovery, elaborating them until it is difficult to determine where facts end and imagined meanings begin, assimilating them into and projecting into them his own feelings and thoughts, making them material for moving expression. They give fresh insight into those colorful and splendid scenes of the battles of the Aztec Knights of the Eagle and the Tiger with the Spanish conquistadors (PLATES 101, 108-110), portrayed on the central wall of the National Palace stairway and in Cuernavaca, or that idyllic and lyrical portrayal of pre-Conquest Mexico on the left wall of the National Palace, or in its corridors, and in the Hospital of the Race. (PLATE 149).

It was characteristic of Diego to give battle precisely on that ground where the attack was most furious and the defense most difficult. Aztec civilization was denounced above all because of its rite of human sacrifice, so it was there precisely that, as devil's advocate, he chose to glorify it.

More than esthetic or archeological theories or material for future murals, these articles and unpublished fragments represent a declaration of faith. We may end the excerpts with one which shows whither that faith was tending. It is from the closing passage of a long and chaotic manuscript by Diego, unpublished also, which traces the history of the folk and its arts and crafts through the pre-Conquest, the colonial period, and the history of independent Mexico:

But now there begins to dawn a hope in the eyes of the children, and the very young have discovered on the slate of the Mexican sky a great star which shines red and is five-pointed. Like the features on the face of the moon, there can be discerned on it a hammer and a sickle. And emissaries have come saying that it is a presage of the birth of a new order and a new law, without false priests who enrich themselves, without greedy rich who make the people die though they might easily, on what they produce with their hands, live in love, loving the Sun and the flowers again, on condition of bringing the news to all their brothers in misery on the American continent, even though for that a new Flowery War might be needed.

"A new Flowery War!"—such was Diego Rivera's Aztec approach to Communism.

15. WHEN ARTISTS FORM A UNION

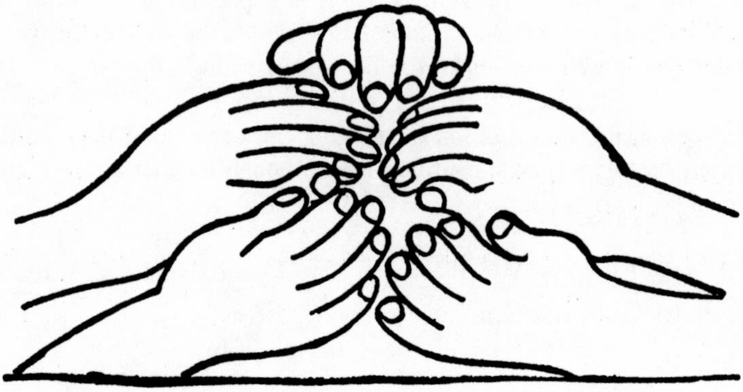

Near the end of 1922 Diego jointed the Communist Party. Almost immediately he became a leader.

His membership card bore the number 992, which would imply that 991 Mexicans had joined before. Yet the reader should not imagine that it possessed so many members. Governors like Carrillo and generals like Múgica, who were among its founders, had already ceased to belong. As the Obregón government began to stabilize, to change from the Revolution organized as government to the "Government of the Revolution," officeholders and office seekers quietly dropped out. Moreover, the Communist International had already passed the high tide of its popularity. Defeats in Germany and Hungary and Italy and at the gates of Warsaw, famine and peasant uprising in Russia, the restablization of war-shaken Europe—had all had their effect. In Mexico the drift towards Communism ceased among the official class and government-controlled labor movement, only to begin among the artists. From a party of revolutionary politicians, it changed to a party of revolutionary painters. At its 1923 convention three artists were elected to its Executive Committee: Diego Rivera, Alfaro Siqueiros, and Xavier Guerrero. They lacked one of making a majority of the Committee.

About the same time—a little earlier, in fact—Diego and his fellow painters formed a "union." Its name was sonorous, the *Sindicato Revolucionario de Obreros Técnicos y Plásticos.* Later they changed it to Revolutionary Union of Technical Workers, Painters, Sculptors, and Allied Trades. Its title was a banner and a credo:

Revolutionary—they would transform the world, and art was to aid in the transformation.

Union—to defend the interests of their craft, to win a place for social painting, conquer walls, reconquer the right to speak to the people.

Workers—down with aestheticism, ivory towers, long-haired exquisites! Art was to don overalls, climb the scaffold, engage in collective action, reassert its craftsmanship, take sides in the class struggle.

Painters, Sculptors, and Allied Trades—did they not all work with their hands? Were they not building-trades workers—like plasterers, stone-cutters, glaziers, cement-pourers? They would unite with the rest of the producers, clarify by their paintings the consciousness of the most important class in modern society, be supported and defended by it, join it in the building of a workers' world.

This was not the first time that artists had banded together. Irrevocable were the days when they had been simple handicraft workers and members of the guilds; painter and sculptor had moved far away from mason, stone-cutter, and roofer. Yet always about the artist, even the most precious of them, there remained something of the craftsman. Even the opulent and elegant Rubens had been denied the title of ambassador though he carried out ably the affairs of state entrusted to him, because that title could not be granted to one who "worked with his hands."

The nineteenth century had been full of attempts of painters to overcome their isolation from each other, to restore somehow the stimulus that comes from mutual defense and labor in common. The Pre-Raphaelites had dreamed of a union, part medieval guild, part Christian brotherhood—a monastic order where love between the sexes was not prohibited. Van Gogh had made fruitless efforts to establish a community of painters, close to each other, to the peasantry, and the soil. Montmartre and Montparnasse had been a sort of union of the self-isolated.

Fresco painting, however, seemed different. Here the division between physical and spiritual labor seemed to be bridged over. The painter was a man in overalls, sitting high up on a scaffold, fitting into a cooperating team of workers, painting, not in random fits of "inspiration," but to cover a given area of wet plaster laid by cooperating laborers within a definite period of time, beginning just so many hours after the plasterers had finished and continuing until the wet surface had become too dry to absorb paint. The veil of mystery was stripped off: idlers could watch him at his work as they watch pile-drivers and steam-shovel operators.

To be sure, these painters were "intellectuals" and handicraftsmen of a highly specialized ability rather than modern industrial proletarians. Even if, as Siqueiros later urged, they should use Duco, air brushes, and paint guns on poured concrete in place of employing earth colors mixed with water and applied by hand-manipulated brush on wet plaster, that fact would not be altered. Their kinship was rather with potters, weavers, woodcarvers, basketmakers, who were still tied to the peasantry. Mexico itself was a land with but little modern industry and machinofacture, and the Mexican Revolution, despite the proletarian verbiage it borrowed from Spanish syndicalism and Russian communism, was essentially agrarian insofar as it was not merely a revolt of a new generation against the mummified Díaz regime, then a succession of struggles between rivals for the place of *Caudillo.* Characteristically, when these "organized workingmen" painters founded a newspaper to speak with word and woodcut to the masses, they did not entitle their organ "The Hammer" or "Hammer and Sickle," but *El Machete.* The name was the measure of their outlook, and the agrarian populist nature of the Mexican Revolution.

El Machete was vast, bright, and gory. It was oversized, the largest newspaper format that I have ever seen, a veritable bed sheet. Its masthead was a huge machete, sixteen and one-half inches long and five deep, held by a fist, printed in black directly from a woodcut and overprinted in blood red. Beneath it was the motto:

El machete sirve para cortar la caña,
para abrir las veredas en los bosques umbríos,
decapitar culebras, tronchar toda cizaña,
y humillar la soberbia de los ricos impíos.

The machete serves to cut the cane,
To open paths in shadowed woods,
To decapitate serpents, to cut down weeds,
And to humble the pride of the impious rich.

Its editors were Xavier Guerrero, David Alfaro Siqueiros, and Diego Rivera. It carried articles on Communism, manifestoes on art, popular ballads by self-appointed poets of the people, engravings printed directly from woodcuts, carved chiefly by Guerrero and Siqueiros. Selling for ten centavos, it was inaccessible in price to the majority of the workers and peasants in a land where many a rural peon did not earn more than thirty centavos a day by labor from sunup to sundown. It was inaccessible, too, despite its popular ballads, by virtue of its language and ideas. Its deficits were made up by subscription among the painters, Diego, whose earnings were larger than those of the others, being the main contributor. After the *Sindicato's* brief life had terminated, the paper became the official organ of the Communist Party of Mexico, which continued many of its peculiar features until the days of "People's Front" respectability, when it was cut down to tabloid size, the revolutionary motto removed, and its name changed to something less belligerent in implication: *The Voice of Mexico.*

The members of the *Sindicato* were a group of strangely variegated temperaments. The union was born in conversations on the scaffold and in the home of Diego, not far from the Preparatoria, where most of them were now engaged in painting. Because it was in fashion, or because they believed it had government approval and would aid them to employment, many joined who were unsuited for the fresco work it exalted and the purposes it proclaimed. The leading spirts of the organization were the three editors, Guerrero, Siqueiros, and Rivera. Diego was regarded by the other two, each more than ten years his junior, as the maestro. But he was soon engaged in the first of the great works, the enormous series of murals in the Secretariat of Education, and was far too busy painting day and night, weekdays, Sundays, and holidays included, to give more than his name and cash to the *Sindicato* and the paper.

The real driving force, people's tribune, manifesto-maker, agitator of the organization, was David Alfaro Siqueiros, who had but recently returned from Europe, where he had been sent to study art on a pension from the government of Carranza. Curly-haired, gray-green-eyed, pallid-skinned, aggressively virile, Alfaro's cheeks seemed to be permanently puffed out by the constant stream of his voluble enthusiasm. Not yet twenty-five years of age, mercurial, high strung, eloquent, bombastic, eager to exhibit himself, trembling with excitement at each of his new enthusiasms, driven by inner turbulence from one uncompleted enterprise to another, Siqueiros was the General Secretary and chief mouthpiece of the Union. His mural in the Preparatoria never got past the initial stages; time and student vandalism have further ravaged the poorly organized fragments. He left his Preparatoria mural to go to Guadalajara as assistant to Amado de la Cueva; then became a mine-union organizer, organizer for the Communist Party, delegate to this conference and that. He was expelled once for indiscipline, again for neglecting to carry out his mission as delegate to a congress, officially announced to have severed his connections when he had dirty work to do which the Party wanted done without taking responsibility, yet was always reinstated, and finally given the accolade of having had "continuous membership" through all these vicissitudes. In jail and out, at this writing, in again; bobbing up in Buenos Aires, Havana, New York, Moscow, Los Angeles, Madrid; author of innumerable manifestoes, theories, and systems of painting, sometimes suggestive, sometimes merely showy or silly, none of which he has had the patience or persistence to work out into reliable processes; painting in a dozen cities and countries and talking in fascinating overflow to gaping young artists about his latest scheme for completely revolutionizing art; fighting in Spain on the side of the Republic and on the side of the Communists when they attacked other Republican parties and tendencies; in 1940, under the inspiration of Soviet secret agents, leading a band of twenty armed men disguised in police uniforms to machine gun the bedroom and bed of Leon Trotsky and his wife under cover of darkness, but succeeding only in wounding Trotsky's grandson, Seva, in the foot, and carrying off one of Trotsky's guards, Sheldon Harte, to be shot in a mountain cabin, and buried under its floor in quicklime; fleeing the country until the storm blew over, only to reappear and talk and paint again, until he landed in jail, not for trying to machine gun a helpless old exile, but for attacking the Mexican Government and arousing turbulent demonstrations against it. In 1961 when the Mexican Government put him in jail, ironically, as is the pattern of his life and of Mexican painting, he was engaged on a large scale mural in the Government's own Chapultepec castle, until recently the presidential palace and now a government museum. Judging from the fragments I have seen reproduced, it gives promise of being one of the best and most carefully worked out of his murals, indeed, the work of a major painter, more carefully designed than anything else he has done. Though it lies unfinished on the walls, amidst his painting materials locked up in the sealed room, and in his mind, the completed parts, showing the influence of Orozco, are full of movement and vitality. He has used some new plastic paint, perhaps pyroxilin, spray gun and air compressor, spraying on as with a carefully controlled, swift and giant brush, in accord with a predetermined structural (and of course, ideological) design, and a strongly marked and sinuous calligraphy that flows from wall to wall, three vivid colors—an industrial plastic, bright orange-yellow, a lime green, and a bougainvillaea, reddish purple. The figures are the familiar ones of the Mexican revolutionary school, Porfirio Díaz enthroned, surrounded by his evil associates while well-dressed writhing women dance before him; the sea of Zapatista guerrillas flowing from background to foreground, and the sea of a proletarian procession—the whole preaching the sonorous and slightly absurd aim for which he has been imprisoned, namely "social dissolution." Like so many of his more ambitious works, it is unfinished, but enough is on the walls to suggest that it is even now the best which his turbulent, disorderly talent has produced. It tells us much of the early painter's union, that he was its secretary and that the *Sindicato* collapsed at a single No from Vasconcelos to the demand for "collective bargaining." And it tells much concerning Mexican politics that Siqueiros was never jailed as the *pintor a pistola* (an artist who paints with a pistol instead of a brush) who tried to murder the old revolutionary exile whom the government had given asylum, but is in jail for trying to foment social disorder, while the same government carefully, and quite properly, protects and preserves his unfinished masterpiece, and permits him to paint in his cell.

Xavier Guerrero, who completed the triumvirate, was in all things the opposite of Siqueiros. A full-blooded Indian, stocky, solid, with straight black "horse-tail" hair, burnished coppery skin, high cheekbones, impassive countenance, he is uncommunicative, slow of thought and action. Among his friends he is known as *el Perico*—the parrot—because he never talks. He assisted Rivera successively in the Preparatoria, the Education Building, and the Agricultural School at Chapingo, did a number of woodcuts for *El Machete,* became a silent member of the Executive Committee of the Communist Party of Mexico, made several unimportant attempts at independent painting and sculpture, gradually drifted out of painting, worked as a Communist organizer among the peasants, where his uncommunicativeness made them feel he was one of them though they never heard enough from his lips to know what he was trying to teach. After spending three years in the Lenin School in Moscow, he devotes himself today to drawing uninspired political cartoons and carrying on his unimaginative, unthinking work for the Communist Party of which he is an official.

The diversity among the leadership of the *Sindicato* was as nothing compared with the nondescript makeup of the membership brought together by the favorable atmosphere and mood that, for a brief moment, prevailed.

Two women were in the union: Nahui Olín (Aztec *nom de guerre* of Carmen Mondragón), more model and camp-follower than painter, unless we except the startling and striking way in which she painted her own person;* and Carmen Foncerrada, fragile, sensitive, a painter of quiet, decorative Indian figures on a carefully planned background of planted fields and native hills, a girl too delicate physically to take an active part in the *sindicato.*

Then there was Roberto Montenegro (born 1885), a painter

* She served as the model for the figure of Erotic Poetry in Rivera's Preparatoria mural.

of the old school, whose exquisite, almost feminine temperament and worship of elegance as the highest painting quality fitted him poorly for participation in a rough-and-tumble, "proletarian" fresco painters' movement. In the more refined and stratified society of Don Porfirio's day he would have made a pleasant and reasonably important place for himself, but in the Mexico of today, as in the time of the *Sindicato*, his work suffers from its refined ambiguity.

Carlos Merida, Guatemalan (born 1893), followed the fashion with the rest of them, though by temperament and inclination he was attracted to abstract art. He had been a pupil of Van Dongen and Anglada Camarasa. While the fresco movement was all-powerful, he painted a fairy-tale mural on the walls of a children's library, then returned to Europe to continue his studies in nonobjective art. He resides in Mexico now and devotes himself almost exclusively to surrealistic and abstract painting, doing work that is sensitive, delicate, a trifle precious, rich, warm and "tropical" in color, "folkloric" in its occasionally hinted representative elements.

Another union member of foreign birth was Jean Charlot, fine-featured, bespectacled, scholarly Frenchman, then twenty-five, with a dash of Mexican and a dash of Jewish admixture in his French ancestry. He left a Paris university to join the French army during World War I, served as an artillery officer, then came to Mexico which had filled his dreams since childhood and adopted it plastically and literally as his country. Later he resided in New York, but his work was still devoted to Mexican motifs. Though fresco work attracted him, he was more at home in small sketches, woodcuts, and paintings. Subtle, erudite, skilled in expressive distortion, he loads each work with the cerebral burden of some aesthetic investigation, succeeding every so often in solving one of his self-imposed problems with startling skill. Charlot is a devout Catholic with a touch of delicate mysticism in his creed, making it singular that he should have been able to work in amity and brotherhood with this Jacobin crew.

The point of contact was his admiration of the humble common folk, women servants and burden bearers whose labors he delighted to represent monumentally within a tiny compass, and a strain of primitive Christian anticlericalism that mingled with his piety.

Still more alien to the group was the temperament and personality of José Clemente Orozco. Born in 1883, he was the oldest of the union members. His approach to life was religious, more deeply and emotionally than in the case of Charlot. Not in a conventional and institutional sense: his murals indicate that for the hierarchical pillars of the Church and the fine ladies who wear their piety as a self-righteous garment he had nothing but contempt. His was a heretical, poor-friar Christianity, taking literally the metaphor of the camel and the needle's eye. In the evangelical cry of wrath against the oppressor and of woe to the rich, lay the sum of his "socialism"; in a miraculous rain of destruction from on high upon the modern cities of Sodom and Gomorrah, his expectation of the destruction of the old order; in love and charity, the balm that would mitigate but not alter the burden of the poor; in a new leader, a Prometheus-Moses-Quetzalcoatl-Cortés, leading a new migration of passive, uncomprehending followers out of the wilderness, lay the hope of mankind—by an act of self-redemption, the Hero Savior might yet destroy the forces of evil that had abused His blood atonement, and thereby redeem man from omnipresent cruelty and baseness.

By nature Orozco was a lone wolf, desiring little association with his fellow painters, giving little to them and getting little in return, holding himself proudly aloof, seeming to paint out of a penumbra of gloom which surrounded him and gave forth flashes of jagged lightning suddenly illuminating the darkness. His life, as he himself summed it up, represented the never-ending and heroic (his word for it was merely "tremendous") effort of a largely self-taught painter "to learn his trade and find opportunities to practice it."

His heroes, too, are solitary beings, and his masses, multiples of nonentity. Modern society was too complicated for him to grasp; his migrations, as Meyer Schapiro has pointed out, are of nude men, devoid of any baggage of intellectual and material civilization as they move over the face of the earth. Their social hierarchy is reduced to varying quantities of physical energy, their leaders being distinguished merely by their dynamism of movement. As with the migrants, so with all the other types he portrayed: they are socially naked, static, unhistorical, their energy the mechanics of mere change of position—a dynamics often vivid, sometimes violent, occasionally overenergetic to the point of becoming declamatory.

Yet no one has illustrated the tragedy of the Mexican Revolution as Orozco has. His murals are the pictorial analogue of Mariano Azuela's *Los de Abajo* (*Bottom Dogs*). If Rivera has painted what the Revolution should be, what it should have become if it were to realize the visions of its Flores Magóns and Zapatas, Orozco has painted what the Revolution had been, its brutality, its senseless pattern of demagogy and betrayal. Negative criticism of the Mexican Revolution is contained in Rivera's work too, but subordinated to an emphasis on dreams of fulfillment. Orozco's outlook was pessimistic and skeptical; he lacked Rivera's confidence in life; his embittered satire is directed no less against the poor than the rich; in all his Mexican Revolution series there is no sign of recognition in its unhappy present of any seeds of a better future. His armed peons are drinking and looting and defiling, his peasant is on his knees praying in anguish; his worker has mere stumps in lieu of arms; his revolutionary soldier is not inspired by the red flag, but blinded by its folds. All is incoherent protest, sardonic bitterness, nay-saying to life as it is and to revolution. Yet this saying no to life because it is evil is saying no to the evil that is in life, and in this sense Orozco, too, may be regarded as a revolutionary.

His strictures on the poor differ from his strictures on the rich in one particular; they are occasionally mitigated by pity, charity, and love—the love of the charitable monk for the crushed Indian, of the old mother for her son departing to the wars, of the *soldadera* following the army for her man. This love is a softening touch of radiance on the solid outline of darkness; it mitigates but does not transform the circumstances of misery. And at these points the work sometimes degenerates from pathos to sentimentalism, for the real power of Orozco's brush is in his bitterness.

His style is violent in composition, crude and powerful in structure, generalized and impersonal in the figures that sparsely fill a space devoid of background or landscape, compassionate, yet sardonic and brutally satirical in its treatment of the human animal. His strong mural work often shows, from a purely technical standpoint, serious defects: changes of color mixture from one day's painting to the next where uniformity was intended; breaking the day's task at points which do not coincide with the basic lines of the composition, so that often the jointure shows disturbingly betweeen the daily stints of plastered surface; poor adaptation to wall space, lack of concern for the relation of design to architecture. Hence the work of Orozco actually gains by reproduction in book form, whereas the work of Rivera loses greatly when it is transplanted to the printed page. But at its best the jagged diagonal design, the violent movement, the bitterness and anguish, the anger of a prophet, attain an explosive force unequaled by any painter since Goya.

A stupid fashion has grown up among professed admirers of Rivera or Orozco of showing their "appreciation" of one by running down the other. As if humanity could not use more than one great painter in a generation. As if art, too, must follow the fashion of one-man dictatorship. I can understand the painter who will deny Velázquez because he admires El Greco, for in his way he is but protecting himself against a self-negating eclecticism, since his admiration may involve setting up the preferred one as master. But when the art lover follows this fashion, he is rooting out areas of his own sensibility; when the critic does so, he is engaging in vandalism. Yesterday the same type of critic was denying El Greco because he admired Raphael or Velázquez, as today he is denying Raphael to exalt El Greco.

Discounting factional motives, which are plainly insensible to aesthetic considerations, one must still conclude that those who proclaim the narrow, self-denying formula "Not Rivera but Orozco" or "Not Orozco but Rivera" must be deficient in their understanding of both and of contemporary painting. Certainly these two unwilling chieftains of the rival feudist bands never agreed with or encouraged those who battled in their name.

Thus, in 1924, when Vasconcelos, yielding under attack by the *gente decente* of Mexico, stopped Orozco in the middle of his work on the Preparatoria courtyard murals, it was Diego who led the battle for his reinstatement. Years later, in 1936, when the Communist Party of the United States exalted the work first of Siqueiros and then of Orozco—discovering proletarian revolution in the latter—as a way of attacking Rivera, I translated for Diego at a lecture he delivered to a summer-school seminar at San Angel Inn. Some questioner asked what he thought of Orozco; his answer was a warm tribute to his fellow painter. To be sure, that was after Orozco's fame was secure and many of his greatest works had been done. But here is Diego's verdict written in 1925, when Orozco had not yet finished his first set of murals:

> José Clemente Orozco, along with the popular engraver, José Guadalupe Posada, is the greatest artist whose work expresses genuinely the character and the spirit of the people of the City of Mexico, in which, though born in Zapotlán, Jalisco, he has lived from early childhood.
>
> Typical *criollo*, of the petty bourgeoisie, he frankly says:
>
> "In a people of Indians we feel as if we were in China."
>
> Sullen and crippled—by an artillery accident as a child—he maintains at bottom a great tenderness, which he hides out of modesty and an instinct of defense.

Excessively conscious of his genius, his character is bitter because he never feels that he is sufficiently recognized and has been too long unappreciated.

Profoundly sensual, cruel, moralistic, and rancorous as a good, semi-blond descendent of Spaniards, he has the face and mentality of a servant of the Holy Office.

And it is with the fury of an Inquisitor that he persecutes sinful love in dens of pleasure and attacks the degenerations and defects of rich and poor.

He mocks the vice of sinners and foolish virgins, but caressing so rabidly the morbidities of those whom he torments that peaceful folk are terrified by his works.

His terrible amorous temperament, restrained by the brake of his pride, his timidity, in daily life, overflows in his painting.

Like Posada, he is an anarchist, instinctive, profoundly romantic; and, as such, in all his work one feels the simultaneous presence of love, of pain, and of death.

His work is profoundly moving, expressive of genius, terrible as a rule, and tenderly and excessively sentimental at times. Never will his passionate transports, despite the heroic effort of the painter, which at times leads him to regions alien to him with lamentable result, altogether succeed in constituting an architectonic material necessary for painting which desires to be monumental. Never will a painting of Orozco's fill a mural role as part of a harmonic construction. But the stormy expression of his genius will endure in the spirit of men, and that suffices.*

Other members of the painters' union were: Fermín Revueltas, just turned twenty, a talented painter who died in his early thirties of illness brought on, it is said, by excessive drinking. Amado de la Cueva, restless experimenter whose love of scorching down dubious Mexican mountain roads on his motorcycle cut short a promising career; Fernando Leal, Emilio Amero, Ramón Alva de la Canal; Máximo Pacheco, Ignacio Asúnsulo, Angel Bracho, Roberto Reyes Pérez and a brother of his whose name I no longer remember, Manuel Anaya, Ramón Alba Guadarrama, and Cahero. All of these were very young at the time

* From notes by Rivera on the various members of the *Sindicato* and other contemporary Mexican painters, in an article that was never published.

of the formation of the *Sindicato*. With the exception of Bracho, Asúnsulo, and Cahero, all worked for shorter or longer periods with Rivera as assistants, learning much of their craft by the time-honored, but today no longer customary, method of apprenticeship. Omitting those who died prematurely and those treated separately above, only one of them, I think, realized the promise of his youth by becoming a significant painter, the then fifteen-year-old Máximo Pacheco.

The career of the *Sindicato* was brief and tempestuous. Despite all the phrases about proletarianism, painting is not a mere skilled craft in which one artisan's day counts substantially like another's. The "proletarian solidarity" is on the surface, the rivalry and jealousy cut deeper. So long as the government is the patron, and a willing one with many walls, there can be collective action to prescribe wages and hours, regulate opportunities, increase their scope. There can, too, be cooperation in defending a painter against censorship, securing opportunities to exhibit, regulating royalities for reproduction and exhibition rights, and similar matters.

But there was no way of convincing government officials that every member who affiliates is equally entitled to walls of public buildings. Moreover, governmental circles were by no means as friendly as the painters imagined when they formed the *Sindicato*. The Governor of Jalisco, José Guadalupe Zuno, who had himself been a cartoonist before taking up politics, sheltered the union members in his state while he was Governor. But other officials thought differently. Even the Education Minister, Vasconcelos, was opposed to the turn the painters were taking, and to the propaganda content that began to show in Rivera's murals. How he looked at the matter is indicated by the following passage from his memoirs:

> . . . I was amused when they organized themselves into a union. Siqueiros communicated to me the formation. Three assistants accom-

panied him, dressed in overalls. For two years I had been patient with Siqueiros, who during all that time never seemed to finish some mysterious snails on the stairway of the small court of the Preparatoria. Meanwhile the newspapers were overwhelming me with accusations to the effect that I was maintaining drones under the pretext of murals that never came to an end, or were an absurdity when they did. I endured the criticisms as long as I believed that I could count on the loyalty of those I was protecting, and from all of them I demanded hard work. On one occasion, through the newspapers, I defined my aesthetics: "Surface and speed is what I demand," I said to them, exaggerating; and explained, "I desire that they paint well and quickly because the day I go the artists will not paint or will paint propaganda art."

To Diego, to Montenegro, to Orozco, it never occurred to create unions; it has always seemed to me that the intellectual who has recourse to these methods does so because he feels himself individually weak. Art is individual and only the mediocre support themselves in the gregariousness of associations which are all right to defend the salary of the worker who can easily be replaced, never for the unsubstitutable work of the artist.

Therefore when there presented themselves to me, organized, precisely those who did not do work, amused, smiling, I answered:

"Very well, I will not deal with your union, nor with you. Personally I prefer to accept from all of you your resignations. The money which has been going into your murals we will employ on primary-school teachers. Art is a luxury, not a proletarian necessity, a luxury which I will sacrifice to the proletarians of the teaching profession."

The face they made was diverting. They withdrew in confusion. But they counted on my friendship and did not have anything to be sorry for. On leaving they begged one of my secretaries:

"Tell the *Licenciado** not to fire us: we will continue working as before."

The whole thing was a tempest in a teapot. It is proper to state at this point that each of the artists earned an almost wretched wage, with positions as clerks, because I had not dared to enter in the budget an appropriation for painters, for they would have defeated me on it in the Chamber. Public opinion had not yet become accustomed to consider the encouraging of art an obligation of the state.

* *Licenciado*, an honorary title of address in Mexico, signifying "attorney." All professional men with university degrees are regularly addressed by their titles of *Inginiero* (Engineer), *Licenciado*, etc., as we do in the case of medical doctors, professors, and doctors of philosophy.

The *Sindicato* did not long withstand this humiliating blow. Siqueiros, Rivera, and Guerrero, having joined the Communist Party, turned over *El Machete* as its official organ. Civil war broke out once more so that the educational budget was cut to the bone in favor of the military. Siqueiros left to work as assistant to Amado de la Cueva under the wing of Governor Zuno in Guadalajara. Diego as the most prodigious worker earned more than the others by several appointments at once, and got more walls, thus arousing jealousy. The conservatives dropped out of an organization that plainly did not enjoy official favor. The *Sindicato* fell apart. The brief brotherhood was at an end.

Postscript: While this book was on the press, Jean Charlot (now Professor of Art at the University of Hawaii) sent me a copy of his new book, "The Mexican Mural Renaissance, 1920-1925," published by Yale University Press in 1963. It gives Charlot's own view of why he was ousted from the Second Court of the Secretariat of Education, along with his associates. This version differs considerably from the one I got from interviews with Rivera and Minister Vasconcelos. Unfortunately, since my book was already paged up and on press, I could neither investigate and make changes nor put the two opposing versions side by side. All I can do is let the reader know that Charlot's version is to be found on pages 271-279 of his new book.

16.
ALL MEXICO ON A WALL

In March, 1923 Rivera began the first of his great works—a series of 124 frescoes on the corridor walls of a spacious courtyard, three stories high, two city blocks long, and one wide, the patio of the Ministry of Public Education.* Rivera decorated all four sides on all three floors, except for three panels on the ground floor and a section on the second floor on which the shields of the Mexican states have been emblazoned by other painters. For good measure, he added murals on the dark approaches to an elevator and all the way up the walls on both sides of an ascending stairway. The task occupied four years and three

* Again the reader should be reminded of the impossibility of conveying in reproductions and page measuring six inches by nine the impact of frescoes that cover walls three stories high, two city blocks in length, and one in width. The total painted surface on the three floors and stairways is 1,585 square meters or over 17,000 square feet, i.e. the equivalent of a painting one foot deep and over three miles long. Of this only the first floor and the stairway, and a few panels on the top floor, something less than half of the total can be counted as among Rivera's best work.

months of intensive if intermittent labor, eight, ten, twelve, sometimes fifteen hours at a stretch, with reluctant pauses for a frugal lunch of fruits and *tacos* brought up to the painter on the scaffold. During the same period, by crowding more than seven normal working days into each seven-day week, and by using a small squad of plasterers, color grinders, tracers, and common laborers to assist him, Diego also completed 30 frescoes in the Agricultural School at Chapingo. In both places all the actual painting was done entirely by his own hand. For "relaxation" he engaged in politics, wrote articles, did innumerable canvases and sketches, and worked on plans for further murals.

It was this series in the Education Building that made the Mexican art movement suddenly known throughout America and Europe and made the name of Rivera famous through the Western world. It initiated a revival of mural painting, decadent since the late Renaissance, a revival felt first in Mexico and then in the United States. Other great works were to follow in incredible succession: Cuernavaca, the National Palace, the Detroit Institute of Arts, Radio City, the New Workers' School, the production of the destroyed Radio City mural in the Palace of Fine Arts in Mexico City, and lesser enterprises such as the Health Building in Mexico City, the Hotel Reforma banquet hall, the San Francisco Stock Exchange and Art Institute, the Hotel del Prado, the Institute of Cardiology, the Hospital of the Race, the Lerma Canal, the façade of the Teatro de los Insurgentes, any one of which would be regarded as a vast undertaking by an artist of lesser fecundity; and several smaller works like the outdoor encaustics of the Mexican stadium, two panels in the International Workers School, some wood carvings in Chapingo, two stained-glass windows in the Health Building, the mosaics in his pyramid museum.

The sum total of this work is striking beyond the power of words and expresses more completely, I think, than the work of any other painter a land and an age. Yet if Rivera's tremendous energies had been exhausted even by this single first work, or if the effort had consumed, as with a less fecund talent it must have done, all of a lifetime, its achievement would still be overwhelming.

Future historians, discovering the ruins of this single building —the frescoes are painted to endure as long as the walls themselves—would be able from them alone to reconstruct a rich and varied picture of the Mexican land, its people, their labors, festivals, ways of living, struggles, aspirations, dreams. From it, too, they could reconstruct some notion of the thought-currents of the Western world in our time. Not since the Renaissance has any work embodied so vast a cosmology and sociology as this. If we can find other contemporary works to match it, they are from the hand of the same man.

It might be supposed that this amazing mass of painting has been achieved by mere brute strength and careless improvisation, yet the 124 Education Building panels constitute a single work, at once simple and sophisticated, its simplicity flowing from the fact that each line is calculated, each gesture planned, each part enriching and merging into the whole. It both utilizes and adapts itself to the architecture, and harmonizes planfully and naturally with the land in which it has been done, the people whose lives it is intended to reflect and serve, the age of which it is an expression, and certain ageless aesthetic needs of man.

The Ministry of Education building is constructed simply and solidly of stone and cement. To visit any of its offices one must enter into this great inner court on which they all open. The court is lined with arches forming a series of traversable passageways all around the great rectangle, a simplified version of Spanish convent architecture. The walls are partly shadowed by the passageways of the two upper floors, the top corridor similarly covered over, the patio itself being open to the sky and the brilliant Mexican sun. Thus each painting is part in sunlight, part in deep shadow, and the walls are broken at frequent intervals by double doors opening outward from the offices and arched passageways leading to the street.

The problems of painting this vast and varied space, not with abstract designs but with living figures and scenes, the main lines of which are an abstraction from the lines of the building, have been solved so simply that they scarcely seem to have existed. Here and there one's pleasure is subtly increased by an awareness of how some recalcitrant rectangular opening in the wall surface has been arched with paint, or surmounted by recumbent figures resting as solidly as architecture. One steps back and sees from the other end of the courtyard how the apparently closed units of painting on the ground floor carry the eye to the second, and from that to the brightly colored niches and arches that top off the third. One sees how the artist has overcome, even made capital of the fact that each painting is part in sunlight, part in shade, how the whole grows lighter and brighter as it climbs towards the open sky. Here and there one becomes even sharply aware, because of the brilliance with which a problem has been solved, of the triumphant assimilation of an ugly gash in the wall surface into the beauty of the artist's plan, as when he manages to assimilate a glass-covered electric switch box as part of his composition (PLATE 60). But for the most part, one feels rather than sees the rightness of the design; the extension of the building's architecture into new dimensions; the enclosure of the multiplicity and movement of Mexican life within the restful monotony of these archways; the balancing of colors in harmony with bright sunlight and intense shadow; the heavy solidity on the first floor as a foundation for the whole; the sky brightness and rounded lightness of design on the third. The subject matter, too, has an earth-to-sky organization.

The observer is invited by a panel to approach close up to it, and it lives by itself; he withdraws, to be caught by the rhythmic design of a whole section of panels, by a unity of three floors of walls at once; he turns slowly around to go, and finds himself

67. Portrait of Guadalupe. Wax on Canvas. 1926

68. Sketch for Portrait of Guadalupe. 1938

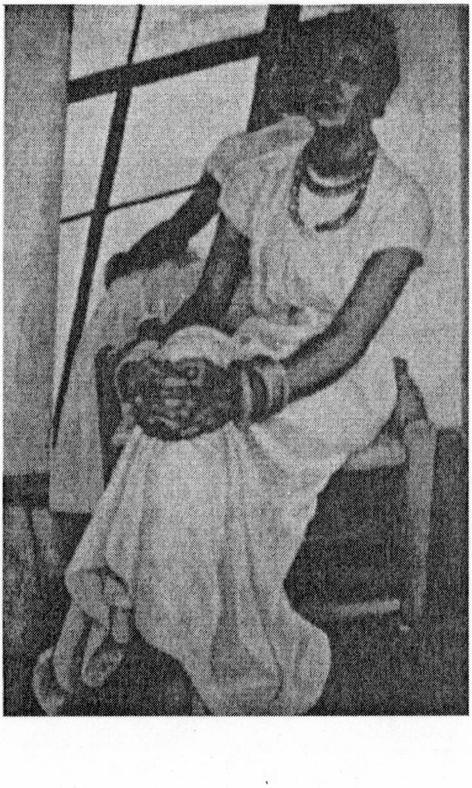

69. Portrait of Guadalupe. Oil. 1938

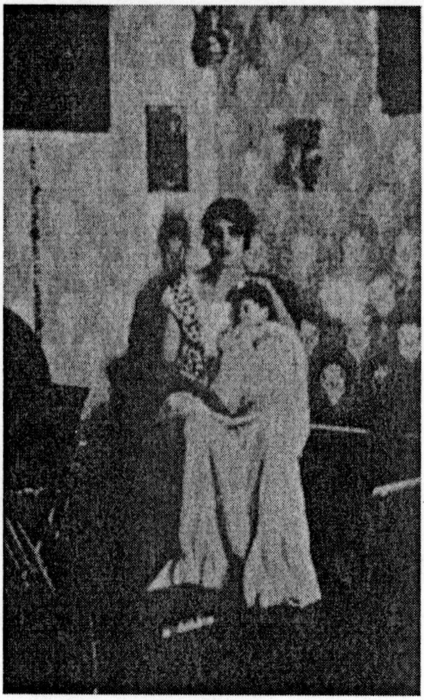

70. Guadalupe and Ruth in the Rivera Home.

72. Portrait of Ruth Rivera. Oil. 1949

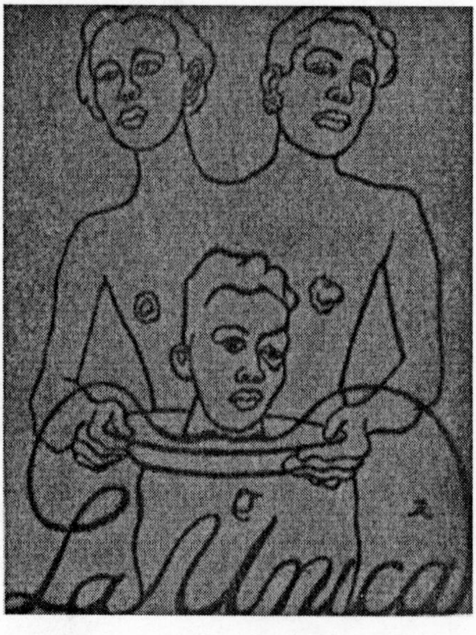

71. Portrait of Guadalupe and her Second Husband. Cover for her novel, "La Unica." 1937

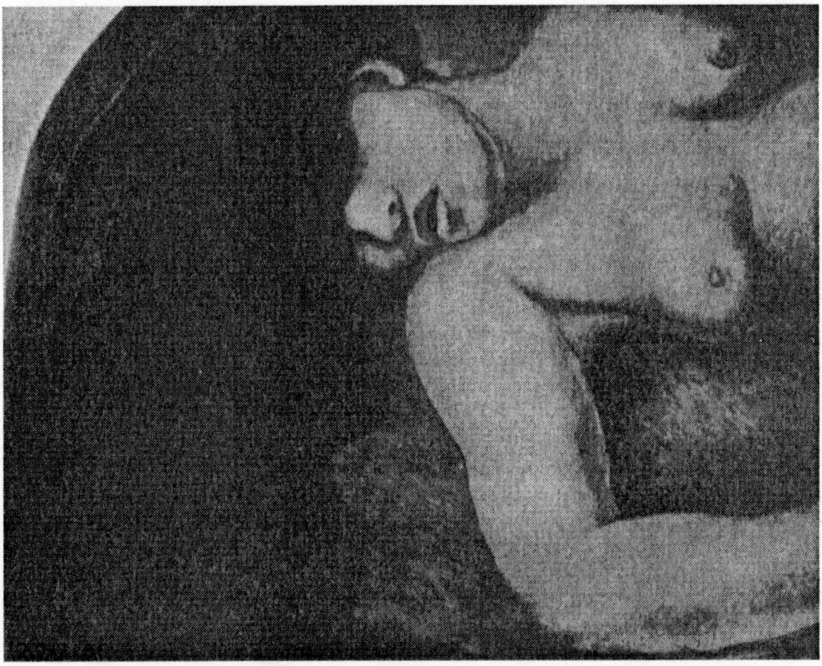

73. Germination. Chapingo. 1925

74. The Earth Oppressed. Chapingo. 1925

75. Distribution of the Land. Chapingo. 1926

76. Bad Government. Detail. Chapingo. 1926

77. Night of the Rich. Detail. Top Floor. Education Building. 1926

78. Night of the Poor. 1926

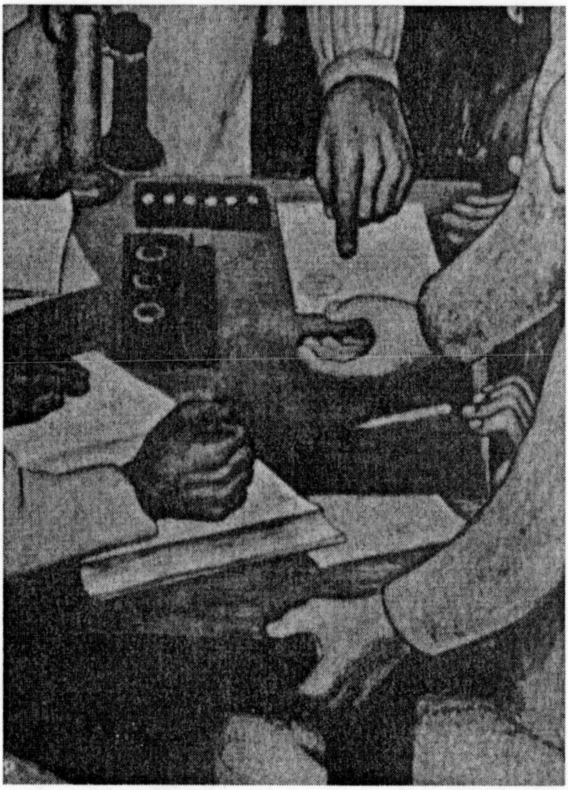

79. Hands. Detail from "Taking Over the Factory." Education Building. 1926

80. The Architect. Self-Portrait. Education Stairway. 1926

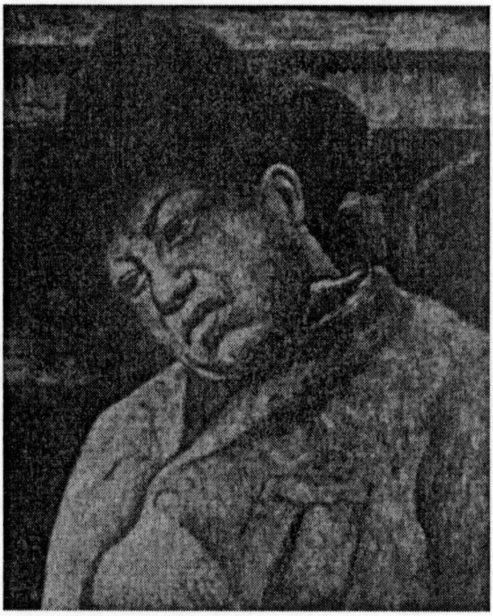

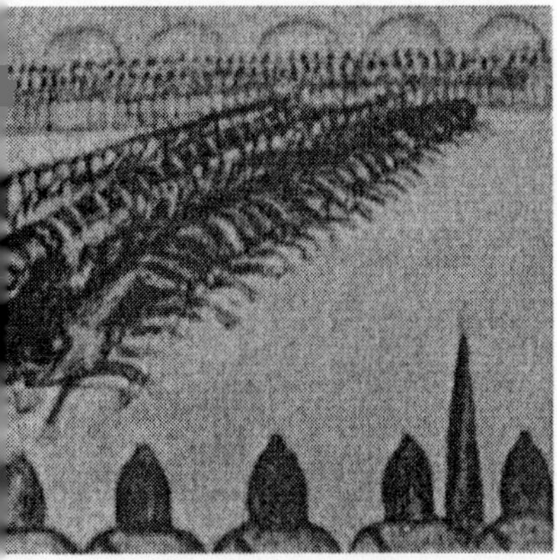

1. Red Cavalry. Watercolor Sketch in Notebook. 1928

82. Red Horsemen. Watercolor Sketch. 1928

3. Red Army Formation. Watercolor Sketch. 1928

84. Red Army Truck. Watercolor Sketch. 1928

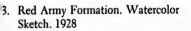

85. May Day in Moscow. Oil. 1928

86. Children Playing in Snow. Oil. 1927

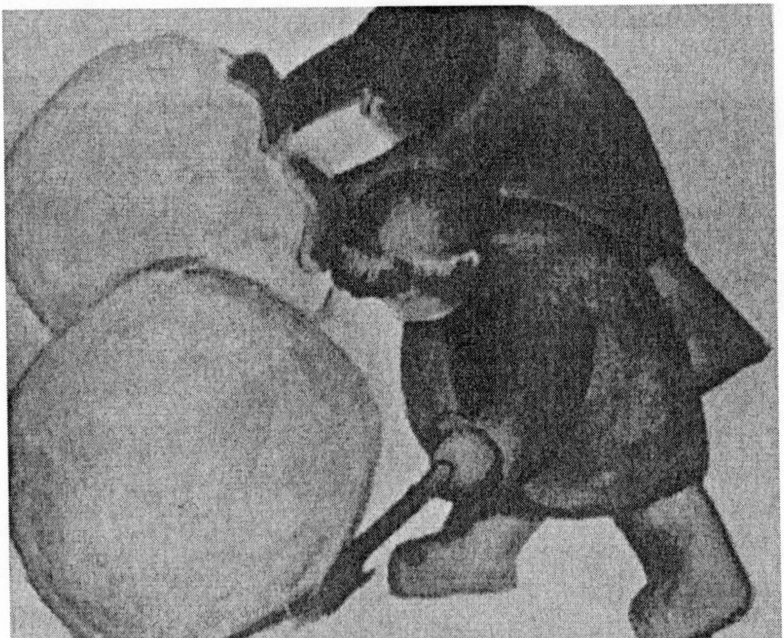

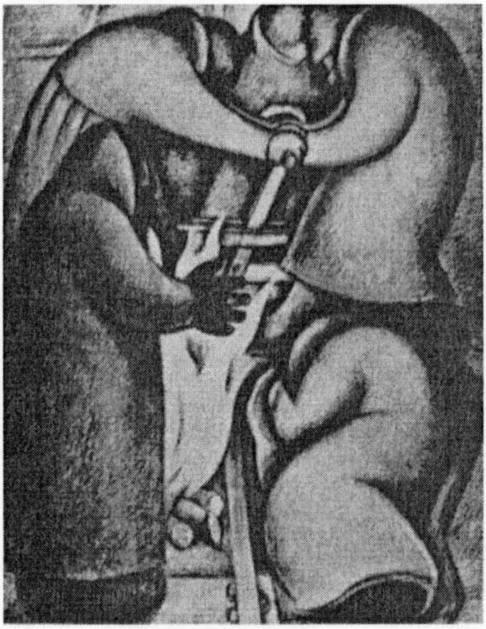

87. Sawing Rails. Pencil. 1927

88. Communards. Color Cartoon for "Krasnaya Niva." 1928

89. Frida at Thirteen.

90. The Author's Wife and Frida.

91. Frida in 1939.

92. Frida and Diego. 1931

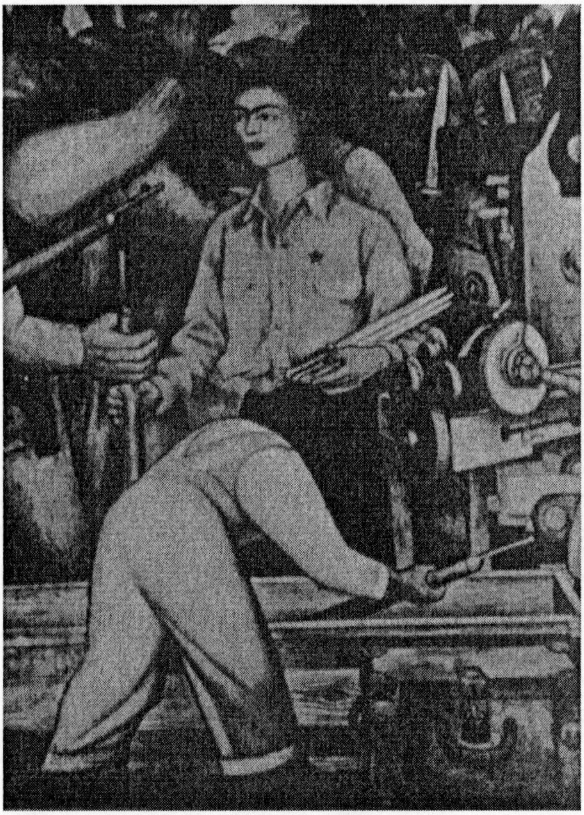

93. Frida Distributes Arms.
Education Building.
Top Floor. 1927

94. Frida and Christina.
National Palace. 1935

95. Frida Kahlo. Self-Portrait.
Oil on Gesso. 1939

96. Knowledge. Health Building.
(Model, Christina Kahlo.) 1928

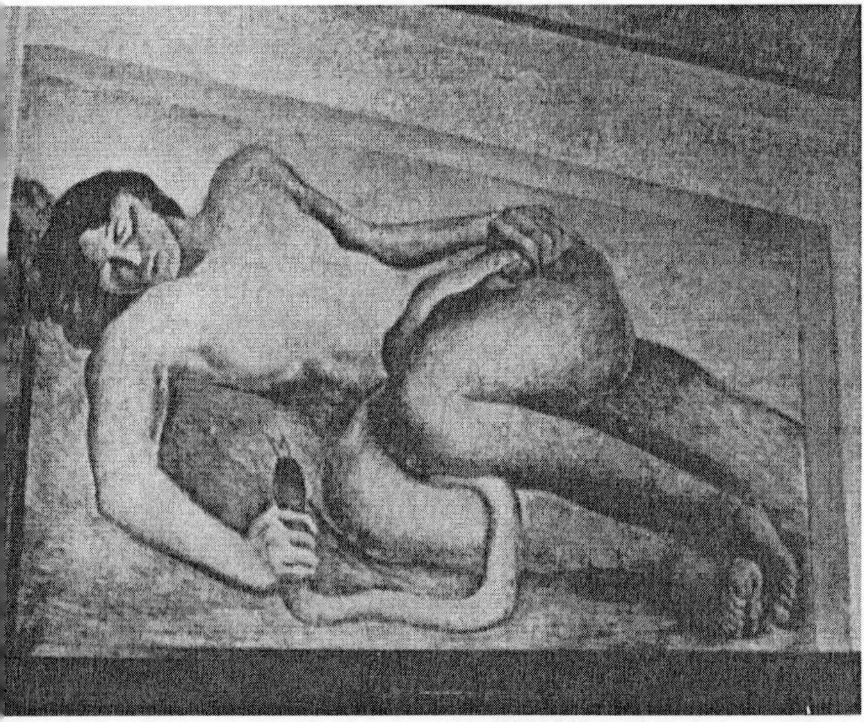

97. Continence. Health Building. 1928

98. Guadalupe and Frida. 1934

99. Portrait of Guadalupe
by Frida Kahlo. Oil. 1932

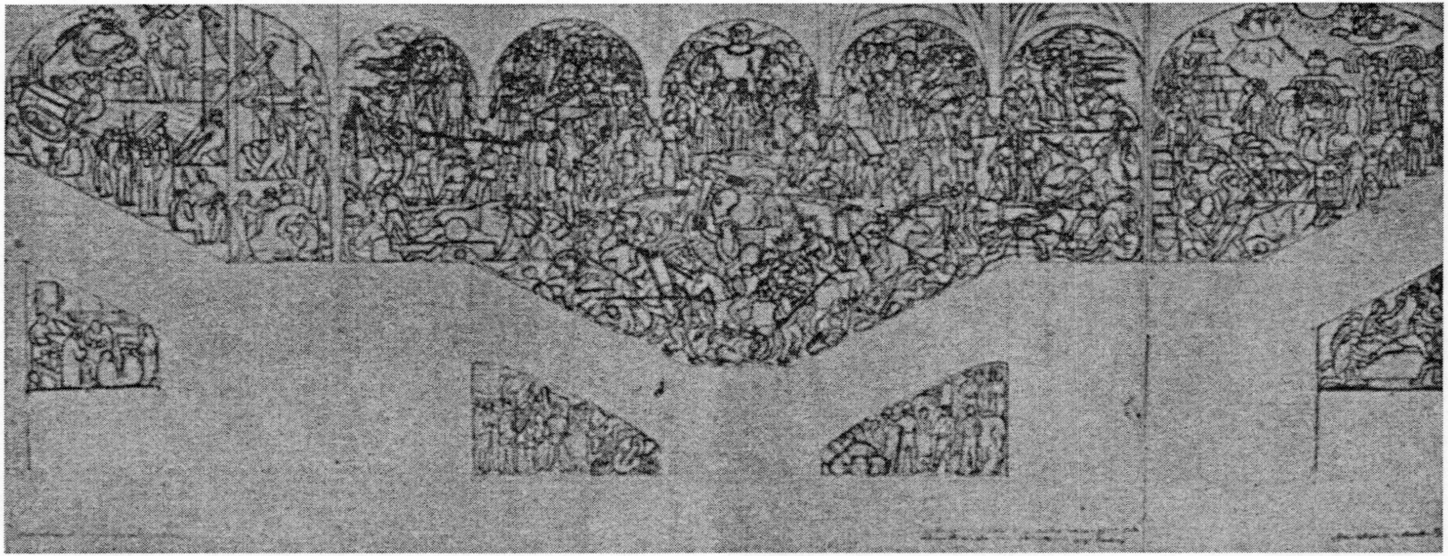

100. Sketch for National Palace Mural.

101. Before the Conquest. Right Wall. National Palace Stairway.

102. National Palace Stairway. Center. Fully sketched and partly painted.

viewing the works as a whole. Always it remains a living organism, obedient to a vast and detailed plan.*

The great rectangular courtyard is divided at a point one-third of the way from one end by a bridgelike gallery affording communication from one side of the building to the other on the levels of the second and third floors. This makes it in effect two patios. The smaller of the two Diego made into "the Court of Labor," the larger "the Court of the Fiestas." The general plan of the work is as follows:

Court of Labor: on the ground floor, the industrial and agricultural labors of the Mexican people; on the second and third, the arts: painting, sculpture, and dance, music, poetry, and popular epic, the drama.

Court of the Fiestas: on the ground floor, popular festivals; on the second, festivals in which intellectual activity predominates; on the top floor, illustrated folk ballads of the bourgeois and proletarian revolutions.

The approach to the elevator and the stairway walls provide a synthesis of the ascending Mexican landscape in which appear symbolic figures representing its social evolution. It begins at the street level with subterranean waters and those that wash Mexico's shores and the islands of the Gulf; then the tropical lands that rise from the sea, the fertile mountain slopes, the high plateaus, culminating in snow-capped mountain peaks. At each level allegorical figures represent the pursuits and social evolution of Mexico from primitive society through agriculture and industry to the "proletarian revolution" and construction of a new social order.

There are significant aspects of paintings that can never be

* In his self-portrait at the head of the stairway, in a trio of building workers—a painter, stonecutter, and architect—Diego has painted himself as the architect, author of the master plan (Plate 80).

conveyed in words. As well try to convey the taste of a mango as the emotion experienced in the presence of so vast a work of art. In one case as in the other, there are aspects that can be treated verbally with some adequacy, others which can be hinted at, others which cannot even be suggested. I do not mean to reduce the uses of aesthetic criticism and interpretation to zero. With the mango one can give a notion of shape and color, texture of flesh, and size and shape of pit and more besides; but when it comes to the taste itself, words are useless. So there are many aspects of a painting which can be conveyed with words, others not even with printed reproductions. If this is true of the single canvas, how much more is it true of a monumental mural, only fragments of which can be reproduced in the pages of a book, and only at the expense of their monumentality, of the qualities which come from scale, and relation to the architecture of which they are a part. All one can do is give a "catalogue" notion of the work in question, falling back in the end on the inevitable truism that such a painting has to be seen to be felt. According to Elie Faure and Walter Pach and many another sensitive writer and artist, it is worth going halfway round the world to see.

The Court of Labor is divided according to the location of its walls to correspond with the main divisions of the country: north, central, and south. The north walls show weavers at work (PLATE 56), dyers tinting the cloth, women gathering fruits and flowers, laborers on a sugar plantation and in a *trapiche* (domestic sugar refinery) (PLATE 54). *The Weavers* shows how skillfully and freshly Rivera has used devices of perspective learned from Uccello; the *trapiche* conveys some notion of the rhythmic dance of the labor of the sugar workers as they grind the cane, pour the juice and stir it in the vats. Work here, as so often in Rivera's paintings, far from being brutalizing and exhausting toil, is a rhythmic dance. Thus his dogmas as a Communist give ground to his vision as a painter, with results that are propagandistically weak in proportion as they are plastically strong.

On the middle wall, without the harmony between man and his environment coming to an end, the disharmonies between man and man begin. Here are silver miners going down to their work in the mine, strong simplified bodies, some naked to the waist, some bearing a wooden beam suggestive of Christ bearing His own cross. The eye is led to accompany them in their descent by the in-curve of the arches, and by traveling downward from beam to beam and tool to tool as they are borne on the shoulders of the descending men. In the next panel the miners ascend once more, an exhausted face and weary upstretched arm just showing from the pit, while one who has emerged is subjected to search by an overseer. His arms, outstretched to facilitate the search, suggest that he is nailed to a cross.

Diego was here beginning the task of creating the symbols for the new content of his painting, symbols for a new age which had to be linked with symbols already accepted; whose long life and familiar presence would endow them with overtones of feeling, provided they could be seen afresh. One of the difficulties of all such ground-breaking in art is that the symbolic aspect of iconography, like the metaphors of poetry, is likely to flourish best in a period when a number of vivid conventional symbols about important subjects already exist and have currency, but have not yet grown trite and stale. Rivera had little or nothing to build on in the imagery of painting or in the Mexican popular mind. He rejected the sentimentalizing of Millet, the elegant idealizing of Meunier, the treating of smoke and industry and labor as a spectacle for the eye as was done by the impressionists in the 1890's, the sentimental pathos of Steinlen and Käthe Kollwitz. None of them was adequate to the sweep of his thought or the nature of his problem. His task was closer to that outlined by Gregory the Great in the sixth century when he wrote to the Bishop of Marseilles:

> What writing is to those who read, that a picture is to those who

have only eyes; because, however ignorant they are, they see their duty in a picture, and there, although they have not learned their letters, they read; wherefore, for the people especially, pictures stand in the place of literature.

While painting the mining panel, Rivera ran into the first of his controversies with his patrons, controversies which made him for years the storm center of representative art. On the timbers which cover the exit from the mine, he decided to paint in explicit words his message. For the purpose, he chose a few lines of a poem by Gutiérrez Cruz:

Compañero minero,	Comrade miner,
doblegado bajo el peso de la tierra,	Bowed under the weight of the earth,
tu mano yerra	Thy hand does wrong
cuando saca metal para el dinero.	When it extracts metal for money.
Haz puñales	Make daggers
con todos los metales,	With all the metals,
y así,	And thou wilt see
verás que los metales	How after, all the metals
después son para tí.	Are for thee.

When these verses were discovered by the metropolitan dailies that were carrying on a continuous campaign against the paintings, a storm broke. To the charges that the paintings were ugly, anti-esthetic, a waste of public money, a defamation of Mexico, was added the accusation that the painter was urging assassination! This was too much for Vasconcelos; he pleaded with Diego rather than insisted, urging that he was under fire enough on the score of the paintings and that if he were to continue to defend them, the offending verses must be removed. The Painters' Union called a council of war; they considered the "revolutionary" possibilities in the series as a whole, the fact that the plastic propaganda which was growing on the walls remained uncensored except insofar as it had been expressed in words "with all their letters." They realized, too, that those people least sensitive to painting were precisely those who objected most strongly to the verbal underscoring of what the pictures said directly in paint. In the end it was decided to yield. One of Diego's assistants smashed the verses off the wall, solemnly wrapped up a copy of the text in a tiny bottle, buried it in the fresh plaster to preserve the verses for posterity, and Diego repainted the timbers at the mouth of the mine without the poetic exhortation.

Then he proceeded to his next panel, worker and peasant in a fraternal embrace, a painting with some of the simplicity and strength of an annunciation by the Italian primitives (PLATE 55), and beneath it on a rock, fresh verses from Gutiérrez Cruz! They urged worker and peasant to join in an embrace of comradeship and love and, thus fortified, take all the fruits of factory and field for themselves. The protest flared up afresh, but there were no daggers in the verses this time; in the end they remained.

The central wall was completed with a scene of potters at work at their craft, pyramidally designed figures of Indian peons resting in a pause at the harvest, a landowner, thumbs inserted in a cartridge-lined belt, superintending the weighing of bags of grain. The peons, bending over the scales, are bowed in symbolic submission.

On the north side Rivera painted metalworkers at crucibles, arms simplified into a single swinging curve as they drive spigots with long-handled hammers, foreshortened so that the hammerheads seem to fly out of the wall; iron miners, a rhythmic repetition of bent backs and picks biting into the ground; revolutionary guerrilla fighters freeing enslaved peasants, a village teacher who instructs young and old while armed peasants stand guard or work the land and build the edifices of the new order; steelworkers who pour molten metal into a mold, illuminating the wall and court with a somber glow.

Having finished the Court of Labor, Diego turned to the larger section of the great patio. This he had entrusted, as director of the entire enterprise, to a number of the younger painters of the *Sindicato*. But the Court of Labor had been filled by his tireless brush and overwhelming imagination while they discussed and wrangled and decorated uncertainly insignificant portions of their still blank walls. Collective work sounded beautiful in theory, but was proving difficult. Perhaps they were insufficiently trained to it, or too strongly divergent in styles and temperaments, or Rivera might have been at fault for scrupling to assert sufficient arbitrary authority as director of the work. At any rate it neither showed the advantages that might conceivably derive from such a procedure, nor did each of the cooperators prove able to give as much, working separately, as he might have done. The "collective" disintegrated into individual painters doing individual panels, with others acting as their assistants. Even so, by the time Diego had finished his patio and a world had come to life upon its walls, the "collective" had completed only four of the twenty-four paintings which, according to contract, they were to have done in the same length of time. Vasconcelos pronounced the collective arrangement unworkable and the contract violated by non-compliance, and asked Rivera to finish the other court, then the entire three floors, except for the section of state shields.

The four panels that the "collective artists" were able to show in a state of completion were the work of two of their number, Jean Charlot, already experienced in fresco painting, had completed three, and Amado de la Cueva one. Rivera accepted two of Charlot's and the panel by de la Cueva as sufficiently adapted to his plans and style to remain upon the walls. One of Charlot's panels he removed.* His own nearby and opposing panels that might be taken in by the observer simultaneously with those of Charlot and de la Cueva, he skillfully adapted, shading off towards their styles and colorings so that they do not merge badly into the whole. Years later, when he got into his controversy with

* A remarkably fine painting, it seemed to me. In fact I committed the indiscretion of telling Diego that it was a marvel of plastic organization and a fit companion for his finest panels, which put him in a fury and may have sealed its doom.

the Rockefellers and they ended by wantonly destroying his entire work in Radio City on ideological grounds, there were not lacking persons ill-disposed towards Rivera, or desiring to give support to the Rockefellers, who whispered around that Diego himself had "once destroyed a mural by a Mexican painter."

In the Court of the Fiestas, harmonizing with the red of the molten metal of the Court of Labor, Yaqui Indians perform the Dance of the Deer and the Old Huntsman (the Dance of Life and Death) around an open fire. Then come the festival of the corn harvest, the festival of the dead in both city and country, that of the flowers, the burning of the Judases on the Saturday of Glory, pagan dances in the Church of our Lord of Chalma representing the movement of the heavenly bodies around the sun. The middle of each of the three walls is occupied by a great composition embracing three panels and the spaces over the doors between them: one showing the division of the land among the peasants, the second a rural market fair, the third a celebration of the First of May.

As Diego moved from wall to wall, his mastery of the half-forgotten process of true fresco gained apace. He made researches into Italian books of the old masters of *buon fresco,* studied Aztec and Mayan mural techniques, experimented with colors and materials. In his first efforts, the wet plaster on which he painted dried too quickly. He tried mixing more water with the pigments, but this made the colors thin. He tried nopal juice as a binding material, the nopal being a native cactus from which came a viscous fluid reputedly used by the ancient Indians in painting. The surface dried more slowly, but in time the organic matter in the juice began to decompose, producing opaque stains. So Diego returned to Italian fresco methods, seeking to refine them with the aid of the latest achievements of chemistry.*

* Rivera's experiments and growing knowledge explain why some of the earliest panels show more signs of weathering and cracking than the later ones.

Fresco is one of the most exacting methods of painting. It involves painting with water colors on freshly laid plaster while the plaster is still wet. The color is absorbed by capillary action, and held and protected by a fine film of calcium carbonate formed by the brush as it moistens the lime. The first reaction of the moistened lime is a film of calcium hydroxide. Time causes its conversion into insoluble calcium carbonate by absorption of carbon dioxide from the air. The painting is then waterproof; if the plaster coat has been properly made, it will last as long as the wall unless actually hammered, scratched, or cracked off. Under a microscope the surface appears as a fine mosaic of pigment.

A knowledge of chemistry is necessary for the preparation of durable work, a mason's skill for the proper laying on of the successive coats of plaster. The sand must be free from salt, as salt ruins the color. It must be free from organic matter or fungus. Lime which has been coal-burnt cannot be used, for sulphur absorbed from the coal may alter the pigments. Ammoniates and nitrates must be rigidly excluded for the same reason. In the process that Rivera finally worked out, lime which had been wood-burnt and slaked more than three months previously, shipped to him in rubber sacks that helped to prevent contact with the carbon dioxide in the air, and chemically tested before using, was employed, and ground marble dust substituted for sand. His pigments were tested in a sodium-hydroxide solution to ascertain that they were proof against alteration by lime, and further tested for resistance to exposure to light and other chemicals to which they are likely to be subjected. At least three coats of plaster were evenly spread on the wall, the third being a fine coat of lime and ground marble dust, thinly spread and carefully smoothed and polished off. Only earth colors were used, oxides of iron, manganese, aluminum, and copper, blending appropriately with the lime and marble dust, which are also earth substances, to become part of the wall which they decorate. The pigments commonly used by Rivera were yellow, golden and dark ocher, raw sienna, Pozzuoli red, red ochre, Venetian red, burnt sienna, transparent oxide of chromium, cobalt blue, vine black (calcined grape seeds), and *amalgre morado*, a Mexican red oxide of iron earth. The colors were ground by his assistants by hand on a marble slab with a small quantity of distilled water to form a paste. These he put upon his "palette," an old "graniteware" plate, and applied them with a brush moistened in distilled water to avoid impurities. Clearly one must be something of a scientist to do durable fresco work.

And a workingman too! While painting in the open courtyard of the Secretariat of Education Diego was one of the "sights" of Mexico City. Artists and tourists came from afar to watch him. Men and women who came to the Ministry would pause to look on, as in New York people follow the operations of a steam shovel. It was on the scaffold here that I first got to know him well: a bulky, genial, slow-moving, frog-faced man, in weather-worn overalls, huge Stetson hat, cartridge belt, large pistol, vast paint-and-plaster-stained shoes. Everything about him seemed heavy, slow-moving, cumbersome, except the vivid intelligence, the alert prehensile senses, the sensitive, pudgy hands, unexpectedly small for this mountainous man and tapering off, despite their pudginess, into slender fingers. The body was that of a giant, planted solidly on a sagging beam for hours on end. The eyes bulged like those of a frog or a housefly, as if made to see a whole crowd, a vast panorama, or a wide mural. The fingers moved easily, steadily, covering space endlessly without appearing to hurry, flexible as the limbs of a dancer, sure as the hands of a knitting woman.

And lucky he was to be a giant, for fresco painting is hard and exacting. After sketches on paper, done in the studio and enlarged to scale, comes sketching with red chalk or charcoal directly on the great surface of the wall, on the rough second, or "brown," coat. Assistants trace this sketch on transparent tracing paper on the wall and run a perforating wheel over its lines to make a stencil. Then they put on the final coat, and, through the stencil perforations, they sift powdered lampblack, reproducing faintly on the wet surface the part of the sketch covered up by the final coat, the rest still remaining on the rough "brown coat." They test the new plaster till it has dried nearly to the proper degree of humidity, then go to wake the painter. Usually it is just about dawn, the masons having worked during the late hours of the night. The plaster will remain at the requisite degree of wetness for six to twelve hours, according to the warmth and dryness of the day. During that period he must cover it with paint—cover it, according to his method of working, not once, but twice. The first time in black, to give the chiaroscuro modeling or sculpturing of his figures, their solidity, roundness, turning in space. Then fresh brush strokes in the chosen color, following the lines of direction of the modeling or the requirements of the design, the painter altering and recomposing as he goes. And so for hours, while a fresh squad of plasterers covers a new section of the wall.

All day he works, if conditions permit, straining his eyes on into the fading evening light, not daring to turn on artificial illumination when he has begun with daylight because the color values would change. Long after the spectator, sitting beside him on the scaffold, can no longer see for eyestrain, his bulging eyes continue miraculously to function and his hand to weave its spell, building figures and volumes into a living world.

At last, heavily, wearily, he climbs down. The patio is deserted by then, except for his wife or a friend and perhaps one or two helpers to receive their orders for the night. He has worn out a squad or two of masons, several assistants, hundreds of observers, scores of friends. You breathe a sigh of relief and exhaustion yourself. He will go home at last to dine and rest. But no, he stands squinting and straining there in the darkness, head cocked on one side, advancing, retreating, looking, looking, looking. He is looking at it as if someone else had done it, as if it were not his painting, as if he were merely asked to criticize it. What can he possibly see in the darkness, you ask, where you can no longer make out anything but a blur? He advances to the scaffold again and wearily clambers up; another stroke here, a deepening of color there, a change of line or form. Again he is down and again up, for alterations must be made now before the plaster dries. Tomorrow will be too late, no palette knives will serve him as on canvas; if he would change things tomorrow, he will have to smash off the surface of the wall and plastering must begin afresh. Often did I see him, after a day's long work was done, lose his temper at the result and tell his assistants, "Clean it all off and put on fresh plaster! I'll be back tomorrow morning at six."

17. WILD BEAUTY

"Call that art?" one college student demanded of another as they stood watching Diego on his scaffold, painting his first mural. "Just look at that naked woman there!" continued the student, referring to the nude at the lower left. "How would you like to be married to a woman that looked like that?"

"Young man," said Diego from his high perch, "neither would you want to marry a pyramid, but a pyramid is also art." The retort became celebrated. Yet in actual fact Diego was in love at that very moment with the girl who had modeled for the nude!

Indeed, Diego was in love as he had not been before, both as artist and as man. The model obsessed him, was to obsess him for years, as the incarnation of exuberant femine form. All the years that they lived together—and the tale of those years, as in the case of Angelina, was seven, though passion diminished till he confided to me that he was beginning to feel towards her as towards a sister—she continued to haunt his vision, reappear in his frescoes, serve for portraits and sketches, model most of his nudes, inspire the best and strongest of his feminine figures. Long after as a man he had ceased to love her, as artist he was still rapt by her physical beauty and wildness of spirit. In 1937 he illustrated her novel *La Unica* with a sketch of her (PLATE 71) and in 1938 painted of her one of his most carefully studied portraits (PLATES 67 and 68).

Guadalupe Marín, when Diego met her, was the wildest and most tempestuous beauty in Jalisco, the state famed in song and legend for its beautiful women. If the reader has turned back to the Preparatoria mural (PLATE 51) in an effort to judge of her beauty, he may have suffered a severe disillusionment or entertain grave doubts as to the writer's taste, and the painter's, in feminine beauty. But the nude whom the student rejected is not a portrait of Guadalupe Marín though she modeled for it; it is an *idealization*—of femaleness, as Diego conceived it. The great curves of arm and thigh, exuberant breasts and rounded belly, really have in them a touch of the solidity and grandeur of the pyramid to which the artist compared her. In the Preparatoria mural, the "pretty" figure is the man's, the vital one the woman's. The only other figure that can match it for vitality is that of primal man, bisexual in the sense of expressing the entire genus, appearing in the crypt that houses the organ. Nor do the other figures in the painting for which Guadalupe modeled possess the same rugged force, though she herself reappears twice more in the same mural: as SONG, holding on her lap the golden Hesperian apples, and as JUSTICE, holding a sword and resting on her shield.

In a preceding chapter I spoke of the impossibilty of conveying fully in words the "taste" of a fruit or of a painting. Is not the same true of the beauty of a woman? The reader is herewith presented with portraits by Edward Weston (PLATES 61-64) and reproductions of other paintings in which she served as a model, but more impressive than these—not a man, nor a woman, that knew her could be heard to deny her beauty.

Long of limb and tall of body, graceful and supple as a sapling; hair black, wild, unkempt, curly; dark olive skin, light sea-green eyes; high forehead and nose of a Phidian statue; full lips ever parted by eager breath and by lively, disorderly, and scandalous chatter; a body so slender as to suggest a youth rather than a woman—such was Lupe when Diego met her. Part of her beauty lay in her wildness: wayward of thought and speech and action; primitive as an animal in her desires and her readiness to scratch, bite, and slash to attain them; clever, spontaneous, untutored, cunning with animal cunning; absorbed in herself as a spoiled kitten, with the same toleration of those who serve and pet and feed her, the same aloofness; the same claws too, hidden in deceptive softness; capable of giving blow for blow in her bouts with her mammoth husband, making up for what she lacked in physical strength by the long nursing of her wrath and the wild tongue; capable of slashing his sketches and fresh-painted canvases before his eyes as an act of vengeance; threatening once to shoot his right arm off that he might never do another painting —a hell-cat when aroused, a graceful, splendid, purring, feline creature when contented. If this narrative has not so far made it clear, be it said at this point that Diego, who was attracted above all by her savagery, had a streak within him which was at least a match for it. Such a woman and such a painter, no one who knew them could doubt that they were well mated.

Lupe fell as wholeheartedly in love with Diego as he with her. She did not have as much experience with men as he with women, nor was her provincial, middle-class background the counterpart of his cosmopolitan man-of-the-worldliness; but she possessed sufficient native intelligence, feminine subtlety, and instinctive egolatry to defend herself. She was enchanted with his physical bigness and attractive ugliness: he was to her *muy feo* and *muy hombre*. He was Paris, the world of art and letters of which she had dreamed as she gossiped with the Bohemian literary and artistic circles of her native Guadalajara. She was flattered by the admiration of one who was reputed Mexico's greatest painter. She was proud to serve as his model, nor did the startling result on the Preparatoria wall alienate her; intuitively she appreciated the "idealization." Lupe was proud too of the terrific controversy that surrounded him: did not she herself love the storms of scandal and delight to be at their center?

Her letters prior to and subsequent to their marriage, and her attempt at a novel fifteen years later, comment little on art, nor do they manifest any sensitiveness in the field of painting. Yet association with him gradually cultivated her sensibilities and gave her flashes of astonishing articulateness, as revealed by the letter to him from Guadalajara, when he sent her a photograph of the Preparatoria mural after the organ crypt was completed:

> Amado brought me the photograph, with the center already painted. In my opinion it is incomparably better than the outside part. . . . How simple! . . . (a beautiful plant such as those of which there are so many on the Isthmus) What life it has! It looks like one we have seen: there is nothing in it of that over-refinement and strain of the earlier part . . . it possesses an incredible vitality. I think that my presence harms you: probably you exhaust your imagination and, with me present, you come to lack strength. Strength which here you have in absolute form and have revealed in the center portion. . . .
>
> I scarce dare to tell you of my sorrows; after what I have just said, it seems to me that speaking to you of love, I interrupt you. . . . Never mind! (Forgive me) . . . I love you so! That nothing, nothing absolutely nothing attracts my attention except you; it seems an enormity to me to wait a month to see you, and there comes to me the fear that someday your offered letter won't come and I think that I am a burden to you and that I take away much of your time when I am with you. And at the same time in Mexico [i.e., Mexico City] I cannot live; the climate terrifies me. . . . Work hard so that you can come soon, and don't regret the time you lose here with your dark girl. Eat well, go out in the sun awhile for a walk, and after that, even if you work the whole day, it won't hurt you. Think (but only during the moment you leave for rest) of your skinny dark girl. . . . Don't forget that she loves you deeply. *Adiós*, fatty.
>
> Lupe

When Diego began his labors at the Secretariat of Education, he no longer had time for even an occasional visit to Guadalajara. Lupe overcame her terror at the climate of Mexico City and came to live with him in some large, *petate*-carpeted rooms, simply and poorly furnished in the Mexican style, in an old house in the heart of Mexico City. This was preceded by a religious ceremony in the Church of Saint Michael with María Michel and Xavier Guerrero as witnesses. There was no civil marriage. Lupe became a familiar figure in the Ministry of Education, where she appeared daily to bring him his lunch on the scaffold. She used no make-up, wore her curly hair in disorder as if no comb had ever passed through it, dressed carelessly, predominantly in black, a *rebozo* flung about her neck, presenting an aspect of studied unconcern as to her appearance. Her one attempt at personal decoration in their early days together ended in discomfiture. Piqued by Diego's admiration of feminine opulence, conscious of her own slender tallness, and schooled by the changes he had made in her body when he painted the nude in the Preparatoria mural, Lupe ventured to put stockings in her bosom. The painter detected the fraud as soon as he glanced at her; reaching into her blouse in the presence of spectators, he fished out the stockings with a delighted roar.* For years thereafter she gave up all efforts to alter her appearance.

The quarrels between Lupe and Diego, thanks to a touch of wildness in each and the overflowing energy of their natures, became celebrated. I was at a birthday party she arranged for him at their house, when Lupe flared up with sudden jealousy because he was showing some drawings with too much tenderness to a Cuban girl with whom he had had an affair. The party came to an embarrassed standstill. Lupe tore up the drawings before our horrified eyes, scratched and pulled the hair of the unfortunate girl, began beating Diego with her clenched fists while he parried as best he could. The guests slunk off without

* At least this was Diego's story, told to me in her laughing presence.

taking leave, abandoning Lupe in possession of the field. But a few hours later, perhaps at three in the morning, my wife and I were awakened from slumber by hammering at our door. We opened to find Lupe, tearful and disheveled. "He has been dragging me around by the hair for the scene I made," she alleged, "and threatens to kill me. Let me stay with you tonight." We gave her a place to sleep. Next morning she was up early, arrayed herself at her prettiest, and went to the near-by national pawnshop to buy him a big beautiful revolver as a peace offering.

Their quarrels were mostly over three matters: his frequent donations from his meager wages for Communist activities and to hard-up people and vagrants; his painting, which occupied so much time that it left little for her; and his susceptibility to women. In this last respect, he was more often pursued than pursuing, for he was not only too busy for Lupe, he was too busy to pay court to anyone. Most of the women literally had to climb his scaffold to talk with him or arrange a rendezvous.

It was when Lupe discovered him making love to her younger sister, whom she had invited from Guadalajara, that hell broke loose in the Rivera household. She destroyed a number of his paintings and, seizing his own gun, threatened to shoot his right arm off. She ended by packing her clothes, bundling off her sister, and departing to their parental home in Guadalajara. Then it became clear that despite his infidelities Diego loved her. He wandered the streets of Mexico City for days, like one lost, unable for once to continue with his murals. He ate little, slept less, wasted away—though not exactly to a shadow. After a week he disappeared from Mexico and did not return till he had won his bride back in Guadalajara. I saw them return one Sunday morning, he in his humble baggy best, Lupe resplendent as neither before nor since have I ever seen her. Diego had bought her an astonishing new hat with a great reddish-pink plume, which had caught her fancy, and her usual simple black skirt and *rebozo* had yielded to a silk dress of lavender. Her wild beauty was tamed into ludicrousness by the outfit, but she trailed along in state, celebrating a triumph. Diego looked sheepish, but visibly pleased at the reconciliation.

Lupe gave birth to a girl, and a few years later to a second. The first was named Guadalupe, but known by her pet name of Pico. She figures in several of Diego's paintings. As she grew up she came to look more and more like her mother, although lacking in the wildness that was the luster of Lupe's beauty. The second, Ruth, brown as an Indian, with pug nose, prominent eyes, a sensitive nature, and more than a touch of a refined and feminized Diego in appearance and temperament, was familiarly known as Chapo, short for Chapopote, the Indian name for tar, pitch, and petroleum. (The painter and his two daughters are shown in PLATE 38.) Ruth is today a painter and architect, and a member of the Chamber of Deputies.

Lupe reveled in her new sensations. Here at last she was doing something creative, too. She was jealous of Diego's work, much of her unruliness and rudeness to his guests being but a by-product of her desire to shine in her own right. At last she felt that she was doing something Diego couldn't do. Into the mouth of the heroine of her novel, *La Unica,* she puts words that suggest an instinctive delight in the experience:

> If you only knew what an agreeable sensation I feel when I am pregnant. Just as the skin on my belly stretches, so I feel all over: as if my lungs were dilating, my heart growing bigger, my nostrils enlarging, my eyes opening wider. I feel the placidity of a cow. I would represent a pregnant woman as a cow lying on the grass gazing at the moon. And all that about the terrible pain? . . . I swear that the bruise I gave myself on my finger the other day hurt me far more than when my child was born.

Lupe pregnant (PLATES 65, 66) was an impressive figure.

She served as model for most of the great nudes Diego now painted in the assembly hall of the Agricultural School at Chapingo. Previously nudes had played but little part in his painting. Lupe had appeared in his frescoes several times, but fully clad, marching, mouth open, on the painter's arm in the *May Day Demonstration* in the Secretariat of Education, and again, open-mouthed as always, walking with him through the crowded market place of the *Fair of the Day of the Dead* in the same fiesta series. But in Chapingo both architecture and theme suggested the need of nudes, and Lupe and Tina Modotti served as the models. The space consisted of an entrance hall and stairway and a chapel now converted into an auditorium. The school occupied the nationalized estate of a big landowner, having formerly belonged to President Manuel Gonzaléz. Its architecture, especially that of the chapel, was Spanish baroque, the nave tripartite, the ceiling built in complicated fashion of arches and pendentives. Many painters regard this as the greatest of Rivera's works because they are amazed by the virtuosity with which he solved the problems of the complicated spatial structure. The lines of the composition are baroque, as befits the architecture. In accordance with the uses of the building, he chose themes related to agriculture; the evolution of the earth, germination, growth, florescence, and fruition of plants, and symbolic parallels in the evolution of society. The whole grows from natural and social chaos to harmony, culminating in the harmony of man with nature and man with man.

Tina appears as *Germination* (PLATE 73), *Monopolized Earth* (PLATE 74), oppressed by Capitalism, Clericalism, and Militarism, a striking composition in which the graceful nude imprisoned in a constricting frame contrasts strongly with the grotesque clothed figures of the three symbolical oppressors and rests disturbingly just above a row of jagged cactus points. She appears a second time as the voluptuous and lovely figure of *Virgin Earth* (PLATE 59) sheltering in her hand a germinating plant, trifoliately phallic in its form. And in the back of the hall, where once the altar stood, Lupe dominates the entire chapel as *The Fecund Earth* (PLATE 66), surrounded by representations of the four elements, Earth, Air, Fire and Water, now conceived of as benevolent and controlled servants of man.

Most of Diego's infidelities, when she knew of them, Lupe had taken lightly and pardoned readily. It seemed to me at times as if she took a perverse pride in the way women pursued him. But when Diego chose Tina to serve for some of the nudes he required in the Chapingo chapel, Lupe suddenly became furious. More than an infidelity of the man, this was an infidelity of the artist. In her novel, though this is not true to the facts, she attributes to his affair with this new model the breakup of their relationship. Here is her account of the matter:

> The time passing thus, home seemed an inferno to her. When she was not being beaten, she was alone or afraid. Often Gonzalo amused himself by playing *volador* [thief] with two enormous loaded pistols, and she felt dizzy with fear; there came a moment when she shook at just hearing his voice or his footsteps. Then he complained to his friends that she did not understand him, and sometimes did not return home all day, giving as pretext her disdain; and also he made frequent and long journeys. Marcela thought that perhaps a woman was the cause of her abandonment and the vexations in which they were living, and did not take long to verify it. She knew that her husband shared a beautiful Italian woman with a Cuban Communist leader. Unfortunately, in those days Cuban Communist youth lost in him its best leader. By order of the then President of Cuba he was assassinated one night while walking arm in arm with the shared comrade. He fell to the ground, pierced by the bullets which had been discharged in cowardly fashion from behind. Immediately the friends of the Italian girl tried to liberate her from the scandal; principally Gonzalo, who was the one most interested in her; but by no device were they able to prevent it. The press spoke a great deal of the matter; there were papers that insisted that she was an accomplice of the killer. The police searched her house minutely, not finding any proof that might connect her with the crime; on the other hand, they did find a great number of love letters from different men, sufficient motive for applying to her the 33 [number of the article of the Mexican Constitution which permits the President to deport "pernicious" foreigners without trial]. . . .
>
> The injustice and her departure saddened Gonzalo, leaving him

very deeply depressed. He wanted to follow her but could not. A thousand mischances oppressed him. He began to take trips in the country; he made great horseback journeys to dissipate his pain.

One day when he left very early in the morning, three hours later several individuals arrived with him on their shoulders; but she soon convinced herself that nothing serious had happened to him even though Gonzalo did not open his eyes and pretended to be dead. The doctor, after examining him, as a preventive against a disturbance of the brain ordered an ice pack, which she applied, knowing that it was unnecessary.

Newspapermen, photographers, political personages, and artists invaded the house a few minutes after they learned what had happened. The sick man fell seriously ill and even went so far as to declare that he had meningitis. Marcela did not become alarmed, she did not believe it; she had always considered him a *farsante* given to exaggeration, and this time she understood perfectly that nothing was the matter with him. . . .

"It is pure farce you are carrying on. I am sure that there is nothing the matter with you, and you are only complaining to make yourself interesting: with me you don't get away with that stuff any more; go on, complain to some other woman who may believe you."

Gonzalo, infuriated, jumped out of bed to grab a stout Apizaco stick which he used to carry in those days, and went running after her all through the house. Marcela wanted to leave by the first door she found, but it was locked; she tried the same thing with all of them, finding them all in the same condition; till at last, the only one left, the one close to the exit, turned out to be open. Rushing out through it, she was beginning to run downstairs when she found various persons who were coming to inquire as to the health of the "patient." She entertained them discreetly, giving him time to return without their seeing him; and when the visitors arrived at the bedside, he was groaning, pretending that he was dying, turning up the whites of his eyes. After, he blamed her for his illness, telling the visitors that she was a witch.

The constant quarrels, and the death which Gonzalo felt so near, showed her that it was only an acute neurasthenia produced by the displeasure of living at her side; and determining to separate from him, she thought of marrying Andrés. But unfortunately, in those days Andrés had no work. . . . Two or three friends between them paid the wedding expenses; and afterwards the recently married couple decided that she, if possible, should continue living in the house of Gonzalo while Andrés was getting work; which was easy to arrange, thanks to Gonzalo's advanced ideas, for he kindly lent himself to the plan. . . .

The account has more than a little truth in it, but is dressed up to put a better light on one of the most scandalous actions of Lupe towards her husband. He did suffer an accident, not a fall from his horse, but from his scaffold. He was painting simultaneously in the Secretariat of Education and in Chapingo. The fever of creation was on him and he spent unbelievable hours painting in one place, only to snatch a few hours' sleep and set out for the other. He drove plasterers and assistants at such a pace to keep up with his painter's fury that, though they worked only in eight-hour shifts, two of them got sick. He himself worked unending stretches, including Saturdays and Sundays. At last, after working all day and all night, he fell asleep in the midst of his painting and toppled off his scaffold to the pavement.

In the middle of the day he was brought back from Chapingo, carried by three men, when Lupe was at her dinner. She was infuriated by his prolonged absences—he had not been home the night before at all—and attributed them to his new Italian model. When the men told her that Diego had fallen from the scaffold she answered, "Throw him on the couch in the corner. I'll tend to him when I have finished my dinner." It was not until one of the men fetched a doctor, who declared that Diego's skull was cracked, that she really paid any attention. The matter became a scandal throughout the city, but the novel permits Lupe to revise life so as to improve the light in which she was viewed.

Tina Modotti was a strikingly beautiful girl who came to Mexico from California with Edward Weston, the photographer. She became celebrated through the nude studies Weston did of her. Lacking Lupe's tallness and stateliness, she made up for it by softness and roundness of contour. Her face, too, was soft and beautifully rounded, her eyes full of wonder at the life around her, her aspect that of a young and virginal Madonna.

Some notion of the effect of this girl upon the intellectual and artistic circles in Mexico may be gleaned from the description of her in the memoirs of José Vasconcelos. He portrays her as a *femme fatale,* thereby expressing not so much her nature as the erotic mysticism that dominated his being and made a good part of his memoirs a succession of would-be Don Juanesque adventures alternating with temptations regretfully resisted because of devotion to his Oriental cult of "self-conservation." He met Tina, whom he disguises under the name of Perlotti, through his friend and collaborator, Gómez Robelo. His account of her reads:

He [Gómez Robelo] was of value more for the occasional sparks of his mind and for his noble heart than for his capacities as a worker, already much undermined by his strange life of possession by the demons of the flesh and the spirit. Member of a group of Bohemian artists of Los Angeles, California, Gómez Robelo, upon repatriating himself to serve in the Department of Education, had dragged all of them along with him. Liking their new surroundings, one of them dedicated himself to writing, another to artistic photography, others simply to international Bohemianism. The photographer brought with him a beauty of Italian origin, sculptural and depraved, who was the axis of the group and held them united by a common desire; divided by bitter rivalry. La Perlotti, let us call her thus, practiced the profession of vampire, but without commercialism *à la* Hollywood and by temperament insatiable and untroubled. She was seeking, perhaps, notoriety, but not money. Out of pride, perhaps, she had not been able to derive economic advantages from her figure, almost perfectly and eminently sensual. We all knew her body because she served as a gratuitous model for the photographer, and her bewitching nudes were fought over. Her legend was a dark one. One husband she had liquidated in California, kept in a lunatic asylum because of venereal excess, and at the time of which I am writing, she kept two strong men pallid and gently rivals: the famed photographer and our friend Rodión [pen name of Gómez Robelo]. Before the photograph without veils of his girl friend, Rodión would pour out tears of sensual tenderness. Slowly the unwholesome passion wasted his body, drugged his will. And jealousy produced a fever in him. She, for her part, maintained herself alert. She utilized Rodión to introduce herself into artistic and political circles. . . .

The beauty was then just entering her thirties, imperturbable and seductive. I met her for the last time in the official auto in which she was to accompany us with a friend of hers on a visit to an abandoned convent in Coyoacán. Her voluptuous silhouette was a powerful magnet in the afternoon full of sun. The car raised clouds of dust and she said: "A splendor of gold envelops us." Sure gift of art it was to find beauty where others found only inconvenience. A glance awakened swift temptation, but then I felt pain in my spine: I remembered her victims sucked dry of their marrow. I never saw her again; years after, she entered the little Communist group, then disappeared, headed for Moscow.

A fearful temptation, valiantly resisted. The more fateful he makes the temptress, the more Vasconcelos can feel himself a hero of renunciation. But in truth his portrayal does not do her justice. Tina Modotti rejected for herself, as do most men in Mexican intellectual and artistic circles—the morality of monogamic marriage. Unlike them, however, she rejected the double standard and hypocritic pretense, which is the chief source of her legend. But she no more lived a life that was purely sensual than Vasconcelos. His memoirs record several mistresses and a host of temptations self-righteously resisted. Hers, if she had written them, might have recorded a somewhat larger number of erotic adventures, no self-righteousness, and no resisted temptations. Her husband, Roubaix de l'Abrie Richey, died of tuberculosis. Gómez Robelo died three months after he had gone alone on a trip to South America and, on his return, taken up with another woman. Edward Weston died full of years, always cherishing bright memories of his friendship with her. Diego long outlived his brief affair with Tina. Julio Antonio Mella died by a bullet from one of President Machado's gunmen. Thus the legend is more Vasconcelos than Modotti.

Tina's association with the artists of Mexico made her into a Communist and an artist. Her work with Weston enkindled in her an interest in photography. He taught her what he knew that was teachable, helping her to become a great master of the camera in her own right, a worthy pupil of a worthy master. On my walls hang works by each of them; people cannot tell which photographer did which without looking for the signature. I am indebted to her for many of the photographs used in this book.

After the assassination of Mella, which belongs to a later chapter, she went to Moscow, then to Paris, then to Spain, in the company of the Italian Communist, adventurer, and Soviet agent Vitorio Vidali (Enea Sormenti; Commissario Carlos), who is now active in the Communist movement in Trieste.

Her end was tragic. According to the story told by her Communist friends, she died suddenly of a heart attack. According to the report in the Mexican press at the time of her death, revulsion at Commissario Carlos's purge activities in Republican Spain caused her to break with him upon their return to Mexico. He gave her a farewell party, from which she fled alone in a taxi, asking the driver to rush her to a hospital, and died on the way, some said of heart failure, others of poisoning. The Mexican press gave many details of the death, but none of the autopsy.

Following Guadalupe's novel and Vasconcelos's memoirs, we have run ahead of our story. There are several things to record before we come to the end of the life together of Diego and his favorite model. And that model was not Tina, though he did some beautiful sketches and paintings of her, but Guadalupe Marín, who lived seven years with him, bore him two daughters, and all his life continued to haunt his painting.

18. THE WAR ON DIEGO'S MONKEYS

Though the Italian cities of the Renaissance have little in common historically with Mexico City, there are curious parallels in the flavor of life in these two so different worlds: some of the same violence and passion, the same blend of cruelty and sentiment, the same lighthearted homicide in casual brawls; dagger and pistol, in lieu of sword and poison, still serve to avenge insults to fragile honor and eliminate obstacles in the path of achievement. There is the same directness in facing life, adorned —but never concealed—by pomp and pageantry; the same aesthetic sensibility and human insensitivity; the same cult of energy and action and will and bravado; the same strong savor of personality. Only the temperament of the Italian is open and sanguine, that of the Mexican closed and melancholy. The *condottieri* are matched by the *caudillos* who fight their way up to places of power in despotisms tempered by turmoil and tyrannicide. For all their urbanism and urbanity, such cities as the Florence of the Renaissance or the Mexico of today seem somehow to be less insulated by walls and paving stones and conventions from blood and soil than are New York or London or Paris. From the standpoint of sociology and economics the resemblances we speak of may be superficial, but from the standpoint of their influence on the will and emotions—in which the arts are rooted—they are in some ways strangely alike. The life of a Rivera or a Siqueiros comes closer to that of a Michelangelo or a Cellini than it does to the pattern of a Jonas Lie or a John Sloan, a Puvis or a Picasso.

Above all, a period of change of presidents in the twenties was a time of unsettlement. There were no genuine elections: the man in office determined who was to succeed him; barring a successful uprising or removal by assassination, the result was a foregone conclusion. But first there was a year or more of uncertainty while the president prepared the succession. It was a time of unrest and speculation, rumors and counter-rumors, elaborate politeness and good-fellowship between men who are coldly wondering about getting the draw on each other. It was a time of reckless demagogic promises and careful calculation of when to jump, and in which direction; a time of intrigue, corruption, bribery, assassination. No public man was exempt, no public employee secure in his post, no institution free from uncertainty.

The presidential campaign of 1923-24 began with an assassination and ended with an uprising. The first victim was Pancho Villa, living in bucolic retirement with his *Dorados* ("Golden Boys") on an estate in Chihuahua. Adolfo de la Huerta, Obregón's Minister of the Treasury, had "pacified" him, negotiating peace between Villa and the Government in return for land and funds for agricultural equipment and permission for his *Dorados* to keep their rifles. Now de la Huerta was planning to "run" for the presidency without Obregón's approval, against the preferred Calles, Secretary of Gobernación. On July 20, 1923, Villa was assassinated by an army officer from ambush. The assassin went unpunished, for this was but the opening gun in the electoral battle.

Even before the uprising the time for painting was over in Mexico. Funds were diverted from Education to War; the fresco movement withered. One by one the painters lost their jobs; only Diego remained.

On December 5, 1923, the de la Huerta rebellion opened. On December 11, a report was delivered on the Education murals by the Controller's Department, professing to show that Diego's contract was being violated and should be canceled. The report is worth our attention for what it shows of the state of governmental accounting methods, the situation of the painter and his helpers, the cost of materials, the nature of Diego's contract:

To Citizen Diego Rivera,

Greetings,

The Auditor of Accounts commissioned to this Secretariat formulates the following observations on the contract entered into between the Secretariat and you for the painting of the walls:

To date there have been painted 281 sq. meters.
Cost of surfacing and painting 281 sq. m. at $1.52 — $421.50*

Material supplied:		
32 cu. m. of sand @ $4.50	$144.00	
1 ton of lime	19.00	
	163.00	
Personnel employed daily:		
1 mason	$4.50	
1 mason	3.50	
1 laborer	1.75	
2 laborers	3.00	
3 decorators	12.00	
1 assistant	3.50	
1 assistant	2.00	
	30.00	

* The dollar-sign throughout the document indicates not American dollars but Mexican pesos. As the peso was then worth fifty cents, the figures should be divided by two to get their American equivalents.

From the 23rd of March to the last of November		
weekly	181.50	
Total		6,534.00
TOTAL		$7,116.00
Which gives an average of $25.32 per sq. meter. If we take into account the wages earned by the contractor		
from the Secretariat at $20.00 daily		$9,300.00
his assistant at $10.00 a day		4,650.00
TOTAL		$13,950.00

It will be necessary to increase the amount by $50.00 per sq. m. and will thus give a cost of $75.32 per sq. m.

In addition the Contractor received for travel expenses	445.00
Paid on account of the contract	4,500.00
Materials and labor	7,116.00
Wages	13,950.00
Paid to date for decoration	26,011.00
Value of the contract	8,000.00
Difference in excess	18,001.00

The contract stipulates clearly that material and labor will be on account of the Contractor.

The contract authorizes	760 sq. m.
There have been decorated	281 sq. m.
Difference	479 sq. m.
That is to say, almost 665	

As the reader with a head for arithmetic can see, the report does not make sense on the face of it. For the item of salaries to "the Contractor" (Diego) to make sense, for example, there would have to have been 465 days between March 23 and November 30 in the year 1923. Without attempting to untangle it, let us examine Citizen Rivera's answer, dated December 14:

To the Citizen Auditor of Accounts,

Greetings.

I answer your kind note of the 11th of the present month re

the contract entered into with the Secretariat of Public Education, for the painting of walls, which contract was in the following form:

1. The contract stipulates $8 per sq. m.

2. The material supplied—that is 32 sq. m. of sand and a ton of lime—was given in payment of that which the contractor had advanced for the work of the second patio of the building [i.e. the one which the *Sindicato* was supposed to be painting]; hence the sum of $163.00 was owing to me.

3. The personnel paid by the Secretariat was so paid because the original sum assigned for the contract made impossible the execution of the work, as decided by the Citizen Secretary, and this personnel was only:

1 master mason at	$4.50
1 journeyman mason at	3.50
1 laborer	1.75
1 helper	4.00
Daily total	13.75

It is necessary to point out that this personnel worked not only in the painting of the first patio but also in that of the second, in the corridors and elevator vestibule, along with the rest of the personnel, with which the contractor has nothing to do since the C. Secretary ordered the works of the interior patio, the undersigned merely directing them as head of the Department of Plastic Crafts in the Secretariat of Education; hence out of the sum of $13.75 (above) there can actually be charged only the following:

One laborer	$1.75
One assistant	4.00
half-day's wage of master mason	2.25
half-day's wage of journeyman mason	1.75
Daily total	9.75

or from the 23rd of March to the last of November, 36 weeks at $40.50, $1,458.00, or a maximum increase of $5.75 per square meter. There have been painted 326 cu. metres and *not* 281 as is said in the observations made by the Auditor of Accounts.

4. As to the wages of Señor Javier Guerrero, he has worked during this time:

1. On the decoration of the patio
2. On the vestibule of the elevator, and

3. On the gilding of the background of the reliefs on the same interior patio.

5. As to the wages of $20.00 daily which the undersigned receives, it has nothing to do with the work, since he earns it by his regular employment as Head of the Plastic Crafts, in which capacity, he directed the works of the second patio of the Secretariat, and in this capacity, and to study matters connected with his job in different regions of the country, the travel expenses were given him by decision of the C. Secretary, to which the Inspector of Accounts refers. Hence 326 cu. m. have been decorated at $8.00 per cu. m.

which makes $2,608.00	
received in regular payment according to the contract	4,500.00
remains to be balanced by work	1,892.00

It should be added that during the entire execution of the work the contractor has paid in overtime to the indicated personnel a quantity no less than that paid by the Secretariat in support of the execution of the work.

The hypothetical reader with a head for arithmetic will perceive that Diego's figures make no sense, either. There is, for example, no way of multiplying a daily wage of 9.75 pesos by the number of days in the week so as to get a weekly total of 40.50 pesos as indicated in his communication. His spelling is more capricious than that of the Citizen Auditor of Accounts, and he slips unaccountably from square meters into cubic ones, but his calculations are more dependable, though it did not occur to him to check the arithmetical mysteries of the original attack upon him. Moreover, his letter is accompanied with a detailed listing of the actual painting surface covered in the brief period under discussion, and it totals—no mistakes in calculation either—326.45 square meters (over 3,500 square feet) of wall plastered, planned, sketched, and covered with frescoes in a period of eight months, with time out for journeys to make drawings from nature!

From the exchange of notes it can also be seen that Diego Rivera, best paid and hardest working of all the Mexican painters, was receiving the princely sum of twenty pesos, or ten dollars a day, out of which he was meeting overtime payments to the laborers assisting him.

We need not follow further the tangled skein of negotiations and accounts between painter and government. Notes continued to pile up through the years, protests, demurrers, explanations, counterprotests, of which the above are but two of the earliest specimens. In the end, according to Diego's calculations, the government left unpaid to him a debt of 1,500 pesos. Correct or not, there is certainly no likelihood that he would ever grow rich from this or subsequent mural ventures. Indeed, Diego had to work furiously at oils, water colors, and drawings, which he sold in the United States, to make up the deficits incurred on his frescoes. The murals were lucrative only as "advertising."

Diego did not wait for a rejoinder to his observations on the "audit," but disappeared into the hills, on the orders of the Communist Party, to attempt to raise up guerrilla bands among the peasantry. The party, after a moment of hesitation, had decided to give conditional support to Obregón against what they considered to be a "more reactionary" opposition, and the President had agreed to provide arms without insisting that these guerrilla bands be subjected to the regular army. Dressed in khaki and puttees, armed with two pistols and two cartridge belts, Diego went off with the others. His sector proved to be a quiet one. When he returned a few weeks later, he resumed his painting without the matter of payment being settled. He painted desperately now, driving himself beyond endurance, for it seemed that his days as a muralist were numbered.

His fears were not groundless. A new contract was signed by him on June 23, 1924, clarifying some of the disputed points and promising terms a little more favorable, but the work itself was suspended by presidential order a month later.

"As soon as Calles is President," Roberto Haberman, close to the President-elect, boasted to me, "his first official act will be to rub off those ugly monkeys of Diego's from the walls of the Secretariat."

The campaign of vandalism against all the mural painters gained headway. Orozco's frescoes, in the courtyard of the Preparatoria where students of high-school and junior-college age congregated, were the most subject to wanton destruction.

Students scratched their names into the plaster, drew faces and scrawls with the point of their jackknives, inscribed wisecracks and obscenities. Rivera's work in the Education Building, where grownups came, was relatively exempt from this sort of "criticism." But in compensation, it was the center of the campaign for destruction. Articles appeared denouncing the *monos* —"monkeys"—of Diego Rivera. They were ugly, not art; the bodies were heavy, unbeautiful; he painted that way because he could not paint in the traditional manner. Where were the classic nudes? Where the magazine-cover faces? Where the finer things of life to which art was dedicated? They were propaganda and hence could not be art. They were degrading to Mexico, representing only peons, Indians, laborers, "the dregs of society." Was Mexico, then, so gloomy a place that there were no smiling people? Where were the elegant allegories? Where the better people of wealth, leisure, culture, good clothes, light-skinned faces? Why give the impression that Mexico possessed no ladies who kept up with fashion?

The figures he painted showed that he could not see straight: look at those workers with arms but a single curve as they swung their hammers! Did you ever see a sleeve of a workingman without wrinkles? If this was not cubism, it was worse—literati coined a new word, *feismo*, "uglyism." The incoming head of the Department of Fine Arts, in his first interview to the press, sealed the fate of the paintings. "The first thing I'll do," he told the reporters, "is whitewash those horrible frescoes."

Thus encouraged, scenting blood, the yelping of critics and

"the respectable public" swelled to a mighty volume. In the burlesque in the Teatro Lírico, a fat actor made up to look like Diego came out on the stage to sing:

Las muchachas de la Lerdo	The Lerdo schoolgirls*
toman baño de regadera	Take shower baths
pa'que no parezcan	So that no one will take them
monos de Diego Rivera	For Diego's monkeys.

The hue and cry was at its loudest when suddenly it trailed off into weak and isolated yips of uncertainty. What confounded respectable critics and the *gente decente* was appreciation of the work in unexpected quarters. They had set up against his "ugly" Mexicanism the refined standards of New York, Los Angeles, and Paris. But rumors of something extraordinary in painting had spread abroad; the admired art critics of New York and Paris began to arrive and to praise Rivera. Enthusiastic articles appeared in the foreign press. Mexican journals, ever sensitive to praise from such quarters, translated them. For some unaccountable reason he was regarded, the respectable public suddenly realized, as one of the attractions of Mexico. Detractors were reduced to uncomprehending silence.

Not that the attacks ceased, but from an abomination he was converted into a tolerated "institution." The Government discreetly forgot that anyone in high office had talked of whitewashing his walls. Papers learned to speak with pride of *nuestro muy discutido Diego*—"our much disputed-over Diego."

As a sample of the more "reasonable" criticism which now appeared, we can take the following by Alvaro Pruneda, in *El Universal Ilustrado* on the inauguration of the stairway of the Education Building:

> The obsession of Rivera in these frescoes is the feminine nude. It seems as if he has only selected from various horrible women the most repugnant lines and colorings, and not even satisfied with that, pur-

* The Escuela Superior Miguel Lerdo, a girls' high school.

posely limited himself to the least suggestive and most wooden forms. . . . Various nudes of women drag themselves on high over a sky, dirty in prelude to a storm, which profoundly wound the aesthetic sense and the gentle and sweet impression which is left in our spirit by the ideal delicacy of our beautiful women. . . . I could not contain my indignation . . . I did not want to suffer more. With bowed head I continued my climb, but—oh, wonder!—on the last step I had to stop, attracted by an impression still more disagreeable. The self-portrait of the painter forms part of a group of workers and adopts the sad situation of an imbecile. . . .*

Strong words, but no longer followed by a demand for the destruction of the murals. Moreover, they are in their way a tribute to the power of the painting. One familiar with the history of art would recognize, even without a single reproduction, that the work Pruneda was criticizing must possess strength and intensity. Mediocrity does not arouse violent reactions, only indifference.

Every change in the standard [Meier-Graefe has written] repels, and must repel, the multitude, for it is accomplished against their will, and consequently appears to them in the light of a humiliation, even when it is solely a question of esthetic things.

But here it was more than a mere question of esthetics: there was also the "message" of the paintings to arouse partisanship. Moreover, Meier-Graefe's dictum ignores that which is more marked in Mexico than in more literate and industrialized countries: the differing layers of taste in different layers of the population.

Diego attempted to generalize the phenomenon of social stratification of taste in an interview he gave in 1924 to Katherine Anne Porter.

Here in Mexico [he said] I find that very simple intuitive persons, in common with a highly sophisticated and prepared type, accept my

* This refers to the self-portrait reproduced here as PLATE 80, one of the painter's best, based on a portrait by Edward Weston.

way of painting. But the bourgeois mind (here as elsewhere called "cultured," I believe does not. This bourgeois mind of Mexico is of a special virulence, for being mixed in race for only a few generations, it is also lamentably mixed in its 'culture.' It is, in a word, saturated with European bad taste, the finer European influences having been almost wholly rejected by the Creole of Mexico.

As intellectual arrogance and spiritual understanding are always enemies, this bourgeois has not really comprehended anything, and has remained insensible to the atmosphere of art about him. He has not only aspired to be altogether European in the manner of his ill-chosen masters of art, but he has attempted to dominate and deform the esthetic life of the true Mexico (the Indian who possesses his own heritage of classic art), and his failure to do this has created in his mind a professional rancor against all native things, all art expression truly Mexican. He has so fouled the atmosphere that for a century art in Mexico has been almost stifled. He accepts without discrimination the dubious cultural influences of Europe, not only in one style, nor from one country, but from all. A monstrous school has thus been created, as one may see by a glance at our popular academy exhibitions. This catholicity of corrupt appetite has spoiled his palate for the pure beauty to be found in America. When he encounters anything so natural and limpid, so foreign to his taste, he is at a loss to classify it. Not being tainted with the flavors he loves, he regards it with enmity, and rejects it. If you should ask him for a reason, he would answer in effect: "Indian art? Absurd! What can a peon know about beauty?" For being in the main Spanish, he even now confounds race with class and has not learned the difference between an Indian and a peon. . . .*

It is instructive to compare this with Orozco's sharp observation: "The bourgeois buys proletarian art at fancy prices, though it is supposed to be directed at them, and the proletarians would gladly buy bourgeois art if they had the money. . . . The halls of bourgeois homes are full of proletarian furniture and objects like sleeping mats [*petates*], rush-bottomed chairs, clay pots, and tin candlesticks, while a worker, as soon as he has a home, buys a Pullman sofa and a breakfast set."

Diego's frequent pronouncements on the necessity of educat-

* Diego Rivera: From a Mexican Painter's Notebook," *The Arts* (January 1925), pp. 21-23.

ing proletarian taste show that in his heart he agreed with Orozco.

The campaign for the destruction of Diego's murals did not die out altogether. In 1929 Governor Benitez Terrones of Durango demanded their removal in the daily *Excelsior.* In 1930 *Universal Gráfico* carried this malevolent item:

TIME, ACCOMPLICE OF THE STUDENTS IN DESTRUCTION OF THE WORKS OF DON DIEGO RIVERA

The rumor that direct action is to be exercised against the pictorial work of Diego Rivera caused us to interview some of the students of the Faculty of Architecture who were the initiators of the campaign let loose against the *discutido* painter.

The attackers of Diego Rivera told us that they would not exercise violent direct action against the paintings of Diego Rivera which misadorn the walls of the Secretariat of Public Education in view of the fact that such action would not give more relief than that which time is exercising on the paintings, which are visibly suffering a great deterioration, thanks, according to the opinion of the future architects, to the deficiences of the encaustic process in which they were executed.

Needless to say, the expectation of the disappearance of the paintings by the action of nature has as much foundation as the statement that they are encaustics. In 1935, not confiding any longer in the elements, a group of students sprayed acid on Rivera's National Palace Mural, defacing but failing to obliterate a section in which he suggested that the clergy employed the image of the Virgin of Guadalupe to get money from the Mexican poor. After his Del Prado murals they tried direct action on his studio windows.

When Diego saw that the tide was turning in his favor, he followed up his advantage by becoming more defiant in the propaganda contained in his paintings. Signs of exhaustion from the intense effort had been visible, I believe, in the frescoes on the second floor and the first court of the top floor of the Education Building. They were, as always, technically skillful, but their allegory was banal, and the revolutionary apostles, with the exception of Zapata, were painted lifelessly, Now, however, with increasing audacity of conception, strength revived: the third-floor arches broke out triumphant in revolutionary song. Not only did he become more audacious in propaganda, but chose a device which made that natural and easy: a series of illustrations, as in a picture book, of selections from three popular revolutionary ballads. Thus he became not a painter of a mural but the illustrator of a brightly colored ballad book painted on the walls of a building. He began with a few verses from a ballad on Zapata; followed with the best stanzas from one of the current folk ballads of the 1910 Revolution;* and since no lightning struck painter or paintings, ventured to complete the series with a *corrido* written by one Martínez, for *El Machete, Así Será la Revolución Proletaria*—"Thus Will Be the Proletarian Revolution." (A few details from the vast ballad series are shown in PLATES 53, 60, 77, 78, 79, 93.)

The lines of the three ballads are painted in bright colors on a bright gray ground, rising and falling in graceful festoons around the court, following and reflecting in reverse the rhythm of the arcades, and reflected by the rhythms of the paint-created arches which contain the scenes illustrating the verses. Everywhere there are curves, weaving in and out and up and down in rhythmic repeats: curving grace in the cartridge belts of workers fighting on revolutionary barricades—a trifle too lyrical for the realities of barricade struggles, but after all, this is a ballad revolution. It is relieved and heightened in turn by elements of ferocious

* The text derived from a broadsheet *corrido* by José Guerrero. The original contains many dull passages, and verses pretending that the Mexican Revolution accomplished more than it actually had. Diego omitted these stanzas which were at the same time the dullest and most pedestrian. His selection is similar to the collective process by which the folk, by remembering more vivid and forgetting less striking passages, gradually make a haunting and beautiful "collective" ballad out of what was originally the mediocre composition of some "popular" poet.

satire and caricature in the treatment of the representatives of the ruling class and existing order. Most celebrated of the illustrations (for reasons not directly connected with aesthetics) is the one denominated *Night of the Rich* (PLATE 78):

Dan la una, dan las dos,
y el rico siempre pensando
como le hará a su dinero
para que se vaya doblando.

The clock strikes one and then two,
And the rich still at it, wondering
What they can do to their money
To keep it always doubling.

The illustration shows Mexican and American capitalists and their womenfolk, at a table before champagne and ticker tape, a bank vault, loudspeakers, the ticker, and a replica of the Statue of Liberty. Those at table include caricatures of John D. Rockefeller the First, the elder J. P. Morgan, and Henry Ford. Certainly, when the Rockefellers hired Diego to decorate Radio City, they could not allege that they were not forewarned, for they were already familiar with this mural.

The ballad of the Proletarian Revolution as painted reads:

Son las voces del obrero rudo
lo que puede darles mi laud
es el canto sordo pero puro
que se escapa de la multitud.

The sound of workers' voices rude,
Hoarse and full and strong
From many-throated multitude,
Rings out our freedom song.

Ya la masa obrera y campesina
sacudióse el yugo que sufría
ya quemó la cizaña maligna
del burgués opresor que tenía.

Of slavish growth we've cleared the ground
And burned the evil weed.
Now with our song the fields resound
As we plant a better seed.

Por cumplir del obrero los planes
no se vale que nadie se raje;
se les dice a los ricos y holgazanes,
"El que quiera comer, que trabaje."

We fought until our cause was won,
A fight that none could shirk.
Now, if he'd eat, the idle drone
Will have to go to work.

Las industrias y grandes empresas
dirigidas son ya por obreros:
manejades en cooperativas
sin patrones sobre sus cabezas.

Now mines and mills without a boss
Are by the workers run.
Nor do we have to "mourn our loss,"
As better work is done.

Y la tierra ya está destinada
para aquel que la quiere explotar.
Se acabó la miseria pasada
cualquier hombre puede cultivar.

Now to him the earth is free
Who works it with his hand.
Gone is the age-old misery,
For all who wish there's land.

La igualdad y justicia que hoy tienen
se debió a un solo frente
que hicieron en ciudades, poblados y ranchos
campesinos, soldados y obreros.

The freedom we at last have won
We could not win until
We formed a strong united front
Of barrack, farm, and mill.

Ahora tienen el pan para todos;
los desnudos, los hombres de abajo;
la igualdad, la justicia, el trabajo
y han cambiado costumbres y modos.

None want for roof, for clothes, for bread,
For useful work to do;
Where justice reigns and greed is dead
Our ways grow better too.

Cuando el pueblo derrocó a los reyes
y al gobierno burgués mercenario,
e instaló sus consejos y leyes
y fundó su poder proletario.

No king, no boss, no bureaucrat
To serve the bosses' cause
Now rules the proletariat
Its councils and its laws.*

When Diego finished the revolutionary ballads and martyrs on the top floor of the Education Building, José Vasconcelos, no longer Minister of Education, denounced the work. He had never liked Diego's painting, but had hitherto claimed credit for it.

* The translation here, contrary to those elsewhere in this book, is not closely literal. I have tried to preserve the ideas and spirit and to give the reader a feeling for the folk-ballad character of the *corrido* by employing English popular-ballad expressions and meters.

Now, as it was becoming more "revolutionary," he himself was becoming more conservative. To the completed work he dedicated the following oft-repeated phrases:

> It was believed till quite recently that the economic transformations which are at present taking place in society would produce a great art—proletarian in Russia; popular in Mexico. For lack of a religious spirit, these movements remained incomplete, both socially and artistically. In Russia they have fallen into the grotesque, and in Mexico into the abjection of covering walls with portraits of criminals. . . .*

Diego responded by painting Vasconcelos in the ballad series among the disseminators of false knowledge, seated, in sign of this theosophy and ill-digested Oriental mysticism, upon a little white elephant. Though he is seated with his back to the spectator, so skillful is the portrait that none could fail to recognize it. What infuriated Vasconcelos was that the inkwell into which he appeared to be dipping his pen looked suspiciously like a cuspidor. A sad ending for an alliance which had begun so hopefully. Without Vasconcelos Rivera would never have had the opportunity to paint frescoes on public walls; without the great fresco renaissance, Vasconcelos would have won less renown.

While Diego was completing the top floor and stairway of the Education Building, he was "resting" by alternating on the entrance, stairway, and chapel of the Agricultural School at Chapingo. Over the stairway he painted: "Here it is taught to exploit the land, not man." The entrance hall represents the four seasons; on the first floor, at the head of the stairway, are good and bad government (a traditional subject of classic painting), the distribution of the land (PLATE 75), and symbolic representations of the sciences which serve the land. (Some of the details from the Chapingo frescoes are shown in PLATES 65, 66, and 73-76.) In the summer of 1927 he finished the frescoes in both buildings.

* José Vasconcelos: *Estética* (Mexico City, Andrés Botas, n.d.). The "criminals" are such Mexican leaders as Zapata.

Even the critics of the Academy were silenced when so reputable a work as Michel's *Histoire de l'art* eulogized the Chapingo frescoes. The comment was written by Louis Gillet, Conservateur du Château de Chaalis, who visited Mexico to do a chapter on Mexican art. Here is what the respectable *conservateur* wrote in the respectable history:

> His art has the function of instruction, the force of propaganda which the Catholic missionaries expected of painting: this aesthetic, violently anti-clerical, is a vehicle of mystic passions and ideas. This is quite visible in the Chapel of Chapingo, stripped of its altars and of everything pertaining to religion, which the painter has covered with naturalistic frescoes—Sainte-Chapelle of the Revolution, Sistine Chapel of the new age.
>
> The artist unfolds there in fiery and violent images at once a catechism and a cosmogony, the double genesis of nature and of man, the profound confinement, the *accouchements* of the Earth and of the human race on the soil of Mexico. One sees there Nature, recumbent giant, holding between her dreamy hands the germ of life, surrounded by ferocious figures of the elements, Water, Wind, and Fire, spirit crowned with a fan of flames and rising from a crater. Elsewhere there are intimate powers and forces in labor in the bowels of the Earth: a feminine spirit, a bizarre squatting sphinx, crouching on her heels in a magic attitude in the depth of a cavern of flames, extends her arms, attracts the divinities of metal, the energies which doze and glide in the form of meteors in the veins of the terrestrial crust.
>
> Finally, on the wall which faces the apse, in place of the old paradise, a vision of harmonious Nature, of an Eden cultivated by a regenerated humanity. One sees the importance of these paintings in which Diego Rivera has created the first revolutionary imagery, the *geste* of his people and the national legend.
>
> This is a work of which one will seek in vain for an equivalent, not only in the rest of America, but also in Europe, and in Russia. Chance has caused to reveal itself in Mexico the first of the great works of art born from Socialist and agrarian materialism. The author himself has hammered out for this purpose a personal dialect: one recognizes in his pictures the complete collection of natural types, the broad flat faces of the Indians, the conical cranium and the beak of the Aztec, the mask, composite and troubled, of the *mestizo*. Sometimes, in certain types of bourgeois, in the painting of the rich and the idle, he does not

hesitate to use the procedures of the pamphleteer, of election-poster satire. But the emotion overflows, an irresistible seduction sweeps criticism off its feet; on that drawing which overwhelms you, an admirable rainbow of colors, a play of all violets, oranges, tender green, rose of fire, unfolds its scarf of delights, all the voluptuous gamut of the light of Mexico. . . .

Diego's long and hazardous battle for recognition and for the right of his works to survive seemed to have ended in victory. He had created two monumental works, each worthy of an artist's lifetime, had won a place for himself in his homeland, given rich and varied expression to its life. If the ballads and martyrs of the top floor of the Secretariat, however bright and decorative, suggested that the painter had changed his theme and became a mere illustrator, Chapingo had demonstrated anew his astounding powers as a master mural painter. Confidently he lumbered down from his scaffold and looked for new lands to conquer.

19. JOURNEY TO THE HOLY LAND

For a while Diego identified himself with the Russian Revolution more completely than any other painter of his time, expressed it more directly than did David the French Revolution, became in some fashion its brush, embodied what he took to be its meaning on the walls of two lands far distant from the country of its origin. It is not what he gave to it, but what it gave to him, that is significant. It was the flame that fused the isolated fragments of his experience and aspirations: his father's Liberalism, the populism of Posada, student rebellion in the art school, Bohemian rebellion on Montparnasse, the memory of the Rio Blanco massacre and Barcelona's bloody week, the excitement of Spanish anarchism, the shock of the birth of total war out of the womb of civilization, the hope of revolution to bring the nightmare to an end, the hope of an art that would reconquer the right to speak to the people and elevate the popular taste to the point where it might once more become the fruitful matrix of great art.

It was the impact of the Mexican and Russian revolutions upon him that extricated him at last from the maze of experiment on Montparnasse, sent him wandering down the Italian peninsula to feed his eyes on fresco-covered walls, then to his native land to paint "the revolution"* on walls of his own. The invitation from his friend David Sternberg, who had become "art commissar," to come to Russia to paint, hastened his homeward journey. He was too creative a personality, too much a generator of his own energy, to be content to go to "Mecca" to worship. He preferred to go to Mexico to work. Yet always he harbored a secret doubt whether he should not have accepted, a longing to go there to see for himself, to learn, and in his own field to teach, to serve with his brush by painting a great mural in the land of the Soviets.

It was Edo Fimmen, President of the International Transport Workers' Federation, who finally arranged for him in 1927 a second invitation to Moscow.

> . . . You will remember that I said I would do what I could to have you invited to Soviet Russia [he wrote in a letter in French, dated Amsterdam, July 25, 1927]. I am glad that I had no trouble arranging that you receive an invitation to attend the celebrations of the Tenth Anniversary of the October Revolution. . . .† The expenses to the border will be on your own, but during your stay in Russia you will be the guest of the government. Probably you will have received the invitation by the time you get this letter. I sincerely hope that you will be able

* The word was as resonant as it was ambiguous, for it embodied two totally different revolutions, and engendered in the mind of the painter an image resembling neither of them.

† We now know why the climate of the Tenth Anniversary was so inhospitable to Diego's art. Stalin spent the very morning of November 7, 1927 in the cutting room of the State Cinema offices, personally cutting out 900 meters of Eisenstein's film *Ten Days That Shook the World,* nor were the cuts limited to such things as the elimination of Leon Trotsky, chairman of the Military Revolutionary Committee that directed the uprising. Episodes involving Lenin were also cut out, including much of the finale, Lenin's address to the Second Congress of the Soviets. (*Pravda,* Oct. 28, 1962.)

to accept it and thus get the opportunity to know modern Russia, its workers, and its life and art, and at the same time to offer them the opportunity to know your talents. . . .

The painter was one of a delegation of "workers and peasants" (mostly intellectuals) from Mexico to the festivities. His pockets bulged with documents, mandates, credentials. They certified him to be a member of the Communist Party, delegate of the Mexican Peasant League, General Secretary of the Anti-Imperialist League, editor of its official organ, *El Libertador*, and many other things besides.

In Moscow Diego was caught up in the pageantry of the Tenth Anniversary celebrations. From his place on the reviewing stand against the old Kremlin wall, he watched the Red Army file through the historic Red Square, followed by a procession that continued all day long. With greedy eyes he watched, notebook in hand, sketching as well on the tablets of his tenacious brain; saw the surging sea of crimson banners, spirited horses rearing as their riders stopped them in their tracks to deliver a salute, caught the rattle of wheel and streak of moving line as horse-drawn artillery flashed by at full gallop, the cubic pattern of trucks loaded with riflemen, solid squares of marching infantry, then the vast banner-plumed, float-bearing serpentine line of the masses of men and women marching until nightfall through the square. All this he noted in forty-five watercolor sketches and innumerable penciled notes, out of which he hoped to build murals for Russian walls (PLATES 81-88). One of the sketches became the cover of an issue of *Fortune*. The notebook was purchased by Mrs. Abby Rockefeller; part of it served as material for the Russian demonstration scene on the wall of the Radio City building which the Rockefellers subsequently destroyed. Several sketches found their way into *Cosmopolitan* magazine.*

On November 9, George V. Korsunsky, young Russian with

* September 1932, illustrating an article by Emil Ludwig on Joseph Stalin.

a command of Spanish, an interest in Latin America, and a love of art, lectured on "Contemporary Mexican Art," with Diego as guest of honor. The anouncement promised:

> Social Views and Life of Contemporary Mexico; State of Artistic Culture; Renaissance of Monumental Art; Diego Rivera; Proletariat of Art.
>
> To be illustrated with photographs. After the report there will be an opportunity to talk to the distinguished Mexican artist, Diego Rivera, delegate to the October celebration from the American Anti-Imperialist League.

Young painters attending were impressed by the pictures, astonished by the huge, homely attractiveness of this painter from a distant land, charmed to discover that he understood and after his own fashion could speak their language. Rivera's star was in the ascendant. He was invited to speak to artists' groups everywhere, made an instructor in the Academy of Fine Arts, besieged with applications of younger painters who wished to serve as apprentices. They felt after seeing the reproductions of his walls that they could learn much from this man. They sensed a new potential in his work that Russian painting had not guessed at.

On November 24 he signed a contract with Lunacharsky, Commissar of Education and the Fine Arts, to do a fresco in the Red Army Club. To facilitate his free movement for the purpose of gathering material and making sketches, Lunacharsky issued to him the following credential:

> We hereby certify that the government of the U.S.S.R. has decided to give a commission to Comrade Diego Rivera to make a fresco of large size according to his own selection. The order is regarded at the same time as a favor on the part of the Mexican people's art of Rivera, and if a favorable result comes of this experiment, the government looks forward to having Rivera prepare serious work for the decoration of the new V. I. Lenin Library at present under construction in Moscow.
>
> People's Commissar
> Lunacharsky

A rash of articles favorable to his painting broke out in the Russian press. *Krasnaya Niva* had him paint a picture for the cover of their Paris Commune anniversary number (PLATE 88).* The note calling attention to the cover told the reader:

Our cover . . . is the work of the famous painter-Communist of Mexico, Diego Rivera. . . . Diego Rivera is one of the few monumental painters of our time, master of mural painting, to whose brush we owe most of the frescoes to be found in the Education Building in Mexico.

At present Rivera is working on the design of the frescoes which are to decorate the Red Army building in Moscow. In an early number of *Krasnaya Niva* the reader will find a special article dedicated to the creation of this great master.

Next Alfred Kurella,† one of the country's intellectuals and an amateur writer and painter, wrote a "fundamental political" article for the Russian party press after a series of interviews with the artist. Kurella was then head of the Department of Agitation and Propaganda of the Communist International. His article is interesting both for what it shows of the state of Russian painting and as a statement of Rivera's views on the social role of the mural, for Diego's language, somewhat muddied by its passage through Kurella's agitprop mind, runs through the article.

Soviet painting [Kurella begins] has not even begun to realize the slogan of art for the masses. The painter works in isolation in his studio, painting neither for a definite place nor for definite persons. In exhibitions his picture vies with a thousand other works for a moment's attention from a stream of visitors, whence it returns to his studio, or in rare and fortunate cases is purchased by some organization.

Now new difficulties arise [the article continues]. The canvas is too big or too small; it needs light from the left and the room in which

* *Krasnaya Niva,* No. 12 (March 17, 1928). The original is in the possession of Dr. Hubert Herring.

† Heinrich Kurella, Alfred's brother, died in one of Stalin's concentration camps, but Alfred, after years of eclipse, is today (1963) culture dictator of Communist East Germany, more rigid and repressive even than the analogous Soviet cultural police.

it is hung is lighted otherwise. In view of its drawing and composition, it should be viewed from close by; but it turns out that the room is too spacious. It is finally hung somehow, but it is seen sad and dispirited. . . . And that's the way we try to introduce pictorial art to the masses!

In reality, the masses will not be permeated by art in that fashion. . . . From the point of view of its social meaning such a work is worth zero. It remains outside of our new social structure, a vestige of an alien individual form of production. The work of art can have influence only when it is linked in some way to the current of social life of the period in which we live or when it is assigned a clearly defined collective function. . . .

The gap between the most advanced artistic expression and the elementary tastes of the masses can be bridged only by following a course which will improve, integrally, the cultural level of the masses and capacitate them for artistic perception of the new ways developed by the dictatorship of the proletariat.*

Nevertheless, it may be possible to begin at once the rapprochement between the masses and art. The road is simple: Paint! Paint murals in clubs and public buildings!

This is, some say, a discovery made in America. And that is true. The discovery does indeed come from the New World. . . .

But where shall we find these artists?

We have them in our midst. Here among us is one of the greatest contemporary masters of that kind of work. He is the most famous mural painter in all the world, the Mexican artist Diego Rivera.

This technical worker in mural paintings—as he calls himself—old revolutionist who has fought, rifle in hand, in the civil war in his own country, is also a revolutionist in art; revolutionary in his compositions and designs, and, what is still better, revolutionary of the masses. He it was that initiated that great artistic movement in Mexico. . . .

And it seems to us that we ought not to wait. Forward! Let's begin from the bottom. Forward! Let's give the opportunity to our fresco painters to show that they are capable of engendering a new art which will draw close to the masses.

In retrospect, the climax of the honors showered upon Diego seems to have come when he was invited to draw from life a

* The reader will bear in mind that this was written in the twenties. In the thirties the "gap was bridged" by degrading the work of the painters to the level of taste of Joseph Stalin and his cronies in the name of *partiinost* (party spirit) and "accessibility" to the masses.

portrait of the General Secretary of the Communist Party, Joseph Stalin. True this mark of favor did not then have the significance which it would have later, for the Byzantine cult of the *Vozhd* had not yet come to full flower. Indeed, it was at that moment, in the spring of 1928, that the apotheosis of Stalin began and his face appeared simultaneously on the cover of every paper and magazine in the country, while every prominent artist was set to do his bust or portrait. To this campaign Diego unwittingly contributed. Judging from the sketch he did, he does not seem to have been impressed by his subject.

An uneasy feeling arose in Diego that all was not well with his plans to paint in the Red Army building. The artists assigned to assist him proved incompetent or unwilling to subordinate themselves to him and their humble auxiliary tasks. The building was a former palace; Diego wanted its hall stripped of its "Empire" decorations, which he considered rubbish, but of which the art experts of the club were enormously proud. They wanted him to paint in Empire style! He caught cold while sketching Russian winter scenes in the snow of a hard Moscow winter, and it complicated the sinus trouble for which he had been operated on in Mexico the previous spring. He was sent to the Kremlin Hospital for treatment. When he came out, he found that a veritable campaign of undercover calumny on the part of the older artists was under way against him. His lectures at the Academy on the deficiencies of Russian art aroused the enthusiasm of the young, but the indignation of the men successful according to the prevailing standards which he was beginning to disturb. He inquired after the fate of some of the earlier painters, his futurist, cubist, expressionist, and other modernist friends of Paris days. He was shocked to hear how they had been silenced, driven out of the land, paralyzed by uncomradely and reckless criticism and hothouse forcing of adaptation, so that many had given up painting altogether. Still more was he shocked by the shoddy banalities produced by those who had hastened to conform.

In his lectures he pointed out the weakness of easel painting for immediate mass consumption. A score of artists rushed to reply as if he had denied the role of easel painting altogether. The Russians had erred, he said, in not seeking to fuse the developed technique acquired in Paris with the peasant and popular tradition of Russian folk art. "Look at your icon painters," he bade them, "and at the wonderful embroideries and lacquer boxes and wood carvings and leatherwork and toys. A great heritage which you have not known how to use and have despised!" Voices answered charging him with glorifying icons and the Church, admiring backward peasant handicrafts, underestimating the role of the machine, of industrialization, of the economic plan. The debate became hotter, Diego began to feel ill at ease and out of sorts. To his daily requests for material and proper assistants, the answer was *Zaftra budet*—tomorrow. He knew that device from his own land.

At that point the Latin American Secretariat of the Comintern took a hand. Although the Mexican party had released Rivera at Lunacharsky's request for an indefinite stay, it suddenly ordered him home "for a few months," as President of the Workers' and Peasants' Bloc, not to run for office, but to manage a presidential campaign. A likely story! But he was glad to go.

He left suddenly in the middle of May, without stopping to say good-by to the Russian sweetheart he had acquired, or to artist friends. One of the latter managed to find his Mexican address and wrote him:

Dear and unforgettable comrade:

I am profoundly grieved by your precipitate and unexpected departure. Do you know that I came to visit you just one half hour after you had left? Can you imagine my surprise, indignation, and afterwards my sadness when I knew that you had gone? I could not believe it. To tell the truth, I did not believe it either when, during our last conversation, you tried to tell me you intended going; still less could I foresee that you would go without saying good-by to me. Don't you remember that the last time we saw each other, I informed you that the University Circle of Art Studies was organizing for next Tuesday a discussion which you were to lead? This was one more reason why I could not suspect your mean intention to leave us so soon.

My comrade students were preparing a meeting in your honor and we all had the intention to arrange also, before you left, an evening affair or banquet for you with the participation of the Communist Academy, the professors and the painters. And now you have gone without being bidden farewell or being accompanied en masse by us who admire you, without receiving the evidences of our general affection for you . . . !

It seems to me that I have some reason to believe that you left with a bad taste in your mouth, with sadness or resentment. . . . I am sure that such feelings were and are without foundation. . . .

I embrace you with immense affection.

Diego did his best to cover up the shabby treatment. When Eugene Lyons, United Press correspondent in Moscow, came to interview him on his rumored departure, this is the story Lyons got from the painter:

Diego Rivera, the noted Mexican painter, is preparing to leave Moscow, where he has been since the November celebrations, for a several months' sojourn at home. He will then return to the Soviet capital to work on a set of frescoes which he has been asked to do for the Ministry of War.

The undertaking is likely to keep him busy an entire year. The commission was urged upon Rivera by the government after it had been suggested by members of the American and German labor delegations at the tenth anniversary celebration. After some discussion the building of the War Commissariat was decided upon as most suitable for the purpose.

It has not yet been determined, however, which of several large halls in the building would be used for Rivera's mural decorations. Some preliminary sketches which he made will have to be altered because the room for which they were intended cannot be used for the purpose. The architects, it appears, fear that the frescoes in that particular room might clash with the general style of the structure.

Rivera has been very much involved in polemics on art matters here. Among painters, as in the other arts, there are conflicts occasioned by the revolution: an effort to adjust both the content and form of art to the new social conditions and viewpoints. Rivera is in the thick of this conflict.

These polemics, he says, have created the impression abroad that his project for decorating the war ministry is being opposed. This he denies. Both the government and the communist painters support his undertaking. He has just been made professor at the Moscow Academy of Art, where he has lectured. Upon his return to Mexico he expects to give several lectures on Soviet art and culture.*

So ended Diego's Moscow expedition. He never finished the Red Army mural and did not return to Moscow until the last year of his life.

A fitting postscript is provided by an article Diego wrote in 1932, summing up his opinions on art in the Soviet Union:

Present-day Russian artists, formed in the aesthetic of the Occidental European world, founded entirely on the culture sprung from the French bourgeois revolution and refined during the period of super-capitalism, find no place in the Soviet regime. They struggle at the same time against the incomprehension and the petty-bourgeois bad taste of the Soviet functionaries—a taste formed, like the art of the artists, within the bourgeois European culture, but infinitely more neglected—and against their own esthetic sensibility and technical modalities which are not meant for the collectivist revolutionary functions of art, but for the individualists of the decadent bourgeoisie.

The Russian masses were right to reject the Paris and Berlin form of art called "ultramodern"; they were right, when they were given the opportunity to choose, to prefer daubings that were at least legible to those inaccessible beauties; for the artists should have given them an art of high esthetic quality, containing all the technical acquisitions of contemporary art, but an art simple, clear, and transparent as crystal, hard as steel, cohesive as concrete, the trinity of the great architecture of the new historical stage of the world. This is an architecture that will come naked and implacable, totally stripped of ornamentation. When men seek repose after their struggle for the conquest of themselves, become

* U.P. mail story by Eugene Lyons, dated Moscow, April 17, 1928.

a strong species instead of sterile individuals, when they feel the necessity for the living form and color that will transport them beyond time and space, then architecture will be the receptacle for the new mural painting and architectonic sculpture, the highest manifestations of the new order, as they were in every historical period in which men found a definition of themselves.

The true artists, especially the painters and sculptors of contemporary Soviet Russia, live in lamentably bad circumstances, but the fault is more their own than that of the inept functionaries who, with the coming of the NEP, restored the academic Russian painters—the worst academic painters in the world.

These bad painters shielded themselves behind mottoes that are good and justified within Marxist dialectic materialism.

If the good artists, instead of maintaining a desperate and sadly heroic struggle to keep alive art forms of other times—*the workers cannot acquire paintings and sculptures on the same conditions as the capitalists*—had accepted the fact that it was necessary to adapt themselves to a living reality and to produce an art that the workers and peasants could absorb and enjoy, they could thus have snatched from the false artists the standard of the true purpose. The bad functionaries would not have been able to hinder them, for the strength of the proletariat would have been with them.

This is one of the varied results of the actual descending curve (transitory degeneration) of the Russian bureaucratized Communist Party, against which the sane revolutionary forces of the entire world are struggling, an opposition which the international functionaries, petty leaders, and intellectual lackeys of Sir Joseph Stalin reward with the titles of renegades, traitors, and social fascists. But these gentleman will have, against the true revolutionary ideology and the true art of the revolution, the same efficacy as a drunkard who, having stolen a pair of scissors, tries to cut with it a ray of light.*

* Diego Rivera: "Position of the Artist in Russia Today," *Arts Weekly* (Vol. I, No. 1 [March 11, 1932], pp. 6-7).

20. THE COMMUNIST WAR ON RIVERA

Back in 1924 I undertook to discuss with Diego his relationship with the Communist Party, thereby straining our friendship nearly to the breaking point.*

He was working that day on his scaffold in the Education Building. I climbed the scaffold and watched the busy movement of his hand and the somnolent contentment on his face. We exchanged pleasantries, a remark or two about the figure on which he was working; he explained the intention of the panel. Then: "*¿Qué hay?*—What's up?"

"Diego," I said awkwardly, "I think you should resign from the Party."

He stopped painting—in the middle of a stroke, twisting his body so that his eyes were looking into mine. When he saw I was not jesting, he put down his brush and with accustomed courtesy motioned to me to precede him down the scaffold. He

* I was then a member of the Communist Party of Mexico and its Central Committee, as was Diego.

lumbered after, giving a single backward glance at the unfinished work, then left the wet plaster to dry beyond the possibility of painting while we paced up and down the courtyard, then along downtown streets, and talked. How many hours, I do not know, but the first half hour seemed a fair slice of eternity.

From the first it had seemed obvious to me that he was a great painter, one of the greatest, beyond question the greatest in the Communist movement. As his work grew in strength as art and as propaganda, as I became aware of his amazing passion for painting, his fecundity and animal strength for labor, I began to begrudge for his sake, and that of the movement it was intended to serve, every moment he spent attending committee meetings, drafting manifestoes, wrangling over trival things, waiting for subcommittees that, with Mexican informality, would start three or four hours late or never get to convening at all—in short, every moment he spent away from painting. It was not that I thought that painters and writers should not be Party members, but here was one "intellectual" who did not need to be imbued with the philosophy and spirit of the movement by constant contact. Here was a monster of fertility that could actually create during all his waking hours and live by paint alone. Even before I felt the necessity of his resigning, it had become increasingly clear to me that the best service he could give was the service of his brush.

Moreover, he was a poor Central Committee member, even in a routine sense of the term a poor member, for he was constantly forgetting what day of the week it was and what hour of the day, so absorbed in his painting that he missed committee meetings and even speaking dates. While the plaster was wet and the vision flowing from brain through hand to wall, time would stand still. He was the "enemy of clocks and calendars" and all discipline save the self-discipline of creative work. He was in constant hot water with the other members of the committee, in constant danger of being expelled for nonattendance at the regulation "three successive meetings" and for forgetting or neglecting to execute assigned tasks.

My negative reason, no less cogent, was more touchy. It lay in his amazing picture-making power. In all my life I have met no one with so vivid, rich, and overwhelming a fantasy as his; even the history of art does not present many parallels. A marvelous talent to employ on acres and acres of wall; but in a party as backward and inexperienced as the Mexican, made up of unskilled intellectuals and newly proletarianized peasants possessed of peasant minds, the impressiveness of his personality, the ease with which he commanded authority in any meeting he attended, the verisimilitude of his rich flow of words and images and his skill at coordination of details into a unified picture—in short, his talents, assumed the proportions of a positive danger. Nobody on the Committee seemed to know anything about the economic and political realities of the land, nor —with the exception of the one non-Mexican member—did anybody seem to care. Diego had no need for such study; he could sense things, build up out of the merest fragments with the aid of extraordinary powers of "composition" a complete, self-consistent, internally logical, overwhelmingly convincing picture. He had a feeling for trends, developments, directions, elaborating them more directly and logically than reality did, not troubling to check with the facts, building them into pictures as complete and rich and detailed as any he ever spread on walls. Occasionally these fantasies were right, foreseeing developments for long periods ahead, predicting things which more plodding methods would not have caught on to; but most of the time he would be just as completely, overwhelmingly wrong. Right or wrong, the picture captured the imagination of the Committee, always carried conviction, hung together with a beautiful rightness that stopped every doubt in advance; always it rested on a substratum of reality which had acted as starting point. When anyone challenged, the fertile mind of the painter would be stirred to bring forth from within himself fresh "proofs," new details more convincing than before. Even when, as was sometimes the case, his long-run anticipations turned out to be correct, the decisions of the immediate moment could not be based upon distant perspective alone, but had to take into account each momentary turn, since politics is a matter of meeting each day's exigencies in such fashion that not only the distant goal is kept in mind, but the next step is grasped which will lead towards and not away from it. When his fantasy elaborated things in the wrong direction, the Committee, swayed by his eloquent verisimilitude, was so far wrong that they might as well be laying plans for work in another country or on another planet.

I explained, as far as I dared and as tactfully as I could, the dangers to an inexperienced committee of his overpowering mind and imagination. Then I shied off from that delicate topic to emphasize the other reasons as no less cogent.

"Look, Diego," I pleaded in summary, for he was manifestly hurt and shocked, "you are today the greatest revolutionary painter in Mexico, probably in the world. Men like you should specialize. Just as one practices teaching, another speaking, a third writing, a fourth trade-union work or activity among the peasants, so should you. No matter how well you do other things, they are not so well done as your paintings. It is a shame to waste for a day, or an hour, such an exceptional talent as yours. The best thing you can do for the movement is paint.

"Besides," I concluded, "you are not a good Committee member or Party member anyway. You are always missing meetings, forgetting assignments, being reprimanded, threatened with expulsion for absence. Your participation is sufficient to disturb your painting, and not sufficient to be of any other service. Don't you see, Diego, as a sympathizer, you would be the best, the greatest, the most valued sympathizer, more valuable than any member? But as a member you are one of the worst. That's 'dialectics,'" I jested lamely, and became silent, awaiting a cloudburst.

We walked for a long time without either of us saying a word, while Diego revolved the idea in his mind. At last, he pressed my hand warmly in token that there was no ill will, and we went to his home to draft his letter of resignation together. I had another battle to convince the Committee that the proposal was for the good of the Party.

After he resigned, Diego's painting became no less propagandistic in content; he contributed more money than before, and continued to speak and write on request. As soon as I left Mexico—in the summer of 1925—both Diego and the Central Committee, by mutual agreement, hastened to undo my efforts. In 1926 he was readmitted into the Party and the Committee, only to be expelled in 1929 under circumstances which discredited the Communist Party and wounded and embittered Diego.

Diego's services to the Mexican Communist Party between 1926 and 1929 were most varied. He brought it prestige, carried on a polemic in its behalf in the press, used his influence with government officials to shield its members from persecution, more than once opening the doors of a cell for one who had been imprisoned. He drafted many of its documents—the theses of the Anti-Imperialist League and of the National Peasant League, and the statutes and program of the Workers' and Peasants' Bloc—and he wrote for it public manifestoes which were posted on the walls. He was the head of the Mexican delegation to Moscow on the occasion of the Tenth Anniversary celebration, representative to the Moscow Peasant Congress and Trade-Union Conference, Chairman of the Anti-Imperialist League, President of the Workers' and Peasants' Bloc, director of *El Libertador*, organ of the Anti-Imperialist League of the Americas, manager of the presidential campaign of 1928-29, Mexican correspondent for Barbusse's *Monde* (he did the cover for its issue of October 20, 1928). He did drawings or covers for *El Libertador*, while every few weeks *El Machete* carried a photograph of one of the murals issuing from his brush. During all this period—except for the six months of the trip to Moscow—he continued painting with the same monstrous speed and fecundity.

Throughout the world he was cited as the outstanding example of a Communist artist, living proof that the Party knew how to treat its artists so as not crush the creative spirit, and that art could be enriched and fructified by the ideas and feelings and experiences involved in participation in its movement. In the United States the *New Masses* published a two-page spread of his *Distribution of the Land among the Peons* (PLATE 75) from the Chapingo series, with the remark that "Going to see the paintings of Diego Rivera straightens you out a little bit."*

In January 1929 the Communist International wrote to the Central Committee of the Mexican Communist Party, and to Diego personally, asking for reproductions of his recent work for an exhibition of revolutionary art to take place in Moscow in March. But within the year the *New Masses*, the *Daily Worker*, and other organs of the Comintern throughout the world were to discover that his "draftsmanship and composition were awkward," his "form crude," that "their monotonous repetition of colors and lack of imagination bore the spectator," that he had never been a Leninist, only a petty-bourgeois agrarian *Zapatista* and had now become a bourgeois painter altogether. Such are the mutabilities of art when it must consort with a mutable party line!

Diego's last important Party task was the defense of Tina Modotti. Tina was walking arm in arm with Julio Antonio Mella on a dark street near her home when, on the night of January 10, 1929, he was shot dead with two bullet wounds in his back. The assassin, it turned out, was a Cuban gunman, financed by the Cuban government, assisted by a Cuban police spy, directed by the chief of the presidential secret service of General Machado, President of Cuba. Mella had led a student strike in Havana, been arrested, and when his arrest led to a general

* *New Masses*, March 1927. The picture was accompanied by an article on his work by John Dos Passos.

strike, was expelled from his native land. In Mexico he joined the Communist Party. His wife had refused to join him when he was exiled; in his new home he had fallen in love with and was living with Tina at the time of the shooting.

There must have been Mexican police complicity; the assassins, after their identity became known, were permitted to escape, while Valente Quintana, detective in charge of the investigation, declared that he had evidence that it was a "crime of passion" carried out by Tina herself, with the aid of hired assassins, because she was "tired of her lover." One of the judges in charge of the investigation also hinted that as an Italian she was a spy for Mussolini.

Convinced that money from Machado agents had been the source of the accusations by Detective Quintana and the judge of the first instance, Diego came to the defense of Tina. The Communist Party decided to initiate an inquiry of its own with the painter in charge. For several weeks he devoted his major energies to this task. He visited the morgue—the by-product of that visit being a portrait of the dead Mella in the *Imperialism* panel of the New Workers' School series five years later—attended the police hearings, interviewed witnesses and members of the Cuban colony, testified himself, spoke at public meetings.

The metropolitan press, delighted with the savory possibilities of the case, hinted broadly that perhaps Diego was the alternative lover who had hired the gunmen, snapped the two of them together at the hearings, ran their pictures with suggestive headlines. A typical front-page streamer, even after the facts had come out, illustrated with a nine-inch double-column photograph of the attractive heroine of the scandal, read:

> THE TREASON OF TINA MODOTTI
>
> Tina Modotti, Lover of Julio A. Mella,
> on Whom Fall Suspicions of Complicity
> in the Sensational Crime.
>
> A series of Charges Exist against Her.

Being the Lover of Julio Antonio Mella,
It Seems that She Was in Connivance
with His Assassins *

Tina bore up bravely, presiding at a protest meeting in the Hidalgo Theater on February 10, 1929, one month after the assassination, at which meeting Diego was one of the speakers. She opened the meeting with these words:

> In Mella they killed not only the enemy of the dictatorship in Cuba, but the enemy of all dictatorships. Everywhere there are people who sell themselves for money, and one of these has tried here to conceal the motive for the assassination of Mella by presenting it as a crime of passion. I affirm that the assassin of Mella is the President of Cuba, Gerardo Machado.

She demanded to know why a full month had elapsed with no light yet shed in official circles on the crime. She charged complicity in Mexican governmental circles, and presented a resolution demanding the rupture of relations with Cuba.

The police retaliated by raiding Tina's apartment and confiscating all her papers, on the pretext that they were looking for evidence of her complicity in the crime. They alleged that they found love letters from a number of individuals which proved that she was "a pernicious foreigner" who had come to Mexico "for immoral purposes," whereupon, in the midst of the investigation, they deported her. But Diego and his friends continued the investigation until they had cleared her name, forced Cuba to withdraw its Ambassador—it was without a representative for over a year—and obliged chief detective Valente Quintana to withdraw from government service.

* *El Universal,* February 3, 1934. This was printed five years after the facts were known. The reader can imagine what the press was like at the time of the murder! "Freedom" of the press has its own "restraints" in Mexico, but among them are neither a sense of responsibility nor decent libel laws.

Diego's defense of Tina Modotti and his management of the presidential campaign of the Workers' and Peasants' Bloc during the same year were the last official acts that he performed for the Communist Party. In September, while he was ill, Diego was expelled from the Party.

Neither he nor the Party leaders were able to give me a coherent account of the causes of the break when, in 1936, I went to Mexico to begin work on *Portrait of Mexico*. This is not surprising, since the causes were "international" in origin. Diego was caught in a world-wide purge emanating from factional politics in the Soviet Union, involving in some countries the exclusion of whole parties, in others expulsion or resignation of the principal leaders and founders, spreading at last in milder and more confused form to the more backward lands. The specific reasons given in Diego's case were hastily trumped up and so palpably inadequate that the Party busied itself inventing better ones. They were so petty and trivial that they were repugnant to Diego's sense of his own dignity and that of the Communist movement; he, too, was concerned to invent reasons of a more becoming scope. Both painter and Party were glad to let it appear later that the real cause had been "Trotskyism"; but actually, Diego did not become an adherent of Trotsky until after his expulsion, and the charge did not figure at all in his trial and defense.

Once he found himself cast out into the void, it was not unnatural for Diego to feel the attractive force of the exiled Russian leader. Diego was prepared by his experience with Soviet art to accept the emphasis that Trotsky placed on Russian bureaucracy as the cause of many undesirable features of Soviet life. There was at least one point of kinship between the temperaments of these two men. To an artist prepared as Diego was to accept the view that every revolutionary movement must be the tail to some Russian faction, the personality of Trotsky was more attractive than that of Stalin, Trotsky's figure was heroic (the leadership of the Red Army in civil war) and tragic (the fall from grace and exile into outer darkness). He was more sensitive to art and literature, more tolerant of its innovations, than any other outstanding leader of the October Revolution, with the exceptions of Lunacharsky and Bukharin. His mind operated like that of an artist, in terms of sudden insights, theoretical formulations possessed of a certain literary elegance, constructs based on a mixture of reality and imagination. Analogy—the building block of the logic of the artist mind—plays a major role in his thinking: the prominence of the "Thermidor theory"* in his programmatic system gives evidence of that.

The chief charge levied against Diego at the time of his "trial" was that he "maintained personal relations with Ramón P. de Negri," Minister of Agriculture, and later of Commerce and Labor. He had been seen in the latter's automobile, the testimony solemnly recited, in a restaurant with him, and at a dinner in his honor. To understand the state of mind which could elevate this to a crime, it is necessary for the reader to know that the Comintern was just beginning to go through a period in which it was official dogma that the closer a man was to Communism (without having actually joined the Party), the more dangerous he was.

The Communist International has since had many another change of heart—or "line." Later the Mexican Party made its own commentary upon the charge by defending de Negri in the columns of *El Machete* as "an old revolutionist whose honor is beyond the reach of all the Pedreros and Britos [two veteran *agraristas* who had attacked him] who have ever existed or ever will exist." † Knowing de Negri personally, I venture to question whether he any more merits the blanket endorsement which the

* The Thermidor theory is an attempt to explain many of the phenomena of the Russian Revolution in terms of their analogy to the events of the 9th of the month of Thermidor in the French Revolution, when Robespierre was executed (*cf.* the exile of Trotsky), power passed over to a bureaucracy representing privileged elements created by the new order, and reaction set in.

† *El Machete,* September 4, 1937.

103. Center above Stairway. Detail. National Palace.

104. Padre Mangas. Detail. National Palace. Main Wall.

105. The Church. Detail. Left Wall.

106. Shooting Agraristas. Detail. Left Wall.

107. Mexico Tomorrow. Left Wall.

108. Betrayal. Cuernavaca Mural. Detail.

109. Clash of Civilizations. Detail. Cuernavaca.

110. The Conquest. Detail. Cuernavaca.

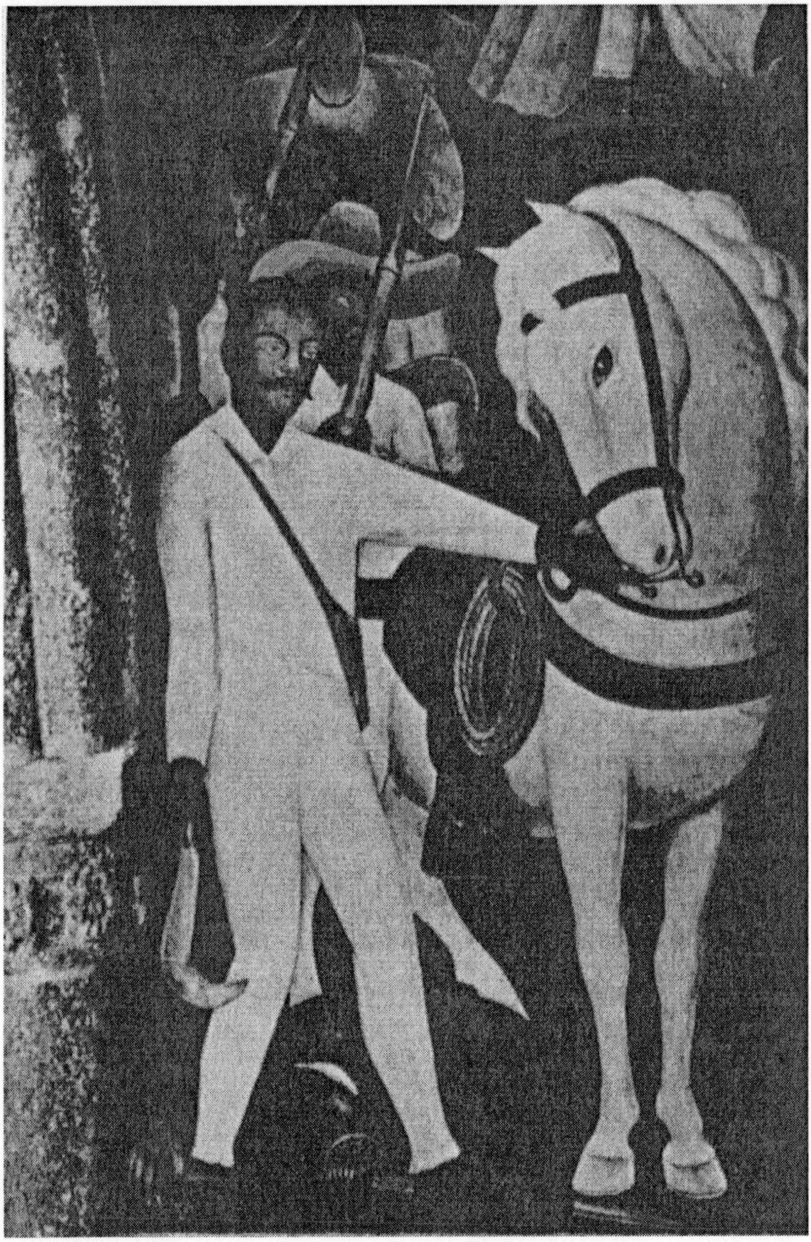

111. Zapata. Detail. Cuernavaca.

112. Sugar Plantation. Detail. Cuernavaca.

113. The Making of a Fresco. (Self-Portrait)
California School of Fine Art. 1931

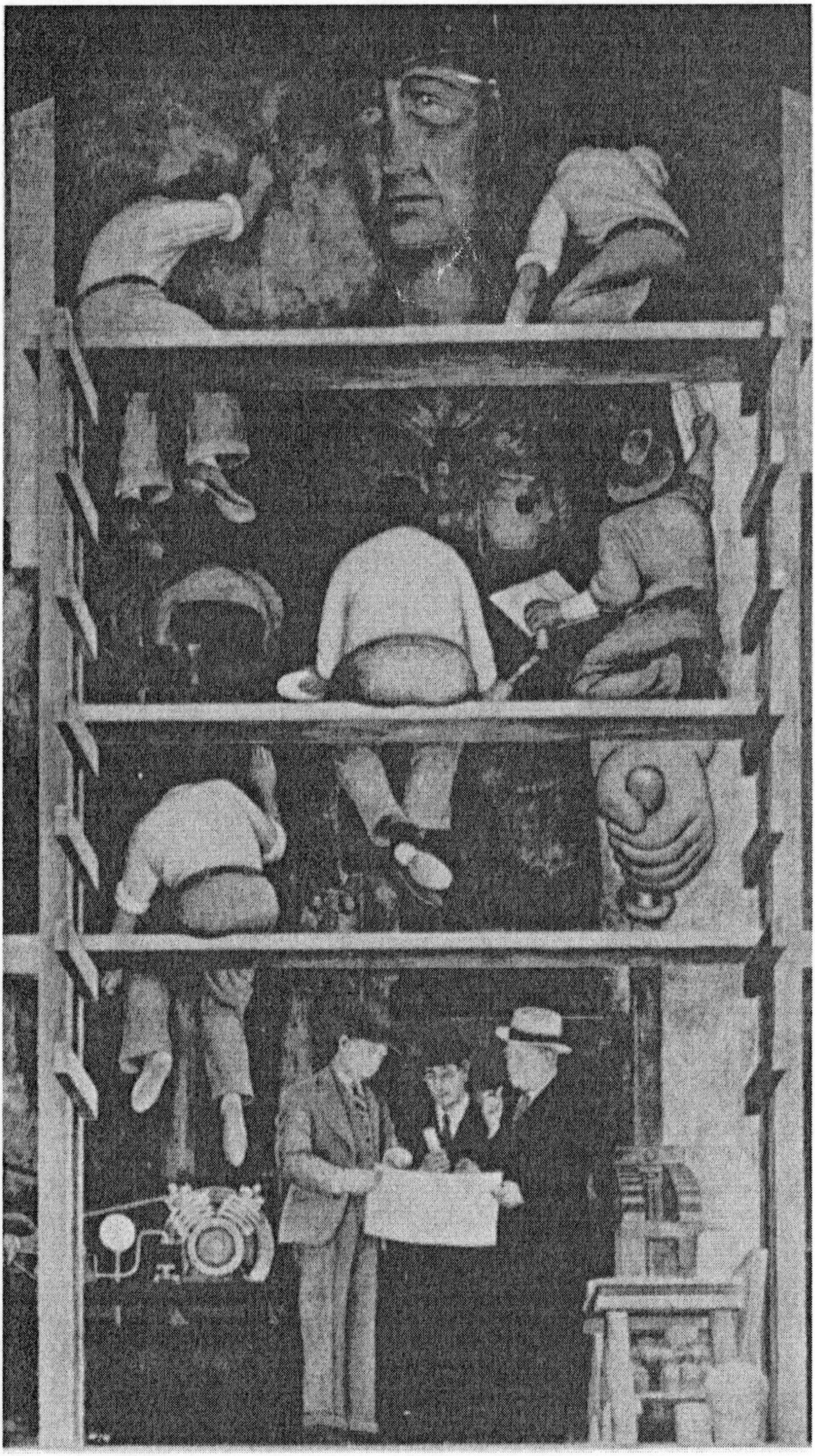

114. Diego Painting in Detroit. 1933

5. The Belt Conveyor. Detroit. 1933 (Showing incongruous architectural decoration.)

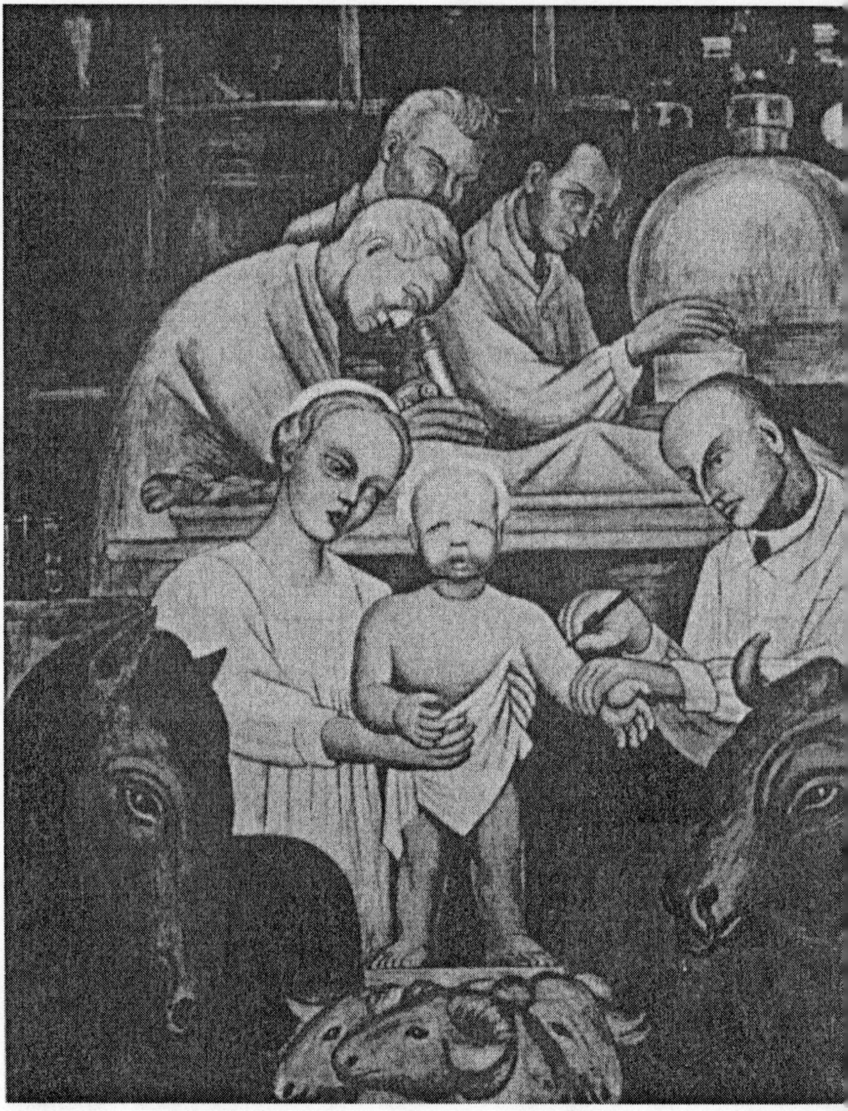

116. Vaccination. ("The Holy Family") Detroit. 1933

117. Turbine. Detail. West Wall. Detroit.

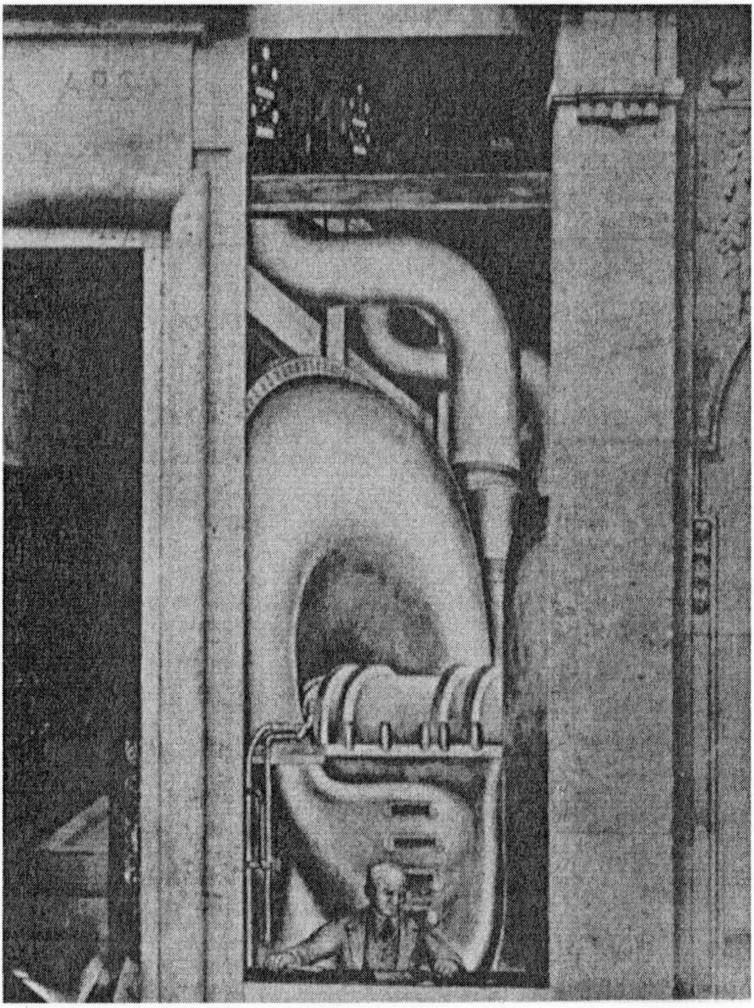

118. Portrait of Edsel Ford. Oil. 1932

Communist Party gave him in 1938 than he did the blanket condemnation that made Diego unfit for membership by virtue of consorting with him.

Other issues arose in the course of Diego's heresy trial. Differences between him and other Party leaders there had been at all times. Indeed, which members of the Central Committee had had no differences with other members? But not until then, when the methods of Russian controversy were imported, had it occurred to anyone to feel that differences of opinion were anything but normal, even helpful to a discussion of complicated, constantly shifting problems by men of diverse personality, experience, and outlook.

Diego brought up his disagreements as accuser more than defendant. He had opposed the Party's new tactic of splitting the trade unions to form special "Red" or Communist trade unions. In this, too, the Party vindicated him a few years later—without reinstating him—by abolishing its separate unions.

Another difference that came out in the trial was one dealing with a recent attempt of the Party to play with the idea of an armed uprising. In Mexico, as we have seen, if you enter into a presidential campaign in earnest, you must be prepared at a certain stage of the election to convert your movement into an insurrection. Of course, the Communist Party was absurdly unprepared for such an attempt, but given to the fantastic and romantic and encouraged by certain dogmas of the new "line" of the Comintern, it proceeded to act as if it "meant business." Their paper gave the order to the peasants to prepare for armed resistance. However much Diego was given to fantasy, this was too much; he had opposed it by voice and vote. The net effect was that the government seized the issue of the paper calling for armed resistance, closed the printing plant, and began a series of arrests which partially outlawed the Party. By a strange logic, de Negri was regarded as responsible because he was closest of the Mexican politicians to the Party, and Rivera because he was friendly with de Negri. Diego did not improve matters by retorting that the Party itself was responsible because its stupidity had given the government an easy weapon.

Only after Diego was excommunicated and a war of words opened against him in the Mexican press did it occur to his erstwhile comrades that the best way to attack an artist is through his art. Now two new charges were added: he was accused of working on the public buildings of a bourgeois government, and of accepting from its hands the post of director of the School of Plastic Arts.

To the first Diego answered that he was painting on the walls of public buildings for the benefit of the masses, and his painting, being revolutionary in content, was of use to the people and the Party. How else, he demanded to know, could he paint for the disinherited in a non-Socialist society? What workers or peasants could purchase his pictures if he were to paint exclusively for private patrons? Here, too, the Party eventually bore him out by having its Revolutionary Union of Artists and Writers, like the analogous organizations in the United States, carry on a campaign for more public walls for painters.

In response to the second charge, he pointed out that the School of Plastic Arts was autonomous, and he had been elected by the mixed council of students and faculty. A little earlier, when President Portes Gil had offered to create the post of Minister of Fine Arts and make him a cabinet member, had he not declined, despite the good he might have been able to accomplish, because he did not want to assume responsibility for the acts of the government?

Diego did not relish a fight with the Communist Party. Communism, he felt, was the very heart of his mural painting, but politics in the narrow sense was a side issue. He was a "revolutionary artist" rather than "a revolutionist who sometimes painted." To paint was the law of his being. Only between spells of plastic activity, when he had worked himself to exhaustion, did he turn to "other forms of politics" as a sort of recreation. If the Party had expelled him and let him alone, he would have continued to paint as before and would have settled down into the relation of sympathizer which I had tried to establish for him. But it would not let him alone! It carried on a noisy campaign against him. The charges mounted continually in magnitude, forcing him to take time from his painting for self-defense, a futile and degrading occupation in view of the level on which the attack was conducted.

In 1936, while I was questioning the Party leadership and examining documents concerning Diego's trial, Rafael Carrillo, whom I had known as secretary of the Mexican Party and who was editor of *El Machete*, acknowledged that Diego should never have been expelled, asserting that if he, Carrillo, had not been in Cuba at the time, it would not have happened. After my discussion with Carrillo, *El Machete* recognized Rivera as an important artist, and criticized the League of Revolutionary Artists and Writers, which it controlled, for having excluded his works from their exhibition. "Naturally," it declared editorially, "the lack of pictures by David Alfaro Siqueiros and by other artists, the failure to undertake afresh the task of fixing the work of Diego Rivera in 1936, and simply ignoring what he is producing, are inexcusable."* But this cautious formulation, the first time Diego's name had been mentioned without insults in seven years, came too late. The Soviet trials and the series of great "purges" occurred during the course of the same spring, and Diego was aroused to hatred towards Stalin and Stalinism and all it represented.

In the autumn of the same year, Leon Trotsky, vainly seeking refuge in some European land since 1927, was ordered out of Norway. Prior to that he had been on the island of Prinkipo (Turkey) and in France. Still the pressure of the Russian government pursued him, and this time, when Norway ordered his departure,† there seemed to be no place on the face of the earth

* *El Machete,* June 10, 1936. Article signed: "The Editors."

† The Soviet Government secured his deportation from Trygve Lie, then Minister of Justice, by placing a large order for Norwegian herring.

for him to go. Country after country refused him a visa. Friends of Trotsky appealed to Diego to see if asylum might not be secured for him in Mexico. The painter went to interview President Cárdenas on behalf of the hunted exile. To his astonishment he got the desired permission. The Communist Party reopened its war on the painter. He had at last really become a Trotskyite.

In December 1936, Leon Trotsky became a personal guest of Diego's, residing, with Madame Trotsky, his secretaries, and bodyguard, in the home where Frida was born, at Coyoacán, a mile or so from the Rivera residence at San Angel.

The Trotskys and the Riveras did not see as much of each other as was generally imagined. They dined together occasionally, conferred lengthily by telephone, took several trips together through the countryside. But Diego was busy at his work and Trotsky at his, both being indefatigable at their chosen tasks. Being men of self-confidence and intense personal pride, their temperaments soon clashed. Trotsky could not stand Diego's fabulous fantasy, but for a time the painter deferred to the politician in the latter's field. For his part, Trotsky showed the increased interest in painting that came from intimacy with a great painter. The following, from an article of Trotsky's in 1938, gives some notion of the impact of Rivera's painting upon his guest:

> In the field of painting, the October Revolution has found her greatest interpreter not in the U.S.S.R. but in far-away Mexico, not among the official "friends," but in the person of a so-called "enemy of the people," whom the Fourth International is proud to number in its ranks. Nurtured in the artistic culture of all peoples, all epochs, Diego Rivera has remained Mexican in the most profound fibers of his genius. But that which inspired him in these magnificent frescoes, which lifted him up above the artistic tradition, above contemporary art, in a certain sense above himself, is the mighty blast of the proletarian revolution. Without October, his power of creative penetration into the epic of work, oppression and insurrection, would never have attained such

breadth and profundity. Do you wish to see with your own eyes the hidden springs of the social revolution? Look at the frescoes of Rivera. Do you wish to know what revolutionary art is like? Look at the frescoes of Rivera.

Come a little closer and you will see clearly enough gashes and spots made by vandals: Catholics and other reactionaries, including, of course, Stalinists.* These cuts and gashes give even greater life to the frescoes. You have before you, not simply a "painting," an object of passive aesthetic contemplation, but a living part of the class struggle. And it is at the same time a masterpiece!

Only the historical youth of a country which has not yet emerged from the struggle for national independence has allowed Rivera's revolutionary brush to be used on the walls of the public buildings of Mexico. In the United States it was more difficult. Just as the monks in the Middle Ages, through ignorance, it is true, erased antique literary productions from parchments to cover them with their scholastic ravings, just so Rockefeller's lackeys, but this time maliciously, covered the frescoes of the talented Mexican with their decorative banalities. This recent palimpsest will conclusively show future generations the fate of art degraded in a decaying bourgeois society.

The situation is no better, however, in the country of the October Revolution. Incredible as it seemed at first sight, there was no place for the art of Diego Rivera, either in Moscow, or in Leningrad, or in any other section of the U.S.S.R., where the bureaucracy born of the revolution was erecting grandiose palaces and monuments to itself. And how could the Kremlin clique tolerate in its kingdom an artist who paints neither icons representing the "leader" nor life-size portraits of Voroshilov's horse? The closing of the Soviet doors to Rivera will brand forever with an ineffaceable shame the totalitarian dictatorship.†

When he became the host of Leon Trotsky, the war on Rivera in *El Machete* became more furious than ever. Yet Diego continued to paint walls intended to serve Communist propaganda, and in the end, with Trotsky murdered, both Party and painter found it convenient to make up.

* So far as I have been able to observe, this charge is not justified.

† Leon Trotsky: "Arts and Politics," *Partisan Review* (August-September 1938).

21. DIEGO PICKS HIMSELF A COMRADE

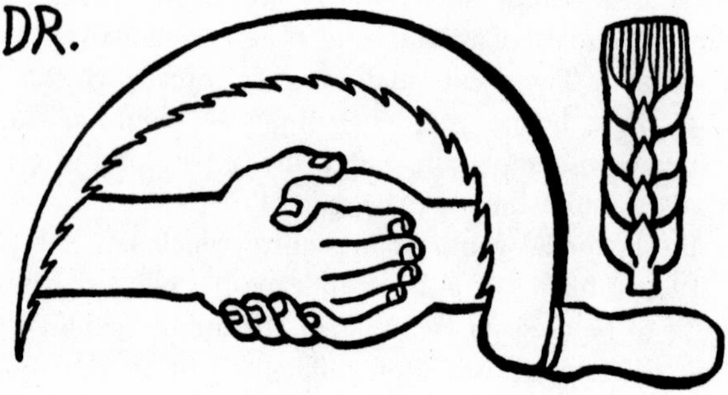

Diego first got to know Frida Kahlo as a mop-haired nuisance at the Preparatoria. She was thirteen then, a bright but neglectful student, a madcap tomboy, ringleader of a gang of mischievous youngsters of both sexes that kept the halls of the Preparatoria in turmoil. Unpopular professors were accompanied with so much noise that they were unable to make themselves heard; paper bags filled with air burst in the corridors; bags filled with water dropped mysteriously over partitions; once a home-made bomb exploded in a reverberating hall, throwing near-by classrooms into uproar; always the provosts would come too late to lay hands on the disappearing mop of Frida Kahlo, sure to have been somewhere near the center of the disturbance.

A photo of her at the time of her entrance into the Preparatoria (PLATE 89) reveals an almost boyish beauty, bright, audacious eyes, long-lashed under thick black eyebrows meeting like a bird's wings above her nose, full lips, black hair cropped short in accord with her hoydenish ways, an undefinable facial cast due to a mixture of German-Jewish and Mexican bloods. She consorted more with the boys of the school than the girls, in comradely rather than flirtatious relationships—though in matters of sex she was wise for her years. Her favorite companions were newsboys in the great city plaza, from whom she acquired a store of street Arab wisdom and the richest vocabulary of obscenities I have ever known one of her sex to possess. She climbed trees, stole fruit, just missed jail on one occasion for stealing a bicycle to take a "joy ride," displayed great ingenuity in devising pranks to plague policemen, professors, and others vested with authority.

At least twice, escapades of which she was the ringleader caused crises in the administration of the school. The second time she was expelled by Lombardo Toledano, then Director of the Preparatoria. She appealed to Minister of Education Vasconcelos: her scholastic record was so high, her appearance so disarming, that the Minister ordered her reinstatement. "If you can't manage a little girl like that," he told Lombardo, "you are not fit to be director of such an institution."

As soon as Frida set eyes on the huge painter who had installed himself in the auditorium, she made him a butt for pranks. She soaped the stairway down which he had to descend when he left the stage where he was painting, then hopefully hid herself behind a pillar. The slow, heavy-footed, work-weary painter planted each great foot so solidly that he didn't slip. She felt compensated only in part when the rector fell down the stairs at assembly next morning.

In those days, the painter was courting Lupe Marín, but on the scaffold he was likely to have any one of the girls who were posing for the mural—most frequently Nahui Olín, who, besides modeling for him, was a painter interested in his methods of work. The energetic Frida saw diverting possibilities in the succession of girls on the scaffold and proceeded to exploit them to the utmost. It was her delight to hide in a dark doorway when Lupe was with him, and call out: "*Oye Diego, ahí viene Nahui!*" Or when he was alone and she spied Lupe coming, she would stage whisper: "*Cuidado Diego, ahí viene Lupe!*"—as if she had been set to give some fair visitor warning.

A group of girl students were one day discussing their ambitions. When Frida's turn came she announced, "My ambition is to have a child by Diego Rivera. And I'm going to tell him so someday."

In time, after a perilous miscarriage in Detroit, followed by an abortion in Mexico and Diego's inexorable refusal to permit a further attempt, her girlhood desire was to become something of an obsession.

In those days Diego paid only casual and amused attention to the little nuisance who, unknown to herself, was developing a "crush" on him, giving vent to it by devising ways of annoying him. He set up house with Lupe and finished his mural at the Preparatoria; for years Frida and Diego saw no more of each other.

Some time after finishing her schooling, Frida met with a frightful auto accident. Her spine was injured, the pelvic bone fractured in three places, a foot and leg badly damaged. Surgeons who have examined the X-ray photos of the triply fractured pelvis found it difficult to believe that they could belong to the living and lively girl who stood before them. "By rights you should be dead," one of them put it to her in my presence.

For a whole year after the accident they did not know whether her bones would mend sufficiently for her ever to walk again. The once irrepressible girl lay flat on her back, strapped to a board, encased in a plaster cast. Desperate with the endless tedium, thoughts racing and roving and deepening since they could not find outlet in immediate action, she underwent a profound metamorphosis in character. It is questionable whether the painter known as Frida Kahlo would have existed were it not for that year of suffering and constraint.

In her boredom she called for paints, brushes, an easel stand within reach of her arms, which alone were free. She had never painted, nor received any special instruction, but, like most Mexican children, she had imagination and a sense of form and color. Her brushwork, from the beginning, was delicate and sensitive. Strapped to the board, not only were her hands free, but her fantasy also; out of the trying ordeal she came forth a painter. When she was able to walk again and had accumulated a few canvases, she remembered the artist she used to tease in the Preparatoria. He was painting now on the top floor of the Secretariat of Education, where she sought him out.

"*Oiga Diego, baje usted*—Hey, Diego, come down here," a voice called to him without any preliminaries; though a newfound bashfulness had made her use the polite form in place of the familiar *tu* which formerly she had employed. She was eighteen now and quite a young lady. Looking down from his high perch at the slender girl with a faint determined flush on her cheeks, Diego did not recognize his old tormentor. "*Venga! Baje usted!*" she repeated with increasing insistence. He climbed down.

From behind her back she drew forth a square of canvas, making a quaint, abrupt little speech as she presented it for inspection. "Listen, Diego," she told him, "I don't want any compliments. I would appreciate your honest opinion and any advice you may be good enough to offer."

The painter's eyes flashed a recognition of talent. "Keep it up, little girl," he said at last. "It's good, except the background of this one—too much Doctor Atl. Have you any more?"

"*Sí, señor*, but it would be hard for me to carry them all here. I live in Coyoacán, Calle de Londres 127. Would you care to call on me next Sunday?"

"I'd be delighted," said Diego. Next Sunday, spruced up beyond his wont, he called. He found her perched on a low orange tree in the patio, from which he had to help her down. Thus began their friendship.

Frida had just joined the Young Communist League. Almost at once Diego painted her into a mural, the *Insurrection* panel of the *Ballad of the Proletarian Revolution:* close-cropped hair, thick heavy eyebrows meeting over a little poodle nose, an unfeminine khaki shirt open at the throat with a red star on it, standing in the center of a group of *insurrectos* handing out rifles and bayonets (PLATE 93). "You have a dog-face," he told her as he painted. "And you," she retorted, "have the face of a frog!" *Carasapo*—Frog-face—became her favorite name for him from that time forward, varied with the epithet *Panzas*—Fatbelly—and sometimes the tenderer *Dieguito*. With such compliments they understood each other and were chummy and comradely from the outset.

"Diego has a new girl," I said as I examined the reproduction of the mural when Rafael Carrillo, passing through New York on the way to Moscow, brought it to me as a present. Certainly there was nothing in the severe lines of the skirt, the long neck, the aspect of an adolescent boy, to tell me so; yet somehow I sensed it.

"You're right, I guess. She's a nice kid. Bright as an eagle. A member of the Young Communist League. Only eighteen. Her name's Carmen Frida Kahlo."

Frida was only one of several candidates for the place left vacant by his break with Guadalupe Marín, for Diego's fame and attractive ugliness seemed a magnet to women. The whole city knew he had broken with Lupe; she had seen to that. While he was in Russia she had told everyone who would listen that he was a pig and without shame, and that he had gone to Moscow never to return, abandoning her with her two young daughters.

I told your sister María to take your things [she wrote to him, trying to arouse his ire] and she did not want to because she has no place to put them. Pablo [probably Paul O'Higgins] does not want to either. No one, no one wants to take your things. Perhaps they will keep them in the Legation [of the Soviet Union]. But you must arrange that. I have two children and cannot be bothered with anything else. I want to move the 15th of April, and if there is no one to take your things, I have thought of giving the pictures to Ramón Martínez; as for the rest, *I will throw it out*. . . .

Probably by that date I shall have married Jorge Cuesta in civil marriage. . . .* In the midst of all these people who have treated me most vilely, he is the only one from whom I have kindness. Even though he seems very intelligent to me [she means *intellectual*—with her a term of reproach] and even though he seems too young, perhaps I shall accept. I don't know if you will like to see us together; but as for me, it does not bother me at all with whom you may happen to be living.

I believe that if you ever return to Mexico, you will have to know the environment which is being made for you here. For everybody says you are vile [*canalla*] and shameless and not much of a man, etc. But those who say it are for me even worse, and it is necessary for you to know how they think of you before you speak with them.

Guadalupe

At no time in his life did Diego have so many affairs as during the year that elapsed from the time of his return from Russia in the summer of 1928 to the summer of 1929. There was the void created by his separation from Lupe—a great void, for she had been model and mistress, source of aesthetic and human satisfaction, a powerful combination to that artist who in his early manhood had written to Renato Paresce that his one ambition was to paint *la beauté devenue femme*. The void was deeper for the disillusion he had experienced in Russia.

It was a year, too, in which he was to paint an abundance of nudes. His frescoes in the Assembly Hall of the Health Building in Mexico City, like the theme of *Germination* and *Fructification* in the Agricultural School, seemed to him to call for

* Lupe and Diego were not legally married, hence no divorce was necessary. They had been married by the Church, but in Mexico only a civil marriage is legal.

a series of nudes, supplemented by decorations of a hand holding voluptuously curving bundles of ripe wheat, another thrusting from the ground, uplifting a great ripe sunflower, and a panel of a young plant sprouting, phallus-shaped, out of the ground. Frida persuaded her sister Cristina to pose for the idyllic and mischievous *Knowledge* (PLATE 96); a second nude portrayed *Strength*, full-breasted, great-fisted and thighed, rough-chiseled and muscular, recumbent on the ground; a third, *Purity*, was seated where a gushing stream of pure water fell into her hand; on the ceiling a nude flew, face downward (Cristina again being the model), representing *Life;* another seated, hands extended in hieratic gesture, was labeled *Health;* not far from the figure of *Purity*, was a slender nude of big boned frame, reclining, eyes closed as if in sleep, holding in her hands a snake whose body, running between her knees, terminated in an erect head with forked projecting tongue, the snake throat firmly grasped in her right hand, the whole representing, not without overtones of irony, the figure of *Continence*. There is nothing aphrodisiac in these voluptuous curves, these unashamed and cleanly painted naked bodies, symbols of knowledge, of life, health, and strength, purity and continence. Still less is there anything of asceticism, merely an understanding and straightforward avowal of the role of sex in life, and a faint, ironical overtone of that sense of the comic inseparable from sex in the Mexican mind. Pornography requires more of a feeling of guilt and denial, aphrodisiac painting implies more of a sense of repression and impotence, than is to be found anywhere in the work of Rivera or his thought or manner of living.

During the time of which we are speaking, Diego had various love affairs—the term covering everything from the most casual encounters to passionate or comradely relationships. These included at least one of the models for the nudes at the Health Building; a brief idyl with a beautiful indigenous girl in Tehuantepec, where Diego went in quest of themes for his paintings; a talented young woman high in official circles whose portrait he painted; several American girls who came to study painting in Mexico; and others whose influence does not show directly in his painting, and who do not concern us.

Some of them had no thought of a permanent relationship; two or three dreamed of becoming the wife of a celebrated painter. One, when she saw that she was not to be his bride and fancied, erroneously, that he was the source of gossip about her, wrote a tart note which began: "Diego—I came to Mexico to paint and not to pose!" To the wounded vanity of this girl, who later married a prominent American intellectual of the Left, Diego attributed—wrongfully in my opinion—much of the ill will he met the following year in American radical circles.

During the same period the friendship between him and Frida was slowly ripening. He discussed her painting with her, then finding that her taste was swift and sure, began asking for her opinion of his own work. So far as I know, he never thus consulted any other person, man or woman, in the years of his maturity. Expressed shrewdly, with tentative interrogation, her verdict was at times quite unfavorable. Then he would grumble or grow bearish, but in a few minutes, or next day, he would alter the offending detail. In the course of succeeding years he became more and more anxious for her approval and dependent upon her sensitive judgment.

He fell into the habit of knocking off work Sunday afternoons and taking a taxi to her home in Coyoacán. After three or four visits her father called him aside. Old Mr. Kahlo was a German-Jewish photographer, skilled in his craft, placid and knowing in his philosophy of life. He had come to Mexico as a young man, married a native girl, and permitted her to bring up his daughters as Mexicans and Catholics.

"I see you are interested in my daughter?"

"Why, yes," stammered Diego, anticipating something not altogether agreeable. "Yes, of course, otherwise I would not come all the way out here to see her. . . ."

"Well, sir, I want to give you a warning. Frida is a clever girl, but she is *un demonio oculto*—a concealed devil. *Un demonio oculto!*" He solemnly repeated the epithet a second time, with still greater emphasis.

"I know it," replied Diego.

"Well, I have done my duty." The old man said no more.

Artistic and intellectual circles in Mexico City (in which, by courtesy, we will include journalism) constitute a great whispering gallery of gossip and scandal. Among the rumors clustering around Diego was one of a coming engagement to the daughter of a minister of an earlier regime. This gained sufficient currency to appear as an official report in the Mexican press on the very day when the following item (authentic except for the spelling of the name of the girl involved) appeared in the *New York Times*:

DIEGO RIVERA MARRIES

Noted Mexican Painter and Labor Leader Weds Frida Kohlo

Mexico City, Aug. 23 (AP). Announcement was made today that Diego Rivera, internationally known painter and labor leader, was married on Wednesday to Frida Kohlo in Coyoacan, a suburb of Mexico City.*

Diego was going on forty-three; and his new bride had just turned nineteen.

Lupe meanwhile had married again, though her second marriage was to turn out more disastrous than the first, and in the end she was to look back gratefully to the time she had spent with Diego. The young man Lupe married was penniless, and though Diego let them live in his house until they should be in better circumstances, and promised to contribute to the sup-

* Issue of August 23, 1929.

port of his two daughters, Lupe was worried. On November 2, she wrote to her successor, in lieu of a letter of congratulations:

Frida:

It disgusts me to take pen in hand to write you. But I want you to know that neither you nor your father nor your mother has a right to anything of Diego's. Only his children are the ones whom he has the obligation to maintain (and among them count Marica, to whom he has never sent a penny!)

Guadalupe

As for the last parenthesis, Lupe herself knew it was untrue —she had grumbled more than once over his sending money to France—but she was not one to be careful of the accuracy of her remarks when trying to hurt somebody's feelings.

Her relations with Frida were not too friendly. She preceded the note just quoted by a visit under circumstances that became celebrated. Pretending to be indifferent about Diego's love affairs, she hinted that she would be "broadminded" enough to attend his wedding. It was a simple civil ceremony—strictly speaking, the first time he had been married according to Mexican law—and no one was present but the required witnesses and officials. But Frida guilelessly invited Lupe to a party they gave afterwards to a few friends and relatives. She came, pretended to be very gay, then in the midst of the festivities, strode suddenly up to Frida, lifted high the new bride's skirt, and shouted to the assembled company: "You see these two sticks? There are the legs Diego has now instead of mine!" Then she marched out of the house in triumph.

Diego did more than pay unofficial alimony. Whenever Lupe wanted extra funds for some special purpose, he found ways of providing them. When she wanted to go to France, remembering his old promise to take her there in the days of his wooing, he "purchased" from her some Aztec and Tarascan idols which she had retained from his collection. Paris she found a veritable wonderland. She wrote letters to Diego and Frida, telling of visits with Elie Faure, her contempt for Ilya Ehrenburg, her seeing Diego's child Marika ("her nose and mouth are just like her mother's; her eyes large and sad like those of the papa she is suspected to have; it gave me much sadness to see her; she is a child who, one can see, has never been happy"); her meeting Picasso, Kisling, Barrés, Carpentier, and other friends of Diego's.

One of her letters (January 16, 1933) records a visit to Angelina Beloff, Diego's Russian wife:

> I must tell you, Frida, that I don't like Angelina Beloff at all. I think she is good because she hasn't enough imagination to be bad; she is a person who has nothing in common with me nor does she interest me in the slightest. I can't understand how Diego ever lived with her. She and —— * believe that I did not know Diego at all, at all. When we speak together I see that for them he is one Diego and for me another. You know that everything depends upon the crystal through which one looks.

In another letter (May 29, 1933) she tells of visiting the gallery of Léonce Rosenberg to see Diego's cubist paintings, and of negotiating to purchase some for the picture gallery she will open in Mexico. The negotiations fell through. The same letter expresses regret that she cannot speak French "to be able to speak evil of you, *Panzas*," and urges Frida to join her for a month in Paris.

Diego and Frida were living in the United States at the time of Lupe's trip. When she passed through New York, they invited her to stay in their apartment on Thirteenth Street. So cordial had their relations become that Lupe accepted.

I visited them at the time and can testify that the atmosphere in this peculiar *ménage à trois* of the painter, his past wife, and

* Here she gives the name of the woman in Mexican governmental circles already referred to.

his present one was amiable. Lupe's hurt vanity and any deeper wounds she may have suffered were long healed: she rather gloried in her freedom and in having been the wife of Mexico's much-talked-of painter.

Three years later I had a still more curious experience, when I visited Diego's sister-in-law, Cristina, and found there Frida, Lupe, and Angelina Beloff, and a fourth woman who had been briefly his sweetheart. I don't know what occasion brought them all together, but hearing that I was working on his biography, they joined in dispassionately dissecting the painter as husband, friend, and lover. After analyzing his faults, they all agreed in speaking well of him. Even Lupe, who began the conversation by telling me that she would recount "horrors" to put in my book, had no more to tell than that she had to scrub him in the tub or he would never bathe, that he was so busy painting that he proved a neglectful husband, and that there was always a horde of "disgusting females" fluttering around him, flattering him, offering themselves, but that he "took what was offered" without letting it turn his head or interrupt his painting. Lupe it was who ended by telling me how much more considerate and comradely he was than other Mexican men, which she attributed to his long absence from the Mexican environment and his "education" in France. Frida sat listening in quiet amusement and saying little, while Angelina merely repeated, "He's just a child, a great big child!"

As I studied the three who had been his wives, I realized how different had been the role of each. Angelina, several years his senior, gentle, soft, maternal, had played mother along with wife to his young manhood. Lupe, savage, stately, extraordinarily beautiful, had been model and mistress to the years of his early maturity. It is noteworthy that he has never done a nude of either Angelina or Frida. During their courtship, Frida secured as his models for the Health Building her sister Cristina, diminutive, rounder, plumper, and two of her girl friends, but served then and later only for clothed models, and that only rarely.

Angelina was all gentleness and kindness; about her was the mark of patience and resignation. Lupe was instinctive femininity, self-centered, demanding, restless for she knew not what depths and heights of sensation and experience, but, for lack of integration in her feelings and views on life, taking it out in a quest for notoriety through scandal. Frida, the vicissitudes of whose life with Diego we shall follow further, played, as the others did not, the role of companion, confidante, and comrade, subordinating her life to his needs as man and painter, and becoming his most intelligent and respected critic. Before the fateful seven years were up that seemed to obey some obscure rhythmic need of Diego's nature, this third marriage, too, was to be strained to the breaking point. But a fresh adjustment was made in time and, with ups and downs, quarrels and strayings by both, their need of and dependence on each other continued until Frida's death. Her last words and acts were full of fierce devotion to the painter she loved and worshiped.

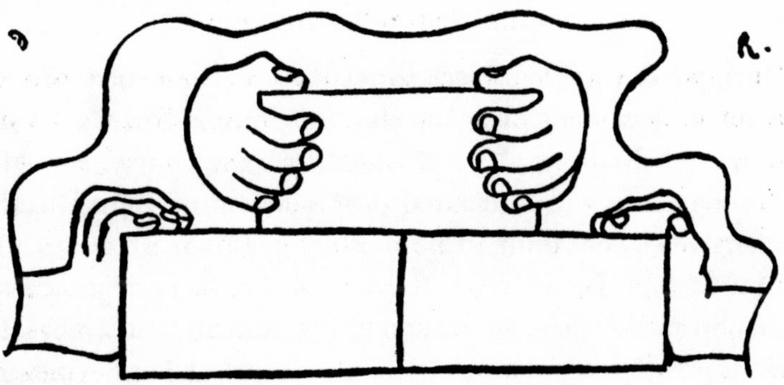

22. A SCHOOL TO TURN OUT SUPERMEN

More than a quarter of a century after he was expelled from the San Carlos Academy, Diego Rivera returned as its Director, elected to that post by the art students, as was the custom. He had become, at the moment, a sort of people's artist. The President offered to create a cabinet post for him. The patio and stairway of the National Palace were awarded to him for decoration.

Letters rained upon him, letters of felicitation with an eye to appointment to the faculty, letters suggesting reforms in the system of instruction, letters from cranks, from people with an ax to grind, from intelligent and zealous men.

Without pausing to reflect or prepare the ground, without stopping his unceasing painting, Diego set out to make a revolution in the Academy. His first action brought the faculty down about his ears, for he established a regime whereby the professoriate, its personnel and methods, were put to the discussion and vote of the student body!

Next, he drafted a project for reform of the course of study that must have made even the statues adorning San Carlos raise eyebrows of disapproval. It provided that the courses should be subordinated to and integrated into a system of apprenticeship; teachers who were unfit to be masters in this master-apprentice system were to be replaced; the school was to be regarded as a workshop rather than an academy; the students, on completing their apprenticeship, had to remain affiliated as journeymen and be given an opportunity to carry out a year of work on some governmental commission, utilizing the materials and workshops of the school for the purpose; they were to regard themselves as skilled craftsmen or technical workers exercising plastic trades and constituted into a Union of Workers in the Plastic Arts; the first three years should be carried on at night so that all pupils could spend the day in shop or factory as workingmen; those who showed aptitude might then enter an advanced five-year day-and-night course of study and apprenticeship; the school must be open to glass workers, foundry workers, engravers, who should be permitted to attend as special students the courses that might serve their craft; each course should end, not with formal examinations, but with a competition and the execution of a practical work by each pupil, embodying the theoretical and technical instruction involved in the course in question; and many more such innovations.

The curriculum the new Director proposed was a work of exuberant fantasy. It was to train men (and women) who were to be skilled factory workers, painters, sculptors, architects, builders, interior decorators, engravers, masters of monumental painting, of ceramics, typography, photography, lithography, and much more besides, all in one and the same person. After they had mastered all these arts and crafts, they might specialize according to their bent. But before they could be specialists, they must be universal artists in the fashion of a Leonardo da Vinci.

For the first three years they were to work in a factory by

day, and study in San Carlos at night: study the various branches of mathematics, mechanical drawing, modeling in various materials, architectonics, drawing and painting as applied to their manual trade, the "beautifying of their dwellings and clothing," the appreciation of "vegetable, animal, and human forms," the ability to construct these forms in various media, carving in stone and wood, forging of metals, modeling in wax for casting, designing of furniture, perspective, carpentry, "composition of abstract forms destined for architecture," the application of plastic creation to the necessities of life, objects of daily use, interiors, exteriors, the arts of book-making. Lest time hang heavy on their hands, "Saturday afternoons and Sunday mornings" would be filled with "a series of lectures by the professors and the most capable pupils" to develop their esthetic education. All this was merely preparatory to their serious training in day courses for the next five (in some cases six) years, after they had completed their three years of night study.

The day courses were essentially more of the same on a higher level, but some new subjects were added, among them "human mechanics," study of materials, "social theory of the arts," "animal mechanics." The would-be nonmonumental painters would take five years of such courses, the monumental painters, six.

All through the eight or nine years of night and day study there were to run "free workshops of plastic specialization." For the monumental painter and sculptor was to be added in the final years four hours a day of work in the section of decorative painting, four hours a day as apprentice to a master of monumental painting, and finally, three hours a day in the last year to be employed in the execution of original monumental work. Not for nothing did Frida write of Diego that he was "an enemy of all clocks and calendars." What clock would yield so many hours? What calendar so many days? What physique support such labors?

A final note to the huge, many-paged curriculum sought to answer these questions:

> It has been borne in mind that both the work of apprenticeship and the professional work of the painter, sculptor, or engraver, have the double character of manual and intellectual work which demands a great quantity of method and physical strength, and that from the pupil must be required great determination, enthusiasm, and love for the art he practices. If these conditions are lacking, it is preferable for society that he exercise any other functions rather than those of the artist. . . .

The program envisaged a race of physical giants, with the enormous physical strength, talents and appetite for labor of a Diego Rivera, and the versatility of a Leonardo da Vinci. Not only the pupils, but the teachers, too, would have to be combinations of a Da Vinci and a Rivera. The pupils would be so deeply enmeshed in the task of becoming omnivorous, omniscient, and omnicompetent, that it is hard to see where they would have strength or time left over to become that highly specialized and highly individualized being, an artist with a style of his own.

Ever since Diego first heard of the versatile life of Leonardo da Vinci and dipped into his notebooks, he had born a grudge against the art school for the narrow specialization which he fancied it had forced upon him. Beginning with the shock of that realization and ending only with his death, Diego was to make many attempts to broaden the range of his creative powers and activities. He designed a stone fountain for a co-operative village near Chapingo, did polychrome low reliefs for the walls of the National Stadium, designed two beautifully carved wooden doors for the Chapingo Chapel, constructed four stained-glass windows in the Health Building in Mexico City, drafted architectural plans for a monumental theater in Vera Cruz, which was never built, and for his own pyramid museum, for which he also directed the construction, designed some sculpture and mosaic decorations. When he painted the outlet of the Lerma Canal, he added some pseudo-archaic, polychrome, high-relief sculpture in its portico. But none of these adventures in the other arts was notably successful or added anything to his stature as an artist. Only the stained-glass windows, the wood carving in Chapingo, and the mosaics in his pyramid even hint at the fact that they are the work of a great draftsman and colorist.

The first skirmish in the war to revolutionize the training of the artists of Mexico Diego won easily. Whether they didn't read it or just didn't understand what they were letting themselves in for, the students enthusiastically approved the new curriculum. And with misgivings the faculty approved it also. It was then proposed in the name of both faculty and student body to the University Council, which routinely gave its approval. The forces of opposition, surprised by the suddenness, daring, and sweep of the attack, now began to gather their forces for resistance.

The old Convent of San Carlos was shared by two independent schools, each attached to the autonomous University of Mexico: two schools that even in the best of times cohabited with ill-concealed animosity: the School of Fine Arts and the School of Architecture. The architects were more numerous, wealthier, more respectable, more conservative than the painters. Painting had been transformed by the revolutionary currents of thought and practice that men like Diego had brought into it; architecture had remained imitative, orthodox, eclectic. The painters were mostly poor devils who thought of themselves as craftsmen. The architects, thanks to the system of building prevailing in Mexico, were closely linked up with building contractors, often acting directly as contractors, with their architecture a subsidiary function, hiring the laborers and purchasing the materials themselves. Sometimes they bought the land and built the houses on a speculative basis. They felt themselves entrepreneurs, if not capitalists.

True, a revolt was beginning among the younger architects, headed by Juan O'Gorman and other youthful pupils of the transitional master, José Villagrán García, who had just been invited to teach in the National Academy by a group of younger men destined to make architectural history in the next decade. But for the moment they represented a minority. Even as late as 1936 the "modernist style" was successfully prohibited by law in many quarters of Mexico City! *

The professors in the Academy of Architecture, and the leading practicing architects, had never lost any love on Diego. They did not like his painting nor that of his colleagues. He had repeatedly poked fun at their proudest (and most absurd) achievements, such as the Italian National Theater, the Venetian Post Office, the blends of Versailles, Baroque, Greco-Roman, Oriental, Operatic, and Gingerbread in the more elegant homes they had constructed along the Paseo de la Reforma and in the new Hipódromo section of the city. He had defeated their leaders in a battle over the design for the National Stadium. He had taken the side of the younger men and their "functional style." Now, when he added to his faculty Juan O'Gorman, who thought that every painter should be something of an architect and every architect something of a painter, and he proposed courses that overlapped their precious preserves, they saw designs for imperialist annexation.

Clashes began between the more numerous student body of the school of architects and the less numerous students of painting and sculpture. The architects secured allies among the conservative professors of Diego's own faculty, and sent declarations to the press against him. They petitioned the University Council to rescind its approval of the curriculum and they petitioned the President to oust the School of the Plastic Arts from San Carlos, on the ground that the old building was not big enough for both of them.

Diego multiplied his public lectures and newspaper interviews on the state of Mexican architecture. He gave interviews, defensive and offensive. The students of architecture told the reporters

* It has been victorious since, only to add to the eclectic mixture in the newer *colonias* of Mexico City.

that they would exercise "direct action" against his "infamous" paintings in the courtyard of the National Palace." * Diego responded that he was armed, and ready for them: he began wearing two pistols on the scaffold and crossed cartridge belts; his assistants appeared armed. "I do not retract a word of my criticisms," he told the press. "With the new plan of studies we are not trying to make architects, but to teach painters and sculptors the amount of architecture necessary to their craft. . . . The courses will be entrusted to excellent architects . . . for what interests me most in the arts is precisely good architecture." †

The architects, students, faculty, and professional groups began raining attacks upon the Director of the School of Plastic Arts. They charged that he was a "false revolutionist," getting their ammunition from the Communist Party, which had just expelled him, and giving wide publicity to every calumny against him. He was a millionaire, they asserted, compelling him to make public the pitiful sums derived from his mural painting and the size of his modest bank account in American dollars derived from the sale of canvases in the United States.

DIEGO RIVERA WANTS TO BE THE MUSSOLINI
OF THE ARTISTS

read one newspaper headline. ‡

He had charged them with being imitative; Lorenzo Fabela of their faculty responded by calling him a "stepson of Gauguin." Some students gave out an interview attacking his craftsmanship by saying that they had not made good their threat to destroy his murals by direct action because his "encaustics" (sic!) in the Education Building were so badly painted that time would soon do the work for them.

Battles between students of architecture and students of painting became a daily occurrence. Appeals against Diego were

* *Universal Gráfico,* April 2, 1930.
† Press release by Diego Rivera, April 2, 1930.
‡ *El Universal,* April 11, 1930.

made to every conceivable authority. Soon all his enemies—he did not know till now that he had so many—from the Communist Party and conservative painters to architecture students and faculty, were banded against him. Twenty-three charges were brought against him in the University Council. On May 10, 1930, less than eight months after he set out to revolutionize art instruction in Mexico, the coalesced bands of opposition were victorious.

Even in defeat Diego was powerful. They elected to succeed him a man who had no experience in the arts, but who had a reputation for radicalism, Vicente Lombardo Toledano (the same Lombardo who was Director of the Preparatoria when he painted there, and who today is a leader of every Communist fellow traveler movement). In his speech of acceptance, the new Director pledged himself "to implant the revolutionary program of Diego Rivera." But of course, nothing came of it. In a short time, "the counter-revolution" was triumphant in the Academy.

23.

PALACES AND MILLIONAIRES

When the walls of the National Palace were offered to Diego—great walls facing and flanking a monumental stairway which rises by steps of low gradient from the ground floor of a large inner court, dividing at the end of the first flight into a right and left staircase—the expanse of wall and the nature of the building suggested to the painter the most ambitious undertaking of his career. He would paint the epic of his people.

The first, the right-hand wall, he would use to paint the indigenous civilization, its myths and legends, temples and palaces, culture and conflicts, arts and crafts—the poetry and dew of morning that seemed to him to surround that civilization before the Spanish conqueror came. On the broad deep central wall at the head of the stairs, with its six rounded arches and inverted, truncated-pyramidal base, he would paint the history of his country from the Conquest to the present, the color and pageantry, the heroism and cruelty, sublimity and folly, woven into the life of the land. At the base he would paint the ruthlessness and power of the Conquest on which the Hispano-Indian culture rested: above, the struggles for independence, the wars of the *Reforma* between Conservatives and Liberals, between Church and State, culminating in the two outermost arches with the battle for independence against the French, and the heroic lost fight against the Yankee invader from the north. Moving inward toward the middle, in the wide curves of the four central arches, the aspirations, struggles, and contending parties of the Revolution of 1910, the crowded, blood-stained years of Madero, Huerta, Carranza, Obregón, and Calles, to the very eve of the day he began the work.

On the left-hand wall, still vague and indistinct in his mind, he would paint the Mexico of tomorrow, an image of the Utopia of his dreams.

Where in all painting was there a comparable project? There would be no Justice holding her scales, no Liberty raising her torch or posing on barricades, no "Washington-crossing-the-Delaware" episodes. Traces there still were of this mode of representation in his first conception, but most of these were eliminated in the course of the gestation of the work. His figures would have to represent social forces, whole epochs incarnated in the country's representative men, popular heroes and villains. Along with the recognizable figures there would be nameless representatives of generations of Indian warriors, slaves, peons, guerrilla fighters, actors through whose blind movements leaders were raised up and history made.

All he knew of his land and its history, all he could learn by study and taking thought, he put into his work—not merely all he knew, but all he felt and sensed, gloried in or thought worthy of contempt or shame. Was this not the Nation's palace? Was it not fitting then that the whole nation, its past, present, and "inevitable" future, should live on these palace walls?

Six years he was to labor on it—or all his life until 1955, two years before his death, if we include the walls of the corridors—draining himself again and again, always seeking rest and restoration in lesser works. Many of these "lesser" works, be it added, were such as only a giant of strength and fecundity could paint. He finished a mural dealing with one aspect of the same theme (the Conquest) in Cuernavaca, went twice to the United States to paint, to store up fresh strength and win time for further contemplation of some new part of the plan. Alternately the responsible authorities cajoled, coaxed, threatened that some *pintorcillo* (dauber) would be employed to finish it, urged that it be completed at least "in time for the next President's inauguration." Three Presidents came and went, and a fourth was assuming the chair before the work came to an end.

When at last he finished, it was not a painting but a world on a wall. It became a treasure mine of iconography for future historians of Mexico. An archaeologist of the future could use it to learn more of Mexico, actual and legendary, than any other single monument in history would reveal of any other civilization.

The first history of Mexico written after Rivera finished, that of Alfonso Teja Zabre,* was illustrated with these murals and details from them, and followed Rivera's plan, spirit, and point of view. Critics called it a "Dieguesque history of Mexico," and the author acknowledged the debt. But Teja Zabre's book lacked Diego's courage: it did not bring the history of the country quite up to date nor analyze critically, as the murals did, the power of the moment, the Calles regime.†

* Alfonso Teja Zabre, *Guide to the History of Mexico: A Modern Interpretation* (Mexico City, Press of the Ministry of Foreign Affairs, 1935). The book was published in Spanish, English and French. The French edition contains the best illustrations.

† Calles was no longer President when Diego undertook the work, but he was Mexico's "strong man" (*caudillo*), the power behind the presidential chair, maker and unmaker of its successive occupants from Portes Gil to Cárdenas. The last, in 1936, threw off the Calles yoke and deported him from Mexico. The stairway mural was completed while Calles was still boss, but it portrays in unflattering terms both him and his puppets, and his partners in the development of the lucrative Callista industries and monopolies, along with the usual lay figures of villainy of Communist propaganda.

It is interesting to compare the sketch (PLATE 100) with the finished fresco. There may be some who imagine that a monumental work is born fully fashioned in the brain of the painter and executed exactly as first planned. Actually, the painter "thinks with his hand," continues to alter his plan even after it is sketched on the wall. A change in one detail suggests changes in another, sometimes a tiny alteration spreads in widening ripples throughout the work. The amazing thing about this sketch is not how much it was altered in execution, but how little. True, it was not the first, but the last sketch done before the actual painting began. Yet how swiftly the vast conception must have ripened in his brain, with what heat been conceived, to be so fully planned at the outset of six years of work! The first wall, as a comparison between PLATES 101 and 102 will show, is designed almost exactly as it was to be executed. The middle wall was to suffer but few changes, the most important being the removal of the allegorical figure of Mexico as a sheltering mother embracing worker and peasant, for the more vital conception of a group of agrarian leaders and martyrs (José Guadalupe Rodríguez, Carrillo Puerto, and Zapata), culminating in the figure of a worker who points for them, over the heads of Calles and Obregón, to Karl Marx on the opposite wall.

The principal changes, however, are in the left wall. And this is natural, since the painter had six years to study and consider the contemporary Mexico he was to portray, years of growing stability and reaction, so that when he came finally to paint it, his last illusions had been dissipated and the negative features of the Calles regime were sharp in his mind. They were years, too, in which he had gone to the United States, and having been in contact with a land of great industry, he could no longer be contented with a tractor, a crane, an airplane, and the return of the feathered serpent as symbols of the recurrence of primitive tribal communism on a higher social level. Painted after he had done the belt conveyers of Detroit and the class-struggle panels of the New Workers' School, this last wall shows their influence and is the distillation of things seen and felt in industrial America.

Art historians have read social attitudes into works of Courbet, David, Delacroix, Van Gogh, Millet, Meunier, Steinlein, Kollwitz, but their paintings and drawings are expressions of social moods rather than of an elaborate ideology. In contradistinction to them, Diego had set out in his complicated and somewhat baroque fashion to express on the walls of the National Palace the complete ideology of Marxist communism. Neither in contemporary Russian nor West European nor American painting, nor in the whole history of art, is there anything to compare with it . . . except perhaps the body of Christian doctrine expressed in "sacred painting." Even the earlier work of Rivera himself does not have the same ideological intention or ideological complexity. His celebration of labor and festival and revolution on the walls of the Secretariat of Education are in this respect but the culmination of nineteenth-century "social" painting, the work of a communist who is painting, not of a painter who is trying to express the complete ideology of twentieth-century communism.

Only after the Russian Revolution could this history of Mexico have been conceived, although, ironically, nothing like it could be painted in the land where that revolution occurred. In the Soviet Union, "revolutionary painting" consists of glorified Lenins towering larger than life over an obedient and worshipful humanity to whom the mighty man gives marching orders, or of bemedaled Stalins looking like Gulliver in the midst of Lilliputians, or of smoking factories, marching myrmidons, and socialistic Sputniks that scatter hammers and sickles amidst the stars. Done with execrable taste, the officially approved paintings and drawings express the execrable ideological clichés of totalitarianism.

Rivera's ideology was crude and fragmentary enough, but in comparison with what passes for socialist painting in Russia, the framework of his National Palace mural is complex in the extreme.

The past, present and future of Mexico are presented as a dialectical march from the glories of primitive, pre-Conquest, Aztec "tribal communism," through the valley of the shadow of Conquest, with its implantation of slavery, feudalism, and capitalism, and its class struggle, or a succession of such struggles, serving as history's driving force, until Mexico climbs once more into the sunlit upland of Marxian Communism, based upon modern industry and a classless society.

The painter strove valiantly to stick to his thesis. He made an attempt to suggest the social role of the nameless masses and the social role of the heroes and villains of his country's history. Armed with the value system of communist thought he strove to make a critical evaluation of Mexico's illustrious and notorious men, and the bright and dark pages of her story. But—fortunately—as he painted, his own visions and feelings and dreams ran away with his ideology. It was not Diego's fault if his dream of Mexico before the Conquest is larger and brighter than life, and his dream of the future society remote and dim and uninspiring.

The painting gained in artistry what it lost in ideology. The history of his country as he knew and felt it was richer, more complicated, at once brighter and darker than that required by his abstract formulas. Nor is it the painter's fault if Marx was a less appealing figure to him that Quetzalcoatl. Still his painting does culminate spatially and diagrammatically in Marx, shown with a full beard and a full quota of appropriate quotations, pointing a monitory hand towards a hill on which can be seen a factory, an orchard, and an observatory—the unattractive *Mexico of the Future*.

With a singular perversity, it was precisely this work of Diego's, the most "Marxist" work in the history of art, that the Communist Party of the United States selected for attack when the painter left Mexico for New York.

First they attacked the site. Rivera was a "painter of palaces" (was the building not called the National Palace?). They ignored the savage critique of the Mexico of the Callista regime painted on the very walls of the presidential palace to charge that he was glorifying the reactionary government of Mexico by painting for it on one of its buildings.

Next they set for one of their writers the task of attacking the very changes Diego had made in order to make the painting more consistently Communist. Diego's earlier sketch had culminated in a picture of Mexico as a nourishing mother, sheltering in her arms a worker and a peasant. His final painting substituted for this empty allegorical theme the portrait of three agrarian revolutionaries and martyrs, with a worker to point out for them the figure of Karl Marx on the left wall, as the road to the Mexico of the future.

Joseph Freeman, writing under the pen name of Robert Evans, was given the task of showing in the *New Masses* of February 1932 that Rivera had been a revolutionary painter until the moment of his expulsion from the Party, and had at that instant ceased to be one. The "proof" was given in the following words:

> The original design for the mural in the National Palace showing Mexico as a gigantic woman holding a worker and peasant in her arms was altered. For the worker and peasant, no doubt a painful sight to government officials who pass the mural every day, were substituted harmless natural objects such as grapes and mangoes.

Diego was furious. For the first time he made an effort to reply directly to his attackers. To the *New Republic,* which on August 16, 1933, published a letter of Freeman against him, he wrote:

Sir: Will you permit me to make clear the facts in the matter?

1. Mr. Wilson's [Edmund Wilson's] statement of the facts in his article "Detroit Paradoxes" * was correct; and Mr. Freeman's letter misstates the facts.

2. Mr. Freeman's original article in *The New Masses* pretended to show a degeneration of my art as soon as I was expelled from the Communist Party. To do that, Mr. Freeman falsified some facts and invented others out of whole cloth. One of those invented out of whole cloth was this statement: [here follows the statement by Freeman on the removal of the figure of the woman] . . .

This strange invention of Freeman's was refuted by the *Workers Age* of June 15, 1933 † by the simple procedure of publishing the original sketch and the final painting. The original sketch shows a woman sheltering worker and peasant. I considered the figure politically false because Mexico is not yet a nourishing mother to the workers and peasants. I removed it, as the *Workers Age* photo shows, and replaced it not by "grapes and mangoes" but by the figure of a worker showing to the martyrs of the agrarian revolution the road to industrial communism. I put that correction on the wall in sketch form as early as 1929.

3. Joseph Freeman pleads ignorance of the final painting when he wrote his article and has now invented a second alteration. But Freeman cannot plead ignorance when he wrote his recent letter to *The New Republic* for two good reasons.

First, because both the sketch and the final painting as printed in the *Workers Age* both show the grapes referred to, and in both cases connected with Hidalgo, who violated the Spanish prohibition against cultivation of grapes in Mexico and taught the Indians to cultivate and utilize the forbidden fruit—an act of defiance analogous to the Boston Tea Party or the Gandhi salt-making expedition. Freeman had only to look at the *Workers Age* of June 15, 1933, which he had in his possession when he wrote to you. He had only to use his eyes and he could have seen the impossibility of inventing his latest fiction. One who cannot see grapes in both sketch and painting, either will not see, or ought to refrain from writing on works of art.

Second, after the *Workers Age* had exposed Freeman's invention as such, he wrote to many people in Mexico, seeking some sort of "explanation," hypocritically assuring those whom he thought might

* *New Republic*, July 21, 1933.

† In an article entitled: "A Shameless Fraud," with reproduction of original sketch and finished painting.

suspect his motive, that he was using the data "for a serious and detailed scientific study of the frescoes and their social role."

Among the answers Freeman received was one from the editor of *Mexican Folkways,* Frances Toor. . . . When Freeman wrote his letter to you he was already in possession of Miss Toor's letter of July 31, 1933, which reads in part:

"I give you my word of honor that I do not remember the change in the drawings you speak of, and my word of honor means something to me and to those who know me. I have asked two or three other people since I received your letter two days ago, and they do not remember it either."

But Freeman hastened into print with his new invention, perhaps too much in a hurry to wait for Miss Toor's further investigation. She did what Freeman might have done—asked the painter himself. She also asked my assistants who worked with me on the job. Then on August 4, she wrote to Freeman the following letter, a copy of which she sent to me:

"My dear Joe:

"I have some further information for you regarding the Palace fresco. I met Pablo Higgins * yesterday and he told me that there never was a change in the project after it was first traced on the wall until the final painting and that the only fruit that ever appeared was the grapevine under Hidalgo's feet, under the central figure. Ramón Alva de Guadarrama, Diego's assistant throughout the work on the Palace frescoes, says the same.

"I could not quite make out from your statements as to whether or not you yourself saw the change or as to whether you based your statement on information given you by others. Now I see that it cannot be the former and that whoever gave you the information and signed statements for you, lied.

"It is really too bad that you weren't more careful.

"Sincerely,
Paca"

I can only say in closing that when a writer who values his reputation for veracity sets up to destroy the character of a painter who is

* Pablo Higgins, painter, was a member of the Mexican Communist Party who had learned the fresco technique by apprenticeship to Rivera.

doing, has been doing, and will continue to do his best to paint revolutionary murals, and for factional purposes that writer invents slanders and falsehoods, he should at least see to it that they are such as cannot be refuted by a mere photostatic reproduction. When slanders are in words only they are harder to refute. But when they concern things that can be photographed and reproduced, then I can only agree with Miss Toor when she says to Freeman: "It is really too bad that you were not more careful."

Diego Rivera

New York City

The *New Republic* delayed the publication of this letter for over a month, until Diego sent in a second letter of protest. Then they published it with the following note:

Mr. Freeman was shown Señor Rivera's letter before publication, but owing to the fact that he is at present in California will be unable to answer it until he can consult various letters which are in New York City—The Editors.

Freeman never did answer. But the *New Masses* took Diego's advice not to try again slanders that could be refuted by photographs.

Barely had the painter begun his labors on the National Palace walls when he suffered another of those breakdowns with which, from time to time, his overdriven body and mind defended themselves from total exhaustion. Dr. Ismael Cosío Villegas worked out the following schedule for him—preserved thanks to Frida, who attempted to enforce it:

1. Get up at 8 o'clock. Before rising, take temperature and make a note of it.
2. Bathe briefly in warm water, guarding against colds, in good weather and at a good time of the day.
3. Paint for three hours from 9 to 12, preferably in the open air.
4. From 12 to 1 repose in the sun.
5. At 1 o'clock dine.

6. After dinner lie down in the shade in the open air in absolute inactivity during two hours.
7. Before lying down take and note temperature.
8. Until 8 o'clock amuse self in discreet form: read, write, listen to music, etc.
9. Sup at 9.
10. Go to bed early.
11. Night and day keep the windows open.

Diego might have kept some at least of these eleven commandments for a while, only just after they were prescribed, he was offered another wall!

The offer came from an unexpected source, that of the American Ambassador, Dwight W. Morrow. Having taken up residence in Cuernavaca, lovely capital of the near-by State of Morelos, Morrow conceived the idea of promoting good will between the two countries by donating a mural to the town. Simultaneously he helped a local curate to restore a chapel, and the Morelos government to repair the Palace of Cortés, now a government office building. Thus he helped state and church, right and left, at the same time.

Painter and "good-will" ambassador sized each other up at table in Morrow's Cuernavaca home. Diego was a good mixer and gracious by nature, except when he was annoyed or his inner fury beset him. Dwight Morrow was an accomplished diplomat. But Diego had strange notions concerning a Yankee ambassador and Morgan partner, while Ambassador Morrow had heard weird tales concerning Diego. Now they ate and drank together, Frida adding charm to the gathering with her swift wit and impulsive gaiety, and Mrs. Morrow contributing the graces of an accomplished hostess. No onlooker would have suspected any strain. Like the men of the world they both were, they talked of anything but the one thing that had brought them together.

When at last they got to the point, all was over and settled almost in an instant. The amount Morrow offered was twelve thousand dollars. From that Rivera would have to purchase materials, pay his workmen, pay commission to a go-between,* maintain and compensate himself. He might decorate as much or as little of the open loggia or balcony wall as his desires and aesthetic feelings and the sum of money permitted. As usual Diego elected to do more rather than less; above the doors, on the side walls as well as the main one, and below the main panels pseudo-bas-reliefs; thanks to his gluttonous appetite for all space and his fecund imagination, the commission netted him but little. Yet dollars were not pesos, and meager as his "profit" was for five months labor, it was still the best paid of his Mexican mural ventures.

Price settled, they went to the question which was worrying the titan of finance as much as the titan of painting: subject matter. But that was arranged even more easily than the price. Morrow disarmed the painter by agreeing that he might select his own theme and execute it as he pleased, with no more censorship than might be involved in painting something acceptable to the authorities of Morelos, to whom the gift was to be presented. The proposal was worthy of the diplomat: in an instant the silent tension was as silently discharged. It is true that Morrow once or twice during the progress of the work suggested, diplomatically, as always, that Diego's clerics were unflattering to the Church and religion. But Diego answered, no less diplomatically, that he was attacking no one, merely presenting the history of Morelos and the Conquest. He pointed out that he was also including good priests: Las Casas, protector of the Indians against the fury of the conquerors, Motilinía, teacher of the arts and crafts of the conquering Europeans. "I do not know whether the Church will like it," said Diego, grinning disarmingly, "but both the good priests and the bad, and the role played by Christianity in the Conquest, are the truth of his-

* In this case William Spratling, who refused his commission, but to whom Diego gave a painting.

tory; and, being the truth, every friend of truth will like it." Thereafter the Ambassador held his peace.

Morelos is in the *tierra templada*, steep-walled, farm- and orchard-covered, well watered, thickly wooded, fertile. The air is softer than in the valley of Mexico, the elevation lower, the rainfall more abundant, the land more joyous. In place of the dry bare melancholy vistas of the top of the *meseta central*, there is a blaze of color and opulence of curve: deep green foliage lines the canyon walls, hangs in festoons down the impenetrable shadowed gloom, glows translucent and golden where the intense sun throws its shafts, is splashed with brilliance of tropical flower and fruit. From this land, gold and silver and semiprecious stones have been garnered, but mainly fruit, corn, and, above all, sugar. Cuernavaca sits high atop the plunging slopes, lording it over the land that Cortés conquered: here he built his palace as a monument to his power and rule. Four centuries later that solid structure still stands, looking out over the broad, deep and pleasant valley where Morelos fought and died for independence, and where Zapata rode the hills with his *agraristas*. All this the painter sought to express in color, form, and substance on the palace wall.

The fresco is painted on an open loggia exposed to sun and air. Through the colonnade opposite, one looks over the green valley and far into the deepening vista of mountains rising range on range until they melt into snow-capped volcanoes and the intense light-filled blueness of sky. This vista too must find expression and reflection in the mural.

The palace is constructed of large *tezontle* (red mountain lava) blocks, covered over with hard gray cement. Now the dimensions have been extended by these frescoes, extended into time to cover the sweep of historical memories clustering around it, and into space to express the land of which it is the capital. Only photographs taken with the specific purpose of revealing such things can show the relation between frescoes, surrounding building, and near and distant views and make clear how skillfully the painter has made the structure of his design give visual support to the ceiling, assimilate disturbing features of the architecture, fit into and harmonize with the straight lines and proportions of wall and arched curve of portals, extend the surrounding landscape audaciously into the composition, reflect its opulent curves against the contrasting solidity of the blocklike figures, as solid and strong as the *tezontle* blocks beneath, heighten the severe color of dull gray cement in the monochrome "low reliefs" near the base, and reflect, in the colored panels above, the brilliant blue-green of the foliage splashed with warm orange and bright red-gold.

The traveler who has once contemplated the foliage of tree and underbrush and canyon wall in PLATE 108 (where an Indian guide, dressed as a wolf, is showing the Spanish the secret crossing over an impassable *barranca* for a surprise attack) will find that thereafter the plants he has passed unseeing along the way take on an unexpected and puzzling intimacy to his eye—a sensation like that of meeting for the first time some person whose portrait hangs in one's room. The rhythm of the turning figures in the twisting, turning foliage catches the rhythm of the plant life all around.

Let the reader contemplate the fantastic stirring spectacle of two civilizations in conflict (PLATE 109), where the Aztec knight of the tiger plunges his flint knife into the steel corselet of the metal-cased, horse-using, firearm-employing Spanish knight, and he will understand, perhaps, what I mean when I speak of the solidity of the blocklike figures reflecting the solidity of the blocks of *tezontle* of which the wall is built.

Then turn to the balladlike beauty of the folk-hero Zapata (reproduction from an unsatisfactory photograph, PLATE 111), standing, benign of countenance while at his feet lies the tyrant his machete has cut down, and leading, as a ballad hero should, a marvelous white horse. Finally if we look at the beautiful, sinuous curves of PLATE 105 and the contrasting curves of whip, human backs, and sugar cane in PLATE 112 we may get some notion of the reflection of landscape and building and history that has been made part of this wall. A representative of the great neighboring power had paid the bill, but it was not frivolous nose-thumbing, as some have implied, that made the artist choose his theme. He felt it a requirement of this building in this land and time that he paint on it a universalized drama of the conflict of a conquering imperialist and a rebellious and resisting native civilization—these memories from the Conquest of Cortés to the revolt of Zapata are the "fourth dimension" that extends the three other dimensions of the building into the life of this people and land.

> It is a hard test for any painting [wrote a sensitive critic] * to be set as a rival to Nature herself. One of Rivera's murals covers the three walls of a court in the Palace of Cortés. The fourth side is entirely open to a view of the valley. The painted landscape which is background for the figures in the Story of the Conquest of Mexico has to stand against the real landscape which is one of the most striking in the world. The result, which has both unity and contrast, proves that man, too, can create a world.

* Philip N. Youtz in the *Bulletin* of the Pennsylvania Museum of Art (February 1932).

24.
THE ART OF A CONTINENT

If Mexico was the base, Russia and the United States were the sides of the great triangle that encompassed Rivera's dreams of contributing through his work to the life of his time. Towards Mexico he was drawn by the ties of birth, nurture, and sensibility, by the compelling voice of natural and plastic beauty, by the promises of its social upheavals. This was the land which he knew best and which could best serve and be served by him. In rediscovering it for himself, he had found himself and worked out the fundamentals of his style.

Russia attracted him as the model land of social transformation. He had dreamed that by painting there he might fructify its art, at the same time enriching his own. That dream had ended in a rude awakening.

There remained the third side of the triangle to explore. He possessed a peculiar ambivalence towards the United States, in which attraction and antipathy mingled. It was the land that had robbed Mexico of half its territory, bribed and bullied, fomented disorder, outraged the sensibilities of a people whose weakness in the face of their giant northern neighbor made them still more sensitive. Yet he knew that it could not be regarded merely as an oppressor.

Above all it was as an artist that the United States attracted him. Its skyscrapers, glimpsed when bound for Russia, seemed to him amazing monuments to man's greed, moving testimonials to his audacious powers of construction, stripped of their sometimes meritricious ornamentation, works of incomparable beauty. Its steel bridges and express highways were works of enchantment. I often sat beside him on speeding autos traversing these nonstop highways, while the smooth ribbon of road, the clean-lined cut-offs, the stone overpasses, the evidence of human intelligence in every detail of the design, held his bulging eyes spellbound, with scarcely a glance at the non-man-made scenery. "Your engineers are your great artists," he told me. "These highways are the most beautiful thing I have seen in your beautiful country. In all the constructions of man's past—pyramids, Roman roads and aqueducts, cathedrals and palaces, there is nothing to equal these. Out of them and the machine will issue the style of tomorrow."

> Now I understand [he told me on another occasion] why painters like Morse [the inventor of the telegraph] and Fulton [the inventor of the steamboat] directed their plastic genius chiefly into mechanical construction.* While our architects are stupidly copying what the ancients did better in accord with the needs of their time, the best modern architects of our age are finding their aesthetic and functional inspiration in American industrial buildings, machine-design and engineering, the greatest expressions of the plastic genius of this New World.

* Both Fulton and Morse were painters as well as famous inventors, therefore to Diego Yankee prototypes of Leonardo da Vinci.

When he sailed into New York harbor at dawn of a winter morning in 1931, a reporter began an interview with him in this fashion:

> It was seven o'clock in the morning as the ship rode up the bay. Mr. Rivera studied the fog, the red sun rising over Brooklyn, the lights in the Manhattan towers, the shadows; he pointed to the tugboats, the ferries, to a gang of riveters at work on the extension of a dock; he waved his great arms and declared, "Here it is—the might, the power, the energy, the sadness, the glory, the youthfulness of our lands."
>
> He picked out the Equitable tower on lower Manhattan, and said, "There we are on our own earth, for whether the architects know it or not, they were inspired in that design by the same feeling which prompted the ancient people of Yucatán in the building of their temples." *

His desire to paint in this land of modern industry and to make his art accessible to a modern working class had by then become an obsession. In a free union of the Americas, in a wedding of the industrial workers of the North with the peasantry of the South, of the factories of the United States with the raw materials of Latin America, of the utilitarian aesthetic of the machine with the plastic sense of the Amerindian peoples, in the mating of the style which glass and steel and concrete were even then engendering with the style that antique Mexican, Central American, and Peruvian art had begotten, he foresaw the dawn of new splendors for the continent.

In the United States his reputation had been growing steadily. His work had first been introduced to a small circle of sophisticated New Yorkers as early as 1915 when Marius de Zayas, painter, connoisseur, and dealer, opened a modest little gallery on Fifth Avenue, and included Paris paintings from his hand. There it was that Walter Pach first "discovered" him.

* *New York Times,* December 14, 1931.

In 1918, at the Second Independent Show, Zayas submitted, without the painter's knowledge, one of his landscapes done in the pointillist manner. In 1919 Zayas arranged an exhibition on "The Evolution of French Art from Ingres and Delacroix to the Latest Modern Manifestation." Once more Rivera figured with five drawings, all portraits, one of a child, one of Eric Satie, and one a self-portrait. When the Anderson Galleries sold the collection of Marius de Zayas in 1923, the catalogue listed "Item 94. Diego M. Rivera, Modern French School, *The Sugar Bowl and the Matches*"; "Item 95, *Portrait of a Woman*," and Item 97, a "*Landscape*, grassy foreground; low walls in the middle ground, above which rises a terrace with houses." The Quinn Collection, too, as we have seen, contained seven Riveras at the time of its liquidation, all of which were sold to American owners.

But it was around 1924 that Diego's fame began to spread in earnest north of the Rio Grande. Rumors had begun to filter northward concerning a great revival in painting, of frescoes simple and strong, moving and powerful as they had not been for centuries, of a painter of legendary proportions and habits who had found a way of bringing art once more close to the life of the people. Artists began their pilgrimages to the new mecca, stayed to watch and study under him, came back demanding walls. Critics and journalists began to fill the press with comment, reproduction, anecdote, evaluation. Collectors returned with fragments of mural sketches, water colors, canvases. Finally, in 1929, the American Institute of Architects, sensitive to the role that a revival of fresco might play in connection with their profession, awarded him the Fine Arts Gold Medal—the second time in its history that the medal was awarded to a foreigner. Diego was not there, but the award was sent to him with an excerpt of the speech J. Monroe Hewlett made on the occasion:

> Mr. Rivera's work seems to embody an appreciation of the wall surface as the theme of his decoration which has hardly been surpassed

since the days of Giotto. It is this quality to which the Committee desires particularly to call attention. . . . If painting and sculpture are to form a vital part of our architecture in the future, it is just as necessary that the architect should arrive at that conception of painting and sculpture as allied to architecture as it is that the painters and sculptors should acquire some appreciation of what architectural decoration requires. . . .

It was in California, not New York, that Rivera got his opportunity to "invade" this country. Californians are a roving people who wander up and down their state, the country, the continent, much more than do the more settled Easterners. Mexico and things Mexican have a special fascination for them. Many of their artists had already visited Mexico: Paul O'Higgins apprenticed himself to Rivera and remained to do murals (he is still there); others studied under Diego briefly, among them Ione Robinson, Earl Musick, Maxine Albro. The homes of California began to display Riveras. His *Flower Day* won the purchase prize of $1500 in the Pan-American Exhibition held in Los Angeles in 1925.

In 1926 Ralph Stackpole, San Francisco sculptor who had known Diego in Paris, returned from Mexico City enormously excited. He brought back two pictures, one a portrait of himself and his wife, the other a Mexican woman holding an infant. The latter he presented to William Gerstle, President of the San Francisco Art Commission. Gerstle did not like the gift, but was too embarrassed to say so. Here is his first impression:

The subjects seemed to be a characterless Mexican woman and her infant. The woman was heavy, coarse-featured, huge-limbed, almost gross. The child in her lap looked like a rather large cloth doll loosely stuffed with flour. Only three colors had been used by the painter: a dismal brown, a washed-out lilac, several shades of much faded overall blue. I thought it a pretty poor painting and was greatly embarrassed when Stackpole gave it to me. To please him, I reluctantly made a place for it on a wall of my studio, where it had to compete with a Matisse and other works hanging there. To my surprise, I could not take my eyes off of it, and in the course of a few days, my reaction to the picture changed completely. The seeming simplicity of the construction proved to come from a skill I had not at first suspected. The colors began to seem right, and possessed of a quiet inevitability. There was about the whole picture a settled, earthy quality: subject, style, design, mood, proved to be in striking and solid harmony, and I began to feel that what I had taken for a crude daub had more power and beauty than any other of my pictures. Without having seen Rivera's murals I began to share Stackpole's excited enthusiasm. When he began to tell me of those walls in Mexico, I agreed with him that we must try to arrange for the Mexican to paint in San Francisco.

William Gerstle thereupon donated fifteen hundred dollars for Rivera to do a small wall in the California School of Fine Arts. The sum was ample for the project, only 120 square feet of space being included in the original contract, but it was scarcely sufficient for a round trip from Mexico City and a stay in California. Diego, still pouring out overflowing thoughts and observations on the walls of his native land, accepted the contract, but delayed four years before he arrived to execute it.

Meanwhile his fame continued to spread in California, while Stackpole continued his efforts to interest other possible patrons. In 1929, when the sculptor himself was engaged, along with other artists, to decorate the new San Francisco Stock Exchange, he induced the architect, Timothy Pflueger, to offer a wall to Diego. Twenty-five hundred dollars were allotted. But when Diego tried to secure a permit to reside for six months in the United States, this "agent of American imperialism and the millionaire Morrow," as the Communist Party press now called him, going to paint in an art school and a stock exchange, was denied admission to the country! * He wrote to his clients and friends in San Francisco, of whom he now had a good number, and they set to work to have the ban lifted.

* This is one aspect of our immigration laws which I have never understood, the pusillanimous fear of a great country that an artist, a writer, or a scientist can menace the foundations of our state by residing briefly among us.

On July 15, 1929, Albert M. Bender, an insurance broker of that city, and a generous patron who had been buying Riveras and persuading friends to do likewise, wrote him:

> I have looked over the telegrams and papers in connection with the same and have no doubt whatever that the trouble is on account of Anti-American activities on your part which have found their way to the State Department . . . the first move should be made by you through the American Consul in the City of Mexico who must visa your passport. Should you receive it and be detained at the port of entry, your friends here will have to render the fullest assistance. . . . If the Consul in Mexico refuses to visa your passport, we could send some telegrams from here to inform him of your purpose in coming to California and of our desire to have you paint murals at the Art School. . . . My opinion is that if the Consul will visa your passport, you will have little difficulty at the port of entry, but if you should be detained, there is every reason to suppose that through the combined influence of your friends, considering the object of your visit, the Department will grant you permission to enter the United States.

Meanwhile Mr. Bender, who had influential friends of his own, had ascertained that the original ban came directly from the State Department. Without any public fuss, he set about to have them remove their objections. On August 13 he was able to write Rivera:

> I think that I can advise you to come through to California whenever you are ready. . . . I feel sure that there will be no further trouble. . . .

The country, it seems, owes to the gentle and elderly insurance broker, whose personal political philosophy was mildly liberal, a debt of gratitude not only for his share in the great stimulus that Rivera's coming provided to American art, but for saving the Government of the United States from the lasting disgrace which would have inhered in the public barring of a great artist who wanted to paint here.

Albert Bender had been a friend of the Riveras and a collector of Diego's works since a visit to Mexico some years earlier. Now he smoothed the way for the trip financially by persuading other wealthy art collectors to add a Rivera or two to their collections. Through him, Mrs. Annie Meyer Liebman, a New Yorker frequently in California, purchased a painting alternatively called *Morning Moon* and *Market Scene in Tehuantepec* * for one thousand dollars, which I believe represented a new high for a single painting of his up to that time.

The connection with Mrs. Liebman proved to be a fortunate one for Diego. She was the wife of Charles Liebman, and related through her brothers and sisters and their respective spouses to a number of generous and discriminating patrons of the arts. One of her brothers was Eugene Meyer, editor of the Washington *Post;* another, Walter Meyer, an officer of the Atchison, Topeka & Santa Fe Railway; a sister, Florence was married to George Blumenthal, President of the Metropolitan Museum; and another, Rosalie, was Mrs. Sigmund Stern of Atherton, California, who not only purchased paintings but contracted for Diego to do a mural in her dining room. Nor does this exhaust the tale of this influential family, none of whom, I believe, agreed with Rivera's political philosophy, but all of whom were capable of appreciating his painting.

The most perisistent and generous of Rivera's patrons in California was Bender himself. Typical of the letters which from time to time he sent Diego is one dated June 21, 1935, in which he informs the painter that he has donated to the San Francisco Museum of Art five hundred dollars for the purchase of a work of the painter intended as a memorial in honor of Mrs. Caroline Walter, mother of the sculptor Edgar Walter and herself "a critical judge of fine art, a stimulating patron, the friend of innumerable artists. . . ."

If Diego does more work than five hundred dollars would ade-

* Published as Plate 62 in *Portrait of Mexico* (New York, Covici-Friede, 1938).

quately compensate, the letter continues, "I should be very grateful for a word from you so that I could make up the difference."

Diego sent in response the strikingly beautiful *Flower Carrier in Xochimilco,** an oil tempera on gesso, a firm and durable ceramic base, erroneously announced in the California press as *Fruit Vendor.* "He has done more than I expected," wrote the pleased Bender to Frida, "and I am too grateful to tell you adequately how much I appreciate it." At various times the same patron presented other Rivera drawings, oils, and water colors to the museum so that he was able to write to Frida during the same year: "It is my ambition to build up a corner of the Museum with more of his work, and when I am 'flush' I will occasionally send a check for other drawings or paintings. . . . The picture of you and Diego is the only one I have kept for myself. . . ." The corner he has built up, be it said, is one of the best museum collections of the work of the artist to be found in this country.†

In September 1930, Timothy Pflueger finally made the announcement that Rivera was coming to San Francisco to do a mural in the new stock exchange. The reaction in local art circles was as violent as unexpected:

> All is not quiet on the San Francisco front, wrote the correspondent of the *Art Digest* for mid-October. A storm unprecedented in recent years is shaking the art colony to its very foundations. Certain local artists are up in arms over the commission given Diego Rivera, famous Mexican artist, revolutionist and communist, to paint murals depicting California's financial and commercial progress on the walls of the Luncheon Club in San Francisco's new $2,500,000 Stock Exchange Building. They contend that although Rivera may be the world's greatest muralist, his communist ideas place him out of sympathy with his

* Plate 93 in *Portrait of Mexico, op. cit.*

† Unfortunately the present policy of the Museum (I visited it in 1962) involves keeping the entire remarkable collection most of the time in the cellar to make room for "action paintings" and "crushed automobile" sculpture.

subject and that the city's own artists were slighted. "Rivera for Mexico City; San Francisco's best for San Francisco," is their cry.

The tide of protest reached its zenith in an anonymous broadside which was circulated throughout Bohemian circles. Grim with the black ink of mourning and wreathed with the imortelles of death, it read: 'Is the San Francisco Art Association dead? Does its president have to go after Rivera to get art for our city? Is he elected for that? Or is he guilty of a frank betrayal of trust?'

The painters, though jealous, were decent in their strictures. Maynard Dixon, painter of Western landscapes and murals, told the press:

> The stock exchange could look the world over without finding a man more inappropriate for the part than Rivera. He is a professed Communist and has publicly caricatured American financial institutions. . . .
>
> I believe he is the greatest living artist in the world, and we would do well to have an example of his work in a public building in San Francisco. But he is not the man for the Stock Exchange Building.*

Other painters, like Frank Van Sloun and Otis Oldfield, were opposed to importing "foreign" artists under any circumstances, though they too were complimentary to his powers as a painter —provided he stayed in his own land to exercise them. Ray Boynton, who apparently had submitted sketches for the same wall, made no statement. But Lorado Taft, the sculptor, without troubling to look at the Rivera paintings available in San Francisco, made the following oracular pronouncement:

> Art, of course, should be simplified; but from what I have seen of Rivera's works he has carried the simplicity to *naïveté*, almost childishness. I have seen only reproductions of several of his paintings, and I do not care for them.†

On the day this declaration was made, Taft might have at-

* United Press dispatch of September 23, 1930.
† San Francisco *Examiner*, November 30, 1930.

tended a preview of an exhibition of Rivera's work at the California Palace of the Legion of Honor. Scheduled to be opened to the public next morning, it contained forty-six Russian sketches, several fresco drawings, and specimens of his work ranging from his Paris days to the year 1930.*

The newspapers, taking the clue from Maynard Dixon, began to reproduce Rivera's anticapitalist murals from the Secretariat of Education, under lurid headlines. The San Francisco *News* ran a cut of his *Twilight of the Gods of the Bourgeoisie,* along with a photograph of William Gerstle and a reproduction of a circular in mournful black which charged him with betrayal and hinted at the death of the San Francisco Art Association over which he presided. The San Francisco *Chronicle* did a composite of the stairway of the Luncheon Club where his mural was to be painted, but by montage placed his *Night of the Rich* (PLATE 77) on the wall, showing Rockefeller, Morgan, Henry Ford, and Mexican capitalists dining on ticker tape! They entitled it *The Kiss of Judas,* and explained that one of the bankers' wives in the picture was "Miss Mexico," whom American millionaires were trying to seduce "from the paths of communism to the fallen ways of capitalism." Next to the illustration of the Luncheon Club wall as they imagined it, they ran a story headed: "Rivera Critics Told to Mind Their Own Business." †

With this auspicious beginning, reinforced, when they arrived, by the attractiveness of Diego's massive frame, genial smile, and unassuming ways, and the lovely charm of Frida in her Mexican costumes, and the fact that Rivera's doings and his forceful painting made good copy, art never left the front pages during the many months that Diego spent in California. When he finally said good-by to the Bay cities, many of the artists who had opposed his coming acknowledged their indebtedness

* The one-man show lasted a month and was augmented by work done in California, including a painting called *San Francisco Breadline.*

† San Francisco *Chronicle,* September 25, and San Francisco *News,* September 26, 1930.

to him. The San Francisco *News,* as if to make up for its earlier scandalmongering, declared editorially:

> His influence has been sane and healthy. . . . His own work is in the great tradition of painting, which it approaches humbly as first of all a craft to be mastered. . . . California's native painters will all profit by the exploitation of Rivera during the past few months; it has meant an enormous stimulation of public interest in art.*

When Diego and Frida reached San Francisco on November 10, 1930, the hostile campaign against him soon died down; the city made every effort to show him the hospitality on which it prides itself. Ralph Stackpole put his studio at 716 Montgomery Street, in the old artists' quarter, at the disposal of Diego for living and working purposes, a studio large enough so that the painter could hang great sheets of paper on its walls and from the rungs of a ladder make his cartoons to scale for the Stock Exchange frescoes. The California Palace of the Legion of Honor put on the one-man show already referred to; galleries throughout the state exhibited his work, among them the Dalzell Hatfield and Jake Zeitlin's in Los Angeles, the Denny Watrous in Carmel, the Fine Arts Gallery of the city of San Diego, the East West Gallery in San Francisco, and the Beaux Arts, the director of which, Mrs. Alice Judd Rhine, had previously publicly deplored the importation of a non-Californian. She it was who busied herself inviting the most incongruous assortment of "notables" to a reception to meet the new social lion, "nearly everyone in San Francisco," as the *Call-Bulletin* said, "who has written a book or a poem, cornered the stock market, painted a picture, sung a song, represented his country as consul, crossed a desert on a camel, edited a magazine, or trod the boards."

Diego and Frida were feted, lionized, spoiled. The city, which can be very hospitable when it wants to, found him thoroughly

* San Francisco *News,* November 18, 1930 and May 9, 1931.

fascinating and her altogether charming, and took them both completely to its heart. Parties everywhere, streams of invitations to teas, dinners, week-ends, lectures with great audiences coming to get a glimpse of them and listening, astounded, to Diego's words on art and social questions. The San Francisco Art Association put the painter on its Jury of Awards. He purchased and praised a work of an aged tailor and Sunday painter, John d'Vorack, who was spending his declining years in the poorhouse: the neglected old man's reputation was made. The University of California offered Diego three thousand dollars to lecture at its summer school; Mills College made a similar proposal; he spoke at the San Francisco Society of Woman Artists, at the Pacific Arts Association Convention, to groups of Latin Americans, to all sorts of gatherings up and down the state. As a prophet he had been without honor in his own country, but now there were thousands delighted to listen to the stirring ideas and tall fantasies that flowed as easily from his tongue as images from his brush. Except to the Latin Americans, he lectured in French, with Mrs. Emily Joseph, wife of the painter Sidney Joseph and writer on art for the San Francisco *Chronicle,* providing faithful translations of his words as she caught them on the wing. Regardless of the theme assigned to him, Rivera used each occasion to defend and explain his theories of painting and win San Francisco for social and mural art. The seed he sowed then is still bearing fruit.*

Capable artists and artisans were delighted to offer themselves as assistants. Viscount John Hastings, radical English lord and painter newly come from Tahiti, Mexico-bound to study under Rivera, found him in San Francisco and enlisted as an

* Lucienne Bloch, daughter of the composer Ernst Bloch, was one of the apprentices he acquired in California "to grind his colors." Today San Francisco has a number of beautiful frescoes done by her. In 1962 I watched her complete a mural in the San Francisco National Bank in a gay and poetic style completely her own, but the wall showed that she had learned well from her master the technique of true fresco. She is only one of a number of painters of the United States who served their apprenticeship in fresco painting under Rivera.

assistant. Clifford Wight, an English sculptor, became his helper, following him later to Detroit. Matthew Barnes, artist, actor, versatile and picturesque personality, became his plasterer. Albert Barrows, engineer, helped with technical advice, and Ralph Stackpole became adviser-extraordinary on any question which arose.

William Gerstle was pleased with the reception of his protégé, yet worried in private over the way he was permitting himself to be fêted, toured, lionized, distracted. He thought ruefully of the four years he had waited for Diego to fulfill his contract, of softheartedness which made him step aside in favor of the Stock Exchange Building, letting its sponsors have first claim on the artist. He knew that Rivera was on brief leave from the unfinished National Palace fresco, that letters and telegrams were piling up from the Mexican authorities demanding the painter's speedy return to finish the job.

Yet Diego was not wasting his time: he was even busier than usual, sizing up California, getting the feel of its people, the curve of its hills, the color of its air, sea, fields, and sky, the nature of its activities, the flavor of its life, making innumerable sketches and mental notes, soaking up like a thirsty sponge the flow of unfamiliar life surrounding him, trying to decide before he put brush to drying plaster what should go into the quintessential distillation of the land and its people.

Everything being new, and his appetite for sensation and experience as always, insatiable, he cared not what came his way. A ride in a swift auto over the skyline boulevard or down the peninsula, a ferry over the Bay, a walk along San Francisco's colorful waterfront or through its grimly tidy slums, eastward into the mountains to a gold mine, south to sketch the silhouette of oil derricks against the blue of the sky—everything was California and America, and he wanted to know it all.

Professor Clark of the Art Department of Stanford sent him his own two tickets to the annual Stanford-California football game. The big, sombreroed, rough-clad Mexican with the slender, dark-eyed girl in native costume attracted almost as much attention as the game, while Diego sat in the stadium, bulging eyes drinking in every detail, his hand making endless rough sketches.

> Your game of football is splendid, thrilling, beautiful [he told a reporter for the *Oakland Post-Enquirer*].* I never imagined anything like it—the crowd in the stadium, the masses of color—a great living picture, spontaneous unconscious art. I marvel at the rooting section . . . at a signal from the leader vast pictures leap into being. . . . Those mosaic pictures have fine color and design . . . made by living men, not by bits of colored stone. It is art in the mass, a new form of art.
>
> Asked to compare it with the Mexican bullfight, he found the latter "essentially a tragic spectacle. A sense of death hovers over it. Football is different. It is not really brutal, it is joyous. It has not the deadly methodological deliberation of the bullfight. It is gay, not sinister.

The artist permitted the interviewer to keep two action sketches from his notebook, which accompanied the article.

At a reception they introduced him to Helen Wills, the then tennis champion. He immediately made an appointment to sketch her and soon had a monumental drawing in sanguine to serve as model for his allegorical figure of California. To his surprise, objections were raised: some thought they had a better claim to be "California's representative woman"; others demanded that the head be made "typical of the finest California womanhood but not a portrait of any one individual." The painter satisfied them with a "compromise" (which he had intended in the first place): he generalized the monumental face and figure that was to represent California, but it is still the generalized head of Helen Wills Moody, and the nude flying on the ceiling bears unmistakable resemblance to her also.† As always, Diego's mastery of the anatomy and dynamics of the human body in motion was such that he was able to

* Issue of November 29, 1930.

† Reproduced as Plate 1 in *Portrait of America* (New York, Covici-Friede, 1934).

communicate life and energy and verisimilitude to nude bodies floating through the air in positions that could not possibly be observed from life. But the "flying" body of Helen Wills he got to know especially well, for he followed her to the tennis courts and made a series of action studies of her engaged in the game at which she was so great a virtuoso. These sketches he presented to her, while the monumental head is now in the possession of Lord and Lady Hastings.

Others whom he met were to become models for his second mural when he finally got to it. The amusingly and sympathetically done trio discussing building plans in the lower foreground of the Art School fresco (PLATE 113) are Timothy Pflueger, architect of the Stock Exchange, Arthur Brown, Jr., architect of the Art School, and William Gerstle, donor of the fresco; while on the scaffold, or on the sides, are visible the figures of Rivera's assistants, Hastings, Wight, Barnes, and other technical and art workers, Michael Baltekal-Goodman, Mrs. Marion Simpson, Albert Barrows. So muralists have done in all ages, selecting faces from among their contemporaries that may appeal to them, giving them universal significance and a life beyond life on durable walls.

The most amusing of the figures in the Art School fresco is the rear view of the artist himself at work on the scaffold, a delightful addition to the long and honorable line of self-portraits that painters of all ages have left as records of their personal presence and conceptions of themselves as artists and men (PLATE 113). How a man must know himself to be able to render his own back so faithfully! Self-portraits are revealing things: plain Citizen Chardin in nightcap and spectacles, proud of being an honest bourgeois; the aged Rembrandt meditating on the vanity of life and the corruptibility of the flesh; romantic nineteenth-century painters in "broad-winged," dashingly tilted berets, boasting their citizenship in Bohemia; elegant and epicurean Matisse, trim-bearded, dignified, carefully negligent and at ease, the delicate black line of a drawing somehow conveying that the rims of his spectacles are of fine gold and his art at the service of a discriminating leisure class dedicated to discreet and fine autumnal pleasures which will still hold out a while longer; the self-portraits of Diego first as bearded romantic Bohemian outsider in Paris (PLATE 12), then as an architect-artisan (PLATE 80), whose work is construction, and as workman-painter on a scaffold (which does not sag for once because the design required straight lines), whose task is mural and monumental. The differences between the self-portraits of a Matisse and a Rivera are as vast as the gulfs that separate their social philosophies, esthetic theories, and modes of painting. (But in old age, he would slough off the philosophic armor and image of himself as workman-painter, to do himself as an aging man who has known the wonders of Paris and New York and Moscow and Teotihuacán—these motifs fill the background—but whose bulging eyes trouble him now with their tearing. He pities but does not spare himself: "Yes," the portrait seems to say, "these things you have been, and done, and seen, but now you are old and soon you will face . . . NOTHING!" See PLATE 164).

This rear-view self-portrait in the Art School was used by a few still dissatisfied cavilers to renew the controversy that had raged about Rivera before his arrival in San Francisco. Typical of these efforts is Kenneth Callahan's letter to the *Town Crier* of Seattle,* in which he complained of the artist's

> fat rear (very realistically painted) hanging over scaffolding in the center. Many San Franciscans choose to see in this gesture a direct insult, premeditated, as indeed it appears to be. If it is a joke, it is a rather amusing one, but in bad taste.

The effort to start a controversy on this issue fell flat; but some noted for the first time something characteristic of all Rivera's painting: that his figures are always engaged in living within the depicted sphere of activity of which they are a part, that no self-conscious glance ever strays with false theatricality

* May 21, 1932.

across the footlights. No figure ever gives one the feeling of being posed in a studio, but rather of being in the midst of the life within the painting, and within the world, internal and external, reflected by it.

The discussion of the notes made in the period while Diego was "sightseeing" has carried us a little ahead of our story, past the anxious weeks and months while Mr. Gerstle waited in growing despair, and tried to hide his fears that the workman-painter was degenerating into the social lion in the too pleasant surroundings of San Francisco. Then suddenly the picture began to crystallize out of the saturated mind of the artist. He attacked the Luncheon Club wall with his accustomed zeal, began driving himself and his helpers to exhaustion with no sense of the passing hours or accumulating fatigue. The local artists and *cognoscenti* were amazed: who ever heard of painters working in that fashion? The Luncheon Club wall was thirty feet high, running up from tenth to eleventh floor on an interior stairway, but in a few weeks the walls were finished and, for good measure, the ceiling also.*

Now Diego was exhausted, and accepted an invitation for himself and Frida to rest "for ten days" at Mrs. Stern's home in Atherton. The ten days lengthened into six weeks while the anxious Gerstle, who had cut short a trip to Europe for the purpose of expediting the long-delayed Art School mural, waited uneasily in San Francisco. But once more Diego was not resting. He had driven down the peninsula in the beautiful season when almond trees are in blossom, and was soon painting a tender, lyrical fresco upon the wall of Mrs. Stern's dining room: rows of almond trees, between them a tractor and men and a boy working the soil; "In the foreground . . . a stone wall on top of which is a large flat basket filled with oranges and grapefruit; peeping over the wall, from behind this basket, three small children with hands grasping the fruit. . . ." Two of them were Mrs.

* The total surface painted is 43.82 square meters.

Stern's grandchildren, the third a dreamchild who lived only in the imagination of one of them and was painted from her description. The skin of the laborers is "swarthy, the color of their garments a rather light blue and yellow, the coping of the wall is pale gray, the earth is a rich brown, the trunks of the trees are, in parts, almost white, like the blossoms, and in others, most dark, in shadow." *

Thus did the painter rest. When, at the end of the six weeks, he returned to San Francisco, he found so many letters and telegrams from the President of Mexico that he forgot about his promised mural and went to say good-by to Gerstle and his other friends, preparatory to leaving for Mexico City. His unhappy patron scarcely protested, though he told friends: "Who knows if he will ever return? If he goes now without doing the Art School wall, it will break my heart." Sensing the unspoken feelings, Diego suggested that Mr. Gerstle and his friends try to get a further delay from the Mexican authorities. Visits to the consul, and cables to President Ortiz Rubio secured the desired extension. Now Diego tackled the wall in the Art School. The 120 square feet he was being paid for looked small, and the wall poorly located, so he chose the largest and finest wall in the building, and without a cent more than originally arranged for, painted over 1,200 feet instead of 120!

We have already described what he painted there. An interesting discussion of what he himself intended is contained in his article "Scaffoldings," † a valedictory to America written just before he left to resume work on the National Palace. It is a dialogue between Myself, My Double, and My Friend the Architect, with brief interventions by The Shade of Renoir, various Memories and a letter from Paul O'Higgins.

MY FRIEND THE ARCHITECT (*together we contemplate a scaffold*): You are right, it is beautiful. And I have jokingly told my

* From Mrs. Sigmund Stern's description of the mural in *California Arts and Architecture* (June 1932), pp. 34-35.

† *Hesperian* (Spring 1931), translated by Emily Joseph.

fellow architects that the beauty of their buildings is most striking when they are still covered by their scaffoldings. The moment they are removed, all beauty disappears.

MYSELF: It is for that very reason that in my next fresco I shall paint a building with its scaffolding, upon which painters, sculptors, and architects are at work. This state of things will last as long as the wall and the beauty of the moment that precedes the removal. . . .

The dialogue turns to other matters, concluding on what had become a favorite theme in Rivera's writing, lecturing and painting. My Double has got out of control in a broadcasting station, and over a Pan-American hook-up declaims:

Listen Americans! Your country is strewn over with impossible objects that are in no way beautiful, nor even practical. . . . Most of your houses are covered with bad copies of European ornament from every known period, mixed up together in a most incongruous fashion. . . . Those among you with better taste have collected a heap of art treasures in the Old World and even ripped off whole façades to bring them back to America. With these costly spoils from the Old World you have made of America a rags-bottles-sacks market instead of a New World. . . .

Americans, America has for centuries nourished an indigenous and productive art, with roots deep struck in their own soil. If you wish to love ancient art, you can have American antiques that are authentic. . . .

The antique, the classic art of America, is to be found between the Tropic of Cancer and the Tropic of Capricorn, that strip of continent which was to the New World what Greece was to the Old. Your antiques are not to be found in Rome. They are to be found in Mexico. . . .

Become aware of the splendid beauty of your factories, admit the charm of your native houses, the luster of your metals, the clarity of your glass. . . .

Let your architects of talent work freely as they will. You possess many such. Do not ask them to give you copies of the edifices you admired while touring Europe. . . .

Take out your vacuum cleaners and clear away those ornamental excrescences of fraudulent styles. . . . Clear your brains of false traditions, of unjustifiable fears, in order to be entirely yourselves. And sure of the immense possibilities latent in America: PROCLAIM THE AESTHETIC INDEPENDENCE OF THE AMERICAN CONTINENT. . . .

It only remains to say that with the triumph of abstract art in the San Francisco Art School a decade later, Diego's fresco was covered up with a canvas screen by a new Art Institute Director of foolishly narrow criterion who found the painting no longer too radical but too "conservative" and too representational." He is gone now, and in 1962 when I visited San Francisco the fresco was as fresh in color as the day it was painted. Diego sat there on the scaffold still, with his back to me, palette in one hand and brush in the other, still alive and at work on the painting.

25. THE PAINTER AND THE MACHINE

On December 9, 1930, the home of John D. Rockefeller, Jr. at 10 West Fifty-Fourth Street in New York City, was the scene of a meeting of a number of persons interested both in Mexico and art. They had come together to form an organization which would "promote friendship between the people of Mexico and the United States by encouraging cultural relations and the interchange of fine and applied arts." The gathering had been prepared with the aid of a promotion fund of fifteen thousand dollars contributed by John D. Rockefeller, Jr., and six months of preliminary work by Mrs. Frances Flynn Paine, art dealer and adviser to the Rockefellers on art, herself related by birth and marriage to several of America's wealthy families.

Those present knew each other either as men and women of a common world of finance, or as contact men between that world and that of art and culture. An organization was set up to be known as the Mexican Arts Association, Inc. Winthrop W. Aldrich, banker and brother of Mrs. John D. Rockefeller, Jr., was elected president; Mrs. Emily Johnson De Forest, whose husband was president of the Metropolitan Museum, was chosen honorary president; Frank Crowninshield, publisher and trustee of the Museum of Modern Art, was made secretary; and Mr. Aldrich was authorized to name all other officers. The following persons had signified their agreement, since their names appear in the articles of incorporation as members of the Board of Directors: Mrs. Abby A. Rockefeller, W. W. Aldrich, Mrs. Elizabeth C. Morrow, Miss Martha C. Vail, T. B. Appleget, Enos S. Booth, Franklin M. Mills, Mrs. Helen B. Hitchcock, Professor C. E. Richards, Henry A. Moe, Mrs. Mabel S. Smithers, Mrs. Emily J. De Forest, Mrs. Frances Flynn Paine, and Frank Crowninshield. If the inquiring reader will check the list against the family names of the boards of directors of America's leading corporations, he will find that they interlock. Names not to be found thus can be located in a second check-up with a list of directors of the leading New York art museums or foundations. A most distinguished company.

Early in its career, possibly at the first session, the association hit upon the name of Diego Rivera as suitable for their first widely publicized undertaking. In the summer of 1931, while Diego was at work once more on the National Palace and dreaming of machinery and walls in Detroit, he was visited by Mrs. Frances Flynn Paine of New York with news that she could secure a retrospective one-man show for him in that mecca of modern painters, the Museum of Modern Art. She could arrange, at the usual dealer's commission, sales of oils and water colors to influential patrons with whom she had connections. Diego knew nothing of the Mexican Arts Association, Inc., nor of the adventures and experiences this opportunity would lead to, but since it fitted in perfectly with his plans, he joyfully accepted the invitation. And well he might, for more than he understood, the doors of America were being opened to him.

The art museums of America today are a big business: their

19. Diego at Work
(after losing over 100 pounds).

120. Lucienne Bloch and Steve Dimitroff,
Assistants to Rivera.

21. Portrait of the Author. Radio
City. 1933 (Subsequently destroyed)

122. Sketch of the Author. New Workers
School. On Rough Coat. 1933

123. Center of Resurrected Radio City Mural in Mexico.

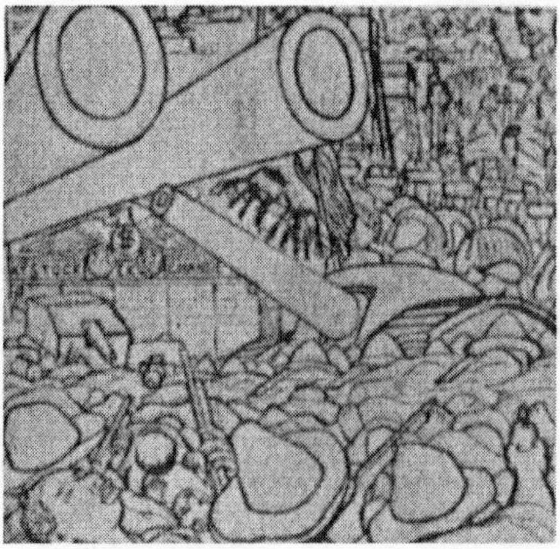

124. Imperialism. Wall Sketch.
New Workers School. 1933

125. Imperialism. Panel.

126. Civil War. John Brown and J. P. Morgan.
New Workers School. 1933

127. The First International.
New Workers School. 1933

128. Communist Unity Panel. New Workers School. Showing "Stalin, the Executioner," Marx, Lenin, Engels, Trotsky and other Communist Leaders. 1933

129. The Bandit Hero. Carnival Series. Hotel Reforma. 1936

130. General Porkbarrel Dancing with Miss Mexico. Hotel Reforma. 1936

131. Loading Burro. Chinese Ink. 1936

132. Woman with Bowl. Chinese Ink. 1936

133. Burden Bearer. Chinese Ink. 1936

134. Basket Vendors. Amecameca. Watercolor. 1934

135. Mother and Children. Watercolor on Canvas. 1934

136. Illustration for Popol Vuh. Watercolor. 1931

137. Pineapple Man. Costume for Ballet, "H.P." 1931

138. Banana Man. 1931

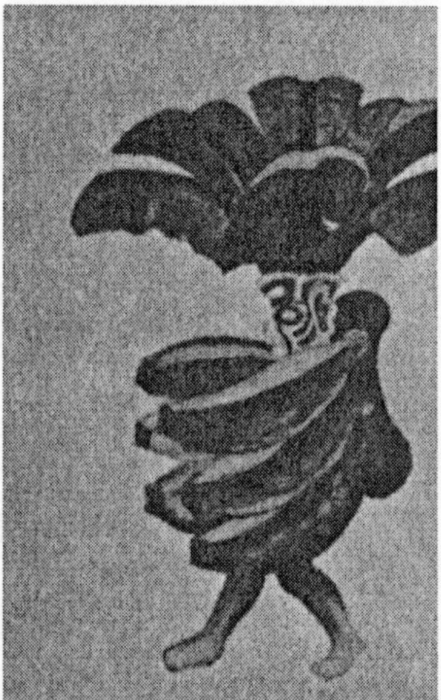

139. Portrait of Roberto Rosales. Wax on Canvas. 1930

140. Girl in Checked Dress. Oil. 1930

141. Sleep. Watercolor on Canvas. 1936

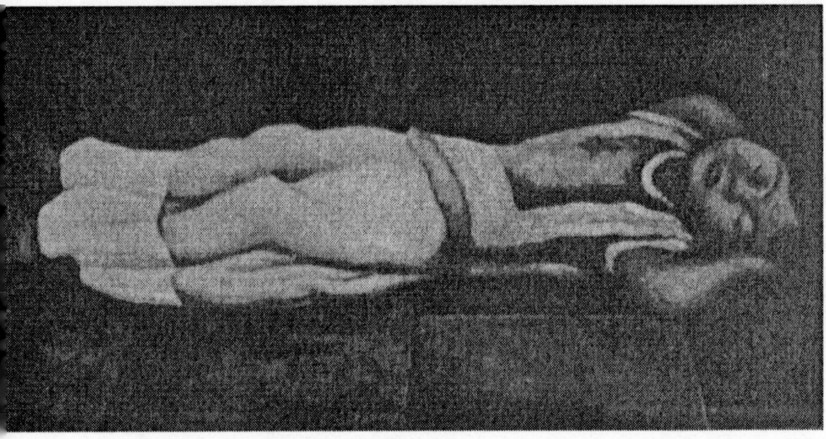

142. Landscape near Taxco. Oil. 1937

143. Vegetable Vendor.
Watercolor on Canvas. 1935

144. The Assassination of
Altamirano.
Tempera on masonite. 1936

145. The Burning of Judas. Chinese Ink. 1937

146. Landscape. Sonora. Wax on Canvas. 1931

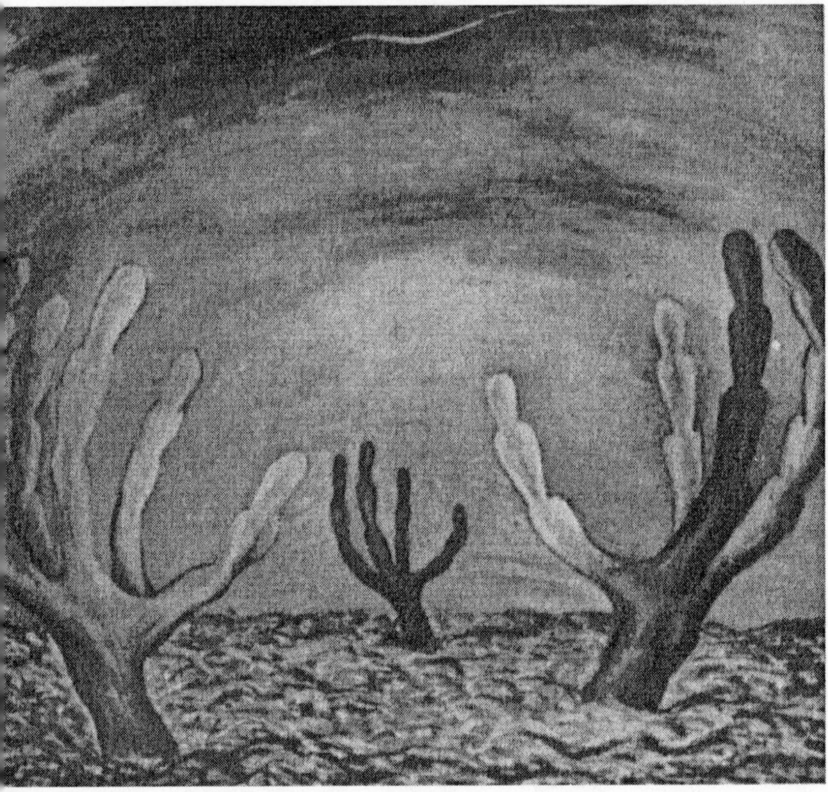

147. Sketch for a Landscape. 1944

benefactors and directors are generally among the richest men in their respective communities; they have interlocking directorates that read not unlike those of any other large corporate interest. No longer do America's wealthy limit themselves to exclusive trading in Old Masters of assured value: the Whitney Museum purchases the work of contemporary Americans; one Guggenheim has set up a foundation for the fostering of abstract art, another the foundation which has helped so many artists and writers; the Museum of Modern Art has Rockefeller backing; a Ford leads the Detroit Institute of Arts; even the Metropolitan buys more work of living artists.

The dominant art family in America is undoubtedly that of the Rockefellers: they may not compete with the older Morgans and Mellons in Old Masters, but they surely predominate in the purchase and fostering of the work of living artists. Many a museum in this country looks hopefully to some member of this family, or a board connected with it, for some share of its maintenance. Where this is not the case, it is usually because some local financial tycoon is the museum's chief sustainer; for example, in Detroit Edsel Ford was chairman of the board that directs the Art Institute.*

In the person of Dwight Morrow, Diego had come into contact with the Morgan partnership. In San Francisco he met and enlisted the enthusiasm of Dr. W. R. Valentiner and Edgar P. Richardson, representatives of the Detroit Institute of Arts. Now Mrs. Paine was offering him the keys to the City of New York. To be taken up by these circles is to be "made"—so far as assured sales, purchase and exhibition by museums, and high-powered publicity can make an artist.

Diego arrived in New York by boat on November 13, 1931, with scarcely more than a month to prepare for the opening of his show. Captain Robert Wilmot of the *Morro Castle* had been

* Edsel Ford was also on the Board of Directors of the Museum of Modern Art in New York.

a most understanding host, arranging a temporary studio on the ship, so that he landed with various works completed from sketches in his notebooks. With a tempo appropriate to the city of speed, he went to work in the large studio-gallery provided for him in the Heckscher Building, at that time the home of the Museum of Modern Art. There he completed, in the brief space of a month and ten days, seven movable frescoes, each six by eight feet in painted surface. These steel-framed, three-hundred-pound panels, he explained to reporters, were not only appropriate to exhibitions, but because of their movability suitable for general use in "a land where the buildings do not stand long." Four were repetitions of details from his Mexican murals, with some modification; three were impressions of New York City. When the exhibition opened on December 23, the museum had gathered together and arranged in a form which showed his evolution and many-sidedness, some 150 items: the seven new frescoes, 56 oils and wax paintings, 25 water colors, and drawings, sketches and fresco studies. Though his best work was poorly represented by the four fresco fragments, the exhibition as a whole was sufficient to give some notion of the stature of the painter. The catalogue, like all those prepared by Barr and Abbott, was a model of what a museum catalogue can be when intelligently edited.

The critics gave the exhibition a friendly reception. They marveled at the long and many-phased imitation of others, finding that even as imitator he had been more prodigious and restless than most painters. When a correspondent denounced the painter as "a conscienceless thief," Jewell of the *Times* answered that the new frescoes showed his originality beyond doubt or possibility of cavil, and "spleen cannot wash these frescoes from the wall"—certainly an unanswerable observation. The best and most poetic of his fresco panels was a beautiful redoing of his gentle-faced Zapata holding the bridle of a white horse, first done in his Cuernavaca frescoes. It is in the Museum's permanent collection and has been reproduced in color in *Masters of Modern Art*, Alfred H. Barr, editor (New York, 1953), p. 154. It was widely admired, for it is one of his most lyrical works.

But his impressions of New York were received with less general approval. One of them was *Pneumatic Drilling*, with drill bits dancing, wraiths of stone dust rising and curling, the men's garments curving round their muscles in lines emphasizing the rhythm of the drills. A second was entitled *Electric Welding*. The third depicted New York on three levels: at the base, a guarded bank vault with immobilized wealth; in the middle, a municipal lodging house with immobilized men lying on the floor like corpses in a morgue; above, the immobilized skyscrapers of New York, like monuments on a tomb of business, the whole denominated by the painter *Frozen Assets.**

This was the beginning of the third year of the great depression, and Americans were very touchy. It was impolite, even a little alarming, for an invited guest to have snapped the host when he was not "dressed for a picture." There were obscure, disquieting hints of what he might paint when he got to know America better. Many critics now had sober second thoughts on the American frescoes which were viewed as "not so successful." They admitted in accustomed critical jargon that the paintings were "closely contained . . . tonally rich . . . forcefully defined . . . significant and characteristic statements. . . ." Then came the "buts," which narrowed down in the end to reservations concerning *Frozen Assets.* Here too the language was usually technical, but each stricture directly or indirectly betrayed the fact that the critic's unfavorable reaction was to that aspect of the painting which so many of them scorned to mention: its social intention.

The controversy over *Frozen Assets* merely served to increase popular interest in Diego's one-man show. The Museum of Modern Art had been founded in the summer of 1929, and had immediately made a place for itself. This was its fourteenth exhibit, its second one-man show, Matisse having been the subject of the preceding one. In the first two weeks 31,625 persons

* *Frozen Assets* and *Pneumatic Drill* were reproduced as Plates 4 and 5 in *Portrait of America* (New York, Covici-Friede, 1934).

paid admission; before it was finished it had broken all previous records.

As we have already noted, when Rivera was still painting in California, the two leaders of the Detroit Institute of Arts, Valentiner and Richardson, had visited the West Coast and been delighted by what they saw of Diego's work. Richardson reviewed his San Francisco show in glowing words. He spoke of Rivera's having "built up a powerful narrative style of painting which makes him, it is safe to say, the only man now working who adequately represents the world we live in—wars, tumult, struggling peoples, hope and discontent, humor and speeding existence. . . . It is interesting, when most of our contemporary painting is abstract and introspective, to see a man like Diego Rivera appear with a strong, dramatic narrative art which takes any story and tells it superbly well. He is a great painter and he has a subject which demands greatness in its telling."*

To Valentiner and Richardson, Diego had communicated his dream of painting in the industrial heart of America the epic of industry and the machine, the beauty of the machine's adaptation of marvelous form to no less marvelous function, the embodiment in it of human intelligence and human cooperation in labor, its potentialities for the mastery of nature and the liberation of man. The Art Commission before which Dr. Valentiner unfolded this plan consisted of Edsel Ford, chairman, Albert Kahn, Charles T. Fisher, and Julius H. Haas. On May 27, 1931, just before Diego left San Francisco, he had received the following letter from Dr. Valentiner:

> At yesterday's meeting the Arts Commission decided to ask you to help us to beautify the Museum and give fame to its hall through your great work. . . .
>
> Now there is only one matter which I hope will not be too diffi-

* *Detroit News*, February 15, 1931, later incorporated in a bulletin of the Institute.

cult for you to understand. Since our funds are limited, the Arts Commission is not able to authorize more than $10,000 for the wall paintings; but I believe that if one would leave a considerable space free on the lower part of the wall where the pillars rise, and possibly on the side, the amount covered by your paintings could be reduced so much that it would amount to about fifty square yards on each side, which at $100 a square yard would be $10,000. . . .

The Arts Commission will be very glad to have your suggestions of the motifs, which could be selected after you are here. They would be pleased if you could possibly find something out of the history of Detroit, or some motif suggesting the development of industry in this town; but at the end they decided to leave it entirely to you, what you think best to do. . . . Everyone in the Arts Commission is very much interested in your work, and knows that an artist must be as far as possible free and independent in his work if something great is to be accomplished. . . .

The ten thousand dollars, donated by Edsel Ford, looked big to Diego after the shoestring budgets, appropriated but often unpaid, on which he had had to work in Mexico. The size of the wall, as usual, did not trouble him; on the contrary, mentally he brushed aside the suggestion that he should leave parts empty to keep the compensation at one hundred dollars a square yard. He loved great walls, and as the National Palace showed, had an abhorrence of vacant spaces. His show in New York coming to an end, he left at once for Detroit to look over the glass-roofed inner court of the Detroit Institute of Arts. Immediately he enlarged his plans to cover four walls instead of two, and such was his enthusiasm for the Detroit factories he visited that only the fact that the roof was glass and a source of illumination prevented him from proposing to paint the ceiling. Edsel Ford, stirred by the first sketches and verbal plans of the painter, generously increased his donation from $10,000 to $25,000, while the Institute agreed to pay the costs of material and the labor of the plasterers.

At the same time Herman Black, Chicago publisher who had seen Diego's work in San Francisco, wrote that he expected to persuade the management of the coming World's Fair ("The Century of Progress") to have the painter do a "machinery and industry" mural in one of its buildings. Word came from New York that the Rockefellers, too, were considering the offer of a wall to him in the new RCA building at Radio City. Diego began to visit Detroit factories, machine shops, and laboratories, his head spinning with these great projects. To have the Rockefellers in New York, the Fords in Detroit, the Chicago World's Fair—probably in the General Motors Building—as his patrons, what more could any painter ask in the twentieth century? Was it not strange that these billionaire sons of the "Yankee Robber Barons" had developed such taste, or the will to engage the corresponding expertise, and the readiness for him to paint on walls so accessible to the masses as the lobby of Radio City, the courtyard of the Detroit Institute of Art, and the central building of the Chicago World's Fair, while Moscow would not give him a wall? Had Michelangelo, "pricked on by your popes and kings," been more favored?

The court of the Detroit Museum in which Rivera was to paint both attracted and repelled him. Its walls set him atingle, but they were decorated in a complicated Italian baroque singularly inappropriate to the theme he had chosen, and broken at frequent intervals by little windows and ventilators framed in wavy molding, by pilasters, by heads of satyrs in rounded high relief, by strips of cross moldings, and doorways, while in the midst of the garden court was a fountain which he characterized to me as *horrorosa*.

The decoration cost him many a headache and many a fit of fury. An art museum which houses styles of many ages may perhaps be justified in making its central courtyard Italian baroque, but what did this decoration have to do with present-day America and a great industrial city? Yet it was precisely here, in this center of modern industry, that he had hoped to offer his contribution to the creation of the new style for his own day.

The problem, he had long been insisting, was never one of deciding which dead style of the past to select. Each past style had once been alive because it had developed in response to the needs of its land and time. But this land and time, and this city which symbolized them, needed the appropriate expressive forms for this new age and style of life.

Always he had done his best to make his frescoes harmonize with the architecture of the structure of which they formed a part, the uses of the building, and the life of the city and people in the midst of which it was located. Often there had been conflict (only if architect and painter were to get together before the edifice was constructed could such conflict be avoided). But this time the gap was unbridgable, between Italy and the age of baroque on the one hand, and America and the age of the machine on the other. In the end he decided to sacrifice the architectural decoration, which he considered false to the spirit of the city, in favor of the city's spirit. With the cunning of which he was master, he set to work to subordinate and assimilate the decoration to his painting in such fashion that the stone trimmings should be overwhelmed and seem to disappear into the painted wall. Even so, this work, which, considered as painting, is the best he did in the United States and one of the best paintings inspired by machinery and modern industry—is not successful in terms of its relation to the other decoration upon these walls. Since the latter, however, is only surface ornament, not involving the fundamental structure and proportions of the courtyard itself, it might easily be removed and the walls as walls simplified thereby into greater harmony with the painting. Perhaps some day a bold museum curator may have the courage to do so.

Diego spent three excited months wandering through miles of machinery, making sketches in the Ford, Chrysler, Parke-Davis chemical, Michigan Alkali, Edison, and other plants, before he even erected his scaffold. The more he saw, the more he was stirred by clean-lined, brilliantly planned laboratories, marvelously designed belt conveyers and precision instruments. As a man may turn over half a library to make a book, and a novelist half a town to make a character, so he went through all Detroit's great industrial plants to paint a single panel of machinery.

> I have had here a very heavy job of preparation [he wrote me in a letter of July 9, 1932] especially a job of observation. The frescoes will be twenty-seven, making together a single thematic and plastic unity. I expect it to be the most complete of my works; for the industrial material of this place I feel the enthusiasm I felt ten years ago at the time of my return to Mexico with the peasant material. . . .

Painting, Diego had long believed, must absorb the machine if it was to find the style for this age, assimilate it as easily and naturally as it had still-life objects, landscapes, dwellings, castles, faces, nude bodies; master this marvelous new material and make it live again on walls as vividly and movingly as ever art had historical scenes, old legends, and religious parables. This was to be no uninformed contemplation from without, as in the case of the impressionists who saw in modern industry only smoke and haze, murky atmosphere and furnace fire, or wavering structure to which no real function could be assigned. Nor was it to be stylized mechanism as with Léger, who reduced every "machine," even the human being, to geometrical *natures mortes*, abstract, ornamental, without passion or power, with no capacity for movement in them, save the movement of the observing eye which follows their sometimes playful geometrical contours. Nor was it to be machinery portrayed as devouring monster, in the fashion of those seekers after the irrevocable past who saw the evil effects but did not see the potentialities for good inherent in these great extensions of man's limbs. He would paint the human *spirit* that is embodied in the machine, for it is one of the most brilliant achievements of man's intelligence and reason; the force and power which give man dominion over the inhuman forces of nature to which he had so long been in helpless subservience; the *hope* that is in the machine that man, freed by it from servitude to nature, need not long remain in servitude to hunger, exhausting toil, inequality, and tyranny. But it did not occur to Diego that the machine might also be used to extend the power of a dictator over the ruled, extend it to something approaching totality.

He would compress acres of machinery into a few hundred square feet of wall, yet make them true to their form and function and movement—they would be so true to the logic and precision of the models that they would "work." Mechanism was to him what it had been to Leonardo, and not many painters in between. "The more one knows," he could say with the Florentine whose inexhaustible intellectual energy and curiosity he shared, "the more one loves."

Rivera's favorite image had always been the wave. Increasingly it had been implicit in his painting, along with subtly modified diagonal structure based upon the "golden section"—a fusion out of which had come his own particular form of what he was pleased to call, after the fashion of artists, "dynamic symmetry." Now he set out to paint the wave explicitly, the wave that runs through electrons, mountains, water, wind, life, death, the seasons, sound, light, that does not cease to undulate in the dead, nor in things that have never lived. It is visible in the geological strata that separate the allegorical figures at the top of the Detroit murals from the machinery panels below, it gives movement and sinuous beauty to the belt conveyers, absorbs in its undulations the movements of the men who work at the machines. As in the Mexican *trapiche,* work here was, in his eyes, not so much toil as a dance. If the reader will examine PLATE 117 he will perceive with what sensuousness Rivera portrayed machinery on these walls. These pipes and tubes possessed more of an erotic quality than his nudes in Chapingo or the Health Building or the "pin-ups" he did in Ciro's night club at the Hotel Reforma.

During the year Diego consumed in this massive work, his health was not good. He was engaged in a fantastically rigorous course of reducing, according to the prescription of a Mexican doctor whose name I think it charity to withhold. Here were the instructions as to diet for a man whose giant body and giant labors entailed enormous need for energizing foods:

QUANTITY OF NOURISHMENT

a) 12 acid fruits daily: 4 lemons, 6 oranges, 2 grapefruit
b) 1 liter of vegetable juice
c) 2 times daily a vegetable salad

MENU

On an empty stomach, fruit salts.
Breakfast: 2 oranges, 1 lemon.
During the day, every 2 hours an acid fruit.
Dinner and supper: a vegetable salad.
Vegetable juice should be drunk during the day.
Fruits of all kinds (except grapes and bananas) may be eaten.
No cooked vegetables. No sugar or oil in salads.
Every night a bath with Epsom salts (½ kilo).

To this drastic diet were added liberal doses of thyroid extract. The frame of the painter was reduced in the course of a year by over one hundred pounds.* When he paid me a visit in New York, he was lean and flabby, his face sunken and sad, his clothes hung about him in elephantine folds. During the whole year he had continued as usual to consume the energy of a dozen ordinary men, painting long hours of the day, especially in summer, under a blazing sun which shone down upon the glass-roofed court until at times the temperature on the scaffold rose to 120°F., continuing far into the hot nights when humidity kept the walls moist enough to paint for many additional hours. This heroic reducing treatment was followed by years of glandular disorder, increased irritability, and increased hypochondria, com-

* Compare Plates 114 and 119.

plicated by a succession of illnesses and collapses, until, in 1936, Dr. Rafael Silva, eye specialist called in to treat an infection of the tear duct of his right eye, ordered him to be "reinflated and not disinflated again under any circumstances."

Frida's condition was another source of worry to Diego. Slender and frail since her accident, Frida did not take kindly to the hot summers of Detroit after a lifetime on the cool uplands of the Mexican *mesa central.* Nor did she take kindly to the bland American cuisine, confining her meals to birdlike pecks at tidbits, supplemented by sucking on hard candies at intervals during the day. She was pregnant when they arrived in Detroit, and it was questionable how the slender waist and fractured pelvis would endure the strain of delivery. As Diego watched her grow pale and peaked and observed her long attacks of morning nausea, he was oppressed with a premonition of impending disaster. What made it worse was the fact that he had a tendency to believe his premonitions were prophetic.

Frida complained that "her baby hurt her," but continued trying to act the gay, reckless girl she had always been. Bleeding gave notice of an impending miscarriage; yet the doctor withheld the truth from her, merely warning her to "take a complete rest." Naturally, Frida ignored the veiled warning, with disastrous consequences. On the night of July 4 she went through the agony of a painful miscarriage accompanied by serious hemorrhage. Diego was terribly frightened, and overwhelmed by a sense of his helplessness. Towards morning she was rushed to the Ford Hospital in a dangerous state. As they wheeled her through the basement directly into an operating room, she opened her eyes, perceived a many-colored ceiling, and in the midst of her agony found the strength and enthusiasm to murmur: "*¡Qué precioso!*" It was typical of that side of her character which made her an artist and a fit companion for a painter.

Frida was heartbroken at the loss of the child, depressed to the point of melancholia. After many days, she asked for oils and a piece of tin and found release from her oppressive sense of futility and pain in a series of highly personal paintings reflecting the experience. Scarcely recovered, she got news of her mother's severe illness, undertook an arduous trip to Mexico, arriving only in time to see her mother die. Diego was unusually thoughtful and tender, more so than he had ever been before towards any human being.

He refused to let her risk a second attempt to bear a child, which aggrieved her at times to the point of obsession. Underneath the wild gaiety and charm which still persisted, her intimates caught a note of profound melancholy. She painted now and again, in disorderly fashion, turning out works at long intervals that are "surrealistic" in a personal but not in the academic sense—strange, witty, fantastic, lovely, highly individual things. They are definitely better than the works done before the loss of her child. Her one-man show in New York in the autumn of 1938 astonished those who visited it for its excellence as painting, its gay, infectious, sometimes troubling wit and fantasy, and its complete lack of the remotest point of contact with the technique and style and subject matter of the work of her better-known husband.*

While Diego was painting in the museum's garden court, rumors of his work began to fill the daily press of Detroit.

> From what is already on the walls, and from the sketches [wrote one reporter] . . . the work in material, manner and enormity, is beyond the conception of the people outside the red drapes [that cover the finished portions of the wall]. When they see it, it will hit them like a bolt.†

After more than a year of superhuman labors, on March 13, 1933, the paintings were finished and officially unveiled. People

* For a contemporary appreciation of it, see my "Rise of a New Rivera," in *Vogue* (October 1938).

† W. M. Mountjoy in Detroit *Sunday Times*, October 23, 1932.

looked for the statuesque female of classic drapes, holding a tiny automobile in one hand and a lighted torch in the other. In place of that, they saw the "spirit of Detroit" at work in laboratories, sputtering in flame from welding torches, writhing through belt conveyers, bending, muscular and absorbed, over sheets of silvery steel being shaped into auto bodies, toiling in overalls, peering through gas masks, alive in crisp shapely gas shells, sunflowerlike motors, and clean-lined, glistening, all-metal planes poised for flight. Nowhere was pomp and luxury, nowhere hollow civic allegory, nowhere leisure-class Detroit—only workingmen and women, engineers, chemists; even Edsel Ford, donor of the fresco, appears in it only to be put at work on the design of an automobile.

Anathema was not slow to descend upon painter and painting. Even before the unveiling, the battle was on. Churchmen and dignitaries and ordinary busybodies who had never concerned themselves with a work of art formed mutual-excitation societies to secure its removal. The vaccination panel dedicated to the glorification of scientific research (PLATE 116), redolent of early Italian painting, aroused particular ire because of its reminiscence of the Holy Family; the stalwart child held by the "halo"-crowned nurse, being vaccinated by a physician, suggested Mary, Joseph, and the Child; the horse, ox, and sheep, whence the serum is derived, carried overtones of the stable of the Nativity; the three scientists working in the background were three Magi bearing gifts. One wonders as one gazes at this beautiful and tender work how anyone could regard this as blasphemy and desire its destruction; or how the same people could have missed the more mischievous allusion to the "temptation of Saint Anthony" in the depiction of the manager of a chemical factory trying to concentrate on adding machines and accounts while surrounded by the exposed knees and calves of girls at work around him. About this panel no complaint was made, except that the painter, amused by the tendency of American designers to give such modern things as radios a "gothic" design, had set the adding machine on a radio cabinet which some people thought looked like a church.

> Señor Rivera has perpetrated a heartless hoax on his capitalist employer, Mr. Edsel Ford [declared President George Hermann Derry of the Marygrove College for Girls] . . . He has foisted on Mr. Ford and the museum a Communist Manifesto. . . . Will the women of Detroit feel flattered when they realize that on the left of the south wall they are embodied in the female with the hard, masculine unsexed face ecstatically staring for hope and help across the panel to her languorous and grossly sensual Asiatic sister on the right?
>
> One may wonder whether Mr. Ford has ever seen a copy of Rivera's fresco, "The Billionaire's Banquet" . . . wherein are presented photographic likenesses of Rockefeller, Morgan and Henry Ford—the latter in the pose of quaffing a glass of champagne? One wonders further how an extra-dry like Mr. Ford [Dr. Derry was not so extra-dry, but any weapon was good against these paintings] will relish himself caricatured in this guise by Rivera on the wall of a neighboring and friendly republic.*

Eight days after the completion of the paintings there was a meeting in the office of the Reverend H. Ralph Higgins, senior curate of St. Paul's Episcopal Cathedral, of people who "represented several different points of view, but all against the murals . . . a volunteer group which has undertaken to crystallize feeling against the murals into a formal request that they be removed. . . ." † Those present included an architect, a structural engineer, three representatives of the art commission of the Detroit Review Club, two representatives of the Catholic clergy, one of the Episcopalian, and a lay member of the board of trustees of the Unitarian Church. Two days later Councilman William P. Bradley presented a motion to the City Council that the "paintings be washed from the walls." He denounced them as a "travesty on the spirit of Detroit, completely ignoring the cultural and spiritual aspects of the city." Assistant Corporation

* Detroit *Evening Times,* March 21, 1933.

† *Ibid.*

Counsel John Atkinson, while prosecuting a local theater-proprietor on charges of "exposing obscene photographs to public view," departed from the indictment to say he thought the Rivera nudes obscene and "would like to see clothes on the slattern and pudgy-bodied" figures.

The authorities of the museum and art lovers of the city had a serious fight on their hands. Several defense committees were set up, one headed by Fred L. Black, President of the People's Museum Association, and the Reverend Augustus P. Reccord, pastor of the Unitarian Curch, another made up of representatives of Detroit labor and radical organizations. The museum authorities gave out interviews defending the paintings, had two young women circulate among the huge crowds visiting the court to find out how sentiment was running, clocked the greatest number of persons the Institute had ever had, appealed to the College Art Association of New York for support. Dr. Valentiner pronounced the vaccination panel "a finely executed, rationalistic interpretation of the beautiful legend of the Holy Family . . . as acceptable to us as a masterpiece on any other subject." The Detroit *News* declared editorially, "the best thing to do would be to whitewash the entire work completely," whereupon Walter Pach wired from New York: "If these paintings are whitewashed, nothing can ever be done to whitewash America."

Mass meetings pro and con were held daily, radio debates filled the air, Sunday pulpits rang with occasional defense and multitudinous fiery denunciations. The Reverend Mr. Higgins of the fashionable Woodward Avenue Episcopal Church, three blocks from the Institute, admitted in a radio debate that he had visited the museum only once in his life, and had not even seen the Rivera murals except in newspaper reproduction. Over station WXYZ he told a radio audience:

> If the genius of our people be unmixed materialism and atheism, if our gods be science and sex, if the brutality of the machine age is the sole virtue which our fair city expresses—if these things be true,

then Mr. Rivera should be hailed as a modern Michelangelo. Of course, are there not sufficient among our people who have not bowed the knee to Baal to warrant the inclusion in the mural panorama of at least a small suggestion of spiritual intuition and aspiration?

Miss Isabel Weadlock of the museum staff invited one of the attackers, Monsignor Doyle, "in all fairness to the artist and the Institute," to give her an opportunity to explain the paintings to him, but he refused to view the frescoes "because he was not an authority on art." Yet he did not hesitate to continue pronouncing the work "an affront to millions of Catholics."

The tens of thousands of visitors to the museum were for the most part enthusiastic, so that popular support grew steadily. What took the wind out of the sails of the opposition forces was the fact that the man in Detroit whom they professed most to respect and look to for leadership, Edsel Ford, issued a declaration in favor of the paintings: "I admire Rivera's spirit," he said. "I really believe he was trying to express his idea of the spirit of Detroit." Feeble as these words of defense were, they were a great help in saving the paintings. Two years later, Dr. Valentiner was able to write to Rivera (letter of May 1, 1935): "Your murals here are still the greatest attraction in Detroit."

It was while Diego was finishing his "machinery" mural that Elie Faure wrote him a lengthy letter (January 20, 1933) on the subject of the machine and its role in modern life, giving his estimate of the Detroit frescoes and the views which had developed in his mind from the seed Diego had sowed there so many years before:

What you tell me of America is preferable to what passes here in France. The machine has become the enemy, all the writers, painters, and dramatists overwhelm it with bourgeois anathemas. *Quos vult perdere. . . .*

Fear reigns. The bourgeois recoils before his monstrous child, which the people is going to take possession of. What an admirable spectacle! . . .

Meanwhile the imbeciles acclaim at the Théâtre Français a piece against the machine. Note that they have reserved their seats by telephone, that they admired the acting with opera glasses, that their autos wait for them at the corner, that they were at the movies the night before, and tomorrow the surgeons, armed with electric drills sterilized in an autoclave, are to trepan their child. Miserable idiots!

You cannot know the pleasure I derive from seeing you utilize the machine as motif of plastic emotion and decoration in your new frescoes, which seem strongly beautiful to me, even though the color element which I admire so much, is lacking [in the photographs Rivera had sent him].

When will I be able to reproduce a few? Soon I hope. But where? The important art reviews, that of Waldemar George especially, are closed to me. "M. Elie Faure," the latter has declared, "is not an aesthetician." *Tu parles, con!* And behold *L'Amour de l'Art,* the only one which still welcomes my articles, disappears. It was there that I intended to publish my article on you, which is written, takes twelve typewritten pages, and is only awaiting a publisher. I affirm, moreover, that it will appear. . . .

There you are, *mon vieux* Diego, that's all I have to tell you for the moment. We have a communion of ideas which I think is complete. It is a great joy for me. You will never know what a capital event was the meeting with you twelve years ago. You were the poetry of the new world rising suddenly before my eyes from the unknown. I felt in knowing and understanding you an unheard-of feeling of deliverance. . . .

Elie Faure finally succeeded in getting the article referred to in the above letter published in *Art et Médecine.** From it I quote the concluding paragraph:

The poetry of the machine which was born in the frescoes of Mexico and San Francisco dominates those of Detroit: flames escaping from drills, dazzling, crackling motors, silent and dancing rhythms of rods and pistons—all these beat the cadences of a new march—the rehearsals of a still hesitant humanity. You see the witchery of mills and of factories, of power-houses, of illuminating arcs over the ocean.

* Elie Faure: "*La Peinture murale mexicaine,*" *Art et Médecine* (April 1934).

Babel towers above the cities—from now on all this becomes a part of our inner being, and woe to those who do not feel it. The hate which you see is really love. Once more man attempts to understand man, in the midst of force itself—these are all new themes, new motives, new causes for emotions. Mexico can well be proud of her great painters who can give expression to this new age.

26. THE BATTLE OF ROCKEFELLER CENTER

The theme offered Diego for execution on the elevator bank facing the main entrance to the RCA Building in Radio City was: *Man at the Crossroads Looking with Hope and High Vision to the Choosing of a New and Better Future.*

The partnership of one of the world's greatest painters with one of the world's richest financial dynasties to give the people of the City of New York a mural with such a theme—a theme not of Rivera's but of Rockefeller's choosing—was the result of protracted and precarious negotiations. The preliminary "wooing" was long and reassuring: Mrs. John D. Rockefeller, Jr. (daughter of the late Senator Nelson W. Aldrich), and the then Mrs. Nelson Rockefeller (the former Mary Todhunter Clark), discriminating collectors both, had purchased examples of his work. As if to evidence that their taste in art was superior to prejudice against his social theme, Mrs. John D. Rockefeller had included among her purchases his notebook of Russian sketches.

Nelson Rockefeller praised Rivera's Detroit murals, deplored the controversy which they aroused, wrote notes such as: "Please let me know when your frescoes in Detroit are finished so that we can arrange to come up and see them. Everybody is terribly anxious to see how you have interpreted the industrial life of Detroit" (letter of October 13, 1932). Finally, Nelson Rockefeller broached the subject of his doing a mural in Radio City. Similar requests were made of Picasso and Matisse.

The written proposal from the construction engineers which followed the oral negotiations invited the three painters to enter into a "competition," the terms of which seemed, consciously or unconsciously, calculated to restrain these turbulent spirits by a series of elaborate restrictions and regulations. They were to submit preliminary projects (for which they were to receive three hundred dollars) for paintings in which no color was to be used, "only black, white and gray"; the scale of the drawings was to be "8 foot, 6 inches for the human figure in the front plane"; the mural was to be done on canvas; the painting to cover "between sixty and seventy-five percent of the canvas"; the instructions even stipulated the number of coats of varnish that were to cover the pigment!

Matisse rejected the commission on the ground that its scale, theme, and character did not accord with his style of painting; Picasso refused to receive the representative of the architects; Rivera turned down the proposal in a letter (of May 9, 1932), written in French to architect Raymond Hood, from which I translate:

> I thank you. Ten years ago I would have accepted your kind invitation with pleasure. It would have helped me start . . . but since then I have worked enough and I am known enough to ask of each one who wants my work that he ask for it on my value. One can always have me make a sketch and take it or leave it, naturally, but no "competition"—I am no more at that point.
>
> Permit me therefore to tell you that I don't quite understand this way of dealing with me; especially when you and Mr. Nelson

Rockefeller have had the amiability to indicate your interest in having my collaboration without the slightest previous solicitation on my part.

"Sorry you can't accept," wired Raymond Hood, the architect. But Nelson Rockefeller intervened and persuaded him to accept without competition. When the painter heard a little later that Frank Brangwyn and José María Sert had been substituted for Matisse and Picasso, there was a fresh crisis. He did not mind so much the frippery that was being dispersed throughout many of the buildings, but the mural canvases of Brangwyn and Sert were to flank his own, and he had contempt for the work of both.

From May to October uncertain negotiations continued. Diego wrote huge tracts in French to Raymond Hood to convince him that he should be permitted to use color rather than mere black and white, and without increase in payment, do a fresco in place of a canvas mural. "Never have I believed that mural painting should have as its principal characteristic that of conserving the plane surface of the wall," he wrote to Hood, "for in that case the best mural painting would be a uniform coat of color. . . . Monumental painting does not have as its object ornamenting, but extending in time and space the life of the architecture. . . ."

"We would accentuate the funereal feeling which is fatally aroused in the public by the juxtaposition of black and white," he argued in another lengthy epistle. "In the lower parts of a building . . . one always has the feeling of a crypt. . . . Suppose some ill-disposed persons should chance upon such a nickname as 'Undertakers' Palace.' . . ."

Again and again relations were strained in these lengthy negotiations between obstinate architect and obstinate painter, but always Nelson Rockefeller, functioning as diplomat, friendly intervener, executive vice-president of Rockefeller Center, Inc., and real boss of the whole undertaking, straightened things out and sustained Rivera in his various demands as a painter.

At last, still in Detroit, Diego began to work on a sketch. To guide him he was given these instructions:

The philosophical or spiritual quality should dominate. . . . We want the paintings to make people pause and think and to turn their minds inward and upward. . . . We hope these paintings may stimulate not only a material but above all a spiritual awakening.

Our theme is NEW FRONTIERS.

To understand what we mean by "New Frontiers," look back over the development of the United States as a nation.

Today our frontiers are of a different kind. . . . Man cannot pass up his pressing and vital problems by "moving on." He has to solve them on his own lot. The development of civilization is no longer lateral; it is inward and upward. It is the cultivation of man's soul and mind, the coming into a fuller comprehension of the meaning and mystery of life.

For the development of the paintings in this hallway, these frontiers are—

1. Man's New Relation to Matter. That is man's new possibilities from his new understanding of material things, and

2. Man's New Relation to Man. That is man's new and more complete understanding of the real meaning of the Sermon on the Mount.

In view of the dispute which followed, it is interesting to examine Diego's detailed verbal description of his intended painting, which accompanied the sketches he submitted.

On the side where Brangwyn is to depict the development of the ethical relations of mankind, my painting will show, as the culmination of this evolution, human intelligence in possession of the Forces of Nature, expressed by the lightning striking off the hand of Jupiter and being transformed into useful electricity that helps to cure man's ills, unites men through radio and television, and furnishes them with light and motive power. Below, the Man of Science presents the scale of Natural Evolution, the understanding of which replaces the Superstitions of the past. This is the frontier of Ethical Evolution.

On the side where Sert is to represent the development of the Technical Power of man, my panel will show the Workers arriving at a true understanding of their rights regarding the means of production, which has resulted in the planning of the liquidation of Tyranny, personified by a crumbling statue of Caesar, whose head has fallen to the ground. It will also show the Workers of the cities and the country inheriting the Earth. This is expressed by the placing of the hands of the producers in the gesture of possession over a map of the world resting on sheaves of wheat supported by a dynamo, expressive of Agricultural Production supported by Machinery and Scientific Technique—the result of the evolution of the methods of production. This is the Frontier of Material Development.

The main plastic function of the central panel is to express the axis of the building, its loftiness, and the ascending echelon of its lateral masses. For this, color will be employed in the center of the composition, merging laterally with the general *clair-obscur*.

In the center, the telescope brings to the vision and understanding of man the most distant celestial bodies. The miscroscope makes visible and comprehensible to man infinitesimal living organisms, connecting atoms and cells with the astral system. Exactly in the median line, the cosmic energy received by two antennae is conducted to the machinery controlled by the Worker where it is transformed into productive energy.

The Worker gives his right hand to the Peasant who questions him, and with his left hand takes the hand of the sick and wounded Soldier, the victim of War, leading him to the New Road.* On the right of the central group, the Mothers, and on the left, the Teachers, watch over the development of the New Generation, which is protected by the work of the Scientists. Above, on the right side, the Cinematograph shows a group of young women in the enjoyment of health-giving sports, and on the left it shows a group of unemployed workmen in a breadline. Above this group the Television gives an image of War, as in the case of Unemployment, the result of the evolution of Technical Power unaccompanied by a corresponding ethical development. On the opposite side, above the representation of the joy derived from sports, the same aspirations created by Ethical Development, but unsuccessful without an accompanying parallel material development of Technical Power and Industrial Organization, either already existing or created by the movement itself.

* Neither here, nor in the next paragraph, is there any suggestion that Lenin would be the "Worker-Leader" joining the hands of worker, peasant, and soldier. In the accompanying sketch, this act was performed by a lay figure wearing a cap, which might in the end have the face of an American workingman or of Lenin.

In the center, Man is expressed in his triple aspect—the Peasant who develops from the Earth the products which are the origin and base of all the riches of mankind, the Worker of the cities who transforms and distributes the raw materials given by the earth, and the Soldier who, under the Ethical Force that produces martyrs in religions and wars, represents Sacrifice. Man, represented by these three figures, looks with uncertainty but with hope towards a future more complete balance between the Technical and Ethical development of Mankind necessary to a New, more Humane and Logical order.

Although, as usual, he was to modify and clarify his project as he "thought with his hand" upon the wall, the general outline here indicated was not departed from. The painter had done his best to incorporate the fuzzy verbiage of the assigned theme into his own description, but it was clear from the outset that he was planning a Communist mural. Here is science destroying the gods (lightning strikes off the hand of Jupiter); the liquidation of tyranny (Caesar beheaded); "the workers of the cities and the country inheriting the earth"; "machinery controlled by the worker"; the union of worker, peasant, and soldier under the leadership of the worker; the implied denunciation of capitalism as breeding wars, crisis, and unemployment; a "popular movement" based on ethics and modern industry; all looking "with uncertainty but with hope towards . . . a New, more Humane and Logical Order."

Moreover, the fact that he was painting for a Rockefeller and that the Communist Party was attacking him as a painter for millionaires strengthened his determination to show what a Communist he was. Whether the Rockefellers expected by gentle persuasion to get the painter to modify his plan, or whether they underestimated from the black and white and verbal sketches the power that the living painting would have upon their central wall in full color, they could not say they were not forewarned as to the intention of the artist. Thus Diego was justified in writing later:

The owners of the building were perfectly familiar with my

personality as artist and man, and with my ideas and revolutionary history. There was absolutely nothing that might have led them to expect from me anything but my honest opinions honestly expressed. Certainly I gave them no reason to expect a capitulation. Moreover, I carried my care in dealing with them to the point of submitting a written outline (after having prepared the sketch which contained all the elements of the final composition) in detailed explanation of the esthetic and ideological intentions that the painting would express. There was not in advance, nor could there have been, the slightest doubt as to what I proposed to paint and how I proposed to paint it.*

"Enough said," wrote Mr. Todd of the construction engineers on receipt of the description and sketch. "We are all happy and looking forward with great confidence and assurance to your larger scale details and to the finished result" (letter of November 14, 1932).

Raymond Hood wired: "Sketch approved by Mister Rockefeller. . . . Can go right ahead with larger scale . . ." (telegram of November 7, 1932).

In March 1933, Diego moved into Radio City and began to paint. The comparatively high fee of $21,000 (nothing to boast of, considering that the space to be covered was 1,071 square feet and that the painter had to pay his own plasterers and helpers) enabled him to hire an unusually large number of assistants to speed up the work. These included Ben Shahn (whose Sacco-Vanzetti series he had admired), Lucienne Bloch and Stephen Dimitroff (who had begun working for him in Detroit), Hideo Noda, Lou Block, Arthur Niendorf, and Antonio Sanchez Flores, his chemist. They prepared the walls while he was still in Detroit and later ground his colors, made tracings of his wall sketches, stenciled them on the wet plaster. The actual painting, as always, Diego did himself. The work progressed smoothly and swiftly; soon the "crypt" in the RCA building began to glow with color and stir with movement. Two great elongated ellipses

* *Portrait of America* (New York, Covici-Friede, 1934), p. 24.

crossed each other in the center of the wall, one revealing the wonders of the microscope—cells, plasms, diseased tissues, bacteria; the other the wonders of the telescope—nebulae, comets, flaming suns, solar systems. To the right, a night club, an unemployment demonstration about to be broken up by the police, a lurid battlefield with searchlights playing, men in gas masks, gleaming bayonets, tanks, planes flying overhead, portrayed the evils of the existing order which man must overcome if his civilization was to continue. To the left of the great "crossroad" was an athletic stadium with girls engaged in sports, a May Day demonstration in a "Socialist" land aglow with flaming red banners borne by marching, singing workers, the figure of the leader joining the hands of a black and a white worker and a soldier in fraternal clasp. The architects and directors of construction became increasingly uneasy. They complained that it was "too realistic," too full of color and life. But on April 3 the painter was reassured by another friendly note from Nelson Rockefeller:

> I am extremely sorry not to have had the pleasure of seeing you as yet since you have been in New York. Yesterday I saw in the Sunday paper your picture working on the mural for the RCA building. It was an extremely good photograph. From all reports I get you are making very rapid progress and everybody is most enthusiastic about the work which you are doing. As you know, the building opens the first of May and it will be tremendously effective to have your mural there to greet the people as they come in for the opening. . . .

"First of May"— suggestive date full of portent for the painter! "Tremendously effective" indeed!

It was not until April 24 that trouble came in the form of a reporter from the *World-Telegram*, Joseph Lilly. His impressions of the painting, nearly two-thirds completed, were published under the provocative title:

RIVERA PAINTS SCENES OF COMMUNIST
ACTIVITY AND JOHN D. JR. FOOTS BILL

The article was no less provocative than the headline:

Diego Rivera, over whose shaggy head many storms have broken, is completing on the walls of the RCA building a magnificent fresco that is likely to provoke the greatest sensation of his career . . . microbes given life by poison gases used in war . . . germs of infectious and hereditary social diseases . . . so placed as to indicate them as the results of a civilization revolving about night clubs . . . a Communist demonstration . . . iron-jawed policemen, one swinging his club. . . . The dominant color is red—red headdress, red flags, waves of red . . . in a victorious onsweep. . . . "Mrs. Rockefeller said she liked my painting very much. . . . Mr. Rockefeller likes it too." . . .

Diego continued painting at inhuman speed, as if the vision was burning him till it had all spread out upon the wall. By the first of May it was nearing completion. For several weeks now the sketch of the "labor leader" on the wall had become an unmistakable likeness of Lenin. (Earlier the likeness had been dimmed by a cap, but by mid-April it had been changed into the familiar bald-headed portrait sketch of Lenin.) Diego was painting from the top of the wall downward; just before the first of May, he converted the sketch into a fully painted portrayal of Lenin's face, standing out lifelike and dominant, the strongest face in the fresco.

On May 4 the painter received the following letter:

While I was in the No. 1 building at Rockefeller Center yesterday viewing the progress of your thrilling mural, I noticed that in the most recent portion of the painting you had included a portrait of Lenin. This piece is beautifully painted but it seems to me that his portrait, appearing in this mural, might very easily seriously offend a great many people. If it were in a private house it would be one thing, but this mural is in a public building and the situation is therefore quite different. As much as I dislike to do so I am afraid we must ask you to substitute the face of some unknown man where Lenin's face now appears.

You know how enthusiastic I am about the work which you have been doing and that to date we have in no way restricted you in either subject or treatment. I am sure you will understand our feeling in this situation and we will greatly appreciate your making the suggested substitution.

With best wishes, I remain sincerely,

Nelson A. Rockefeller

Diego summoned a council of war. For several weeks he had been receiving tactful hints from architects, construction heads, renting offices, from Mrs. Paine and other emissaries of the Rockefellers, to tone down color, subject matter, "realism." If he yielded on the head of Lenin, would one demand lead to another until the whole conception would be destroyed? Was Lenin merely the pretext they had been looking for? Did he not have the right, as painters have ever done, to use any model which seemed suitable for each generalized figure?

As one of those called in to advise him, I urged that he offer to yield on Lenin's head, take Nelson Rockefeller at his word, and save the rest of the painting. Other advisers thought otherwise. His assistants were all for an open break. "If you remove the head of Lenin," they told him, "we will go on strike." It was not hard for them to persuade Diego. He had been uneasy with such a patron from the first, the years of merciless criticism by the Communist Party having left their scars. This made it harder to accept advice which would be deliberately misinterpreted.

On May 6 he sent Nelson Rockefeller the following answer:

> In reply to your kind letter of May 4, 1933, I wish to tell you my actual feelings on the matters you raise, after I have given considerable reflection to them.
>
> The head of Lenin was included in the original sketch now in the hands of Mr. Raymond Hood, and in the drawings in line made on the wall at the beginning of my work. Each time it appeared as a general and abstract representation of the concept of leader, an indispensable human figure. Now, I have merely changed the place in which the figure appears, giving it a less real physical place as if projected by a television apparatus. Moreover, I understand quite thoroughly the point of view concerning the business affairs of a commercial public building, although I am sure that the class of person who is capable of being offended by the portrait of a deceased great man, would feel offended, given such a mentality, by the entire conception of my painting. Therefore, rather than mutilate the conception, I should prefer the physical destruction of the conception in its entirety, but preserving, at least, its integrity.

In speaking of the integrity of the conception, I do not refer only to the logical structure of the painting, but also to its plastic structure.

I should like, as far as possible, to find an acceptable solution to the problem you raise, and suggest that I could change the sector which shows society people playing bridge and dancing, and put in its place in perfect balance with the Lenin portion, a figure of some great American historical leader, such as Lincoln, who symbolizes the unification of the country and the abolition of slavery, surrounded by John Brown, Nat Turner, William Lloyd Garrison or Wendell Phillips and Harriet Beecher Stowe, and perhaps some scientific figure like McCormick, inventor of the McCormick reaper, which aided in the victory of the anti-slavery forces by providing sufficient wheat to sustain the Northern armies.

I am sure that the solution I propose will entirely clarify the historical meaning of the figure of leader as represented by Lenin and Lincoln, and no one will be able to object to them without objecting to the most fundamental feelings of human love and solidarity and the constructive social force represented by such men. Also it will clarify the general meaning of the painting.

The letter was meant to be conciliatory in tone, and leave the way open for further negotiation. For four or five days there was ominous silence. Diego engaged a photographer to preserve a record of the almost finished work; guards prevented him from taking pictures, declaring that they had just received orders barring all photographers from the building. Thereupon, Lucienne Bloch, a Leica concealed in her blouse, moved around the scaffolding taking such details as her secret operations would permit, which alone saved the work from total obliteration.*

The further progress of the affair we can follow in Rivera's "military dispatch," recorded in his introduction to *Portrait of America*:

A mysterious warlike atmosphere made itself felt from the very morning of the day that hostilities broke out [May 9]. The private police patrolling the center had already been reinforced during the

* These are all reproduced in *Portrait of America*, but Diego preferred not to publish the preliminary sketch where the "worker-leader" was a generalized workingman with a cap pulled down over his forehead.

preceding week, and on that day their number was again doubled. Towards eleven o'clock in the morning, the commander-in-chief of the building and his subordinate generals of personnel issued orders to the uniformed porters and detectives on duty to deploy their men and begin occupying the important strategic positions on the front line and flanks and even behind the little working shack erected on the mezzanine floor which was the headquarters of the defending cohorts. The siege was laid in strict accordance with the best military practice. The lieutenants ordered their forces not to allow their line to be flanked nor to permit entrance to the beleaguered fort to anyone besides the painter and his assistants (five men and two women!)* who constituted the total strength of the army to be subdued and driven from its positions. And all this to prevent the imminent collapse of the existing social order! I wish I could have been equally optimistic!

Throughout the day our movements were closely watched. At dinner time, when our forces were reduced to a minimum . . . the assault took place. Before opening fire, and simultaneously with the final maneuvers which occupied the strategic posts and reinforced those already occupied, there presented himself, in all the splendor of his power and glory, and in keeping with the best gentlemanly tradition of His Majesty's Army, the great capitalist plenipotentiary, Field-Marshall of the contractors, Mr. Robertson of Todd, Robertson and Todd, surrounded by his staff. Protected by a triple line of men in uniform and civilian clothes, Mr. Robertson invited me down from the scaffold to parley discreetly in the interior of the working shack and to deliver the ultimatum along with the final check. I was ordered to stop work.

In the meantime, a platoon of sappers, who had been hidden in ambush, charged upon the scaffold, replaced it expertly with smaller ones previously prepared and held ready, and then began to raise into position the large frames of stretched canvas with which they covered the wall. The entrance to the building was closed off with a thick heavy curtain (was it also bullet-proof?), while the streets surrounding the Center were patrolled by mounted policemen and the upper air was filled with the roar of airplanes flying round the skyscraper menaced by the portrait of Lenin. . . .

Before I left the building an hour later, the carpenters had already covered the mural, as though they feared that the entire city, with its banks and stock exchanges, its great buildings and millionaire residences, would be destroyed utterly by the mere presence of an image of Vladimir Ilyitch. . . .

* Rivera here includes Frida among his assistants.

The proletariat reacted rapidly. Half an hour after we had evacuated the fort, a demonstration composed of the most belligerent section of the city's workers arrived before the scene of battle. At once the mounted police made a show of their heroic and incomparable prowess, charging upon the demonstrators and injuring the back of a seven-year-old girl with a brutal blow of a club. Thus was won the glorious victory of Capital against the portrait of Lenin in the Battle of Rockefeller Center. . . .

The affair now became a *cause célèbre.* Bigger and bigger demonstrations picketed Radio City, each demanding the unveiling of the covered mural. Messages of protest poured in to the Rockefellers; messages of solidarity and support came in a constant stream to Rivera. Andrew Dasburg wired the support of the artists and writers of Taos; Witter Bynner those of Santa Fe; John Sloan and the Society of Independents, Ralph Pearson and his students, Walter Pach, Lewis Mumford, Carleton Beals, Alfred Stieglitz, Suzanne La Follette, Peggy Bacon, Niles Spencer, A. S. Baylinson, George Biddle, Van Wyck Brooks, Stuart Chase, Freda Kirchwey, Hubert Herring, George S. Counts, Helene Sardou—are a few names culled at random from the mountain of telegrams that poured in, giving Diego and Frida days and nights of sleepless excitement.

Hostile voices were heard too. Harry Watrous, president of the National Academy of Design, declared the head of Lenin "unsuitable" for an American mural; Alon Bement, director of the National Alliance of Art and Industry, expressed his "disappointment that so great an artist should . . . condescend to become a mere propagandist." A group of conservative painters formed the Advance America Art Commission—which did not outlive the controversy—to "sound the death-knell for all existing beliefs in the pseudo-superiority of foreign artists."

If artists and intellectuals, liberals and radicals,* rallied in the main to the support of the painter, businessmen who were plan-

* The Communist Party was caught in no man's land. It did not want to defend nor praise Rivera, nor take the side of his millionaire patron, nor did it have any "Marxist explanation" to offer. A revolutionary painter for millionaires, a millionaire patron of revolutionary painting, and a Communist Party silent on the fight between them, constituted a triple absurdity.

ning to act as his patrons were not lacking in "class solidarity" either. Rivera had already prepared his sketches for a mural to be called *Forge and Foundry,* ordered by General Motors for their building in the World's Fair at Chicago. On May 12 he received a wire from Albert Kahn, architect for the building:

> Have instructions from General Motors executives discontinue with Chicago mural. . . .

All the promised walls in America vanished with that telegram. The painter was cut off from further murals in the land of modern industry and machinery which had fascinated him so deeply.

In a radio address over WEVD, Diego summed up the issues involved in his controversy:

> The case of Diego Rivera is a small matter. I want to explain more clearly the principles involved. Let us take as an example an American millionaire who buys the Sistine Chapel, which contains the work of Michelangelo. . . . Would that millionaire have the right to destroy the Sistine Chapel?
>
> Let us suppose that another millionaire should buy the unpublished manuscripts in which a scientist like Einstein had left the key to his mathematical theories. Would the millionaire have the right to burn those manuscripts? Or suppose that an engineer has invented a machine which would solve a vast number of economic problems because of the ease and low cost of production if the machine were placed in operation. Would the buyer of the plans of that machine have the right to destroy them?
>
> There are only two real points of view from which to choose: the point of view of capitalist economy and morality (that is, one in which the right of individual property takes precedence over the interests of the human collectivity), and the point of view of socialist economy and morality (that is, one in which the rights of the human collectivity take precedence over the isolated individual and private property).
>
> From the capitalist point of view, the reply to our questions must be *yes.* And as a matter of fact, thousands of inventions are brought each year precisely for the purpose of keeping them from use and to prevent the competition which they might originate, even though they

be useful to the majority of human society. There is not a single cultured and sensitive man or woman who would not be indignant before the destruction of the Sistine Chapel, because the Sistine Chapel is the property of all humanity. So are the high mathematical acquisitions represented by the theories of Einstein, and there is not a single man of science nor a single man of common sense who would not be indignant at the idea of the destruction of an unpublished manuscript which contained them.

We all recognize, then, that in human creation there is something which belongs to humanity at large, and that no individual owner has the right to destroy it or keep it solely for his own enjoyment. . . .

So powerful was the storm let loose by the ousting of the painter that the Rockefellers found themselves obliged to give a pledge that "the uncompleted fresco of Diego Rivera will not be destroyed, nor in any way mutilated, but . . . will be covered, to remain hidden for an indefinite time . . ." (New York *World-Telegram*, May 12, 1933).

But six months after this solemn assurance as to the public trust, on midnight of Saturday, February 9, 1934, the Rivera mural was removed from the wall by the process of smashing it to powder! The destruction was undertaken deliberately, though experts had explained how the mural might be removed without damage to it or the wall, though interested parties had offered to meet the expense of its removal and preservation, or the painting, safely covered over with canvas, might have remained so indefinitely, for future generations to decide whether it was worth conserving.

They had chosen the moment when a municipal art exhibition was being prepared in Radio City. Many artists withdrew their paintings, among them Baylinson, Becker, Biddle, Gellert, Glintenkamp, Gropper, Laning, Lozowick, Pach, Sardeau, Shahn, and Sloan. Other artists wavered. There were hints that those who withdrew promised paintings might have trouble getting invited again.* Many painters became silent, timidly returning their pictures to the exhibition. Watrous issued a declaration

* See Walter Pach, *Queer Thing, Painting* (New York, Harper & Brothers, 1938).

calling the protest "poppycock." But the men whose names I have recorded above, and many others, including José Clemente Orozco and Gaston Lachaise (who had done an important sculptural group in Rockefeller Center), steadfastly refused to lower their dignity as artists and men by exhibiting in this hall haunted by the ghost of a murdered mural.

As a sort of comic coda to the Rivera-Rockefeller controversy came a disagreement between the conservative Frank Brangwyn and his Radio City employers. He had been commissioned to paint a mural canvas allusive to the Sermon on the Mount, to flank Rivera's fresco on one side, while the work of Sert, also on canvas, was to flank it on the other. When his painting arrived in December it was rejected because he had painted Christ as a figure in it!

Diego told reporters:

> I take the part of Brangwyn as an artist, and I defend his right, like mine, to express him own feelings and ideas in his painting. . . . I must say I don't like the painting of Brangwyn. I find he is the type of painter that the bourgeoisie merits today, and this conflict with him proves the present crisis of capitalism and its internal contradictions. If the owners of the building don't want in it the figure of their Christ because it is a commercial building, this means that business is contrary even to the Christian commandments—and today, nineteen hundred years after He scourged them from His temple, the money-changers take their revenge on Christ by scourging Him from the temple of commerce.
>
> The proprietors by forbidding a Christian painter to paint Christ and a Communist painter to paint Lenin prove that when they hire a painter, they think that they are buying him body and soul. . . . They are mistaken.

But the Rockefellers were in no mood for fresh controversy, nor was Brangwyn the kind to defend too fiercely his right to paint his vision as he saw it. The quarrel was patched up before it had well begun, by arranging that the figure of Christ should withdraw a bit, become more shadowy, and turn His back—

ironic symbol!—upon the "temple of the money-changers." Perhaps the quarrel with Rivera over the figure of Lenin could have been patched up similarly if the painter had not felt the pressure of the Communist Party, which, even though he took an uncompromising stand, did not relax its drumfire against him.

For years the wall remained blank where Rivera's fresco had faced the main portal. After negotiating in vain with a number of American artists to induce them to paint over the haunted spot, the Rockefellers at last engaged Sert to produce another colorless work, similar to the ones which he had already contributed to the building. Thus did life for once follow the laws proper to poetic justice, for the Sert mural canvases were exactly such paintings as the place now merited. People go by his melancholy monochromes without so much as a glance. Rivera's mural, whatever else may be said about it, could not have been passed by unnoticed. By agreeing to fill in the blank space left by its destruction, perhaps, after all, Sert has assured himself of a place in the history of art.

When they drove Rivera from the scaffold they paid him to the penny the amount stipulated in the contract. This deprived him of the possibility of appeal to the courts. The law will recognize such rights as may be settled in money, but knows naught of the artist's rights in the work he has been paid for, nor the rights of society either. In Mexico the law provides that an artist retains a right over the integrity of his work despite its sale and that no change may be made in it without his express consent. But in the United States a billionaire could use his fortune to buy up all the art treasures that constitute man's cultural heritage, and then destroy what he had bought and paid for; there is no law on our books to stop him. However, a painter has his own ways of taking revenge.

Diego held the check for $14,000 in his hand and meditated on its possible uses. Out of it, $6,300 (30 per cent of the original price of $21,000) was to go to Mrs. Paine as commission. An additional $8,000 had gone in wages and materials. But that left almost $7,000 of "Rockefeller money." His painting was covered (he did not yet know it would be destroyed), but he was determined that he should not be prevented from speaking to the people of New York through a mural. "So long as this check holds out," he announced to the press, "I will use it to paint in any suitable building that is offered, an exact reproduction of the buried mural. I will paint free of charge except for the actual cost of materials."

The painter was besieged with offers of walls, but in each case either the dimensions were not suitable or he did not like the uses to which the building was put. In the end he selected none of the places proposed, but one of his own choosing: a crazy, ramshackle old building on West Fourteenth Street, the home of the New Workers' School. The building was merely rented, and so old that it would soon be torn down, so the painter constructed movable walls. The school, for its part, had not dreamed of offering itself as a place for painting, since it had no funds to pay for materials. But his assistants agreed to continue to work with him for reduced wages, he moved from the Barbizon Plaza to cheaper quarters near by, and paid for all the material himself.

> For the first time [he wrote afterwards in *Portrait of America*], I painted on a wall which belonged to the workers, not because they own the building . . . but because the frescoes are built on movable panels. . . . They all helped in the work, and there, in the modest premises of an old and dirty building on Fourteenth Street, at the top of a steel staircase as steep as those of the pyramids of Uxmal or Teotihuacán, I found myself in what was for me the best place in the city. . . . I did all that I could to make something that would be useful to the workers, and I have the technical and analytical certainty that those frescoes are the best that I have painted* . . . and informed with the greatest enthusiasm and love that I am capable of feeling. . . .

* Diego's latest, while he was doing it, was always "the best that I have painted." Although I had a hand in helping him with the planning of this mural, I could not share his view that it was the best, or even one of the better, of his frescoes.

Diego's intention had been to repaint the Rockefeller mural, but the building was not suitable in size or structure. In harmony with that structure and the uses to which the building was put, he planned a new work, his *Portrait of America.* Because he was painting in an auditorium usually crowded with people, he filled the foreground of each panel, just a little above the level of the heads of the seated public, with human figures slightly larger than life-size, so that the people filling the hall seem to be continued into the wall, giving the stuffy, crowded quarters an extension and feeling of amplitude. These painted figures represent real or symbolic heroes of our country's history; thus the painter fulfilled the ambition of Rodin, who had sought to set his *Burghers of Calais* almost level with the street, "*mêlant leur vie héroique à la vie quotidienne de la ville.*" The upper or middle ground of each panel is occupied by masses of men in action, those masses whose representative heroes fill the lower foreground. At the top rises and falls all around the hall the landscape of America; while in each panel (except one in which the painter deliberately set out to give a feeling of confusion) some tree trunk, edifice, or other solid, uprising object gives visual support to the ceiling, maintaining the function of the wall and seeming to increase the height and amplitude of the long, narrow, low auditorium.

The frescoes—in all, twenty-one occupying seven hundred square feet of wall space—were painted on movable sectional panels of the painter's own design: each panel framed in wood, fastened at the corners with metal cleats, backed by wooden crosspieces, composition board, chicken-wire and various coats of plaster, topped off with the painted surface of ground marble and cement, held in place by wooden supports and metal strips. A single panel weighs about three hundred pounds. In the land which builds its structures so that they shall not endure, or tears them down before they are really old, Diego was preoccupied with this problem of movable walls. Eventually these stood the test for which they were intended: the old building had to be abandoned, and the paintings moved with the school from Fourteenth to Twenty-third Street, without the paintings' suffering a single crack or scratch.

Years later, when the New Workers' School was dissolved, it donated the paintings to the International Ladies' Garment Workers' Union. They were moved again, this time to the dining hall of the union's Recreation Center in Forest Park, Pennsylvania (Camp Unity). Once more no physical damage occurred, thereby proving that Rivera's technique for movable murals in America's perishable buildings is entirely feasible. But his experiment in "painting for the workers" was less successful, for once more his painting was subject to censorship, not by capital but by labor. The officials of the Union considered two of his small panels and the large one which he intended to be the culmination of his "portrait," a panel entitled *Communist Unity*, too communistic—or perhaps too overtly communistic. The three panels were not put up with the rest but found their way into the hands of a private collector. When last I heard of them, they were, rather inappropriately, on the walls of the home of Mr. and Mrs. Joseph Willen of New York. Ironically, when the painter himself was supplying photographs for the monograph on his fifty-year retrospective in Mexico City in 1949 (published in 1952), being on one of his many humble quests for readmission to the Communist Party, he himself no longer wished his panel concerning the unity of all Communist factions to be reproduced and committed the same act of self-censorship. Hence the monograph reproduces only eighteen of the twenty-one panels. However, since each of them had a kind of separate existence in historical time and in architectonic structure, the remaining eighteen panels look reasonably at home and complete in the dining hall filled with workingmen and women on vacation. If the *Portrait of America* lacks the internal life and magnificence of Diego's living world of Mexican history on the walls of the National Palace, it is but natural, for how could the painter have as deep a knowledge and feeling for Daniel Shays, Abe Lincoln, John Brown, Thoreau, or Emerson as for Hidalgo, Juárez, Quetzalcoatl, Flores Magón, or Zapata? Moreover, the faults of interpretation are in many respects more the writer's than the painter's, for I was the chief mediator between Diego and the history of the United States. But an appraisal of the interpretation, which one critic viewing the frescoes called "a Wolfe's eye view of American history," would carry us out of the realm of the painter's life and into the autobiography of his biographer.

The theme of this mural is the history of the country—a portrait of the America of yesterday and today. It is interesting to record how the painter acquired an insight into the history of a land not his own. Obviously, for the purposes of art, mere factual knowledge is not enough: it must be felt as well as known, reacted to as well as apprehended, absorbed until it becomes "second nature," before it can become the stuff of painting. It was the task of the painter's assistants and members of the faculty and student body of the school to make this material accessible and vividly alive to Rivera. We avoided the standard histories in favor of contemporary documents and contemporary iconography; not so much for lack of confidence in professional historians, but because only thus could the artist acquire a "feel" for the impact of living events upon sentient human beings. We ransacked libraries, reference rooms, museums, for contemporary prints, woodcuts, oils, newspaper caricatures. We ran through speeches and writings of each representative personage selected, excerpting the most vivid and characteristic passages; viewed them through the eyes of their enemies, distilling the latter's hatreds, and through the eyes of their admirers, distilling their loves. Words were checked against deeds, promises against performances, outcomes against gloomy and sanguine anticipations. And beneath and beyond we sought to dig to the moods of the nameless masses in whom these men had inspired love or hatred, the masses who had followed and sometimes created them. How well this method succeeded at its best—thanks principally to Rivera's amazingly prehensile mind—is testified alike by the general sweep of the history of our land and by the beauty and vividness of such portraits as those of Ben Franklin and Tom Paine, Emerson and Thoreau, Walt Whitman and John Brown. Or by the power of such social caricatures as that of J. P. Morgan the First. Many may disagree with his interpretation of our history, but none can deny its impact or its strength, nor regard it as a mere cold exercise in learning facts by rote. Indeed, whatever its shortcomings of propagandistic onesidedness, there is no example by one of our own painters that comes anywhere near giving so moving a portrayal of our people, our history, and our land.

When Diego had finished his murals in the New Workers' School, he still had a little "Rockefeller money" left, so he moved into the headquarters of the New York Trotskyites and did two small panels there representing the Russian Revolution and the "Fourth International," which Leon Trotsky was then beginning to proclaim. With this his funds were exhausted. There was nothing to do but return to his home in Mexico, there to consider the problem of: What next?

He felt he had gotten even with the Rockefellers by using their money to paint for the movements that claimed to challenge their rule. And in the New Workers' School he had done with malicious glee two mordant portraits of the founder of the Rockefeller dynasty and his son. But when he learned in Mexico that his fresco in Radio City had been smashed to bits, his anger flared up afresh. He applied to the Mexican Government for a wall on which to paint anew the mural the Rockefellers had destroyed. He received a wall in that monument of ugliness, the Palace of Fine Arts. This time the building was no real concern of his: he was not seeking to paint a fresco which would express its architecture and use, he was looking for a public place where he could let men see what kind of painting it was that the Rockefellers and their builders had chosen to destroy. They had tried to prevent his work from surviving, even in a photograph; now he would bring it to life in full color and monumental scale upon a wall, that it might haunt them, and that the world might judge between them and him.

Some changes the building forced him to make. The elevator shaft in the RCA building had been a "triptych," a main wall flanked by two sides; but this new wall was flat. The figures which had been on the sides of the elevator bank he now introduced into the two sides of a single main design, and, there being some extra space to fill, he added a few additional figures, among them Trotsky and Marx. There is, too, less simplicity and solidity of structure, more emphasis on line. As painting it is less powerful and, in this site, it has lost its dramatic impact and original intention, which was, quite literally, *épater le bourgeois.*

The most interesting change from the original was one not required by the architecture: the introduction into the night-club scene, not far from the germs of venereal disease, of a portrait of John D. Rockefeller, Jr. "Let them be well used," Hamlet said of the players, "for they are the abstracts and brief chronicles of the time; after your death you were better have a bad epitaph than their ill report while you live." Perhaps it is more dangerous to use painters ill, since epitaph and report are one.

Thus ended Diego's invasion of the United States. The last word on his American painting we will leave to Elie Faure, who from his sickbed, which he was not to leave until his death, wrote to Diego (letter of July 20, 1933) his reactions to the Rockefeller affair:

> I am writing you from my bed, where I am spending all my afternoons for the past two months as I have been told that I am very sick. . . . I know now, however, of your great adventure, principally from

an article in *Lu;* for the daily press here would save itself from whispering the least word which might risk, as this does, troubling the quiet atmosphere which surrounds the brain, if I may call it such, of the French bourgeois; which might disturb his digestion and risk introducing into his ideas, again if I may call them such, the imaginary structures which might upset the flat harmony of his stagnant perspective.

Your daughter [Marika] also proudly brought me the fragment of an American magazine where you are addressing the people, as well as the representation of the fresco where Lenin soiled the wall. I envy your power to awaken in the heart indignation, the spasm of anger. You have found a way of *acting* through thought, which ought to be the ambition of all true intellectuals, of all true painters or writers. Yesterday it was still mine. Alas, no one here wants to understand me, doubtless because I speak a language too hermetic. You have the luck of having at your disposition painting, and of knowing how to handle it. Your plastic language is hermetic, too, but its very strangeness puts it across as painting. One has to look at it well. One can ignore what I am saying—one can avoid the opening of a book. In fine, bravo! Hurrah for the success of your action! The artistic glory of a Matisse or even of a Picasso does not count alongside of the *human* passions which you arouse, and there is not at this hour in the world's course another painter who can say as much. . . .

My dear old Diego, I embrace you tenderly.

Elie Faure

27. ALONE

The late thirties and early forties were for Diego a confused and lonely time. The opportunity for walls was narrowing. The Soviet Union, which had haunted his painting for a decade, had rejected him as not pliable enough for their formulas of "socialist realism." The Mexican Party was losing its colorful indigenous character; absurdly imitating the Russian purges, it had expelled its unmanageable painter. If his membership had always had something faintly ludicrous about it, the attempt to convert him into a symbol of counterrevolution was downright comical. The gods might laugh, but Diego grieved . . . and became still more extravagant in revolutionary gesture.

The land of machinery and modern industry to the north, which loomed so large in his fantasy, had canceled his commissions and driven him from its walls. In Detroit his frescoes hung on precariously. The American Communist Party, and its fellow-traveler artists, outdid Rivera's Mexican comrades in slandering the "painter for millionaires."

Yet his brief stay in the United States had left its mark upon the country. In San Francisco, Detroit, New York, artists had learned from him the technique of fresco. Aided by the depression with its work relief program, they cried out for walls, state patronage, a chance to substitute social charades for the hitherto colorless civic allegory. Good, bad, and indifferent—mostly bad—the public buildings of the land broke out in a rash of murals.

Not that the Blashfields and Alexanders, whose work has as much to do with art as a school history text with literature, lost all the town halls and courthouses. Sert took the place of Rivera in Radio City; Blashfield died twice a millionaire; Randall Davey contrived a Will Rogers in a "shrine" in Colorado Springs with none of the color, salt, or ruggedness which characterized the homely sage; Sargent's offenses against his own better knowledge in such works as the marching soldiers at Harvard continued to beget monstrous progeny like Savage's "Gold Standard Threatened by Greenbacks" * on the stairs of the Harkness Library of Columbia University. But the old school of civic allegory waited only for an authoritative voice to call for a coroner's inquest. The Mexican movement had won its counter-invasion of its mighty neighbor to the north. Rivera, in seeming defeat, returned to Mexico City crowned with laurels. Orozco, Charlot, Tamayo, and other Mexicans won guerrilla battles, too, until the flotsam and jetsam of crushed automobile sculpture and spaceless, lineless, formless nonrepresentational painting at the mid-century washed over the ramparts where they had fought.

> If my Detroit frescoes are destroyed [Rivera wrote in words of moving simplicity as the campaign for their destruction gained momemtum], I shall be profoundly distressed, as I put into them a year of my life and the best of my talent; but tomorrow I shall be busy making others, for I am not merely an "artist" but a man performing his biological function of producing paintings, just as a tree produces flowers and fruit, nor mourns their loss each year, knowing that next season it shall blossom and bear fruit again.

* My name for it, not the university's nor the painter's.

"Tomorrow I shall be busy making others." Yes, but where? The chance to exercise his "biological function" on walls seemed to be narrowing in Mexico too.

> Diego Rivera all but did a song and dance yesterday [reported the New York *Herald Tribune* of August 10, 1933]—when the mail from Mexico City brought him "the greatest opportunity of his career." . . . "They have guaranteed me freedom," he cried exultantly, "I shall do the triumph of science over superstition. . . . I shall show to the human mind the way of reason."

The occasion was the offer of a wall in the new Medical School. The school was housed where once had been the headquarters of the Inquisition in New Spain. The contrast between the old uses of the building and the new stirred thoughts of painting the struggle of religion and science. He would paint the great myths: Creation, the Deluge, the Immaculate Conception, and, alongside these, the scientific achievements which he thought should have freed the mind from belief in them: geological and biological evolution, birth and embryology, death—the wonders of the Bible against the wonders of the laboratory—Copernicus, Galileo, Darwin, Pasteur, Marx, Einstein.

But the offer was made while Diego was still the headline hero of the battle with the world's richest oil magnate and the press filled with his name. When he got back to Mexico, his halo growing dimmer with familiarity, somehow the money was not forthcoming. It was not until ten years later that he got a chance to commence his mural in the Institute of Cardiology. By then the dream of painting the war between science and religion had faded. The two walls, monotonously organized, are little more than a series of portraits of medical researchers and heart specialists of various lands and times, with a great deal of green in their garments and of red in their faces. Even the flames consuming Michael Servetus as he burns at the stake on the orders of Calvin fail to give life to the fresco.

Yet another ten years were to pass, and once more, in 1953-54,

Diego returned to the theme of medicine, in the "Hospital of the Race" of the Mexican Institute for Social Security. The Institute has given more splendor to its buildings and the perquisites of its officials than security to the peons and *braceros* of Mexico, but on its walls Rivera's frescoes were full of poetry again, as he painted, alongside the operations of modern medicine, an opposing wall which embodied his fabulous myths concerning the wonders of Aztec medical science. With primitive instruments of obsidian, ancient priest-healers bind a fractured arm, perform a trepanning, treat a tooth, administer an enema, assist at a birth, operate on the thorax, and perform other medical miracles under the magnificent aegis of the appropriate Aztec deity in full regalia. The painter lacked only two years of turning seventy by then, but he finished the walls in record time, working the same long hours with the same enthusiasm as he had shown in his thirties.

A glance at the two murals in medical institutions has carried us far from the lonely time of Diego's return to Mexico, rejected by Russia, cast out by his party, his fresco in Radio City destroyed, his American commissions canceled.

It was a difficult time for Diego as a mural painter though two walls still awaited completion. One was the often worked on but unfinished frescoes on the stairways of the National Palace; the other was the opportunity to do again in the Palacio de Bellas Artes the mural that Rockefeller had destroyed in Radio City.

He had returned to the National Palace in an angry mood, tired of his long labors on it, a little short of funds, for he had long ago used up the modest original allotment and had difficulty getting more to pay for helpers and materials. On the left side he had painted an idyllic picture of pre-Conquest Mexican civilization, in which, under a bright sun and the presiding genius of Quetzalcoatl, Indian warriors fought their "flowery wars," slaves toiled with burdens of stone up the sides of the pyramids they were building, men and women of beautiful body and serene face danced, played prehistoric instruments, and plied the arts and crafts that Quetzalcoatl had taught them. In keeping with his idealization of Aztec culture, the composition is graceful in its beautiful curves (PLATE 101).

Now, at the head of the stairway and on the opposite side, he strove to finish his vision of *Mexico Today and Tomorrow.* The lower part of the right wall is restless and crowded, full of satirical cartoons and clashes. Burden bearers are carrying bricks to build factories instead of blocks to build pyramids. The Virgin of Guadalupe presides over a machine for extracting coins from the faithful, near a priest who is carrying in his arms a wanton woman. There are strikes, soldiers wearing gas masks engage in combat, agrarian leaders face a firing squad, a Communist agitator is haranguing a crowd, machine pipes with no visible function frame the heads of Mexican and American exploiters and politicians, one of whom is manifestly ex-President Calles. In place of the bearded god Quetzalcoatl on the left wall, the presiding genius over this disorder and turmoil on the right is the bearded god of the future, Karl Marx (PLATE 107). One has only to compare the skill and tenderness with which Rivera did the images of Quetzalcoatl with the stiffness of his Karl Marx to see where the painter's heart lay.

Whatever the defects of the third wall, it completed at last Rivera's remarkable history of Mexico. "My National Palace mural," Diego said later, when a few years before his death he returned to paint yet other walls in the shaded corridors of the Palace, "is the only plastic poem I know which embodies the whole history of a people." In this the painter is not exaggerating. For all its propagandistic and legendary distortion and fantasy, it is the most ample, complete and wide-ranging plastic expression and portrait ever done of Mexico, or indeed, of any country by any painter. Only a giant of physical strength, plastic fecundity, large talent, audacious imagination, and limitless ambition would ever have undertaken to capture thus on three giant walls the entire history of his country. In a riot of color and a marvel of organization, what lives on the stairway walls is not a painting but a world, full of a life of its own, intellectually, emotionally, plastically. While the ideas which guided him to see this and not that, to select particular representative men, heroes, villains, and prototypes of the nameless masses, to picture Mexico in one way rather than another, may not bear scholarly or critical examination, yet the world he created here on such a colossal scale will live and stir the senses and imagination as long as pigment and cement hold together and the walls endure. After Rivera's fresco no historian of Mexico will ever quite see the history of his country the same. None will lack for marvelous iconographical illustrations of the country's illustrious and infamous sons. Men will go back to these walls to learn how this world lived and was, how it viewed itself through the perspective of a not inconsiderable sector of the intellectuals of Rivera's day, and how this painter with his own sweeping, impetuous, unself-critical vision of it, viewed his land and his time. The propaganda is already as stale as yesterday's fashions, often trivial, spiteful, faintly ludicrous. But plastically and humanly the world he created continues to live a life abounding. The Secretariat of Education, the graceful chapel walls and ceiling in Chapingo, the walls of the National Palace, and those of the Palace of Cortés, separately, or added together as one single vision, may be added to any list of the world's wonders.

Mexico Today and Tomorrow was the title of the last, or right hand side on the Palace stairway. If in the United States he had lost a wall for painting his vision of tomorrow, in Mexico it was his image of today which got him into trouble. Vision sharpened by his contact wtih the realities of industrial life in the United States, Diego saw more deeply into Mexico as it really was, and could not choose but paint it as he saw it.

The "socialism" that was on the lips of every politician and job-holding intellectual now appeared to him mere demagogy.

The Calles crowd, calling themselves the "Men of the Revolution," had found that the Revolution could not fulfill its large promises to the people of this poor land, but there was enough in the treasury to make them, as men risen from the people, into shining symbols of the Revolution fulfilled. They set up stock companies to pave roads, build buildings, refine sugar, supply cement and other building materials to the government. They fought "Yankee imperialism" by compelling every foreign development company to give native Mexicans positions on its boards of directors. They enacted laws which crippled the work of the foreign investment companies, laws which could be circumvented for a consideration. They subsidized and domesticated the labor organizations of Mexico, put labor and agrarian officials on government payrolls, furnished headquarters for unions, paid the cost of publication of journals by direct subsidy or huge advertisements of the National Lottery and other national enterprises. Labor and agrarian leaders who would not accept *chambas* and *huesos* (government appointments and sinecures), nor submit to becoming comfortable appendages of the machine, were arrested and "shot trying to escape" (there is no capital punishment in Mexico, but there is the *ley fuga*) or deported to the Islas Marias penal colony.

Successive presidents might continue, at varying rates, to redistribute the land, but there was not enough to go round, nor enough water nor seed nor capital. They might nationalize an occasional industry, which, if it did not make the poor any better off, gave vicarious satisfaction. They could, and did, give the Indian an equal legal and social status with the *mestizo* and the *criollo*, even if he remained almost as poor as before. All this, added together, was "Mexican socialism."

In unflattering portraits, on the very National Palace which they occupied as rulers and officials, Diego painted the "Men of the Revolution." Recognizable figures discussed the sharing of the spoils with each other. Other recognizable types held forth on Mexican "National Socialism" to bemused auditors, while on the side stood knowing workingmen, laughing derisively. The wall contrasted the lyricism of demagogue-intellectuals with the reality of strikes broken, agrarian leaders arrested and slain. Perhaps too harshly, but not altogether untruthfully, Rivera painted on the Palace in which the President transacted business, the regime he saw around him.

It was the criticism being advanced, less effectively, by the Communist Party, but just for that party pundits struck out the harder at one who was not acting out properly the role assigned to him as arch renegade.

As for the politicians who had welcomed him as a hero on his return from the United States, given him a wall in Bellas Artes to repaint what Rockefeller had destroyed, negotiated for him to go to Geneva to paint in the United Nations Building a fresco to be donated by the Government of Mexico, and invited him to paint the new Medical School—they had learned too much from their experience with him in the twenties to tangle again directly with *nuestros muy discutido pintor*. His reputation was too great, public notice too sure; in any war of words in the press he had demonstrated that he was a master of sharp retorts. But it is not hard to understand why the money for the Medical School walls was not forthcoming, why the Geneva negotiations died without issue, why walls in so many new buildings could still be found for a dozen other painters, but for Diego for nine long years there was no government wall in Mexico.* It was during this time of solitude and frustration

* In the late 1940's when the government had once more found walls for their great painter, Rivera told his "autobiographer": "Following the affair of the Hotel Reforma, poor health kept me from painting murals for several years. In his biography of me, Bertram Wolfe dramatizes this period of languishment as a kind of artistic exile which I incurred because of my political beliefs, but his interpretation is not in accord with the facts" (*My Art, My Life* [New York], p. 222). The tale of the "several years" was nine. His health was not so poor that he could not tackle a private wall in the Hotel Reforma—which got him into yet deeper hot water—and a huge wall on Treasure Island in San Francisco. Can the reader blame me for concluding that the "poor health" was political? Incidentally, this is the one criticism Diego made of my earlier attempt at a biography.

that Diego took stock of his work thus far. The result of that stock-taking was his two works done with me, *Portrait of America* and *Portrait of Mexico*, and the encouragement given me to examine his papers and write my first biography of him.

If this was Rivera's exile to Elba, then his brief sortie on the walls of the Hotel Reforma may be compared to Napoleon's "hundred days," for they ended just as disastrously. It was the summer of 1936. Alberto Pani, shrewd political figure and financier who had managed to keep afloat in all the storms and changing tides from Carranza in 1917 to Cárdenas who had just become President, was building a large hotel on the Paseo de la Reforma to accommodate well-to-do American tourists. Pani prided himself, rightly, on his taste in painting. He was one of the first to recognize Diego's large talents in his Paris days, having smoothed the painter's path on more than one occasion. His private collection included many Riveras. Diego was turning out an endless succession of oils, water colors, drawings: the painter did not lack for money, but he did lack for walls. Pani saw a way to satisfy Diego's hunger for public walls, get a good bargain—for Diego was always paid much less proportionately for walls than for easel paintings—and use the painter's unfailingly public name to start his hotel off in a blaze of publicity. He made thrifty offer of space in the banquet hall, at a price that would scarcely cover material and wages for the helpers: four great panels for four thousand pesos. With the shrinking peso of the thirties this amounted to about a thousand U.S. dollars. Some instinct, whether of Pani or the painter, prompted a plan to make the panels movable. Both painter and patron got more publicity than they bargained for.

Since the hall was to be devoted to dining and dancing, Diego chose the *Carnival of Mexican Life* as his theme. At one end two panels deal with earlier Mexico, one presided over by the ancient Aztec God of War and Human Sacrifice, Huichilobos, masquerading now in the stylized, time-dimmed echo of a village fiesta figure; the other dominated by the popular bandit-hero, Augustín Lorenzo, who fought the French invaders, held up silver-trains, and tried to kidnap the Empress Carlotta on the highroad to Puebla (FIG. 129). Behind the bandit dance luminous flames, in front of him muskets discharge their roman candle fire. In color and composition it is the best of the four panels.

At the other end of the hall, folk festival yields to the irony of a sophisticated city carnival. One, *Folkloric and Touristic Mexico,* is no more than a picturesque jest: Yankee savants bedecked with asses' ears and fat fountain pens are interpreting the country to the world; an American "miss," of blonde locks and arms thin as sticks, presides over the scene; faintly unpleasant masked types wave banners and hold bags of gold, while a plucked chicken represents Mexico. In the lower right corner the hooded mask of death has ETERNITY emblazoned on its forehead.

The last panel is dedicated to the Mexican political scene, conceived as a masquerade. Over it rules a single smiling figure, directing the gaiety in all the rings of this colorful and mordant circus: a huge macrocephalic dictator, holding in his left hand a quartered flag composed of the colors of Germany, Italy, Japan, and the United States, his face made up of features borrowed from Hitler, Mussolini, the Mikado, and Franklin Roosevelt, while the composite portrait manages to remind one of Pani himself, surveying the festivities in his banquet hall. The caricature is overburdened with too many symbols and too many bits of ideas. Confused in draughtsmanship and meaning, it is one of the worst figures Diego ever did.

But the carnival over which this composite showman presides is quite another matter. It is made up of political personages in all-but-human animal masks. A figure with long, horselike face suggests the lineaments of the fellow-traveler labor leader, Lombardo Toledano; a general of porcine visage dances with a girl who signifies Señorita Mexico, while from the basket strapped to her back, General Marrano (General Pig, or as we might say, General Porkbarrel), robs his partner of her fruit (FIG. 130).

Immediately the *cognoscenti* were buzzing with conjecture: did the puzzlingly familiar features of General Marrano resemble more those of President Cárdenas or those of his Secretary of Agriculture, General Cedillo? Were not the lineaments of the fat-faced bishop familiar? In the other masked figures and their baubles were there not obvious references to the ruling group of "Men of the Revolution," and the various industries over which they had acquired control? Señor Pani had wanted publicity for his hotel and colorful decorations for its banquet hall, but he knew enough about art to see that what he was getting was more than he had bargained for. To Diego he spoke nothing but praise. As soon as the job was finished, however, and the artist had been paid off and departed, Pani called in his two brothers, architects who knew how to wield a brush, and the three Panis undertook some "slight changes."

"Do you know, *maestro*," a mason told Diego a few days later at a Building Trades Union meeting, "they have been making alterations in your mural?" Accompanied by the union's lawyer and several members, Diego hurried over to the Reforma. The tiger-faced dancer that looked a bit like Calles had changed his physiognomy; the flag in the ringmaster's hand had lost its red-white-and-blue segment; General Marrano was no longer lifting a banana out of the basket of the girl with whom he was dancing.

Engineer Pani appeared; guns were drawn; the police were called. Diego spent the night in jail charged with "breaking and entry," and with possessing "five pistols"—three more than he carried. A Building Workers' strike was called, a picket line was set up in front of the hotel, an old guild law was invoked that made punishable the falsification of the work of an artisan.

"I made the changes with my own hands," explained Arturo

Pani, brother of the hotel owner. "As owners of the building, if we want to make some changes in our property and if we work without wages, no law has been broken and no union is involved. Besides, my changes show how easy it is to paint like Diego Rivera."*

The court thought differently. Alberto Pani had to pay to Rivera 2,000 pesos damages and to the union compensation for the work lost during the strike. In addition, he was obliged to permit Diego to restore the painting. "The hotel does not want to offend any one," Pani announced. "As long as a political issue has been made of the murals, it is best to take them down," Mirrors took their place in the banquet hall, reflecting perhaps a not dissimilar carnival. The panels were placed in storage—a stage higher in human culture than the vandalism which had destroyed the frescoes in Radio City. Sold to Alberto Mizrachi of the Central Art Galleries, they remained in his warehouse in Mexico City for more than two decades. Now their iridescent color and flame decorates a tourist agency.

For the moment, Diego's opportunity to get walls was over. He had quarreled with the Communist Party, with the Government, with many of his fellow painters, with Pani who had so often sponsored his work from his Paris days on. "Diego has only two friends in artistic circles here," Carlos Chávez told me in 1937, "Miguel Covarrubias and me. We are his friends because we have no reason to be jealous of him." Later, Diego would break his friendship with Carlos Chávez, too, in the battle over his *Peace Mural.*

Viewed from a distance, it still seemed as if there were a glorious brotherhood of painters banded together to decorate the city's walls. But from close up, one could see the mischief wrought by jealousy, spite, gossip, factionalism, the love of controversy, the natural desire of younger men to get out of the shadow of the great masters who had dominated the scene, the

* New York *Post,* Nov. 21, 1936; *Herald-Tribune,* Nov. 24; *Times,* Nov. 22 and 24; *Excelsior,* Nov. 21 and 25.

vices of inbreeding that affect the thin layer of urban politicians and artists living at the narrow top of a pyramid, the foundation of which is the nameless mass of Indian peasants and peons. All the artists and writers, except the few of enormous talent, are ineluctably part of the bureaucracy which runs the land in the name of a people that knows not itself and knows not them. The system of government patronage, along with its advantages, has the disadvantage, too, that every intellectual, except the handful of the greatest, depends on the political leadership for his livelihood. Together they hunt in packs against the solitary few.

Of course, Diego had not made things any easier for himself with his garrulousness, his quarrelsome disposition, his love of a controversy and of a headline, and his more than human capacity for creativity and labor. But the taciturn Orozco was no less lonely. When artists band together, they are a band of difficult and solitary ones, so many porcupines huddling together for warmth.

All heroes of art—and glancing backward over Diego's life I am sure that he is entitled to be called one—are likely to be solitary beings, for their way of life is not like that of other men. Perhaps in ages when art was closer to the core of life, this was less so. Today at any rate, even those artists who become the spokesmen of their age and land do not cease to be its critics and antagonists. What they express is not their time as it is but as it might be, not the never altogether satisfying reality but the transforming possibilty. In any of its applications, the intellect, being in its essence a striving for excellence, cannot help but be a goad—to itself, its land, its time.

I do not wish to exaggerate the solitude that now surrounded Rivera. Though walls were denied him for a decade, commissions he had aplenty, and purchasers for anything from his hand. Admirers and disciples were many, but few he could treat as equals, or, if that is too much for genius to ask, then as comrades.

Even in his solitude, his art continued to link him with men and women in many lands. People came from afar to watch him. Letters piled up in his files, more letters than he ever knew what to do with. In 1936, I undertook to organize his correspondence files. I found letters containing checks, which he had never opened; letters from friends; opportunities for the sale or exhibition of his work. Everything lay in disorder, important and unimportant, opened and unopened, trash and treasure. Frida had tried before to dig Diego out of the avalanche. She had purchased cardboard accordion files, then steel cabinets. But we found the letter "P" stuffed and overflowing with opened and unopened epistles, while the rest of the alphabet had virtually nothing in it. "Oh, that?" Frida explained. "We put them under "P" for "*Por contestar*—to be answered." The system had been abandoned when the letter "P" refused to hold another scrap.

I cannot give more than a faint idea of the scope and variety of this answered and unanswered mail: personal begging letters, requests for donations (including evidence that organizations controlled by the American Communist Party were asking for and receiving thousands of dollars from Diego during the very period when they were attacking him most harshly); individual requests, often granted, to help this poor student to publish his thesis and that unknown peasant to purchase a mule; letters from museums, more often unanswered than not, offering Diego the opportunity to exhibit, from dealers, offering the opportunity to sell; letters from artists, expressing admiration, acknowledging a debt of gratitude, asking advice or criticism of photos of their work, requesting permission to study under him, soliciting a foreword to a catalogue, looking for guidance and help in some fight against censorship; letters from bores, cranks, people who wanted to know about Mexico's divorce laws or the cost of living in such and such a village; letters asking whether he hadn't some "little, unimportant sketch or painting" which he would be willing to give away; letters warning him of plots against him, threatening letters, letters preaching some new faith—all the wide range of mail likely to descend upon one who is continuously in the headlines.

Especially interesting are the letters throwing light on his relations with his fellow painters. More often than not, he failed to reply (despite the invariable notation in his own hand: "To be answered"). But when he did, it is always to be generous to young and struggling artists.

When Pedro Rendón, working on a mural in the Rodríguez Public Market, was attacked and his painting threatened with obliteration, Rivera wrote:

"I find his painting extremely interesting, and am amazed at the unfavorable judgments against it. . . . I am determined to defend his work personally on the field of esthetics and the field of justice and will appeal to art authorities on an international scale in its favor. . . ." Despite his laziness to write, he actually did gather testimonials from local and "international esthetic authorities" on Rendón's behalf. The frescoes are still there.

The range of Diego's sensibility was wide. Painters as diverse as Ben Shahn, Paul O'Higgins, Angel Bracho, María Izquierdo, Caroline Durieux, Kandinsky, Klee, Covarrubias, received a word of public praise, an introduction to some catalogue or publication of their work. Even men whose reputation was already big and market assured were pleased at such help. Thus I found this letter from Vassili Kandinsky, dated May 21, 1931:

> Believe me, you have caused me *very great* pleasure with your opinions on my art. You can well imagine that I have periods of great loneliness, but at the same time I know that it will not always be so. . . . It pleased me greatly to know that you own some of my pictures. . . .

At the other end of the spectrum, there is the case of Mardonio Magaña. During his brief period as Director of the Art School, Diego had had this simple Indian raised from janitor in the school to teacher of wood carving. He purchased some of his remarkable wood sculptures, wrote letters and articles about him, interested Frances Flynn Paine, and through her, the Rockefeller family, in the purchase of his work, bought for the old man, already over sixty, a piece of land, a hut, some chickens, some pigs, and a cow, so that Mardonio might be economically independent and devote the precious remnant of his life to the fulfillment of the talents so belatedly revealed. A noble chapter could be added to Diego's life to uncover the many unobstrusive acts of encouragement to fellow artists whose still unrecognized talents aroused the painter's enthusiasm: the courtesy of offering to exchange one of his pictures with an unknown, the timely yet critical word of advice and praise, the deliberately publicized purchase of some painting.

Many letters record lost opportunities. "While you are looking through my papers," he said to me in 1936, "see if you can find one from Jack Hastings about an exhibition I am to have in London. I want to accept, but I have mislaid the letter and don't have his address." I found it in the end, because I looked through every scrap. It was a letter from Lord John Hastings, arranging for an exhibition in the important Tate Gallery in London, lying inside an envelope from the New York publishers, Covici-Friede, and bearing the date March 31, 1935! I answered it for Diego, a year and twenty days after he had received it, and many months after the season which the gallery had reserved for him. Though I succeeded in renewing diplomatic relations and even getting a later invitation for Diego before I left Mexico that year, he never did get to exhibit in London. I am sure it is not Tate's fault, nor Hastings's: somewhere in his files there was doubtless another letter from the latter bearing in Diego's hand: "*Por contestar.*"

In a packet neatly tied with one of Frida's hair ribbons and labeled by her, *Cartas de las mujeres de Diego*, I found her own letters to him, and those of Angelina, Guadalupe, and a number of other women who did not sufficiently influence

Diego's life and art to figure in our story. Both Frida and Diego conceived that these letters, too, should be read by his biographer, and gave their permission.

Yet Frida knew that there were letters in that packet which had caused her bitter anguish. Several of Diego's affairs with other women were carried on while he was wooing her, others after their marriage. One of them, which occurred after they had been married for seven years, came close to breaking up their union. It strained the bonds more than all the rest because it had been more secret, because it had in the end become more scandalously public, but mostly because it involved that one girl in Mexico who, more than any other, was indebted to Frida, and had been her most intimate companion since childhood. When Frida learned of this, she felt she could not condone it as an escapade "proper to genius."

A lonely miserable time followed for both. Frida moved into a room in another part of the city, raged and wept in secret, tried listlessly to knit to some other being or interest the raveled threads that had bound her life so completely to Diego's. Too restless to paint, she left suddenly for New York, told her bitter tale to my wife and me as her most intimate friends there, vainly tried to "get even" by "affairs" of her own. As the flames of resentment died down within her, she knew it was Diego she loved and that he meant more to her than the things that seemed to stand between them.

As for Diego, he had long regretted the episode. He was tactful and patient, and did not reject for Frida the standards he had set for himself. Wiser now as a result of this bitter test, Frida wrote him at last that she knew now that

> . . . all these letters, liaisons with petticoats, lady teachers of "English," gypsy models, assistants with good intentions," "plenipotentiary emissaries from distant places, only represent *flirtations,* and that at bottom *you and I* love each other dearly, and thus go through adventures without number, beatings on doors, imprecations, insults (*mentadas de madres*), international claims—yet we will always love each other. . . .

All these things have been repeated throughout the seven years that we have lived together, and all the rages I have gone through have served only to make me understand in the end that I love you more than my own skin, and that, though you may not love me in the same way, still you love me somewhat. Isn't that so? . . . I shall always hope that that continues, and with that I am content.

With this wise, brave letter, dated July 23, 1935, Frida reconciled herself, not blindly but open-eyed, to the man she had chosen. And, in due course, to the girl who had been the will-less cause of their rift. When my first book about Rivera came out in 1939, Frida thanked me for the care I had taken (and still take here) to conceal the identity of the girl who was by then closer to her than ever.

The love and comradeship of the Riveras came out of this crisis, not the same, but on the whole solider, franker, truer than before. In a country where intrigue, concealment, deception, double standard in extramarital affairs, is deeply rooted, particularly in middle-class and intellectual circles, this marriage became unusual in its honesty and mutuality. "Affairs" became for both of them more casual, while dependence and trust became deeper.

A characteristic letter of Diego to Frida, written on her next trip to New York for a one-man show (letter of December 3, 1938), reads:

Mi niñita chiquitita:

You have kept me so many days without news of you and I was uneasy. I am pleased that you feel a little better and that Eugenia is taking care of you; give her my thanks and keep her with you while you are there. And I am glad you have a comfortable apartment and place to paint. Don't hurry with your pictures and portraits, it is very important that they turn out *retesuaves* [extrascrumptious], for they will complement the success of your exhibit and may give you a chance to do more portraits. . . . You ought to do the portrait of Mrs. Luce even if she doesn't order it from you. Ask her to pose for you and you will get a chance to speak with her. Read her plays—it seems that they are very interesting—it may be that they will suggest to you a composition for her portrait. I think it would be a very interesting subject. Her life (Mrs. Moats told me it) is extremely curious; it would interest you. You can get Mrs. Moats's daughter to tell it to you. She is in New York now, working on *Vogue*. . . .

What will you give me for good news that you surely must know already? Dolores the marvelous is going to spend Christmas in New York. . . . Have you written to Lola [pet name for Dolores del Rio, who was a good friend of both of them]? I suppose it's silly of me to ask you.

I am pleased with the commission of your portrait for the Modern Museum; it will be magnificent, your entering there from your very first exhibit. That will be the culmination of your success in New York. Spit on your little hands and make something that will put in the shade everything around it, and make Fridita the Grand Dragon [*la mera dientona*]. . . .

Tell him [Mr. Kaufmann, the Pittsburgh department-store owner] that the tapestries are now well advanced; I have made a great many changes. Make clear to him that I have worked ten or twenty times more than I had imagined, for the more I look at the house of Frank Lloyd [Wright], the more it seems a masterpiece to me and I want my work there to be the best I am capable of. Tell him I have at last found someone who can execute them for me, that as soon as the series is complete I will send him photographs, that I have not done so yet because I want him to see the compositions as a whole, for together they make a single unified composition. The chance to go to Pittsburgh interests me greatly, but the economic part of it troubles me. I think I might be able to go to put the things in their places; if I went by car I could go very cheaply. On Juan's affair [referring to Juan O'Gorman, whose mural in the Mexico City airport had been partially obliterated by the Mexican government because it pictured Hitler and Mussolini in uncomplimentary terms] it would be interesting if they wrote something, giving the dogs what they deserve. It is very important, and let them publish the answer so that people may know what culture and art are worth to the "socialist" government of Mexico.

. . . Don't be silly. I don't want you for my sake to lose the opportunity to go to Paris. TAKE FROM LIFE ALL WHICH SHE GIVES YOU, WHATEVER IT MAY BE, PROVIDED IT IS INTERESTING AND CAN GIVE YOU SOME PLEASURE. When one is old, one knows what it is to have lost what offered itself and one did not know enough to take it. If you really want to please me, know that nothing can give me more pleasure than to know that you have it. And you, my *chiquita,* deserve everything. . . . I don't blame them for liking Frida, because I like her too, more than anything. . . .

I am well in eyes and liver, a foot pained me because of rheumatism but Fede [Dr. Federico Marín, brother of Guadalupe Marín] cured me swell. I am fit now, but above all content because you are better and the loveliest thing in this world and I send you millions of kisses. Thanks for the flowers, they are lovely.

Tu principal sapo-rana
Diego

To Sam A. Lewisohn, author of *Painters and Personality,* Diego wrote on October 11, 1938 to call attention to Frida's forthcoming one-man show:

I recommend her to you, not as a husband but as an enthusiastic admirer of her work, acid and tender, hard as steel and delicate and fine as a butterfly's wing, lovable as a beautiful smile, and profound and cruel as the bitterness of life.

As for Frida, "loving Diego more than her own skin" was no mere rhetoric; to my own knowledge, it was verified more than once. In 1936 I visited the Riveras when they were occupying adjoining rooms in the British Hospital in Mexico City, she for one of the endless series of operations on her foot and skeletal frame, he in preparation for a possible operation on his right eye, the tear gland of which had become dangerously infected. When I visited Frida's room I found her crying bitterly as she lay in bed—weeping, I thought, because of her pain. But to my futile words of comfort she wailed: "It's Diego's eye that I'm worried about. He'll go blind. Why does it have to happen to him? If it were only me instead. He needs his eyes so much!"

A year later, when four gunmen came over to his table in the Restaurant Acapulco in Mexico City to pick a quarrel intended to end with his assassination, this slight girl leaped up in front of her husband, denounced the *pistoleros* as cowards going four against one, demanded that they shoot her first, and in general created such a scene as made the assassination impossible. She was brave enough while it lasted, but sick to her stomach afterwards.

More than my own skin—she proved the truth of the words in many ways. It has been my privilege to be an intimate witness of the deep ties of mutual dependency that bound these two, this slight, partly maimed girl in her twenties and this huge bulky giant then in his fifties, two painters who, in their styles and the exercise of their craft, had scarce a point of contact, two spirits so dissimilar that, did they not need each other and complement each other, they would not seem to have the slightest thing in common.

"In the tenth year of their marriage," I wrote in my earlier biography of the painter, "Diego grows more and more dependent upon his wife's judgment and comradeship. If he should lose her now, the solitude which besets him would be much heavier than it is."

Shortly after the book appeared, he secured a divorce. To celebrate, he arranged a large party, inviting to it one of my best friends. "Martín," he announced loudly before the assembled company, "tell Bert that I have divorced Frida to prove that my biographer was wrong." The message was delivered.

A year passed, a year of personal unhappiness for both. Then, when Diego was painting once more in San Francisco, he sent for Frida on the pretext that only Dr. Leo Eloesser of that city could properly treat her continuing ailments. On his fifty-fourth birthday, Diego Rivera remarried Frida Kahlo. When I sent my congratulations in December 1940, I could not resist the impulse to ask whether he had remarried Frida to prove that his biographer was right?

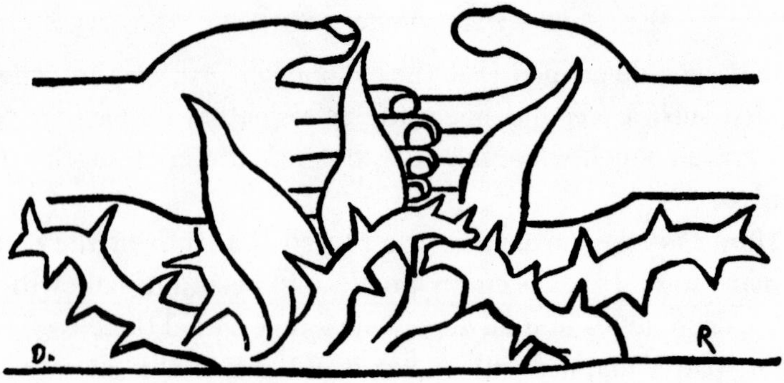

28.

PEACE WITH THE YANKEE

From 1935 to 1943, for nine years, the Mexican Government had no walls for its great muralist. His caricature of General Porkbarrel in the Banquet Hall of the Hotel Reforma, dancing with Miss Mexico while robbing fruit from her basket, made him more than ever unpalatable to the "Men of the Revolution."

No walls in Mexico. No walls in Russia. No walls in the United States. As always, he turned out an endless succession of sketches, oils, water colors. Sometimes he repeated himself with fatal ease. Sometimes he tackled a new esthetic problem. He found joy in his work; he sold all he could turn out; commissions showered upon him beyond even his Gargantuan capacity. The fresh correspondence between thought and hand in the sketch, between what he saw with his penetrating eyes and what he put on paper or canvas, was often more suggestive than the less intimate and less immediate elaboration in his murals. But this was not enough: he longed for walls.

In the middle twenties, critical acclaim in the United States

148. Day of the Dead. Oil on Masonite. 1944

149. Mexico Before the Conquest. National Palace Corridor. 1945

150. El Comalero. Oil. 1947

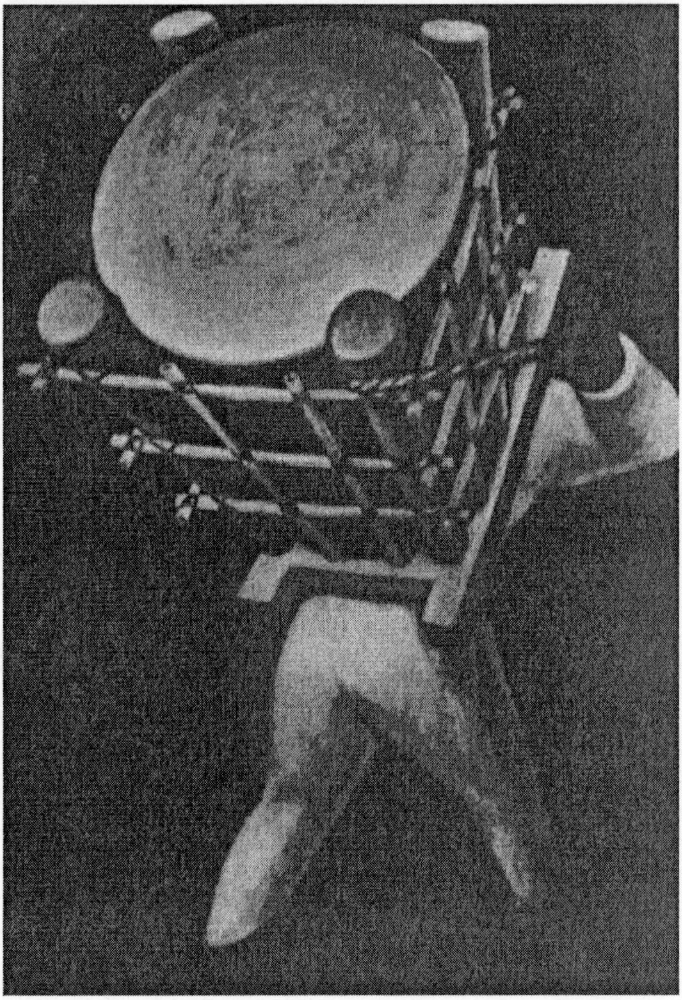

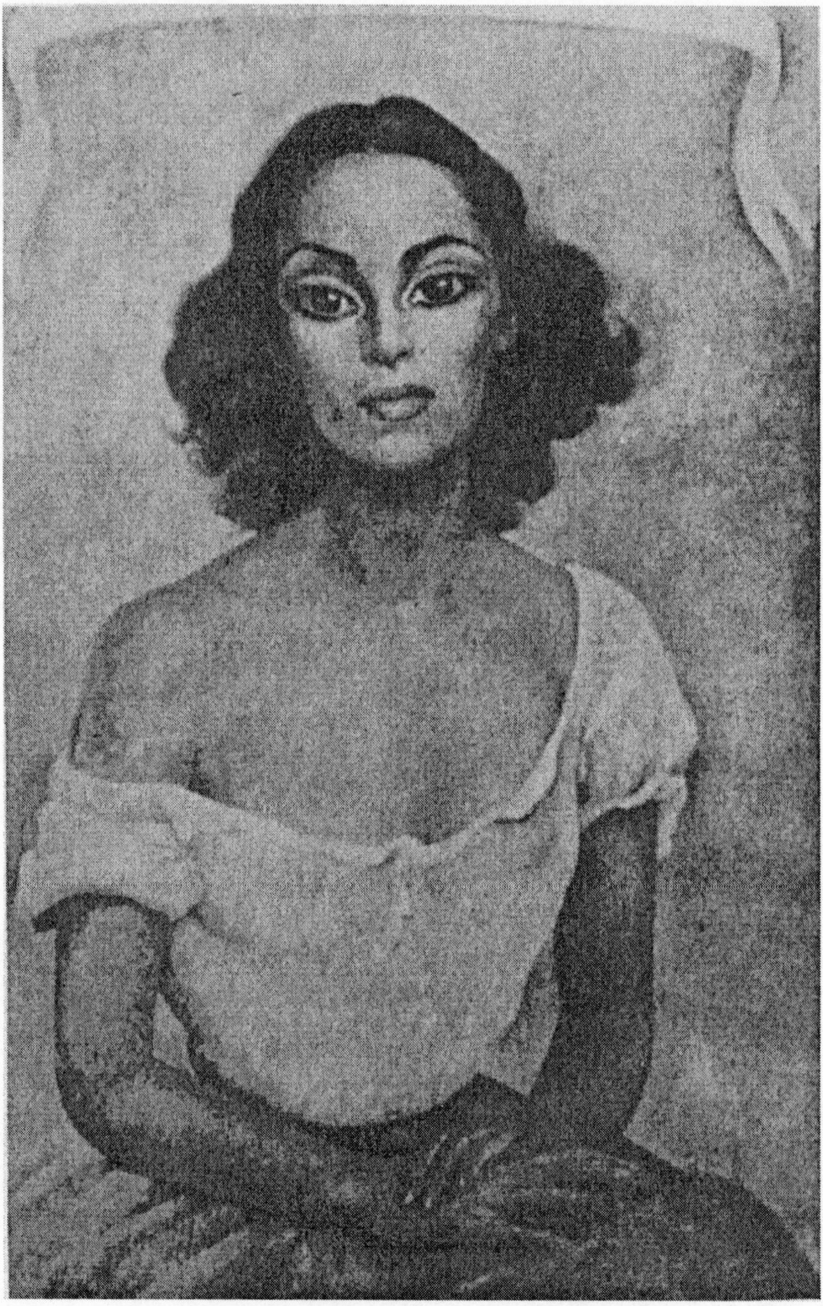

151. Portrait of Dolores Del Rio. Oil. 1938

152. Portrait of Modesta Combing Her Hair. Oil. 1940

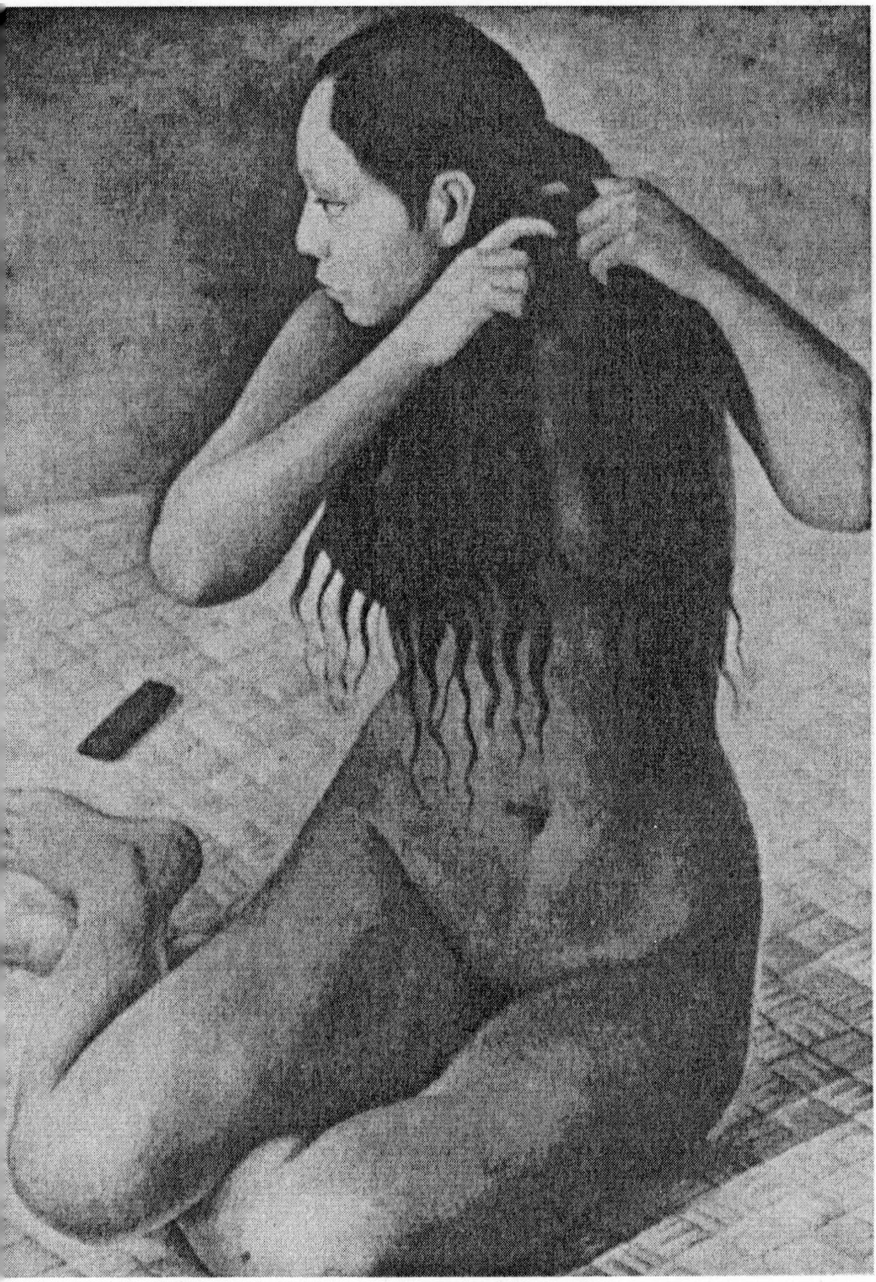

153. Cantinflas. Detail. Insurgentes Theater Facade. 1951

154. The Boy Diego, Festive Death and Posada. Detail of Del Prado Mural. 1947

155. Sketch for the "Peace" Mural. 1952

156. Diego and Frida. Oil by Frida Kahlo. 1931

157. Frida Kahlo. Self-Portrait. 1940

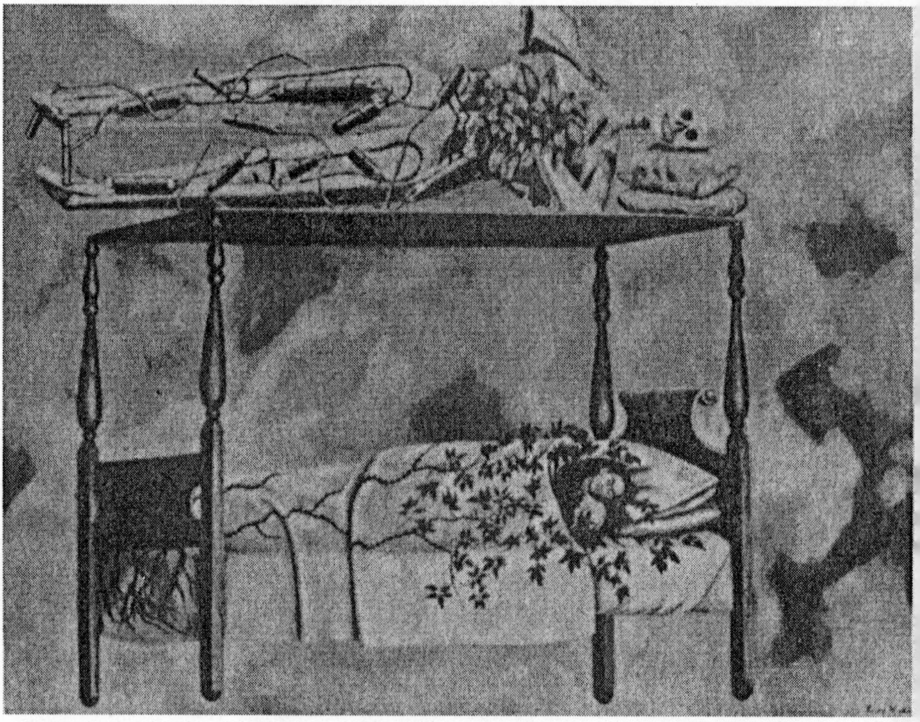

158. Emma Hurtado de Rivera.

159. The Rivera Home. San Angel.

160. Corner of Rivera's Studio.

161. Rivera Pyramid.

162. Self-Portrait. Oil. 1906

163. Self-Portrait. Crayon. 1927

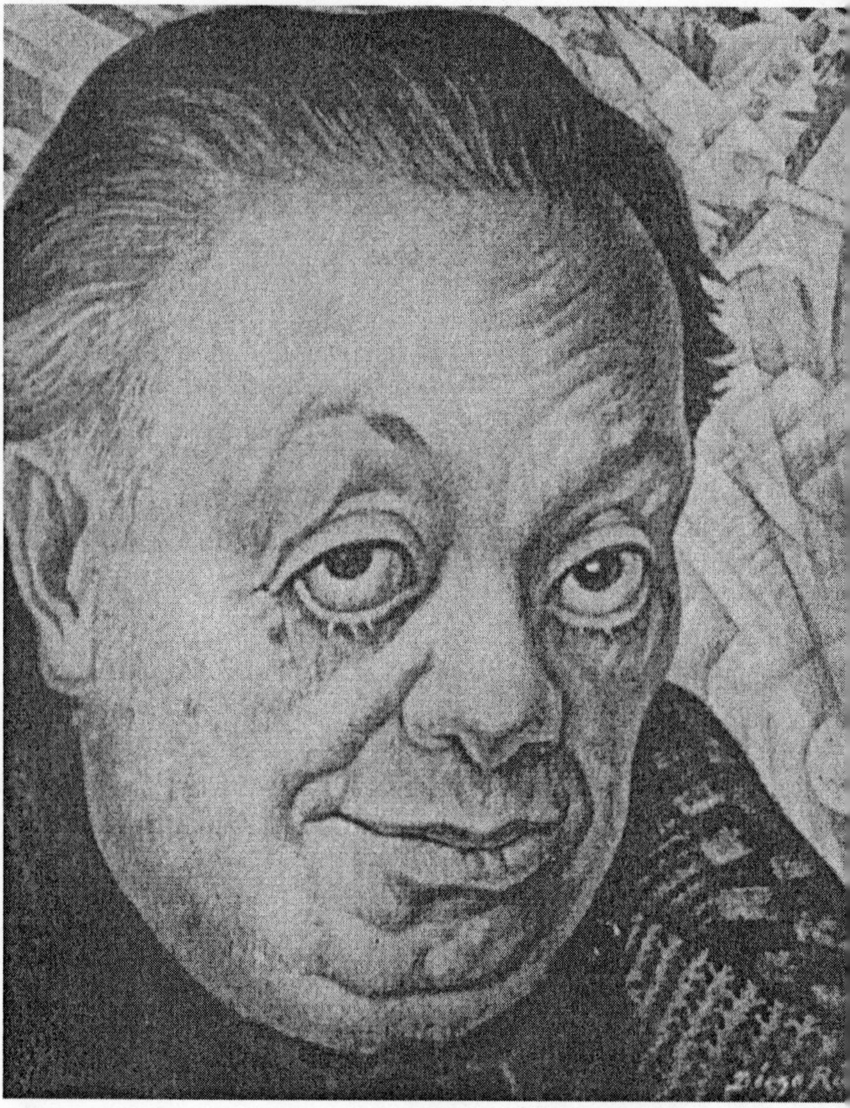

164. Self-Portrait. Watercolor on Canvas. 1949

had prevented the scraping of his "ugly monkeys" from the walls of the Secretariat of Education. Now it was once more the United States that broke the barrier keeping him from walls.

To his "autobiographer," Diego told a weird tale of having been suspected by the Mexican police of machine-gunning Trotsky's bedroom (in which, indeed, two painters were involved, Siqueiros and Arenal). Paulette Goddard, whose portrait Diego was painting at the time, and Irene Bohus, a painter of Hungarian descent, had smuggled Diego into the latter's automobile under the very noses of Police Colonel de la Rosa and thirty of his men; concealed on the floor of the car, Diego had escaped to a hideout where he was provisioned by Miss Goddard until he could escape to San Francisco. "Paulette Goddard," he told newsmen in San Francisco, "saved my life."

The truth was somewhat less sensational. Admirers in San Francisco, particularly Albert Bender and William Gerstle, had been buying his works and giving them to the San Francisco Museum of Art, which in 1939 put on an exhibition of loaned and donated sketches and paintings by Rivera.* San Francisco was getting ready for her Golden Gate International Exposition. It was not concerned with Diego's battles in Radio City, Chicago, and Detroit. Timothy Pflueger, the architect who had arranged his earlier commissions to paint in the Stock Exchange and the School of Fine Arts, made a trip to Mexico to invite Diego to paint movable frescoes in public during the exposition, in a section of Treasure Island to be called "Art in Action." Not secretly like a thief at night, but with regular passport, from Mexico City's great airport, surrounded by the usual fanfare of publicity, Diego flew to San Francisco. He was met by Pflueger and Albert Bender and installed in a studio apartment on Russian Hill, overlooking one of the world's loveliest harbors.

Frida Kahlo, divorced from him at the time, came to San

* Diego Rivera: Drawings and Watercolors from the Collection of the San Francisco Museum of Art and the Collection of the San Francisco Art Association in Custody of the Museum, 1940.

Francisco too, on Diego's invitation, to have her endless succession of skeletal ailments diagnosed, this time as osteomyelitis, and treated by Dr. Leo Eloesser. Then she flew to New York for a happy visit with her many friends, and back to San Francisco, where Diego and she were remarried, on December 8, 1940. Both of them were gladdened by their reunion. Frida painted their new marriage in more sorrowing and mystical fashion than she had their earlier one (PLATE 156). Diego painted her in his fresco on Treasure Island as "Frida Kahlo, Mexican artist with sophisticated European background who has turned to native plastic tradition for inspiration; she personifies the cultural union of the Americas for the South." Even if I had not been in touch with them at that moment, I should have known from the mood of the two paintings that they were together again. But Frida's face in the new portrait looked grimmer, ravaged by illness and pain. For woman as incarnate femininity, in this fresco he chose not Frida but Paulette Goddard.

Diego painted on Treasure Island while the Exposition was on, and for three more months after it closed. His theme was the union of the cultures of north and south in a common America: the blending of the art of the Indian, the Mexican, the Eskimo, and the Yankee, to produce the great continental art of the future. On the right side was the northern culture, predominantly industrial; on the left, the southern, predominantly esthetic and pantheistic. On a background of California's landscapes, San Francisco Bay, Mount Lassen, Mount Shasta, he painted pioneers, inventors, artists, sculptors, architects, engineers, titans of the industrial revolution like Henry Ford (a much kinder image than the caricature he had done before meeting him); the cinema, with Charlie Chaplin as its central hero; idealized figures from the world of sports. On the left side, against the background of Ixtacihuatl and Popocatepetl, he painted pyramids, idols being carved in stone, Indian dances; the pre-Conquest arts and crafts as he imagined them, not without an indigenous

"Leonardo da Vinci," Netzahualcoatl, King of Texcoco, great poet complete with "model of flying machine." And, as a fresco within a fresco, he did a self-portrait, back to the viewer, painting a mural containing portraits of Bolívar, Morelos, Hidalgo, Washington, Jefferson, Lincoln, and John Brown—"the great liberators" of the continent.

In the central panel, uniting left and right, divided like the others into an upper and a lower panel, he fashioned a presiding god, half Mexican earth-goddess with fangs and skirt of snakes, half machine. Beneath it, flanked by Frida Kahlo as the artist of the south and Dudley Carter as the engineer-artist of the north, an "old man of Mexico" (a back view of Diego) and a young girl of the north, reminiscent of Paulette Goddard, joined hands to "plant a tree of love and life."

Completed amidst general plaudits and a feeling that Diego had made his peace with the United States, the frescoes nevertheless had a difficult life for the next twenty years. The movable mural was so big that there was no building to accommodate it. Timothy Pflueger had intended to install it in the San Francisco City College Library he was then working on. But the architectural plans were altered so that there was no library with walls adequate for the frescoes. For years they were stored in vaults, closed to the public view. There were not lacking busy tongues to attribute this to the artist's political views. In 1957 both the architect and the painter died, with the frescoes still in storage.

Finally in 1961, Milton Pflueger, brother of Timothy, who had originally commissioned the work, designed a building area suitable for the fresco, the lobby of the Arts Auditorium of San Francisco City College. Either in storage or in the repeated moving, someone had broken the surface, making a roughly circular gash more than a foot in diameter, which had then been surreptitiously plastered over with gypsum. Who did the damage and who ordered the more damaging "repair" was a well-kept secret. Dr. Archie Weydemeyer, Director of the Art Department of the City's Board of Education, secured the services of Emmy

Lou Packard, a former assistant of Rivera's (herself a figure in the mural). She tested the gypsum plaster for alkalinity and acidity, smoothed the surface, then painted the missing portion according to the original sketches and photographs, in a more recently developed and easier technique, with plastic paints. In color the repair is impeccable, but the hand of the colonial woman embroidering a sampler has a lifelessness that no hand from Rivera's brush ever has.

For the rest, the colors are as bright and alive as the day they were painted; the installation is perfect, as is the illumination. But as I looked at it in its new home in late 1962, reborn after two decades of burial, I could not help thinking how much more beautiful the parts were, especially on the "Indian" side, than the mural as a whole. Once more Diego had demonstrated that he really did not understand, nor feel, the color, form, and meaning of the civilization of the United States as he did that of his own country. If the "history" on the Aztec-Mexican side is in large part absurd myth, as in the case of the flying machine of the King of Texcoco, it is nevertheless living myth. But the painter's misunderstandings and mystifications of the Anglo-American culture are no more than superficial literary clichés. Their roots were not deep in his spirit, hence he did not succeed in giving life to them in paint.

In general, as I review in my mind the entire fruit of his several invasions of the United States, I cannot help thinking that Diego gave us much in technique and example, sowed disciples in three of our cities and throughout the land, added much to his public fame by such episodes as the Battle of Radio City, but except for his murals in Detroit—added little to his enduring work as a painter.

29. THE GOLDEN AGE

On Diego's return from California, Mexico seemed ready to make peace with its embattled painter, too. His sketches showed that he was getting ready for monumental work again. In 1943 he did a series of nudes on the walls of Ciro's night club, works which he himself characterized as pin-ups. Then he painted the long delayed history of medicine on the walls of the National Institute of Cardiology.

Preoccupation with the history of medicine, and his ever-present hypochondria, led him to believe that his life was nearing its end ("my father died at seventy-two, my mother at sixty-two, both of cancer. I must die of cancer soon, for I am nearly sixty"). Two dreams he wanted to realize before death: "to paint the ancient capital of Mexico, Tenochtitlán, as it had been before the barbaric Spanish invaders destroyed its beauty"; and to build a home for the collection of pre-Conquest sculpture which he had been assembling over a lifetime—actually the only wealth he had accumulated by his unceasing labor.

To realize the first of the two dreams, he found new walls in the corridors of the inner court of the National Palace. He began painting day and night again—had he ever really ceased?—as if death would not wait. Portraits, sketches, easel paintings, a lovely children's Christmas Eve festival (*las posadas*) in fresco in the home of Santiago Reachi in Cuernavaca. And, from the pale light of dawn to the dim light of dusk, his idealization of Tenochtitlán on the walls of the corridors of the National Palace (FIG. 149).

His painting was more lyrical now, the curves more graceful, the composition less crowded, the theme was more myth and legend than propaganda, the effect more monumental and rhythmic than in the paintings on the stairway walls. Research, rumor, and overflowing fantasy combined to make of this vanished Aztec world a painter-poet's dream of the Golden Age. Rivera's *Mexico of Tomorrow* under the aegis of Marx, Lenin, and Stalin (or Marx, Lenin, and Trotsky—the painter wavered as to his trinity) with its machines, its tractors and its worker, peasant, and soldier ritually clasping hands, cannot compare with the plastic beauty and poetic fantasy of this *Mexico of Yesterday*.

In Diego's dream there is nothing modern civilized man can do which Aztec, Zapotec, and Mayan have not done more elegantly, intensely, and skillfully. Men and women of graceful bodies, vestments and movements, plant the corn, harvest the ear, grind the kernels, bake them into flat corn cakes in scenes which are a rhythmic dance of worship to the corn god. On sites of topographical distinction they erect their pyramid temples or bustling markets. Chieftain-priests don garments and headdresses at once terrifying and beautiful for the performance of sacred rites. Before the temple, dancers dance their rounds, musicians play sweet, unheard music. Craftsmen weave, smelt, hammer, plait, make jewels of splendor. All these labors are pleasant and joyous, a rhythmic dance. Gentle rivers flow through idyllic landscapes in which dark figures bathe, rhythmically wash clothes, separate bright gold from dark earth. Huntsmen draw their bows in poses of sheer grace, a grace possessed as well by the game they are about to slay. Over all presides the watchful *zopilote* or vulture, who takes upon himself the ungrateful task of scavenging to keep this world clean, a benign nature thus supplying the answer to the vexed question of latter-day scoffers: "In Utopia who will clean the streets?"

Only in the scenes of the Conquest do rhythm, mood, and color change. Here the composition is crowded, the diagonals disturbing; the burden-bearers have lost their elegant outline, the rhythmic dance of labor has changed into a crushed, crowded, bowed shuffling of a chain gang of slaves. From the trees corpses hang, while famished dogs snarl, their ribs showing. The horse on which the conqueror sits has a noble face, but ass and mule, even with noses in feedbags, scowl their discontent, while the very flames have lost their bright glow and lambent grace. The light has grown dim, the color is raw and harsh in its contrasts.

Twice Hernando Cortés appears as the presiding genius of this evil scene. The research of the painter's friends, an "expert in legal medicine, Dr. Alfonso Quiroz Cuaron," who developed "the pathology of the case," and Eulalia Guzmán, who did the "historical research," and Diego himself, who let his wayward fancy and inventive malice give the vision form and body, have produced the Cortés nobody knows. Together they proved, according to the painter, that Cortés had never been properly portrayed before. The real Cortés "had a small head made of small bones . . . elongated from front to back, laterally narrow, a bit conical at the top, asymmetrical in several places; the sternum thin and raised at the center, forming an angle . . . bones spongy, swollen . . . shin bones curved outward, a dwarfish condition caused by congenital syphilis of the skeletal system . . . bird's-beak nose, receding chin, ashy-colored skin and vein that swells at the forehead." Such, according to the painter's fantasy, is the man who, with a handful of horsemen, a few firearms, a dubious patent, and a firm hold on his men, aided by the belief that he looked like Quetzalcoatl, the white-bearded god (!), was able to conquer this multitudinous golden kingdom. Such is the painter's vengeance on behalf of the lost innocence and beauty of the Aztec, Mayan, and Zapotecan civilizations. The caricature is little more than an imprecation.

If Diego expected a great public controversy about his "historical reconstruction" of the portrait of Cortés, he was woefully disappointed. Cortés did not have as many ardent friends and partisans in modern Mexico as a Calles or a Cárdenas or that Juan Diego who was granted a vision of the Virgin. No one demanded that his spiteful, ineffectual, no doubt untruthful, and certainly artistically weak caricature be scratched from the wall of the National Palace, where men who bear in their faces and in their spirits the mixture of Spanish and Indian bloods and cultures today carry on their rule.

Still thinking on death, his own, which he foreboded, and the death around him brought on by the Second World War, Diego began the construction of his museum-pyramid-tomb. He persuaded, or coerced, Frida into giving him title to a barren acreage she had set up with her own money on the lava bed of the Pedregal, to house a Spanish refugee and his family. On the ancient lava bed, nothing grew but cactus and thorn. Her Spaniard had tried to raise cattle there, but Diego wanted it as a house of the dead, a tomb for the ancient gods of Mexico, a modern ruin, the first pyramid to have been built in his country in over a thousand years.

Out of the lava bed, slabs were hewn that were to form its walls. He designed the building from his own plans in a composite of what he himself called "Aztec, Mayan, and Rivera traditional styles." What was "traditional" in the Rivera-traditional, archaeologists would call Toltec. What was "Riveran" came out of the stuff of his dreams of the ancient pre-Conquest world. As one looks at it, one cannot say whether one is looking at a temple, a pyramid, a museum, an artist's studio, or a tomb.

On the land buried by the congealed flow of a long-dead volcano, with no rivaling topographical feature visible in any direction, the monumental temple rises, dominating the dead land. Its walls are built solidly, as if to resist attack, out of irregularly cut stone, with huge solid slabs over doorlike apertures, with false arches such as the ancient Mayans used in their temples, with narrow apertures in place of windows. The stairways, cut of the same lava, run through false arches, too. Huge vertical slabs add solidity to the walls and sustain the arches, admitting light to the galleries where Rivera has set the idols and images acquired over a lifetime, in niches formed by yet other vertical and horizontal slabs. The "halls" of the temple wind and open into each other like those of a labyrinth. In unfaced stone, the walls are gray and cold, but always some strategically placed aperture lets in a dramatic shaft of light to illuminate some idol in its niche. The ceilings are imbedded with brightly colored mosaics, designed by the artist in abstract forms derived from pre-Conquest art. The sculptural decoration, also from the painter's hand, is inspired by the colossal serpent heads, gaping jaws, and curved fangs which are found in Aztec and Toltec pyramids. Many deceptive tricks have been used in the construction to give spaciousness, ample galleries, monumental outlooks and verandas, windows filtering golden light through translucent sheets of marble used as panes—modern comfort, ventilation, lighting, spaciousness, disguised in the forms of the pre-Conquest pyramids which were constructed as they were because Aztec and Mayan did not then know how to form large enclosed spaces.

The uppermost section (there are three floors or levels) Diego intended to be a studio in which he might work. He designed it with wide terraces and outlooks to admit ample light and give a distant view of the lava-flow which reached to the horizon. But he never quite completed it nor found it comfortable or convenient to work there, remaining in his old studio to the end.

On the upper floor is the Chamber of the Rain God, Tlaloc, with appropriate polychrome mosaic decoration, and from it descends, a little absurdly, a stairway to a *Cenote Sagrado* or sacred well such as the Mayans built in their so-different porous, limestone soil, because in Yucatán water will not stay on the surface. The "sacred waters" of Diego's temple extend under the walls to the outside of the building, forming mirrors of water, little pools of quiet light and color in the severe grim waves of frozen lava of the Pedregal.

Other halls of the strange edifice bear such names as Nuptial Chamber, Hall of the Kings, Hall of the Sacred Tamazcal, Hall of the Purifying Bath, and the like. The goddess of night occupies a little cubical almost totally dark. In the mosaic decoration of one of the halls a speaking serpent emits from between its fangs hieroglyphs of a toad (Frida's pet name for Diego) and the Nahuatl sign for the date of the painter's birth. From the terraces and lookouts of the upper floor one sees only the undulating sea of lava, broken up, as it is gradually being broken up over cycles of centuries, by cactus and thorn bush and emerald moss, and far off on the horizon the two majestic snow-capped volcanoes, Popocatepetl and Ixtacihuatl.

From 1943, when Frida acquired the land, until Diego died in 1957, he worked intermittently with a little force of hired laborers on the building and furnishing and designing of this temple, as his imagination, his funds, and his time permitted. He was his own architect and builder. Counseled by such archaeologists as Alfonso Caso, he spent many happy hours planning the grouping and location of those cherished toys, his idols, according to their styles, their subject matter in relation to the respective halls, their chronological order. Those that were most striking were given especially strategic location and dramatic light.

All his life, Diego painted prolifically and unceasingly, sold his paintings easily and for gradually increasing prices (though nothing to compare with the prices they fetch now that he is dead). Every cent that he could spare beyond the needs of his reckless, seignorial, unplanned way of life, he spent on the acquiring of these ancient gods and images, carved masks of jade, jewelry, objects of obsidian, stone, clay, ceramics, semiprecious stones. In 1954 he counted "four hundred pieces in stone and ceramics, some hundred of which are important, and nearly four thousand small objects from all parts of the country and all the ancient civilizations." At his death, some forty-two thousand pieces were inventoried as his legacy to the Mexican people.

Though Diego always spent his money recklessly, gave freely to artists in need, and contributed to the Community Party or whatever cause sent emissaries, he himself lived frugally. He and Frida supported a whole retinue of servants and the families of those servants in feudal or patriarchal fashion, but Diego wore only work clothes and paint-stained overalls, and often lacked for a change of underwear or money to replace a torn tweed suit. Every cent he took in, and great quantities passed through his hands (sometimes in lump sums, as when Rockefeller paid him off), every spare peso was spent on his idols. His taste was sure, he was good at detecting forgeries, not prone to haggle about prices. When he was in money for a moment, all who had idols to sell knew that this market was available.

At his death, I calculate from such data as he made available —he really did not know himself!—he must have spent about $100,000 on the planning and construction of the temple, then near to completion. And there is no telling how much he spent —at least an equal sum—on the thousands of stone idols, clay and ceramic pieces which now fill its niches and line its walls. Undoubtedly the greatest private collection anywhere, any museum in Mexico or elsewhere would envy it.

On his death he left this as his last monument, a gift to the Mexican people to be administered by the Government of Mexico. As the pharaohs left the pyramids (but without so many deaths built into it), so Diego has left his. But he will be remembered better than the pharaohs, not because of his strange, wonder-filled museum-pyramid, but rather because of his canvases and drawings, and above all, because of his walls.

30. "GOD DOES NOT EXIST!"

Still looking for fresh walls to paint, and fresh controversies to add to life's gaiety and his renown, Diego got his next chance in the dining hall of the Del Prado Hotel. The hotel was going up in the very center of the city's elegant life, across from the Alameda. The alliance of hotel and painter was a natural one, insofar as both sought publicity to attract the wealthy tourist trade. It was American tourists that were buying most of Diego's paintings and sketches, and ordering their portraits done; it was visiting American girls who sought a brief moment of notoriety in the limelight surrounding him; it was American patronage which the hotel sought for its swank dining hall, rooms, and suites.

The proximity to the Alameda, and Diego's increasing preoccupation with the thought that his life was nearing its close, combined to determine his theme: *Sueño de una Tarde Dominical en el Alameda Central* (Dream of a Sunday Afternoon in the Central Alameda Park). After a number of repetitious and rather second-rate works, now, in this combination of his childhood memories and fantasies with the complex sophistication of his maturity—a maturity, moreover, in which he remained in so many respects a child—Rivera seemed to enlarge himself again. In color, in composition, in the juxtaposition of figures which could only coexist in a dream, in the images drawn from childish history books, national legends, boyhood memories, thoughts and fantasies—in all respects it is a dreamlike composition.

To the Alameda, Diego had so often been taken in his childhood, back in the days of Don Porfirio Díaz. He had gone there with father and mother, or one of his aunts, to stroll in the shade of the poplars, to sit on a bench and watch the passing show, to rent a seat at twenty-five or fifty centavos (no small sum then) near the bandstand, where a military band played its Sunday afternoon concert. The park was frequented by the respectable, the *gente decente*, by men and women and children in their Sunday best, by *charros*—without their horses, of course—decked out in their flamboyant Sunday horseman's outfits with silver frogs and silver buttons on elegant leather jackets and tight leather pants. Though the police, as Diego remembers it, were on hand to keep out the ragged Indian, the beggar, and the pickpocket, always some light-fingered artists managed to circulate among the crowd. Newsboys were there with their papers, deftly lifting a fountain pen or a purse as they brushed by with their headlines on display. Peddlars strolled by with bright pinwheels turning in the wind, many-colored dancing balloons, *tacos,* sweets made of sugar-sticky fruits, rainbow-hued drinks for the thirsty. How many things there were for a little fat-boy with bulging eyes and an innate artist's vision to see, remember, speculate, and dream about. In later years, too, on his rare days of *fiesta,* Diego would sometimes promenade here with the talkative Lupe and her two daughters, and later, more rarely, with Frida, who found it difficult to walk.

In colonial days there had been a monastery on the end of the Alameda, where, according to tradition, a little embellished perhaps by Diego's fantasy, the Inquisition had burned its victims alive at the stake, until the better residential sections around had forced it to shut down this edifying activity because of the intolerable smell of burning flesh in the park and surrounding streets.

In this park, in 1848, the invading Yankee army had encamped, so the painter must pay his respects, or disrespect, to President Santa Anna, for "betraying the country and handing it over on a silver platter to the invaders." In this square, too, meetings had been addressed to stir up resistance to the French invader, one such demonstration being led by Ignacio Ramírez, affectionately known as *El Nigromante,* along with others by Benito Juárez. Hence these favorite heroes of the painter, along with the usurper-emperor Maximilian surrounded by his notables, are in the mural, too. Naturally, Porfirio Díaz, the perpetual president of Diego's childhood and youth, is here, surrounded by top-hatted, bemedaled, doddering old councilors, the *Cientificos.* Madero, of course is here, gently tipping his hat to the crowd, as if from a political poster, and initiating the campaign to overthrow Porfirio Díaz. There are peasants on horseback, for when Zapata and Villa occupied Mexico City, their armies camped on the Alameda, too.

In a long panel covering the dining room's entire side wall, close to 50 feet in length and almost 16 feet high (15 meters by 4.80 meters), all these memories, fantasies, visions, and dreams are painted—the fashionably dressed Sunday throngs, the newsboys and pickpockets, the weary old men and country yokels snoring on the park benches, the venders of gay pinwheels and balloons, of *tacos* and *dulces,* the heroes and villains of a boy's dream of his country's history, the flames and victims of the Inquisition, the police manhandling the intruding poor, the poets and writers and warriors, invaders and defenders, tyrants and revolutionaries, placards and banners, the bandstand with its band, all elements of a single dream, held together by the writhing branches of the Alameda's trees, by Rivera's skill in assembling them into well-composed groups, by the dreamlike quality of the whole in its rainbow hues of red, blue, yellow, brown, gray, white, and black. Held together, too, by the fact that all the elements are but parts of the single cluster of memories and fantasies in the head of the little frog-faced fat-boy with bulging eyes, a frog sticking out of one pocket and a snake from another, who occupies the center, holding by the hand a fantastic figure of death in her Sunday best (FIG. 154). The little fat-boy is one of the most engaging self-portraits Diego has done, and surely one of the most characteristically Mexican in its mood. The elegantly dressed female skeleton, with winglike ostrich plumes on her hat and noseless, eyeless, lipless visage of a death's head, is an adaptation from a *calavera* (drawing of a skeleton for the Day of the Dead) by José Guadalupe Posada, who had drawn so many *calaveras* to express the mordant-reckless-festive-friendly-familiar Mexican attitude towards death. The *Calavera* wears a feather boa or fur stole around her neck, made of sheaves of withered corn, ending on the right in a snake's head with projecting fangs, and on the left with a snake's rattle, reminiscent of the older Mexican goddess of death. Her one hand holds that of the little fat-boy, while her other bony hand rests on the arm of a Posada, dressed in derby and Sunday suit, a folded silk umbrella in his hand. Behind the corpulent little boy stands Frida, holding in her hand, like an apple, a little sphere painted with symbols of yin and yang, the conflicting principles of life, while to his right, in plumed hats and richly embroidered, wasp-waisted gowns, are his two daughters pictured as elegant, ladylike adults. Only in a dream fantasy could all these heterogeneous elements be juxtaposed in a single mural, and only a master of baroque composition could have given unity to the design. The coloring, with its predominant yellowish-gold, so different from Rivera's usual palette, adds to the dreamlike quality. Despite the elements of pseudohistory (a history so full of tragedy, treachery, bloodshed, and failure), and the central presence of death, the mood is at once festive, humorous, and lyrical.

The new mural got no chance to be judged on its merits, for, as he was painting it, it occurred to Diego to put into the hand of one of his historical heroes, Ignacio Ramírez, a scroll held up directly under the head of Benito Juárez. On the scroll in clear letters one could read: *Dios no existe!*

Ignacio Ramírez was no mere vulgar atheist, but one of the intellectual leaders of the Reformation under Benito Juárez, which aimed at the separation of Church and State, the curbing of the immense economic and political powers of the clergy, the abolition of monastic orders and public religious processions, the secularization of education. His work needed no scroll, while the single sentence emblazoned here was by no means an adequate representation of his thought. Yet, as every educated Mexican must know, he had indeed pronounced these words in the course of one of his polemics. As so often happened with Diego, the people who could not appreciate the force of painting but could read words "with all their letters," might pass over, unnoticed, his sharp satire and propaganda in plastic form, but became indignant when they saw in so many words what they were supposed to be looking at. Moreover, if the quotation was not representative of *El Nigromante's* total body of thought, it was indeed the sentence which best represented him in Diego's own mind and in his dreamlike vision of his country's history.

When the mural was to be unveiled and the hotel opened, Archbishop Martínez refused to bless the edifice until the offending placard was covered up. As the news hit the headlines, young Catholic students raided the hotel, made a gash on the fat-boy painter's face, and scratched out the legend in Ramírez's hand, chanting as they rioted, "God does exist!" and "Long live Christ, the King!" Then mobs of young men paraded in front of

Rivera's studio in San Angel and his home in Coyoacán, shattering the picture windows of his studio with stones. Rivera and his fellow painters and supporters rallied in turn, parading in front of the hotel and taking possession of the dining hall to repair the mutiliations. All this kept the Del Prado Hotel in the headlines, but it was not the kind of publicity that the Director, Señor Torres Rivas, had bargained for. He had the mural covered with a movable screen, which could be removed when desired, to satisfy the curiosity of some distinguished guest. On such occasions a hush settled over the noisy dining room, for the *Sunday Dream* exercised a spell of its own, unrelated to the battle over the existence or nonexistence of God. The screen would be put back in place again, and the controversial painting and the dream would disappear. It did not occur to the proprietors to smash the painting off the wall, for by now Mexico had established the civilized principle that a painter did not lose control over what he sold to the extent that it could be altered at will, much less completely destroyed. Ironically, the Committee on Fine Arts of the moment, which alone had the power to approve such an act of vandalism, was composed of Diego Rivera, José Clemente Orozco, and David Alfaro Siqueiros. Thus neither God's existence nor the painting's could be further called in question. So, throughout the next nine years, the matter stood.

31. RETURN TO THE BOSOM OF THE CHURCH

In May of 1949, as the controversy over the existence of God in the Del Prado Hotel was dying away, Mexico bethought itself of the fact that its celebrated artist was rounding out fifty years of work. In Bellas Artes, the magnificently inappropriate edifice of white marble which Diego had so often ridiculed, the National Institute of Fine Arts opened a fifty-year retrospective exhibition of his work.

Five hundred pictures were gathered from many lands and many stages of his long and fruitful life. The great murals could not leave their walls, but all that was movable was well, if not exhaustively, represented. Museums and private collectors lent their pictures. The Nelson Rockefellers and Mrs. John D. Rockefeller, Jr., without regard for the controversy which had ended in the destruction of one of his frescoes, lent their large collections of his sketches and water colors.

On one wall was the permanent reproduction of the destroyed mural. An entire section of the exhibition was dedicated to blown-up photographs of the details of other murals. Those not content with photographs had only to walk a few blocks to see the National Palace, the Education Building, and Rivera's other works in the city. A bus ride would take them to the manificent chapel in Chapingo which remains one of the best of Rivera's walls and ceilings.

The retrospective was a resounding triumph. It was followed by a beautiful and comprehensive Symposium Monograph entitled, *Diego Rivera, 50 Años de su Labor Artística,* published in 1951. The planning of the monograph was done by Fernando Gamboa, undoubtedly guided and advised by Diego and Frida, who supplied much of the material. It contained essays, good, bad, and indifferent, concerning the various aspects of Rivera's personality and work, an excellent catalogue checklist and bibliography by Suzanna Gamboa, and a rich selection of reproductions, in black and white, with a few in color. There were photographs of the painter in childhood, as an art student, in his home, sketching on the street, painting in his studio and on walls; self-portraits at various ages, including one of the aging painter done by him in 1949, reproduced in the present work as FIGURE 164. A verbal portrait by Frida Kahlo was full of passionately fierce defense of her painter husband against all his detractors. One section reproduced his early efforts: a train drawn by him when he was three years old; pencil drawing of plaster casts done in the Art School; landscapes of the period before he left for Europe; reproductions of his work in Spain; his cubist and post-cubist derivations from the Parisian painters. There was a rich selection of the better known work of his later years.

The nation had become proud of its controversial painter, the controversies having helped to increase their pride, for headlines are the stuff of celebrity in our time. As one looked at the exhibition or the monograph, one could not doubt that the country had reason to be proud of its painter, and the painter reason to be proud of so opulent an exhibition.

In the self-portrait Diego did for his retrospective, he looked unflinchingly at the tearing eyes and sagging features of one whose prodigious energy was beginning to wane. Old age was creeping up. He must make haste, for time, the portrait seemed to say, was running out.

And indeed, during much of his later life as a painter, Diego had largely been repeating himself. He had long ago found his style, his subject, his palette, his calligraphy, his manner of work. He had developed a sure sense of composition and structure. He thought so easily with his hand and brush, saw so swiftly and selectively, drew so skillfully, knew so well how to capture the effects he intended, that he had ceased to experiment or strain to enlarge his large talents.

One dream still attracted him—to be a "universal man," something as he imagined Leonardo to have been. Leonardo had his scientific notebooks, so he too kept pronouncing on all the latest achievements and visions of science. The pronouncements were far-fetched and unimportant. Wanting to be a "universal" artist, he made several more attempts to do sculpture and architecture and mosaics.

In 1951 he got an opportunity to decorate the aqueduct of the canal from the River Lerma. Part of his decoration is polychrome high relief of the god Tlaloc, sculpture that was grotesque, bulky, and unimportant. In the aqueduct itself he painted writhing watery forms which were to continue to exist under water when the sluices were opened: protoplasmic life, undulating water serpents, fishes, tadpoles, and, emerging from the waves, nudes representing the varieties of man. Above them were action scenes of men at work tunneling through the mountains to construct the aqueduct, and a consultation of architects and engineers such as Diego had already done in San Francisco on a smaller scale. The best thing in the work is a huge pair of hands, through which water drips. In this mural Rivera experimented with new pigments, plastics, and techniques, which he believed would stand against the racing and pounding of the water. Before he died, he knew that he had failed. In less than five years the colors were visibly deteriorating; the prospect now is that sediment and water flow will before long obliterate the world he tried to paint under water.

After his fifty-year retrospective, Diego's standing in Mexico was at its highest. His friend Carlos Chávez was Director of the Fine Arts Institute. The intelligent Fernando Gamboa had completed the monograph-symposium which recorded and celebrated Rivera's life and work. President Alemán, whom but yesterday Rivera had been caricaturing on a wall, spoke of declaring the painter's work "a national treasure"—flattering but inconvenient, for it would have stopped the sale of his paintings to tourists (no "national treasure" may be exported) and even their sale for permanent possession to Mexican collectors ("national treasure" in private hands, according to Mexican law, must revert to the government on the death of the possessor). To honor Mexico's "celebrated painter" further, Chavez and Gamboa, with the President's approval, arranged a new commission.

The collection of Rivera's work assembled for the fifty-year retrospective would be sent to Paris, along with paintings by Orozco, Siqueiros, Tamayo, and a host of other stars of the Mexican renaissance. Mexico would show Paris what it could do, how much its artists had learned from the capital of European art, and yet, how much they were themselves. Diego was to paint a new movable fresco especially for the show. A fee of 40,000 pesos ($4,628) was allotted. Neither size nor theme was stipulated, merely that it was to be a movable panel, fresco on beaverboard. It seemed a wonderful arrangement. To understand how it ended in another scandal, we must take a backward glance at Diego Rivera's political career.

Whatever Lenin may have said of the duty of his followers to be "professional revolutionaries," Diego was a professional only in painting. In politics, he was an amateur and a passionate dilletante. In Spain and France he had been an anarchist. When he returned to Mexico in 1922, he was caught up by the Mexican Revolution, becoming, insofar as we can define the subject matter of his murals in political terms, a Mexican national revolutionary, a populist and Indianist, hostile to the Spanish and European element in Mexico's (and in his own) culture. With this vague assortment of feelings and ideas, Diego joined the Mexican Communist Party, at that moment more a painters' party than anything else.

What had given his murals their notoriety was not his amazing fecundity nor his skill but the controversies the paintings had set off. Whereas the nineteenth-century "Ishmaelite" painter had been content to *épater le bourgeois* on squares of canvas in a studio, Diego whipped up his controversies by breaking ground with new forms and by painting obvious Communist propaganda on walls belonging to a government which was not Communist. He satirized the mestizo middle-class intellectuals of which he formed a part and the officials who were his patrons. He painted the head of Lenin in Rockefeller Center. Many of the controversies erupted not over the forms and design nor even the theme, but over words painted on placards *en todas sus letras*—an injunction to the miners to "make daggers of your metals" or a scroll proclaiming, "*Dios no existe!*"

What gave his murals their finest sections was never the routine worker, peasant, and soldier clasping hands, nor the cold, poorly painted, bushy-bearded Marx and Engels. How much more lyricism Rivera could put into the dreamlike figure of Zapata leading a white horse! He could put much more plastic and human feeling into a scene of labor conceived as a rhythmic dance than into an attempt to illustrate the dogma that he who labors is exploited. As a propagandist he was more often than not a mere illustrator of rather shallow propositions. But when he let his deeper feelings take over, love of his country, love for the humble, common folk, love of Indian children, a feeling for the dramatic beauty of the land, his painting could be rhythmic and tender, the design at once sophisticated and simple. His statements concerning the utopia of the future were elementary and trite. Their illustration in paint showed that they had not enlisted the whole of his being. But what a wonderland he could make of the lost innocence of the golden age before the Spaniard came!

Ideologically this might not stand up well against the formulas of textbook Marxism, but this need not have prevented the Communist Party from enlisting his large talents in its services. Still the Party had expelled him, for trivial reasons. After trying in vain to find in Trotskyism a more worthy ground for his enforced separation, his concern in his declining years was to return to the bosom of the church which had sanctified his early murals. In 1946, having denounced himself as a bad Communist and denounced the quality of all his painting done while separated from the Party, he made his first application for readmission. It was roundly rejected. A few years later he tried again. Another rejection!

Diego knew only too well what was in the way. It was not his Trotskyism, which no one, Diego least of all, had taken seriously. It was not his absurd ideological pronouncements, nor his heresies, nor, certainly, the quality and general theme of his paintings, nor the fact that he had painted in government buildings (as all the Communist painters did), nor for wealthy patrons (who else could be a patron?). It was something graver which stood in the way, something *serious* which he had done in paint upon a wall: a portrait, more deeply felt, more intensely and truthfully painted, than his hollow images of Marx, Engels, Lenin, and Trotsky—a portrait of the only man who really mattered in the world-wide Communist movement after 1929. He had seen Joseph Stalin but once, in 1927, but had seen him with that sudden clarity which an artist's vision sometimes gives. He had painted "the greatest genius of all lands and all times" with distaste and revulsion. A bullet-shaped head, low forehead, narrow, cruel yellowish eyes, a touch of red rimming the eyelids, the face of a vengeful and arbitrary tyrant.

This might not have been noticed by the party nabobs, many of whom were insensitive to plastic expression. But he had committed two more sins. He had grouped the head of Stalin in a trinity with Trotsky and Bukarin, as a preachment in favor of "the restoration of Communist unity"—unity between those of his comrades whom Stalin was to execute as traitors and the executioner himself!

Worst of all, he had put his feeling concerning Stalin into words which even the esthetically blind could not overlook. In *Esquire* he wrote:

> I will always remember the day that I met the undertaker [of the Revolution]. At eight we entered the offices of the Central Committee . . . my fellow guests smirking with satisfaction, drooling with superiority . . . they might have been entering paradise. . . . Suddenly a peanut-shaped head, surmounted by a military haircut, decked off with a magnificent pair of long moustaches, rose above them . . . one hand slipped into his overcoat and the other folded behind him à la Napoleon . . . Comrade Stalin posed before the saints and worshipers.

How was Diego to live that down?

When Chavez and Gamboa approached him with a commission to paint a movable mural for exhibition at the Mexican show in Paris, he saw his chance. The world was rocking with Stalin's campaign for "peaceful" coexistence. The Comintern, or Stalintern, had been officially dissolved, and the center of overt Communist energy transferred to a galaxy of fellow-traveler movements and fronts, of which the most important was the Stockholm Peace Congress. That was what he would paint for Paris: "peaceful—offensive—coexistence," the spirit of Stockholm, the glory of Stalin. Paris was a great metropolis and art center; the whole Western world would take notice.

Diego drew his sketch in secret. To Chavez's inquiries he merely answered, "I am painting a mural which will be dedicated to peace." The mural must be huge, he decided, so that it would be the first thing to catch the eye at the Mexican exhibition in Paris. Despite the modest sum allotted, he painted a picture 33 by 15 feet. With the salvation of his Communist soul at stake, he did not count the cost, nor spare himself. In exactly thirty-five days from conception to finished painting, he covered the 495 square feet of surface, working day and night. He called it *The Nightmare of War and the Dream of Peace.*

As painting it was pretty bad; Rivera had rarely done worse. But as an illustration or propaganda poster it had its points, and the painter used his skill in composition to make the points. In the upper right-hand corner, dominating the entire painting, larger than life, the largest figure in the painting, is a portrait of Joseph Stalin, huge left hand resting on a square of paper (the Stockholm Peace Petition), with hand and paper resting on a globe, covering the earth. The eyes are serene and clear, the face confident, benevolent, firm, almost smiling. His right arm and hand extend over the globe, holding out a pen asking mankind to sign for peace. Next to him, almost as large, and also looming over the globe, is an apple-cheeked, dreamy-eyed, benign-looking Mao Tse-tung. The rest of the huge surface serves as counterpoint to this beatific and heroic pair. Facing them, ill at ease and scowling, are Uncle Sam, John Bull, and Marianne, the objects at that moment of Stalin's proposal for a five-power peace pact to force them to recognize all the puppet governments he had set up in the Eastern Europe his troops had occupied during World War II.

Uncle Sam has a thin, sharp face, a machine gun strapped on his back, a Bible in one hand, a sack of money in the other. Just behind him are men hanging on a scaffold, a Negro nailed to a cross. "This shows the United State's double face," Rivera was to explain later for the benefit of those who couldn't see the visual image for what it was. "The United States has lost the spirit of the Bible, but still carries it for show."

John Bull has the tough nobby face of a thug, hat slanted over his eyes. Marianne is treated a little more equivocally, for the picture was to be shown in Paris, but she has a hatchet face and her expression is bewildered and rather dumb.

These three figures are smaller and on a plane that recedes a little from the foreground where the two heroes stand. Below, in the foreground, are figures from the common folk, bearing burdens, discussing some issue, signing copies of a petition. Behind them, a firing squad is executing an unseen victim and men are lashing slaves tied to posts. As the composition lines of the sketch show, the pen held out by Joseph Stalin, whether to mankind or to the three ugly prototypes in front of him, actually is directed past them; a line runs directly from it on a diagonal to the central figure in the lower right: Frida Kahlo, who has risen from her bed of pain, her face ravaged by traces of the advanced stage of her illness, but full of determination as she sits in a wheel chair and holds out a copy of the Stockholm Peace Petition for Mexican men, women, and youth to sign.

The intention is clear: yesterday's "executioner of the revolution" has been glorified. Stalin and Mao represent the "dream of peace"; the nations to which he is offering his five-power peace pact represent the nightmare of war. Thus Diego's art has been put 100 per cent at the service of the current campaign of the Communist Party and its offensive Stockholm Peace Conference campaign, while Frida, the painter's own wife, has been enlisted, in her wheel chair, performing her Communist duty to the last. Such was the illustrated charade of Diego's third petition for readmission.

The painting attracted all the attention Diego had hoped for. Carlos Chávez, after pleading with him to do something else for the Paris exhibition, formally notified him that the Government of Mexico could not exhibit in Paris, nor hang permanently in its museum at home, a painting deliberately calculated to insult and slander governments with which Mexico was on friendly terms. Rivera announced a rupture of all friendly relations with Carlos Chávez, "who has heretofore treated me more like a brother than a friend." He cried "fascist censorship," and aided at last by the Communist Party, arranged a public showing of the rejected mural that was more a political demonstration than an art show.

Leaders of the Communist Party, fellow-traveler intellectuals, Communist artists, officials of the Mexican Peace Committee, diplomats from iron curtain countries, all graced the exhibition. In New York, the *Daily Worker* of May 13, 1952, carried a letter from nine American artists to Diego Rivera: Russell Cowles, Philip Evergood, Hugo Gellert, Robert Gwathmey, Jacob Lawrence, Jack Levine, Rockwell Kent, Anton Refregier, and Charles White. They praised him as a "great artist . . . spokesman of the Mexican people . . . leader of the progressive art tradition. . . ." Rather absurdly, they linked his name with that of the American Communist Party's agitprop director, V. J. Jerome, whose pamphlet, *Grasp the Weapon of Culture*, they claimed was to be suppressed by the Government of the United States. Nine artists, whose names had been linked with so many campaigns espoused by the Communist Party, men who had never lifted their voices while Soviet artists were being censored, suppressed, and purged—this was quite a comedown from the days when hundreds of artists of all schools and creeds had rallied to Diego in the battle of Rockefeller Center. Yet the letter in the *Daily Worker* was evidence that Diego had played his stakes well, and won. Once more, as in the twenties, he was a "hero of progressive art." Once more, he was not a renegade but a revolutionary painter. The day the Mexican Art Exhibition opened in Paris, *l'Humanité* reproduced his *Peace Mural* for distribution to those attending the opening. His operation palimpsest had succeeded: his old portrait of the "executioner" had been overlaid by a new one of the apostle of peace and hope of mankind. Stalin the Terrible had been overpainted with a portrait of Stalin the Good.

The scandal in Mexico also had its muted echo in Detroit.

There a number of people, including former Mayor Van Antwerp, petitioned the Detroit City Council to remove or cover up Rivera's *Age of Steel* frescoes in the inner court of the Detroit Institute of Art. To the earlier arguments against it, they added the fresh one that Rivera had just attacked the United States in his *Nightmare of War and Dream of Peace.*

The City Council asked the Detroit Art Commission to re-examine the paintings and bring in proposals. The commission's report, made while the press was still filled with the *Peace Mural* controversy, reads:

> We regret that Rivera's present behavior has revived the old controversy. There is no question that Rivera enjoys making trouble. . . . But this man, who often behaves like a child, is one of the outstanding talents of the Western Hemisphere. . . . In the Detroit frescoes we have one of the best as well as one of the most serious of his works. No other artist in the world could have painted murals of such magnitude and force. . . . We recommend that the paintings remain on exhibition.

The commissioners who signed the report deserve to have their names recorded. They were Robert H. Tannahill, Mrs. Eleanor Clay Ford, widow of Edsel Ford, who had commissioned and then valiantly defended the work, and K. T. Keller, Chairman of the Chrysler Corporation. Their report, and the city's action, do credit to the good sense and respect for art of all concerned.

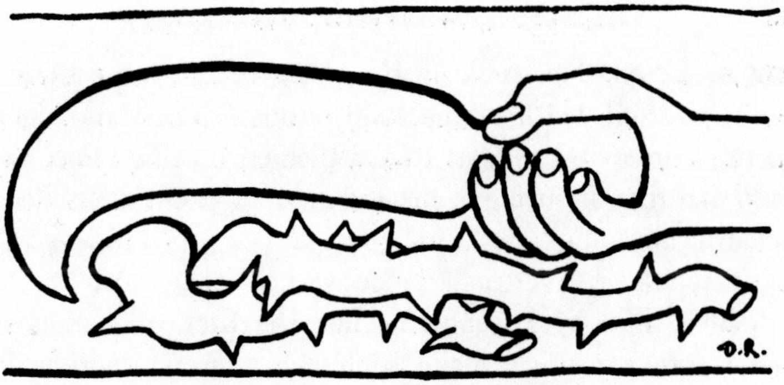

32. THE DEATH OF FRIDA KAHLO

On one of the broadest and busiest boulevards in Mexico, the Avenida de los Insurgentes, a new motion picture theater was built by José María Dávila, of whose pretty wife Diego had done a somewhat too "pretty" portrait. Dávila commissioned the architects, Julio and Alejandro Prieto, to design the great and glittering theater and Diego Rivera to decorate the long, convex façade above the pillar-supported marquee. As many of those who would see the painting would be passing quickly by in the flow of boulevard traffic, Diego planned the composition so that those flying by would carry away a striking image, while those who paused to look up could take in all the detail which was his constant delight and which gave a baroque character to so much of his mural work. At the center, establishing the theme of theater, he painted a huge mask, from which two eyes peered out, held in place by two dainty feminine hands in delicately laced, fingerless evening gloves, from which long slender fingers with lacquered nails projected. This took up the entire center, more than half the height and width of the total façade. To left and right of the mask are many familiar Rivera themes, modified to convey a sense that they are being re-enacted on a stage. On the far left his "scientifically established" image of Cortés as a bowlegged, decrepit syphilitic, presses a lance which seems to have been handed to him by an angel against the back of a crouching, bound Indian captive, while Malinche interprets with a little balloon of speech such as was used in the Aztec codices (and less gracefully in our comics). Over Cortés looms the mask of a stage devil. These are all figures in a play. Below them three musicians in native dress play a fiddle, a drum, and a horn, and a *China Poblana* dances with a *charro* the Mexican dance known as the *jarabe*.

As the eye moves towards the center, we see Mexican historical plays, with the huge masklike faces of Juárez, Hidalgo, and Morelos. Behind them rises a gigantic clenched fist, symbol of Communism (was not Rivera's Communism a species of play-acting, too?). On the opposite side of the façade, matching Morelos, Hidalgo, and Juárez, are Zapata and scenes from the Mexican agrarian revolution. Beyond these on the far right are portrayed the music, dance, and religious ritual drama and pantomime of the days before the Spaniard came.

But it was the central panel directly above the giant masked face and gloved hands that captured public attention, as indeed Diego intended it to. In the very center is a wonderful lifelike portrait of Cantinflas, Mexico's great comedian, with *pelado* (tramp) face and perpetually falling pants, flanked on one side by wealthy Mexicans, caricaturing capitalist, courtesan, militarist, and cleric. The wealthy and powerful gaze admiringly on their comic entertainer, handing him money which, in Robin Hood fashion, he hands over to the hungry, the mendicant, the crippled, and the poor, who cluster around his other hand. The impudent climax of the painting lay not in picturing the comedian, Cantinflas, as a Robin Hood, but in the fact that behind his head rose the towers and stars of the Church of the Virgin of Guadalupe, patron of Mexico, and emblazoned on him was her sacred image. In short, Cantinflas was not only the Mexican *pelado* and Robin Hood, an incongruous enough combination, but at the same time, the beloved, humble and devout Indian, Juan Diego, to whom the Virgin had appeared thrice though she would not vouchsafe her presence to the high dignitaries of the Mexican Church. This trinity of incarnations of Cantinflas might be amusing to the irreligious or religiously indifferent. To the devout Mexican Catholic, however, the byplay was a wound to his deepest feelings.

A new storm broke loose around the painter's name, a storm which Diego hoped would strengthen his next application for membership in the Communist Party. So deep are the feelings of so many humble Mexicans about the Virgin of Guadalupe that the Party did not venture to rally to his defense. Still, to the controversy over the long covered Del Prado mural with its *Dios no existe!* and the controversy over the rejected *Peace* mural with its image of Stalin the Good, Diego felt he could now add the outraged cries of clergy and devout believers over his Tramp-Robin Hood-Juan Diego-Cantinflas as merits on judgment day, when his fourth application for readmission would be taken up. "There is nothing contradictory," he informed the press, tongue in cheek, "between Cantinflas and the Virgin of Guadalupe—Cantinflas is an artist who symbolizes the people of Mexico; the Virgin is the banner of their faith." To make sure that the party bosses would not miss the Communist implications, there was the huge clenched fist, and, under the feet of the wealthy, a legend reading "1,000,000 x 9,000," signifying that there were nine thousand millionaires in Mexico, while under the feet of Cantinflas and the needy mendicants Diego painted "20,000,000=000," that is, Mexico's 20,000,000 poor have nothing. "They are more than poor," he explained to reporters. "They are three times poor, they have three times nothing."

That same year (1953), Frida Kahlo had a one-man show. It proved to be a deeply moving affair. Frida's highly personal painting resembles no other body of work in the whole history of art. It combines the naïve simplicity of a self-taught primitive with the sophistication of a poetic sensibility which might be called surrealist, were it not for the literary nature of salon surrealism which it in no way resembles. It is compacted of nightmare, grim jest, and poetic fantasy indigenous to the Mexican spirit. Every work she has done, except one portrait of Diego, has Frida's own image in it. They are not so much self-portraits as plastic records of some aspect of her adventurous life and evocative dreams. They give plastic form to her awareness, her sufferings, her feeling of childlike wonder (childlike until the day of her death), her love of life in all its wayward, uncontrollable manifestations.

To add to the pathos of the show, Frida, bedridden now, with her life force manifestly ebbing, arrived in an ambulance for the opening, presiding over it in a wheel chair, surrounded by admirers and friends, excited and happy despite her pain.

Later that year, her train of doctors, who had never succeeded in arresting the slow decay of her skeletal frame by all their tormenting operations, persuaded her to undergo yet another, her fourteenth operation in sixteen years! This time it was major, for they insisted that gangrene was setting in in her foot and would eventually spread if they did not cut off her leg at the knee. They told her there was no hurry, the development they foresaw would be slow but their prognosis was sure. "Then amputate now," she said, and it was done. The maiming was a severe blow to her spirit as well as a tax on her waning strength.

As she had first learned to paint after her auto acident in girlhood, lying flat on her back confined in a plaster cast, so she did her last painting for the show of 1953, once more on a bed of pain with an easel fastened over her. Between the first painting and the last, her life had never been free from pain.

It had been a life in all senses out of the ordinary. The flame of vitality had always burned with a peculiar incandescence in that slender, suffering, slight-appearing body. High-spirited, imbued with intense and infectious gaiety, warm and generous in her art as in her person, her sensibility was served but not dominated by an unusually keen and subtle intellect. She made up for the accidental crippling of her frail body by turning herself into one of the most effective of her works of art. Barbaric pre-Conquest jewels, colorfully embroidered skirts and blouses drawn from the Mexican popular costume at its best, bits of brightly colored wool in her braids, long skirts filled out by many petticoats, skillful use of paint and mascara and whatever else her sensibility taught her to use to express the flame that burned so bright in her and to conceal the maiming effect of her accident —her appearance would have seemed outlandish were it not for the artistry with which she designed and adorned herself.

From her tomboy girlhood to the last year of her life, all her days she knew the depths of joy and the depths of suffering, but few conditions in between. From the moment when she told her classmates at the Preparatoria with characteristic deviltry that her one ambition in life was to have a child by the great, ugly, frog-faced Diego Rivera (an ambition which life had thwarted), she began to conceive a passion for him which later ripened into a love filling every fiber of her being.

As is natural with two such strong characters, each totally directed from within, each wayward in impulse and intense in sensibility, their life together was stormy. She subordinated her waywardness to his; otherwise life with Diego would have been impossible. She saw through his subterfuges and fantasies, laughed with and at his adventures, mocked at and enjoyed the color and wonder of his tall tales, forgave him his affairs with other women, his wounding stratagems, his cruelties, his ruthless absorption in his own feelings and his art to the exclusion of consideration for any one or any thing else. Wounded to the depths of her being by the one affair which involved the girl to whom she had given the greatest fullness of her generosity and love and trust, she had struck back with extramarital affairs of her own, until they came to be part of her life, as of his. Despite quarrels, brutality, deeds of spite, even a divorce, in the depths of their beings they continued to give first place to each other. Or rather, to him she came first after his painting and after his dramatizing of his life as a succession of legends, but to her he occupied first place, even before her art. To his great gifts, she held, great indulgence was in order. In any case, she told me once, with rueful laughter, that was how he was, and that was how she loved him. "I cannot love him for what he is not."

This logic of the heart was irrefutable. In her last years Frida became ever more fiercely passionate in her defense of Diego's foibles and monstrous ways, ever more proud of his monstrous creativity. Her indignation had been boundless when she told me how Diego had tried to borrow the very pen which "the old man" (Leon Trotsky) had given her, his name engraved on it as a token of affection and gratitude, in order that this *farsante político* (clown politician), Diego, could sign with Trotsky's pen his application for readmission to what had become unconditionally Stalin's party. Yet dragging her feet, she followed Diego as he moved closer to the Communist Party. Though she could never bring herself to the ridiculous and humiliating ceremony of self-abasement required to apply for readmission, she did lend her name to such fellow-traveler purposes as the Stockholm Peace Petition. One corner of her being, however, she reserved against Diego's pressure—she never lent him Trotsky's pen to sign his application. If she had, Diego would have delighted in publishing this "exploit" to the world!

A strangely matched couple they were. This frail, slender, dynamic girl with her colorful raiment, jewels, ribbons, and make-up resembling some pre-Conquest Indian princess, with the ribbons in her hair barely coming up to her male companion's shoulder, accompanying this clumsy, lumbering giant of a frog-faced man in huge sombrero, ill-fitting tweeds or paint-stained overalls. Wherever they appeared together, they became the immediate center of attention. When they entered a theater, all eyes left the stage. Their appearance in the streets of New York, Detroit, and San Francisco was enough to stop the flow of traffic and pedestrians. Yet nobody laughed at their unusual appearance; even those who had never seen their pictures nor heard their names felt that they were contemplating an extraordinary pair.

At one period, it occurred to Diego to buy for a season a box at Mexico's concert hall, where he would appear, always a trifle late, with both Lupe and Frida, his two daughters, and some current model or mistress, like a sultan with his harem. It was hard on his friend Carlos Chavez, conducting on the stage, when Diego and his train entered his box.

In the 1951 memorial volume devoted to Rivera's fifty-year retrospective, the warmest, in some ways the most penetrating, in all ways the most generous tribute to Diego was written by Frida. She began by apologizing that she was using an unfamiliar medium, namely words, of which she was no master. But her six large folio pages of poetic exaltation and glorification, entitled "Retrato de Diego Rivera," showed that she could use words as imaginatively, vividly, and precisely for her purposes as she could pigments. Her verbal images match the romantic-tender and legendary portraits of him which she has done in some of her paintings. She had painted him as an overgrown babe in her arms, as her bridegroom in a rustic, primitive wedding portrait, and even, rare indeed, perhaps unique in all her painting, in a portrait in which she did not appear at all. But the portrait she did with words is better than that overromanticized painting:

> With his Asiatic head, above which rises dark hair, so delicate and fine that it seems to float in the air, Diego is a huge boy, immense, of amiable face and glance that is somewhat sad. His protruding eyes, dark, filled with intelligence and large, are retained with difficulty—almost starting from their orbits—by swollen and protuberant eyelids

like those of a frog. Widely separated from each other, more so than other people's eyes, they serve to enable his glance to take in a visual field much more ample—as if they were made especially for a painter of spaces and multitudes. Between those eyes, so distant one from the other, one catches a glimpse of the ineffability of oriental wisdom, only rarely does a smile, ironic and tender, the flower of his image, disappear from his Buddha-like mouth.

Seeing him naked, one thinks immediately of a boy frog, standing up on its hind legs. His skin is greenish-white, like that of an aquatic animal, only his hands and face somewhat darker, burned by the sun. . . .

His shoulders, infantile, narrow and rounded, continue without angles in feminine arms, ending in hands that are marvelous, small, delicately drawn, sensitive and subtle like antennae communicating with the whole universe. It is astounding that these hands should have served to paint so much and that they still work so tirelessly. . . .

The rest of the profile discusses and exalts Diego's genius and defends him against all the familiar attacks which his stormy and provocative life as painter and man had called forth. In fact, there is nothing about him any more which Frida does not justify and defend.

His so-called mythomania [she writes] is directly related to his tremendous imagination, he is as much a liar as poets and children who have not yet been turned into idiots by schools or their mammas. I have heard him tell all types of lies from the most innocent to the most involved stories of persons whom his imagination combines in fantastic situations and procedures, always with a great sense of humor and a marvelous critical sense; but never have I heard him tell a single lie that was stupid or banal. . . . And the strangest thing about the alleged lies of Diego is that, sooner or later, those entangled in the imaginary combination grow angry not because of the lie but because of the truth contained in the lie, which always comes up to the surface. . . .

When Frida's profile of her famous husband was published, both of them were nearing the end of their powers as painters and of their days. Frida had only three years to live, Diego but six. Except for the portrait of Cantinflas already referred to, he was to paint scarcely anything worth noting. More and more he was finding it fatally easy to repeat himself. Even when he strove to attempt something new, he no longer had the energy and will required for the further enlargement of his powers.

The wisdom Frida had learned in her last years was profound, a trifle cynical, tolerant of life's waywardness and unreason, fiercely and passionately loyal even to the foibles of her beloved Diego. "*La vida es un gran relajo,*" was her summary to me of the bitter wisdom she had garnered, a summary, unfortunately, untranslatable into English.

Those who knew and loved her watched with sadness now the slow stages of her decline, the devices she used to ward off incessant and intolerable pain, her consuming of endless gulps of three-star Hennesy (she always carried a number of miniature bottles of her anodyne, and sometimes even a pint bottle, too, in her ample purse); and then, as pain grew more unbearable, her tentative, steadily more frequent recourse to more powerful narcotics, which exacted stupor as the price of relief.

Even in her decline, there were occasional flashes of incomparable gaiety, festive humor, tenderness, thoughtfulness for those dependent on her, infectious laughter, which would communicate itself to all who surrounded her bed of pain.

After the amputation of her leg, the periods of stupor and enfeeblement grew longer, her naturally bright and joyous spirit emerging only rarely to the surface. Hitherto unfailing, mischievous good humor gave way to fits of petulant irritability, quarrels and rupture of relations with some of her dearest friends, sensitivity and anger about what earlier she would have considered secondary things.

On her forty-fourth birthday, she drowsed all morning while those who had come to wish her joy waited around her bed. It was the same room in which, forty-four years earlier, she was born. For the first time, she received her friends without adornment or make-up. In the late afternoon she called for her most splendid dress and jewels, made herself beautiful and radiant, then gaily, even happily, held court. That was on July 7. On July 13, 1954, at three o'clock in the morning—death's favorite hour—she died mercifully in her sleep.

When a reporter from *Excelsior* came to snap pictures and interview Diego, he found the painter standing helplessly by her bed, to which he had come from his studio in his work clothes when the faithful servant, Manuel, came to tell him, "*Señor, murió la niña Frida.*"

A friend at her bedside (Ella Paresce) wrote me, "Diego became an old man in a few minutes—pale and ugly." For once he had no words for the press. To the reporter, eager and excited as Mexican reporters are wont to be in the presence of celebrity, beauty, and death, he said, "I beg of you don't ask me anything. . . ." Then he turned his face to the wall without another word.

But by seven o'clock that same morning, Diego had recovered his composure sufficiently to bethink himself of what sort of ceremonial spectacle should be made of Frida's funeral. At that early hour he began calling the home of an old classmate of hers, Andrés Idurate, who was now Director General of the Institute of Fine Arts. He kept ringing insistently until Dr. Iduarte's servants woke him. Diego gave him the news of Frida's death, then said that he, and many other painters, thought she should be given the honor of lying in state in the hall of the Institute. Dr. Iduarte loved his boyhood friend and greatly admired her art. But knowing Diego's ways and the ways of the painters whose names Diego invoked, Alfaro Siqueiros, Xavier Guerrero, and the like, he stipulated: "Yes, she merits honor from her country, but, Diego, there must be no political banners, no slogans, no speeches, no politics."

"Yes, Andrés," Diego answered meekly.

Late that afternoon, the bier was duly installed in the portico, and Dr. Iduarte descended from his office with several other officials of the Institute. Iduarte and three of his aides were to post themselves, as is the Mexican custom, at the four sides of the body to serve as the first guard of honor. As they opened the elevator door, someone standing in the knot around Diego advanced and placed the flag of the Communist Party, red with a hammer and sickle in gold, on the corpse. Iduarte and his assistants retreated in confusion; they did not want to cause a scandal by public argument, nor tolerate the political scandal that Mexico should honor one of her greatest children not with the Mexican flag but wtih the banner of Communism. From his office Iduarte sent an urgent message to Diego, reminding him of their talk and pleading that scandal be avoided. The note came back with the word that Diego was too immersed in grief to be disturbed. Dr. Iduarte called up the Secretary of the President of the Republic (President Ruiz Cortines was out of town) and asked for advice. "Make him remove the Communist banner," was the advice, "but try to avoid a scandal." The Director and his staff returned to the portico, where they found Diego the center of a band of Communist painters and "workers in the arts." The body of the dead Frida, who but a few moments before had been arrayed in her accustomed robes and jewels like a defunct princess, was now almost completely covered by the red flag. When Iduarte protested in a whisper, Diego answered insultingly in a loud voice. He and his comrades, if necessary, would take the body out onto the marble steps and do it honors there. At that moment, General Cárdenas, the ex-President who in his last years had become in more ways than one a fellow traveler of the Communists, entered the hall to take his turn in the guard of honor. Again Dr. Iduarte retired to his office to call up Presidential Secretary Rodriguez Cano. "If General Cárdenas is standing guard," the Secretary answered, "you should stand guard, too." Thus Diego and his band had their way.

At the cemetery, before the cremation, things were arranged with more dignity. Carlos Pellicer recited some poems; the only address was a beautiful and feeling tribute by Andrés Iduarte. The story was well reported in the morning papers next day, but an afternoon scandal sheet carried the huge headline: "*Iduarte Responsable de la Pachanga de Bellas Artes*" (Iduarte Responsible for the Scandal at Fine Arts).

"The funeral orations," *Excelsior* reported a day later, "were not so much in honor of the dead artist as in praise of Communist ideas." The scandal continued to grow until an expiatory goat had been chosen and sacrificed. Angel Ceniceros, Minister of Education, reported that he had "received" Dr. Iduarte's resignation, and had accepted it because the Director of the Institute had "permitted" the painter whom Mexico was honoring to be covered with "a Soviet flag." How Frida would have laughed at the spectacle of her funeral. "*La muerte, como la vida, es un gran relajo*," she would have said.

Andrés Iduarte, who had spent many years serving his country abroad in the diplomatic service and then teaching Latin American literature at Columbia University, returned sadly to his chair at Columbia. The Communists rejoiced, for they had made a party demonstration of Frida's funeral, and it had served to rid them of an obstacle to their intrigues in the Department of Fine Arts as well.

For Diego the stratagem paid off, too. He made a new application for readmission to the Party—his fourth. In each of his successive applications he had engaged in "Communist self-criticism." He had pronounced his painting since he left the Party "a work of degeneration"; he had called it "the weakest period in the plastic quality of my painting." He had labeled himself successively "coward, traitor, counterrevolutionary, and abject degenerate." Impressed by these qualifications, and by the deeds of service which we have narrated, on September 26, some two months after the scandal attendant on Frida's death, the Communist Party reaccepted Diego Rivera as a Communist and a "revolutionary painter."

In his reminiscences for his intended autobiography he told Gladys March: "Reactionary officials raised a cry against this display of a revolutionary symbol, and our good friend Dr. Andrés Iduarte, Director of the Fine Arts Institute, was fired from his post for permitting it. The newspapers amplified the noise and it was heard throughout the world . . . July 13, 1954 was the most tragic day of my life. . . . My only consolation now was my readmission into the Communist Party."

To be officially confirmed once more as a revolutionary painter, to have turned Frida's funeral into a Communist demonstration, to have had the "noise heard throughout the world," to be readmitted to the Communist Party so that he might make one more journey to Moscow, this was the apotheosis Diego had been seeking.

Her ancient house in Coyoacán is today the tomb, and memorial museum, of Frida Kahlo. It is a long, low rectangular house with one room leading into another, all looking inward on a garden patio and a small orchard. The bed in which Frida died is of an ancient type with a roof supported by columns, curtains which can be drawn, and a mirror within its antique confines. Everything is as it was at the moment of her death, even the *lares* and *penates* of the moment which Diego had set down for her to contemplate, Marx, Lenin, Stalin, Malenkov and Mao Tse-tung, three of whom have already proved to be something worse than mortal—out of favor and out of style.

The outer walls of the old house are a pastel blue, floor and walls within are painted a greenish lemon-yellow such as is seen only in Mexico. The furnishings are in the gay style of the Mexican folk. The tall cabinets are filled with dolls of all nations which the childless Frida delighted to collect, while from the ceilings, and in every corner are suspended skeletons, death's heads, Judases and other objects of Mexican popular art. There are paintings by Frida, *retablos,* a landscape by Velasco which Diego gave her, a few wonderful ancient stone sculptures of pre-Conquest Mexico, also gifts of Diego. In the garden, Diego constructed a pre-Conquest place of worship engraved to remind the visitor, a little incongruously, that in Coyoacán Cuauhtémoc was tortured, and in Coyoacán Frida Kahlo was born, lived, painted, rejoiced, suffered, died. The final Mexican touch, which Frida would no doubt have approved: on the high bed is the torture instrument in which for so many years she was encased, a plaster cast on which she had had many of her friends sign their names with brush or pen, and a carved and polished urn containing her ashes. Over the bed with its drawn curtains presides a skeleton death made of cardboard or papier-mâché, painted to resemble bones, the bones held loosely on springy pivots, so that death dances grotesquely in the gentle breezes that sweep through the room.

33.

BOTH MOSCOW AND ROME

Readmitted to the Communist Party, Diego vowed: "Henceforth my sole service will be to Marxism-Leninism-Stalinism, the only just and true political line out of which alone can come good painting." His first work under the new dispensation was disillusioning. It was the crudest propaganda poster of his career, a picture of the revolution which had just overthrown the pro-Communist government of Guatemala. The revolution was pictured as the work of "Yankee imperialists." The center is filled with the villains of "the counterrevolution," John Foster Dulles, American Secretary of State, smiling, in paratrooper uniform, his brother, Allen Dulles, Director of the C.I.A., with a bestial face, American Minister John Peurifoy, Monsignor Verolina, Papal Legate to Guatemala, some tough-looking Guatemalan military men, and the new President, Castillo Armas, who was subsequently assassinated by a Communist terrorist. Castillo Armas is a hateful-looking subhuman creature, with lynxlike face, servile smile, and crouching, obsequious stance, grasping the right hand of the American Secretary of State. The latter's left hand rests on a heavy missile-bomb adorned with the features of President Eisenhower. From Castillo Armas's pants protrudes a bulky revolver; in his skimpy leather jacket is a package of American dollars. At the feet of these distasteful creatures lie in profusion dead children, bleeding from great numbers of lurid, red-mouthed wounds. To the left are bunches of green bananas, a sack of green coffee with the label "Made in the U.S.A.," a ship of the United Fruit Company, the Stars and Stripes. To the right, with hate-filled faces, some Guatemalan peasants lean forward, machetes upraised as if to strike the Papal Legate who, with one hand uplifted in heratic gesture and the other holding a prayer book, blesses the scene. All the faces but one seem to have been painted with aversion, the machete-wielding rebels faring no better than the rest. Seen from a distance, the painting as a whole, the grouping of masses of heads and figures, the curves of banana tree leaves and bunches of bananas show, as always, the painter's skill in composition. But the closer one approaches, the worse the painting seems. Only in the face of John Foster Dulles, strange to relate, does the skilled portraitist prevail over the sensational cartoonist. As political caricature the huge poster may have been pleasing to the Communist Party and to the country to which Diego was meditating a pilgrimage. But looking at it, Diego knew that the Stalinist line had not performed the miracle of restoring his powers as a painter. He sent it off to Warsaw for a traveling exhibition behind the iron curtain, and did not so much as mention it among his late works in his autobiography.

Diego's power of working tirelessly was waning. He began to dream that a journey to mecca would restore his strength as artist and man. A skin ailment around his mouth, which some of his doctors diagnosed as cancerous,* gave an added impulse: "Moscow is the only place in the world," he told reporters, "where doctors really know how to cure cancer."

In his sixty-ninth year, on July 29, 1955, he married for a fourth time, this time secretly, without the usual fanfare. His bride was a woman much younger than he, Emma Hurtado, a friend of some ten years' standing (FIG. 158). Their friendship, she wrote me some time after his death, began the first day they met, when she asked him to do the drawings for the front and back covers of a symposium on *Mexico Prehispánico*, which she was about to publish.† "Since our first meeting," she wrote, "we have been inseparable." In 1946, Diego gave her the valuable right to exhibit and sell all his easel paintings and sketches not done on commission. In those years he was still enormously prolific so that her Galería Diego Rivera, opened especially for the sale of his work, was highly profitable. Now, in his solitary, infirm old age, she became traveling companion, worshiper, and nurse, accepting these tasks and the title of Diego's wife with pride. "He has been the greatest love of my life," she was to write me. "I have always had the deepest admiration not only for his art but for his way of thought, without ever being able to find anything at all in which I could be in disagreement with him." Today, since the Spanish language does not permit of our locution, "Mrs. Diego Rivera" (in Spanish it would have to read: Mrs. Emma Hurtado, Widow of Rivera), she has had recourse to French and imprints her stationery: "Madame Diego Rivera."

Diego's late propaganda pictures and controversies got him the invitation he sought, from the Academy of Fine Arts in Moscow and from some of the other capitals of Eastern Europe. Just before he set out with his new bride for this autumnal honeymoon, he called a "national and international press conference," in

* One of his physicians assured his friends that the true diagnosis was "warts."

† Editorial Hurtado, México, D.F., 1945.

which he made public his marriage, his plans for the trip, his expectation of being healed of cancer by the superior medical science of Moscovy. On August 24, the pair left by plane for Europe.

Diego spent the better part of a year being lionized in Pankow, Prague, Warsaw, and Moscow. In Moscow he rested in a sanatorium reserved for the new privileged class and their honored foreign guests. When he returned to Mexico with Emma, he told reporters that Moscow doctors had cured his cancer with a "cobalt bomb." "With the rest and the superior medical treatment I received in Russia," he added hopefully. "I should live ten years more. Right now my fingers are itching to start my next mural." He did not look as well as his words suggested.

The exhibition at his wife's Galería Diego Rivera, made up of the sketches, oils, and water-colors he had done in Russia and Poland, was an undistinguished one. On his trip he had done nothing either emotionally or plastically significant. Renewed contact with the world of Communism had not renewed his powers. Out of piety, the critics were silent, or irrelevantly anecdotal.

With that same sense of comic fitness which had prompted him to ask Frida for Trotsky's pen to sign his application to the Stalinist party, it was from Moscow itself that Diego chose to send a letter to Carlos Pellicer, a poet and a prominent Catholic churchman, suggesting a reconciliation with the Church in their long feud over the covered mural in the Del Prado Hotel with its placard: "God does not exist!" He had taken his first step for reconciliation some time before this, when, without fanfare, he removed the image of the Virgin of Guadalupe from the portrait of Cantinflas which he was doing on the façade of the Teatro Insurgentes. But this had been only a cease-fire in the long war between Diego and the Church.

Always one to relish a sensation, after first authorizing Carlos

Pellicer to arrange the deletion of the offending placard, Diego sent him a wire from Moscow asking that nothing be done until he himself should return.

On April 15, 1956, the screen was removed and Diego in person climbed a specially erected scaffold before the mural which had been covered for nearly nine years, to make a "secret" alteration. He chose for this *coup de main* one of the busiest hours of the day, 6:30 P.M., contriving to alert the press that something sensational was about to take place in the Hotel Del Prado. He took two hours for the little job of resurfacing and repainting, then climbed down from the scaffold to tell astonished reporters, "I am a Catholic." Linking up his old change in the Cantinflas portrait with this new act of conciliation, he added, "I admire the Virgin of Guadalupe. She was the standard of Zapata, and she is the symbol of my country. It is my desire to gratify my countrymen, the Mexican Catholics, who comprise 96 per cent of the population of the country."

For a man who had boasted that his father was a freethinker and he himself an atheist since the age of five, for a painter who had done pictures of gross and fat priests extricating the coins of the faithful from chutes placed under the image of the Virgin, priests blessing brutal reaction, priests carousing with or carrying in their arms disheveled, skirt-lifted courtesans, this was startling. In a country where anti-clericalism is imbedded in the Constitution of 1857 (that of Juárez), and in that of 1917, and in the Jacobin revolutionary tradition which forms part of the stock-in-trade of so many run-of-the-mill politicians, it was more astonishing still.

One of the reporters asked, "Diego, why did it take you two hours to make that small alteration?"

"I had to make other changes," he answered. "For instance, the face of the little boy of ten that I was in my dream, during the eight years that he was covered up, became old and wrinkled, and I had to restore his lost youth."

Within the course of a single year, his sixty-ninth, Diego Rivera thus effected a reconciliation both with Rome and Moscow.

A few years later, when Diego was dead, the uncovered Del Prado mural was found to be in grave danger. The hotel's foundations, like those of so many heavy buildings constructed on the filled-in lake bed of ancient Tenochtitlán, were discovered to be sinking into the ground, more each year. Moreover, they were shifting unevenly. The pressure thus created on the surface of Rivera's fresco had caused its right side to be fretted with many tiny cracks.

There was much consultation of experts. Then the hotel management decided to try to remove the whole dining room wall from its supports, a difficult and perilous operation. The 17,500-pound wall was placed in sections in a specially constructed steel boxcar, to be moved on rails the few feet necessary to install it in the hotel's lobby. The job was carried out perfectly. It is to be seen now to much greater advantage, for its surface is no longer obstructed by pillars, as it was in the dining room. It is open to a wider public, too, which is fortunate, for now that the little placard that attracted so much attention has been altered, people for the first time are seeing the mural rather than the controversy. It is as if people were seeing the beauty of a palace for the first time after a shocking obscenity scrawled on the face of it had been erased, for actually this is the finest work of Diego's late years, beautiful in composition and color, lyrical in its dreamlike quality, the most poetic of his major works after Chapingo, and of all his works the most playful.

34. DEATH COMES FOR THE PAINTER

In December, 1956, Diego turned seventy. As is customary when a country becomes aware that one of its illustrious sons has lived out three score and ten, Mexico celebrated. The journals devoted special supplements to the painter, but as he had done nothing of importance in the past year, they reproduced self-portraits, less known easel paintings, fresco details which seemed novel because they had not been used before.

In his statement to the press, Diego spoke again of getting back to fresco painting. But as 1957 marched by, his plan to ascend the scaffold remained unrealized. He worked at his pyramid and the disposition of his idols in their niches. He visited the School of Cardiology, where a new wall was being offered, made some preliminary sketches, asked a doctor friend for slides of cancerous tissue, began a portrait of Ruth Maria de los Angeles, infant child of his daughter, Ruth.

In September he suffered a blood clot and an attack of phlebitis, losing the power to move his right arm. He did not complain of the pain, only that "the brush no longer obeys me." All his life he had had two fears, that an infection of the lachrymal gland should blind his eyes or some affliction paralyze the hand which transferred to wall and canvas what eyes saw and fantasy created.

His heart grew weaker, yet he would not hear of hospitalization. Instead, he had himself installed in a bed in his San Angel studio, surrounded by idols, ikons, masks, gods, Judases, skeletons, and, at his bedside, two easels with unfinished paintings, the one of his granddaughter and the other of a smiling Russian child. When he recovered control of his brush, there they would be, waiting.

Near midnight on the 24th of November, he called the faithful Emma by ringing a bell. "Shall I raise the bed?" she asked.

Contradicting his interlocutor as was his wont, he answered, "On the contrary, lower it. . . ." Those were his last words.

Next day a death mask was taken by Federico Canessi, while Ignacio Asunsulo made a mold of that right hand which had filled the land with his paintings. The body was dressed in a dark blue suit and a red shirt; then in a coffin of metal, painted to look like mahogany, it was transported to the rotunda of the Palace of Fine Arts.

Notables of the art world and the world of politics took turns in fours as a guard of honor. The Under Secretary of Education represented the President; ex-president Cárdenas stood at the head of the coffin looking bored; old Dr. Atl, who had encouraged him in his youth, mourned as he stood guard on crutches; Alfaro Siqueiros, who had so often attacked him, was grief stricken and stony faced; some politicians looked self-important, others chatted or turned expectant faces to the cameras.

Outside the Palace, dense throngs crowded the rotunda, the stairways, the surrounding streets. Next day thousands of men and women from all walks of life marched in his funeral procession. Both the Communist Party and the Government said their say at his cremation, in words not worth remembering. For his intimates and family, the poet Carlos Pellicer, who had been his friend and Frida's, delivered the last farewell. "The great throng" *Tiempo* reported, "watched the ceremony with tears in their eyes."

In his will, Diego had asked that his ashes be placed next to Frida's in her bed in Coyoacán, but President Ruiz Cortines ordered the urn to be installed in the Rotunda de los Hombres Ilustres, where it now rests. Reporters interviewed his widow, Emma Hurtado de Rivera, on his last moments, the size and disposition of his estate. She calculated his goods were worth twenty million pesos, *Tiempo* reported; she valued the pyramid and its treasures as more than fourteen million. The rest consisted of his house in San Angel, Frida's house in Coyoacán, pictures, art objects, and an automobile. As always, there was little actual cash. The heirs were his widow and Diego's two daughters by his marriage with Guadalupe Marín, the architect, Ruth Rivera de Alvarado, and the law-school graduate, Guadalupe Rivera. But the chief heir was the nation itself, to which he left his lifetime of painting, his walls, his pyramid, and his archeological treasures.

Thus ended the huge, fantastic, colorful fresco, perpetually overflowing with invention and adventure, which was his own life. Only when the excitement engendered by the continually changing image he created of himself has died away will Mexico be able to ask itself what kind of painter lived among its people, what was transient and what enduring in his work.

It would be presumptuous for one writing so soon after Rivera's death to undertake that assessment. Moreover, such estimates are never final, for time gives ever-fresh perspectives, not necessarily sounder one than another, but in any case different. The works themselves, insofar as they possess vitality, will live lives of their own, independent of the intentions of their creator. Parts will seem to disappear into the wall, others stand out ever more boldly, beget their own offspring, say new things to new generations. The measure of their creator, too, will vary with changing moods, fashions, values of succeeding ages. All that a contemporary biographer can do (we were contemporaries though there was ten years' difference in our ages) is leave some tentative notes for a future biographer. . . .

35. NOTES FOR A FUTURE BIOGRAPHER

The Revolution which took possession of Diego Rivera and made him its painter, was the Mexican Revolution not the Russian. The upheavals in Mexico that began in 1910 and continued for more than a decade, preceded the Russian Revolution, developed independently, had causes which sprang from Mexico's own condition. Its aims, however, vague, were entirely its own. Its agrarian revolution produced not a new state-controlled serfdom as in Russia but an independent peasantry.

When the Tsar was overthrown by spontaneous rebellion in the Spring of 1917 and the new Russian democracy was in turn overthrown by Lenin in the Fall of that same year, the Mexican Revolution had already been going on for seven years.

In 1917, for a moment a few of Mexico's ideologues turned their gaze uncertainly towards Moscow, then again looked inward, rejecting as alien Russia's influence, her dogmas, and the arrogant commands and instructions of her new rulers.

The Mexican Revolution was above all an attempt at self-discovery. A poor, unhappy land, which for the first century of its independent existence had been colonial and imitative in its culture, sought to find its roots in its own past, to assert thereby the worth and dignity of its own folk. If in several decades the Mexican Revolution has not accomplished much else, this much it has accomplished: the reversal of some of the social consequences of the Spanish Conquest and the rise of the Indian to full citizenship in his country. And this, it seems to me, leads us to the essence of Rivera's painting in Mexico, not in his murals alone but in most of his easel paintings and drawings, as well.

To be sure, this suggests that Diego Rivera was a populist rather than a Communist. And that indeed is what his painting says concerning him.

The first sketch Diego did on his return to Mexico in 1921, a sketch for an intended painting, with color notations still written in French, was entitled "Zapatistas."*

Once before, some six years earlier, when there was as yet no Russian Revolution, in mid-1915 Diego ceased for a moment his endless succession of Paris cubist scenes, Paris studio objects, and Paris cubist portraits, to do a unique canvas, bright with colors almost never used in somber cubist painting. Its background was a geometrically stylized Mexican mountain landscape with nothing cubist about it. Its foreground, on a flat surface of the deepest Mexican blue, was a cubist construct, made up of bits and pieces, colors and shapes, abstracted from the equipment and costume of a Mexican agrarian revolutionary. The core of the construct is a small bore rifle such as the *agrarista* carried into battle. The gun is surrounded by elements derived from a sombrero, a bright *sarape* of Saltillo, a mule's head, saddle bags, a water canteen, white patches suggesting peasant raiment, fragments of rock, grained wood, deep green foliage with bits of its own shade. All this forms a single cubist

* Reproduced as plate 219 in *Diego Rivera: 50 Años de su Labor Artística*, Suzana Gamboa, ed, (Mexico, D.F., 1951).

object, resting on a deep blue ground behind which rises the Mexican sierra. Its granite craters and cones, the highest topped with perpetual snow, rise into a remote, clear, light-filled, pale green-blue Mexican sky. The painting was entitled *Paisaje* Zapatista. (FIG. 16). The colors, the mixture of poetic elements, cubist and noncubist, and, above all, the subject itself, tell more of the nostalgic landscape of Diego's spirit at the moment than they do of Paris painting or the Mexican Revolution. It is a fall from cosmopolitan-Parisian grace, a ballad in cubist language to the Mexican agrarian revolution, a cry of longing for home and country. Its title foreshadows the protagonist of some of the most poetic passages in Diego's future murals: Emiliano Zapata.* Its fragments of folk garb, revolutionary folklore and folk uprising, against the background of Mexican soil and sky, constitute an inventory of elements in so many of Diego's future frescoes. The little rectangle of paper, nailed with a painted nail near the lower right-hand corner of the blue foreground, is worth noting, too. When such scrolls appeared later, they were taken to be a conventional expression of Communist leaflets and posters, but here we have such a placard done before Lenin seized power in Russia or founded his Communist International. Actually it was taken not from Communism but is a common feature of Mexican primitive painting and of the Mexican *retablo*. The painters of primitive portraits generally put the name of painter and subject in such a placard or scroll, while the *retablo* painter used the same device to recount the miracle which called forth the votive offering.

In 1917 when the two revolutions occurred in Russia, Rivera went on doing much what he had done before. Only in 1921, when he set foot once more on his native soil, or rather in late 1922, after a journey through the strife-torn land, when he got his second wall (in the Secretariat of Education), did the Paris studio painter become the Mexican painter we know. Only then

* In Rivera's frescoes the most frequently repeated figure is Emiliano Zapata.

did he find his characteristic style and subject matter. And, as panel after panel proclaims, at last he had found his epic subject: the Mexican folk.

Diego was then thirty-six. He had left Mexico, already an accomplished landscape painter, at the age of twenty-one. Abroad he had worked hard and wrestled to wring their secrets from all the great pictures and schools of European painting, modern and classic. Despite his awesome productivity, his marvelous draughtsmanship, his chameleonlike ability to take on a hundred styles without altogether losing himself, he had not found himself. His work remained the derivative-original work of a talented "provincial" or "colonial" who had spent fifteen years in Europe, more than a decade in Paris, yet was still a stranger in the *Quartier Latin.*

Only when he renewed contact with his native earth was his strength renewed for the great labors he was henceforward to undertake. One cannot help but feel that if he had remained for the rest of his life in Paris, as so many painters do, though he would have done many excellent paintings, the final verdict would likely have been little different from that which was pronounced on him when he first made the Autumn Salon in 1914 and Guillaume Appollinaire wrote: "*Rivera n'est pas du tout négligeable.*"

Thus Diego's return to Mexico and his contact with the Mexican Revolution was for him what the Revolution itself was for his country—an experience in self-discovery an enhancement of his appreciation of his native roots and autochthonous plastic sensibility.

That he at times confused the Mexican Revolution with the excitements of anarchist and socialist ideological fragments picked up in café conversations in Madrid and Paris is not surprising. Diego was not the only painter in Paris, nor in St. Petersburg either, to confound the studio-and-café revolutions aimed at upsetting, astonishing, defying the "bourgeois" with

Lenin's hatred of the bourgeoisie or determination to liquidate whole classes of men. By "bourgeois" the artist meant little more than someone insensitive to modern art, possessing bad taste, subservient to habit and routine, neglectful of living art and the living artist. But Lenin, as I have shown elsewhere,* was ready to include under the category "bourgeois" the entire intelligentsia of Russia and of Europe, and to regard as "petit-bourgeois" those workers who concerned themselves with economic and political reform in order to improve their lot in "bourgeois society." And, for good measure, Lenin added the real hero of Rivera's painting, the agrarian peasant revolutionary, to the category of the bourgeoisie, to be distrusted and eventually eliminated.

None of the painters ever took the trouble to study the writings of the Marx and Lenin whose names on occasion they invoked. Even Modigliani, whose brother was an outstanding leader of the Italian Socialists, knew nothing of the literature of Marxism. Mastering political and economic treatises was not their *métier*. All that Diego ever knew of Marx's writings or of Lenin's, as I had ample occasion to verify, was a little handful of commonplace slogans which had attained wide currency. Even if Diego and his fellow artists had wanted to study Lenin's works, they would not have found the more horrendous and dogmatic part of his doctrine available in Spanish, or French, or English, nor would they have understood its meaning without considerable effort. Indeed, specialists in political theory have learned to understand its meaning only with the benefit of hindsight.

Up to 1914, the doctrines of this ardent pedant of totally centralized, totally organized power, and total terror were rejected by every serious socialist leader, insofar as they themselves understood what Lenin was driving at. After 1907, the influence of Lenin's sect in Russia itself dwindled rapidly.

But in August, 1914, began four terrible years during which the crisis in European civilization manifested itself in total war

* In *Three Who Made a Revolution.*

without definite aims or visible limits. During those years, statesmen and generals treated their own people as human matériel to be expended in pursuit of undefined and unattainable objectives. Universal war so brutalized civilized man that it became possible to beguile him into fresh brutalities by the fury of his resentment against brutality. This it was which made Lenin's fantastic prescriptions for the waging of the class war ("kerosene rags to start fires; tacks for horses' hoofs; children and old people to pour acid and boiling water from roof tops") * seem less fantastic. Men no longer shuddered at his proposal to continue the endless world war by prolonging it into universal civil war. With whole nations under arms, his plans for the military discipline of his party and of society seemed less strange, too.

Before there could come what Churchill was to describe as the reign of "the bloody minded professors of the Kremlin," there first had to be the bloody mess of Flanders Field, of which no less a one than England's wartime leader, Lloyd George, would write: "Nothing could stop Haig's compulsion to send thousands and thousands to their death in the bovine and brutal game of attrition."

In Paris, Diego was a close witness of the secular crisis in European civilization, of which this century's first total war was striking evidence, and Communism and Nazi Fascism two characteristic by-products. Born in the trench psychology of the First World War, these twin isms with their paramilitary organizations turned the streets of every great European city into battlefields, destroyed the young democracies of Germany and Russia, then joined hands in the Stalin-Hitler Pact which engendered the Second World War. How could Diego and his fellow painters understand this when neither historians nor statesmen nor philosophers understood it?

* The same secret instructions of Lenin to his followers include the use of knives, brass knuckles, cudgels, bombs, the casing of banks for holdups, the killing of isolated policemen to get their weapons and many other such carefully thought out instructions. They are to be found in the Fourth Russian Edition of Lenin's Collected Works, Vol. IX, pp. 258-59, 315, 389-93.

All that painters and poets heard of Lenin's words and meanings was the echo of their own longing in their ears. "Since it was a time of horrors," they told themselves, "at least let violence have peace as its objective, and as its enemy the civilization that had made the sterile carnage possible." That Lenin meant to prolong the carnage into an all-inclusive and universal civil war was a fine point which escaped them. That he expected the time of violence to endure for an entire epoch until man had been remade in accordance with his blueprint and for that blueprint he had won the world, escaped them, too.

Above all, how could a Picasso or a Rivera imagine that the Lenin to whom they attributed their dreams of freedom was actually possessed by the dream of subjecting all forms of human activity, including those of the spirit, to the total control of state and party and dictator?

Only because Communist Parties did not conquer the lands in which they lived and painted, were Rivera and Picasso able to paint in such un-Communist fashion and continue to call themselves Communist painters. Because they remained outside the walls, each could paint according to his vision, which is the moral imperative of the artist. Rivera was expelled once, resigned once, was hectored and harassed, but since he lived in a country where the Communist Party did not possess a monopoly of power, neither expulsion nor condemnation was fatal. In 1927, before the mold constricting the arts in Russia had hardened, the relatively liberal Lunacharsky invited Diego to Moscow to do a mural. After the party bosses (Lunacharsky was not one of them) had seen Rivera's sketches and heard his views, the opportunity to paint on a public wall in Moscow was denied him.

Two years later, it was completely impossible for anyone with the esthetic sophistication of a Rivera or a Picasso, with their mastery of the officially condemned impressionist, cubist techniques, to paint in Russia at all. The Russian artists whom Diego had known in Paris, returning to their homeland to serve their people and the Revolution and enjoy its new freedoms, either fled again to the West, or were denied the right to be true to their own vision and esthetic conscience. Some ceased to paint; others were forced to debase their art to vulgarity and flattery; many ended in concentration camps.

Rivera and Picasso loved freedom and took the freedom to follow their own vision for granted. They never dreamt that in the modern world direct censorship of painting was possible. But under the Communist dispensation in Russia, to censorship by the powerful has been added total ownership and total control of all museums, all galleries, all institutions that might commission, purchase, or display one's painting. To censorship and total ownership has been added positive dictation to the painter of both theme and method of treatment. The writer's situation under totalitarianism was no better, for here, too, along with censorship and dictation of style and theme, the party controlled a monopoly of all journals, printing presses, and publishing houses, all bookstores and libraries, all reviews, and all reviewers. One can hide an occasional manuscript "for posterity," but where can one hide a stack of paintings or find a wall?

Unlike Picasso, Diego cherished the additional dream of painting for the people. In the Soviet Union, to be "accessible to the masses" meant painting to suit the tastes of a Stalin or a Khrushchev, and of their culture overseers, for the Party bosses claim to speak for the masses in the arts as in all other respects.

To Diego's credit be it said that he openly rejected the notion that the unformed taste of the esthetically illiterate masses should determine what and how a painter should paint. Though he did not emphasize the fact that he was opposing the Soviet dictators, his answer to them was direct and forthright:

> The workman, ever burdened with his daily labor, could cultivate his taste only in contact with the worst and vilest part of bourgeois art which reached him in cheap chromos and the illustrated papers. This bad taste in turn stamps all of the industrial products which his salary commands. . . .

Popular art produced by the people for the people has been almost wiped out by [an] industrial product of the worst esthetic quality. . . .

Only the work of art itself can raise the standard of taste . . .

This is clear enough, but when Diego said it in the Soviet Union it was not printed. When he got back to Mexico he made the same statement for an American art journal.

On another occasion, when he was in the United States and had gone to a gallery which prided itself on always following the *dernier cri*, Diego delivered himself of some judgments on spontaneous action painting," on painting which welled up from the "subconscious" without guidance from the conscious, and on painters who scorned to master their technique or to study the great inherited tradition of the past.

Do we have to discard all our modern technical means and deny the classic tradition of our *métier?* Just the contrary—it is the duty of the revolutionary artist to master and use his ultramodern technique. He must try to raise the level of taste of the masses, not debase himself to the level of unformed and impoverished taste. He must allow his classic training to affect him subconsciously while he sees with his trained eye and thinks with his trained hand. Only thus can he form of the masses an audience worthy of the best work of which he is capable. Only thus can he make their life more beautiful and joyous, nourish their sensibility, help great art to come out of the masses.

When I asked him what he thought of nonobjective art, he expressed admiration for such painters as Klee and Kandinsky, and, as always, for the restless experimentation of Picasso. But then he added:

The painter can and must abstract from many details in creating his painting. Every good composition is above all a work of abstraction. All good painters know this. But the painter cannot dispense with subject altogether without his work suffering impoverishment. The subject is to the painter what rails are to a locomotive. He cannot do without it. Only when the artist has selected a congenial subject appropriate to his purposes and attractive to him, is he free to create from it a thoroughly plastic form. A subject properly selected frees the painter for abstraction from it, yet guides him. When he refuses to seek a proper subject for his plastic experiments, don't think he is without a subject altogether. His own plastic methods and his own esthetic theories become his subject. He becomes nothing but an illustrator of his own state of mind, which is likely to be a smallish matter for painting. That is the secret of all the boredom which one feels from so many of the expositions of modern art.

If Diego managed to get back into the Communist Party in his old age, three years before his death, it was not because the Communists considered that he would be easy to manage. After so many wayward deeds and heretical pronouncements, they knew he would continue to be unmanageable. But they decided that "on balance" he was "useful." As with Picasso, many things have to be forgiven to "useful" artists working in the "bourgeois world" which would not be permitted to workers in the arts in the Soviet Union.

When a friend went to Picasso after one of the latter's pro-Communist gestures, to remind him of the fate of painters such as he in the Soviet Union, Picasso lost his temper. Then he grew silent and thoughtful and at last he said:

If they threw me into jail, I would sever an artery in my arm, and on the floor of my cell with my last drop of blood, I would paint one more Picasso.

A magnificent gesture! But some scrubwoman or warden would take care of the "last Picasso."

What then induces a Picasso or a Rivera—or, for that matter, a Siqueiros—to serve the Party which, if it takes power in his country, will make some Thorez or Fajon the arbiter of their painting? What makes such freedom-loving painters help a movement which, in power, would destroy the one freedom which matters most to an artist? To this question Karl Marx has no answer. Nor has Lenin, nor Stalin, nor Khrushchev. Perhaps Freud does though: he called it the death wish.

Near the end of his life, Diego said one day to Gladys March:

Looking back on my work today, I think the best I have done grew out of things deeply felt, the worst from a pride in mere talent.

A wise judgment. To "mere talent" I would add "mere cleverness."

If we look at Rivera's portraits of Marx and Engels, we see lifeless faces, clichés not men. Had Diego looked at his Marx portrait critically he would have used against it one of his favorite Paris epithets for hollow rhetoric in art: *pompier*. Nor are the various portraits he did of Lenin any more alive. Paradoxically, the benevolent, smiling Stalin Diego did in the *Peace Mural* is less endowed with vitality than the jovial face of John Foster Dulles in the Guatemala poster, whom he meant to lampoon. But the malevolent Stalin of the portrait which the painter called "the executioner of the Revolution" is completely alive, for in it the artist's intensest feelings were enlisted.*

On the ground floor of the Secretariat of Education Diego painted the labors and the festivals of his people. Despite a few lines of propaganda verse from Gutierrez Cruz and an occasional symbolic gesture, labor is not an object of exploitation or a subject of class struggle, but a rhythmic dance. There is great beauty in the *Trapiche* (Sugar Mill) with the graceful rhythm of bodies bending in the foreground to pour the juice of the cane, the veritable dance movement of the men in the center stirring the molasses with great poles, and the contrasting severe geometric perspective of ground and beams and pillars. What

* Picasso too had his difficulties when he tried to do a portrait of Stalin to honor "the greatest genius of all lands and times" on the latter's seventieth birthday. His portrait failed to satisfy either the great art experts of the French Communist Party or the Soviet dictator.

commands the eye in the *Entrance to the Mine* is the curve of vaulted arches and the curve of bent backs carrying straight beams. In *Waiting for the Harvest,* Indian women are grouped in tenderly treated little pyramids, as is an Indian man completey wraped in his *sarape* and tilted sombrero, the human forms echoed by the conical mountain peaks in the background against the Mexican sky. If, as Lenin wrote, "Class hatred is the prime mover of revolution," then clearly the man who painted these scenes informed with love of the common folk and love of the spectacle of their labor and the landscape in which it takes place is no Leninist.

Indeed, as we go through the vast body of painting by Rivera, it is hard to think of any passages of real anger and hatred. One finds neither the bombastic rhetoric so frequent in Siqueiros's social painting, nor the prophetic denunciation which at times moves Orozco. When Rivera strove hardest for such effects, what he achieved was sardonic laughter or mocking caricature. Only rarely, when he lost his remarkable control of his medium or tried to shout too loud, was he likely to degenerate into melodrama, as in the excessive number of what are intended to be piteous red wounds in the children strewn around the foreground of his Guatemala poster. Or the ludicrous, overliterary imprecation in his "scientific" portrait of the knock-kneed, chicken-breasted Cortés in his later painting. Rivera was not born to be a Savonarola in paint as Orozco was, nor a strident soap-box orator like Siqueiros.

On the stairway of the National Palace Diego painted a striking history of his country, and a pageant of *Mexico Yesterday, Today, and Tomorrow. Tomorrow,* it must be said, fares badly. It is presided over by an oversized, pompous, stiff-bearded Karl Marx, holding a scroll with some of his apothegms in one hand while with the other he points out to a bemused and far from bright-looking trio of Mexicans, a worker, peasant, and soldier, the Mexico of the future. The landscape he points to lacks the beauty possessed by so many of the landscapes in the upper reaches of Diego's frescoes; it is cluttered with a dam, a mine shaft, some smokestacks, a grove of fruit trees, and an observatory. It is more intellectual cliché than hope or dream. But when Diego got to Detroit, in the America not of tomorrow but of today, he fell in love with the beauty of the machines he saw, finding in them a design to delight the eye, even, as in his *Turbines* (FIG. 117), something of the voluptuous beauty generally associated with other painter's nudes.

In contrast to the drab Mexico of Tomorrow, the Mexico of Yesterday on the left wall of the Palace stairway, the Mexico of authochthonous Indian civilization before the Spaniard came, is lyrical in organization and in the treatment of its nameless figures, in the poetry of the arts and crafts of that vanished Golden Age, the graceful flowery wars, the idyllic landscape overhung by a personified and animated sun, presided over by three legendary incarnations of Quetzalcoatl. He rises out of a volcano as the feathered serpent in tongues of flame; he rides the sky in a serpentine boat; he presides, as Marx fails to on the opposite wall, over a group that forms a graceful circle around him, while with majesty, benevolence, and wisdom, he expounds the arts and crafts and imparts learning to men.

The landscape of the *Future*, does not loom large enough in Rivera's scheme to fill the right wall, the lower part being occupied by a spill-over from the *Mexico of Today*, a caricature of millionaires worshipfully watching a ticker tape, which feeds some of its profits to a trio of the Mexican military man, the politician, and the priest. But the Golden Age of Mexico's past cannot be completely contained on its single left wall. It spills over onto the lower part of the central wall to provide a magnificent spectacle of knights in armor battling Aztec warriors dressed in the barbaric-poetic dress of knights of the eagle and the tiger, opposing to the cold steel of the Spaniards wooden lances and swords tipped with obsidian.

This Golden Age may never have existed, or may have been

rude and barbarous and cruel, but no matter. Its temples and codices, its sculpture and remnants of poetry and artifacts, testify to the fact that it was a profoundly esthetic culture, more cruel and passionate and mythopoetic than logical and rational. It stirred the artist in Diego. He believed in it, idealized it, was moved by its real and imagined splendors. Wherever he has painted it, in Cuernavaca, on the stairway and later on a wall of the corridor of the National Palace, in the Hospital of the Race, his painting moves the beholder. Rivera's true Prometheus is not Marx but Quetzalcoatl. His golden age is not in the mine shafts, smokestacks, and observatory of the *Future* (in the real future the smokestacks will disappear), but in the morning splendors of the Golden Age that has vanished, insofar as it ever was, this painter of his country's epic has found his utopia.

From infancy, Diego drew and painted, early becoming one of those virtuosos of pencil and brush who could do what his eye and hand and mind and heart wanted to do. His draughtsmanship was superb; his artistic sensibility great; his capacity for work, almost until the very end, that of a tireless giant. Indeed, he was a monster of nature, a prodigy of fecundity, rapidity, and prodigality of creation. Such sheer fecundity occurs but rarely in the history of man. He is for painting and drawing what a Lope de Vega is for literature. Such men, by the ease and volume of their work, and by the excellence of so much of it, enlarge one's faith in the capacity of man.

If Diego had not been thus fruitful and overflowing, he would not be the painter we know, but another. His work might have gained in rigor and self-discipline; he might to the end of his days have set himself fresh plastic problems; but his work would have lost in opulence, in abounding vigor, in the insatiable appetite to embrace, to create, a world—on paper, on canvas, on walls.

If he was at times too complaisant with himself, if it was too fatally easy for him to paint well, and to repeat himself, yet he turned out more really good works in a year than many another painter, who has limited himself to a handful of paintings, in a lifetime. With unflagging energy and never idle pencil and brush he covered miles of canvas and paper and wall.*

Though much of his work is less than his best, there is little indeed which is lacking in skill. There are literally hundreds of paintings and drawings, along with a half-dozen or so of his great walls, which will take their place among the notable fruits of artistic creation.

When time has finished the task of selection which that amazing "biological urge" to create did not permit him to attempt, the "complete works" will reveal him as one of the most fecund of men of plastic talent, while his "selected works," I am convinced, will show him to have been at his best one of the most fruitful and sizable of geniuses.

He has had large aims and achieved them on a large scale. His total work from his thirty-sixth year on is undoubtedly the most ample, complete, and wide-ranging plastic portrait of Mexico. Indeed, I doubt if any other land has had so much of its life set down on wall and canvas by another painter.

Not alone, but surely in the forefront with a handful of others, Diego's work broke ground for the Mexican renaissance in painting and the contemporary revival of the art of fresco on the walls of public buildings. He took the issues and the aspirations of art from the studio to the street, made them a subject of newspaper headlines, parlor conversation, music-hall satire. Issues of esthetics became public issues.

What lives on his walls and in his sketches and paintings is the Mexico of his dream as seen by the gifted eyes of a painter of sharper vision than the normal. His eye and hand taught outsiders and Mexicans alike to see a Mexico which until then had escaped their vision. Who can any longer lift his eyes to

* Suzana Gamboa made a computation of the number of square meters he had covered on walls alone up to 1949 in *Diego Rivera: 50 Años de su Labor Artística* (Mexico, D.F., 1951), pp. 297-315. According to her mensuration the total surface painted up to that point was approximately 4 kilometers long by one meter deep (3,969.39 square meters), or about 2½ miles of painting one yard deep.

the mountains, behold the villages and the folk, without seeing everywhere "Riveras"? As long as his walls and paintings will endure, men will go back to them to delight the eye, to learn how this world was and how this painter saw it. The propaganda in his painting is already stale, as is the propaganda in Bertolt Brecht's *A Man Is a Man,* but Brecht's work will continue to be living theater as Rivera's will continue to be alive plastically, living a life that is rich and abundant. Then as now, no one could look at his work without having his vision sharpened, his sensibility intensified, his joy in the forms of the visible world increased, and his understanding of those forms deepened.

Neither the "decent folk," nor the "masses" whom he hoped to "nourish" esthetically, liked his frescoes. At first only artists, critics, a handful of Mexican intellectuals, and Communists hailed his work, the latter generally for reasons which had nothing to do with art.

"As a social person," Samuel Ramos once wrote, "Diego is democratic, but as an artist he possesses a distinction and a refined taste which separate him from the multitude." Yet even if their taste has not been "formed and nourished" as he had hoped, by the refinements in his art, the multitudes have become more aware of their world as seen through his eyes than before. The Mexican nation has come to regard him with pride, as they do the "ugly" plumed serpents and Aztec gods. At the very least, he has become a "national monument" like the pyramids and temples. But thereby, half unconsciously, the Mexican people has become more aware of itself and its heritage, and the rest of the continent more aware of Mexico.

Diego's composition began with dogmatic theories about geometrical structure, the "golden section" and "dynamic symmetry." As he painted tirelessly, thinking with his hand and the sophistication acquired by his search of the secrets of all the great works of Europe, of ancient Mexico, and of the cosmopolitan world of modern plastic sensibility, his construction of a painting became increasingly instinctive, freer, easier, with more play of delight in the wonders he saw everywhere. The geometric design remained a scaffolding, but flowing curves, echoing, repeating, and modifying themselves, gave his works more graceful and more abundant life. The baroque sensibility which is part of Mexico's precious heritage prevailed over severer theories of composition, baroque curve and opulent detail straining at the painting's structure, yet, as a rule, firmly contained by it.

It has been a fashion to deplore the folkloric, the decorative, the lovely, and the opulent in recent Mexican painting. Beauty is a word for the moment out of fashion. "I say we have had enough of pretty pictures of grinning peons in traditional Tehuana dress," Siqueiros rudely told the press in his last attack on Rivera less than two years before Diego's death. "I say, to hell with ox carts—let's see more tractors and bulldozers. Mexican art is suffering from primitivism and archaeologism."*

But the weakest passages in Rivera's painting are precisely his tractors and bulldozers, or their equivalent. Nor have tractors and bulldozers yielded any plastic beauty in the work of Siqueiros, not to speak of Orozco or Tamayo. The unfinished painting on the walls of the Chapultepec Palace, which, even unfinished as it is, seems to me the best of Siqueiros, is concerned not with tractors and bulldozers but with the epic of the Mexican agrarian revolution and masses of primitive peons on the march.

As for Rivera, the tenderest and most lyrical sections of his work are precisely those inspired by the love of his people, by the beauty of the Mexican landscape and the life of the Mexican folk, a life which, for all its misery and poverty, is the expression of a civilization more passionate and esthetic than rational in its quality. In his weavers and fishermen, in invaders climbing the branches of trees to cross a canyon, is neither the cruelty and brutality of war nor of exploitation, but the harmonious arabesque of a plastic dance. In the awkward grace of his Mexican children and the simple, elegant, abstracted curve of the back

* *New York Times*, Dec. 11, 1955.

of one of his burden-bearers, it is not poverty we see but the tenderness of the vision of a painter who loved his country and his people.

The world he finally idealized, as we have noted, was not the grim world of Communism, but the poetic world of pre-Columbian civilization as seen by his fantasy. The colors of that world are brighter, the forms more solid, the air flooded with a brighter light. Here is joy and beauty in labor, preternatural skill in primitive surgery and science, plastic splendor in the ceremonies of human sacrifice. The terrifyingly beautiful and monstrous gods and temples are free from the feeling of terror and somehow full of splendor. What can bulldozer and tractor offer to compete with this vision? Or with the beauty which Rivera sees in the disinherited, impoverished descendants of this splendid people, the simple Indians and Indian children of modern Mexico whom Rivera portrays with such tenderness and affection, and in whose name he claims their lost inheritance?

The last words in these notes should be given to Frida Kahlo, who knew Diego Rivera best, and knowing his weaknesses and experiencing his cruelties, yet gave him unstinting love as a person, and admiration as the great artist she saw in him.

> No words [she wrote] can describe the immense tenderness of Diego for the things which had beauty. . . . He especially loves the Indians . . . for their elegance, their beauty, and because they are the living flower of the cultural tradition of America. He loves children, all animals, especially the Mexican hairless dogs, and birds, plants and stones. His diversion is his work; he hates social gatherings and finds wonder in truly popular fiestas. . . . His capacity for energy breaks clocks and calendars. . . . In the midst of the torment which for him are watch and calendar, he tries to do and have done what he considers just in life: to work and create. . . .

Let these words be the painter's epitaph. And the starting point for the study of his life and work by the future biographer for whom these last random notes are written.

SELECTED BIBLIOGRAPHY

I. *Autobiographies.*

"Autobiografía," *El Arquitecto*, Mexico, March-April, 1926, pp. 1-36

Das Werk Diego Riveras, with an autobiographical introduction by the painter, Berlin, 1928, 70 p 50 il

Memoria y Razón de Diego Rivera, an autobiography dictated to Lolo de la Torriente, 2 vols. Mexico, 1959. il

My Life, My Art, an autobiography dictated to Gladys March, New York, 1960

Confesiones de Diego Rivera, by Luís Suárez, containing both comment by Suárez and material dictated by Rivera, Mexico, 1962, 192 p 15 il

II. *Books and Pamphlets by Rivera*

Portrait of America, by Diego Rivera and Bertram D. Wolfe, New York, 1934, 232 p 60 il

Amerikas Ansikte (translation of above), Stockholm, 1934

Portrait of Mexico, by Diego Rivera and Bertram D. Wolfe, New York, 1938, 211 p 249 il

Posada, Monograph with 406 engravings of José Guadalupe Posada, Introduction by Diego Rivera, Mexico, 1930

La Acción de los Ricos Yanquis y la Servidumbre del Obrero Mexicano. Mexico, 1923

Abraham Angel, Mexico, 1924

III. *Books and Monographs on Rivera*

Ancient Mexico, Three Murals of the National Palace, Mexico, n.d., with a text by the painter.

Architectural Forum, special edition devoted to the New Workers' School murals, two panels in color, rest in black and white, text by Diego Rivera and Andrés Sánchez Flores, Jan. 1934

Chávez, Ignacio, *Diego Rivera, sus Frescos en el Instituto Nacional de Cardiología*, Mexico, 1946, text in English and Spanish, 13 il

Edwards, Emily, *The Frescoes of Diego Rivera in Cuernavaca*, Mexico, 1932, 27 p il

Evans, Ernestine, *The Frescoes of Diego Rivera*, New York, 1929, 144 p 90 il

Frescoes in Chapingo by Diego Rivera, Mexican Art Series, No. 3, edited by Frances Toor with a text by Carlos Merida, Mexico, 1937

Frescoes in Ministry of Education, Mexican Art Series, No. 2

Frescoes in National Preparatory School, Mexican Art Series, No. 6

Frescoes in Palace of Fine Arts, Mexican Art Series, No. 8

Frescoes in Salubridad and Hotel Reforma, Mexican Art Series, No. 4 (all the Mexican Art Series have the same editor, text writer, and date)

Gual, Enrique F. *Cien Dibujos de Diego Rivera*, Mexico, 1949

Guido, Angel, *Diego Rivera: los Dos Diegos*, Rosario, Argentina, 1941

Guzmán, Martín Luís, *Diego Rivera y la Filosofía del Cubismo*, Mexico, 1916

Hanson, Anton and Rue, Harald, *Arbeiderkunst: Diego Rivera*, Copenhagen, 1932

Maceo y Arbeu, Eduardo, *Diego Rivera y el Pristinismo*, Mexico, 1921

Ramos, Samuel, *Diego Rivera*, Mexico, 1935

Diego Rivera: Acuarelas (1935-1945), 25 watercolors, 14 drawings, from the collection of Frida Kahlo, text by Samuel Ramos, Mexico, 1948

Diego Rivera (*stutsåld*), Stockholm, n.d., probably, 1934

Rodríguez, Antonio, *Diego Rivera,* Mexico, 1948
Secker, Hans F., *Diego Rivera,* Dresden, 1957, 283 il, 15 color
Weissing, H. L. P., *Diego Rivera,* Amsterdam, 1929
Wolfe, Bertram D., *Diego Rivera, His Life and Times,* New York and London, 1939, 420 p 174 il, 1 color, bibliography
Same in Spanish but badly translated, Santiago de Chile, 1941

IV. *Principal Museum Exhibitions and Catalogues*

California Palace of the Legion of Honor, *Diego Rivera,* Catalogue, San Francisco, 1930, 38 p 14 il
Detroit Institute of Arts, *Illustrated Guide to the Frescoes of Rivera,* texts by George Pierrot and Edgar P. Richardson, Detroit, 1934, 22 p 6 il
Minneapolis Institute of Arts, Bulletin, Minneapolis, 1933
Museum of Modern Art, *Diego Rivera,* New York 1931, biographical note by Frances Flynn Paine, text on style and technique by Jere Abbot, 64 p 75 il
———, *Frescoes of Diego Rivera,* text by Jere Abbott, New York, 1933, 15 il black and white, 19 color
Pan-American Union, *Diego Rivera Exhibit,* text by Bertram D. Wolfe, Washington, 1947, 33 p il
Pennsylvania Museum of Art, Bulletin, Philadelphia, 1932
Diego Rivera, The Story of His Mural at the 1946 Golden Gate International Exposition, San Francisco, 1940
San Francisco Museum of Art, *Diego Rivera, Drawings and Watercolors,* San Francisco, 1940, 31 p 12 il, text by Dr. Grace McCann Morley
Worcester Museum of Art, Bulletin, Worcester, Apr. 1928 and Jan. 1931
Diego Rivera 50 Años de su Labor Artística, Exposición de Homenaje Nacional, Museo Nacional de Artes Plásticas. Based on an exhibition in 1949, this big book, published in 1951, is a retrospective survey of his work by many writers, with great numbers of illustrations in black and white and in color from all periods, from childhood drawings up to work done in 1949, 468 p, checklist of 1196 works, bibliography

V. *Books and Articles Illustrated by Rivera*

Antología. Esta Semana en México (1935-1946), Mexico, 1946
Beals, Carleton, *Mexican Maze.* Philadelphia, 1931
Berliner, Isaac, *La Ciudad de los Palacios,* Poemas en Yiddish, Mexico, 1936
Brenner, Leah, "Moon Magic: A Story Based on the Boyhood of Diego Rivera," *The Virginia Quarterly,* Winter, 1945
Chase, Stuart, *Mexico: A Study of Two Americas,* New York, 1931
Convenciones de la Liga de Comunidades Agrarias de Tamaulipas, Mexico, Vol. I, 1926, 51 drawings; Vol. II, 1927, 42 drawings; Vol. III, 1928, 40 drawings
Forma, "Proyecto para un Teatro en un Puerto del Golfo, Mexico," Oct. 1926, 4 il
Fortune, New York, Covers and Illustrations in issues of Jan., 1931, Nov., 1932, Feb., 1933, Oct., 1938
Krasnaya Niva, Moscow, Mar. 17, 1928, cover
El Libertador, Mexico. Covers and illustrations in various issues in the later 1920's
Lopez y Fuentes, Gregorio, *El Indio,* Indianapolis, 1937
Ludwig, Emil, "Joseph Stalin," *Cosmopolitan Magazine,* New York, Sep., 1932
Marín, Guadalupe, *La Unica,* Mexico, 1928
Medioni, Gilbert y Pinto, Marie Thérese, *Art in Ancient Mexico,* New York, 1941 (Selected and photographed from the collection of pre-Hispanic art of Diego Rivera).
Mediz Bolio, Antonio, *La Tierra del Venado y el Faisán,* Mexico, 1935
Monde, Paris, Oct. 20, 1928 (cover)
Teja Zabre, Alfonso, *Guía de la Historia de México,* published in Spanish, English and French, illustrated with murals of Diego Rivera, Mexico, 1935
Velazquez Andrade, Manuel, *Fermín* and *Fermín Lee,* Mexico, 1927, textbooks illustrated by Rivera

VI. *Articles by Rivera*

"Architecture and Mural Painting," *Architectural Forum,* New York, Jan. 1934
"Art and the Worker," *Workers' Age,* New York, June 15, 1933
"Children's Drawings in Mexico," *Mexican Folkways,* Mexico, Dec-Jan 1926-27

"Dynamic Detroit," *Creative Art*, Apr 1933
"La Exposición de la Escuela Nacional de Bellas Artes," *Azulejos*, Mexico, Oct 1921
"From a Mexican Painter's Notebook," translated by Katherine Anne Porter, *Arts*, New York, Jan 1925
"Genius of America," Committee on Cultural Relations with Latin America, New York, 1931
"The Guild Spirit in Mexican Art," *Survey Graphic*, New York, May 1, 1924
"Los Judas," *Espacios*, Mexico, Spring, 1949
"Lo que opina Diego Rivera sobre la pintura revolucionaria," *Octubre*, Mexico, Oct 1935 and *Claridad*, Buenos Aires, Feb 1936
Manifesto: "Towards a Free Revolutionary Art," Diego Rivera and André Breton, *Partisan Review*, Autumn, 1938
"Mardonio Magaña," *Mexican Folkways*, Mexico, 1930, Vol. 6, No. 2
"Mardonio Magaña," *Espacios*, Mexico, Sept 1948
"María Izquierdo," *Mexican Life*, Mexico, Dec 1929
"Nationalism and Art," *Workers Age*, New York, June 15, 1933
"The New Mexican Architecture," *Mexican Folkways*, Oct-Nov 1926
"La Perspectiva Curvilinea," *El Universal Gráfico*, Mexico, Dec 1, 1934
"La Pintura Mexicana: El Retrato," *Mexican Folkways*, Feb-Mar 1926
"Pintura Mural y Arquitectura," *Arquitectura*, Havana, Sept 1939
"Position of the Artist in Russia Today," *Arts Weekly*, New York, Vol. 1, No. 1, March 1932
"Protesta contra el Vandalismo en la Destrucción de las Pinturas de Juan O'Gorman," *Clave*, Mexico, Dec 1938
"Pulquería Painting," *Mexican Folkways*, Mexico, Vol. 2, No. 2, 1926
"The Radio City Murals," *Workers' Age*, New York, Jun 15, 1933
"Retablos," *Mexican Folkways*, Mexico, Oct-Nov 1925
"Revolution in Painting," *Creative Art*, New York, Jan 1929
"The Revolutionary Spirit in Modern Art," *Modern Quarterly*, Baltimore, Autumn 1932
"The Stormy Petrel of American Art on His Art," *Studio*, London, Jul 1933
"Talla Directa," *Forma*, Mexico, Vol. I, No. 3, 1927
"Verdadera, Actual y Unica Expresión Pictória del Pueblo Mexicano," *La Sierra*, Lima, Peru, Sept 1927
"What is Art For?", *Modern Monthly*, New York, Jun 1933

VII. *Books, Articles, Catalogues Dealing in Part with Rivera*

Abreu Gómez, Ermilo, *Sala de Retratos*, Mexico, 1946

"Los Alumnos de los Tres Grandes," *Tiempo*, Mexico, Jun 27, 1947

American Federation of Arts, Catalogue of the Exposition of Mexican Arts, organized by the Carnegie Corporation, 1930 (a traveling exposition, 1930)

Art Institute of Chicago, International Exposition of Contemporary Prints for the Century of Progress, Chicago, 1934

"L'Art Vivant au Mexique," *L'Art Vivant*, Paris, Jan 1930, 85 p 100 il

"Berdecio, Roberto," Sobre la Crisis en la Pintura Social, *Espacios*, Mexico, Sep 1948

Brenner, Anita, *Idols behind Altars*, New York, 1929

"Bomb Beribboned," (Frida Kahlo), *Time*, New York, Nov 14, 1938

Camp, André, "Peinture Mexicaine, Reflet d'un Peuple," *Le Monde Illustré*, Paris, Aug 1948

Cardozo y Aragón, Luís, *La Nube y el Reloj: Pintura Mexicana Contemporanea*, Mexico, 1940, 372 p 135 il

Charlot, Jean, *Art from the Mayas to Disney*, New York, 1939, 285 p il

Charlot, Jean, *The Mexican Mural Renaissance, 1920-1925*, Yale University Press, New Haven, 1963

Cheney, Martha Chandler, *Modern Art in America*, New York, 1939

Cheney, Sheldon, The Story of Modern Art, New York, 1945

Coquiot, Gustave, *Les Independants, 1884-1920*, Paris, 1920

Cossío Villegas, Daniel, "La Pintura en Mexico," *Cuba Contemporanea*, Havana, Apr 1924

Cossío del Pomar, Felipe, *Neuvo Arte*, Mexico, 1939

———*La Rebelión de los Pintores*, Mexico, 1945

Craven, Thomas, Modern Art, New York, 1940

De la Encina, Juan, "Diálogo del Arte Mexicano," *Mañana*, Mexico, Sep 25, 1943

De La Torriente, Lolo, "Conversación con David Alfaro Siqueiros sobre la Pintura Mural Mexicana," *Cuadernos Americanos*, Mexico, Nov-Dec 1947

D'Harnarncourt, René, "The Exposition of Mexican Arts," *International Studio*, New York, Oct 1930, 5 il

———"Four Hundred Years of Mexican Art," *Art and Archaeology*, Washington, D.C., Mar 1932, 10 il

———"Loan Exhibition of Mexican Arts," *Bulletin of the Metropolitan Museum of Art*, New York, Oct 1930, 6 il

"Diego Rivera y José Clemente Orozco," *Tiempo*, Mexico, Nov 13, 1942
Faure, Elie, *Art Moderne*, Paris, 1921
———"La Peinture Murale Mexicaine," *Art et Medicine*, Paris, April 1934
Fernández, Justino, *El Arte Moderno en México*, Mexico, 1937, 473 p 6 il
———*Prometeo*, Mexico, 1945, 219 p il
———Sobre Pintura Mexicana Contemporanea. Mexico, 1949
García, Granados, Rafael, *Filias y Fobias: Opúsculos Históricos*, Mexico, 1937. Pages 15-35 deal with Rivera and Ambassador Morrow
Goldschmidt, Alfons, *Auf den Spuren der Azteken*, Berlin, 1927
Gómez de la Serna, Ramón, *Ismos*, Madrid, 1937, 386 p 72 il; pp 329-50, "Riverismo"
Gruening, Ernest, *Mexico and Its Heritage*, New York, 1928
Gutiérrez Abascal, Ricardo, *La Nueva Plástica*, Mexico, 1942
Helm, Mackinley, *Modern Mexican Painters*, New York, 1941, 205 p, 95 il
Lewisohn, Sam A., *Painters and Personality*, New York, 1937
Maillefert, E. G. "La Peinture Mexicaine Contemporaine," *L'Art Vivant*, Paris, Jan 15, 1930
Michel, André, *Histoire de l'Art*, Paris, 1929
Moreno Villa, José, *Lo Mexicano en las Artes Plásticas*, Mexico, 1948
Museum of Modern Art, various catalogues.
Pach, Walter, *Ananias, or the False Artist*, New York, 1928
———*Queer Thing, Painting*, New York, 1938
"Paintings by Two Artists, the Diego Riveras," *Art and Decoration*, New York, Aug 1933
Payro, Julio E. *Pintura Moderna*, Buenos Aires, 1942, 106 p
Philadelphia Museum of Art, *Mexican Art Today*, Philadelphia, 1943, 104 p 83 il
Pijoan, José, *Art in the Modern World*, Chicago, 1940
Plaut, James L. "Mexican Maxim," *Art News*, Dec 15-31, 1941
Robinson, Ione, "Fresco Painting in Mexico," *California Arts and Architecture*, Los Angeles, Jun 1932
Salazar, Rosendo, *México en Pensamiento y Acción*, Mexico, 1926
Salmon, André, *L'Art Vivant*, Paris, 1920
Schmeckebier, Laurence E., *Modern Mexican Art*, Minneapolis, 1939
Siqueiros, David Alfaro, *No hay más Ruta que la Nuestra*, Mexico, 1945, 127 p
Vasconcelos, José, *El Desastre*, Mexico, 1938
———*Estética*, Mexico, 1936

Velazquez Chavez, Agustín, Contemporary Mexican Artists, New York, 1937
Venturi, Lionello, *Pittura Contemporanea,* Milan, 1948
Villaurrutia, Xavier, *La Pintura Mexicana Moderna,* Barcelona, 1936
Zigrosser, Carl, "Mexican Graphic Art," *Print Collector's Quarterly,* London, Vol. 23, No. 1, 1936

VIII. *Selected Articles on Rivera*

Alden, S. "Further Query: Reply to Men, Machines and Murals," *American Magazine of Art,* New York, Jun 1933
Allen, Harris C. "Art to the Rescue of the Tired Business Man," *California Arts and Architecture,* Los Angeles, Dec 1931 (On the San Francisco Stock Exchange Murals)
Amabilis, Manuel, "La Obra de Diego Rivera," *El Arquitecto,* Mexico, Sep 1935
American Architect, New York, 1935
"An Artist's America," *Argus,* Melbourne, Australia, Jul 15, 1935
"Archbishop vs Rivera," *Newsweek,* New York, Jun 14, 1948
"Art and the Capitalist," *North China Daily News,* Jun 11, 1935
"Art for Propaganda's Sake" New Republic, New York, May 24, 1933
"Artist in Difficulties," *Commonweal,* New York, Dec 11, 1936
"The Art of Diego Rivera," *Survey,* New York, Oct 1, 1928
Barry, John D. "Characteristics of Rivera," *Stained Glass Association Bulletin,* 1931
Blunt, Anthony, "The Art of Diego Rivera," *Listener,* London, Apr 17, 1935
Born, Ernest, "Diego Rivera," *Architectural Forum,* New York, Jan 1934
Craven, Thomas, "Diego Rivera, Mexican in the United States," New York Herald Tribune, May 6, 1934
"Diego Rivera," *De Vlam,* Amsterdam, Jun 8, 1948
"Diego Rivera, Artist of the People," *Pictorial Review,* New York, Oct 1933
"Diego Rivera's Mural in Rockefeller Center Rejected," *Newsweek,* New York, May 20, 1933
"Diego Rivera Murals in the California School of Fine Arts," *Creative Art,* New York, Jan 1932
"Diego Rivera's Portrait of America," *Connoisseur,* New York, Jun 1935
"Diego Rivera, Raphael of Communism," *Creative Art,* New York, Jul 1930

Dos Passos, John, "Diego Rivera Murals," *New Masses,* New York, Mar 1927
"Einstein on Rivera," *Worker's Age,* New York, Mar 15, 1934
Erskine, John, "A Defense of the Murals of Rivera," *Art News,* New York, March 3, 1934
"Evolution of a Rivera Fresco," Interview with Mrs. Sigmund Stern concerning the fresco in her home, *California Arts and Architecture,* Los Angeles, Jun 1932
Frankfurter, A. M. "Diego Rivera," *Fine Arts,* New York, Jun 1933
García Maroto, Gabriel, "La Obra de Diego Rivera," *Contemporaneos,* Mexico, June 1928
Gómez Morín, Manuel, "Los Frescos de Diego Rivera," *Antorcha,* Mexico, Feb 14, 1925
Gregory, Horace, "Texts and Murals," *New Republic,* New York, Mar 7 1934
Hastings, John, "Renaissance in Mexico," *Architectural Record,* London, Aug 1935
Hellman, Geoffrey T. "Profiles: Enfant Terrible," *New Yorker,* New York, May 20, 1933
"H P, 25 Designs for Ballet," *Theatre Arts,* New York, Vol. 16, No. 4, 1932.
Johansson, Gothard, "Världens Störste Muralmålere, *Svenska Dagbladet,* Stockholm, Jan 20, 1935
Kahlo, Frida, "Retrato de Diego," *Hoy,* Mexico, Jan 22, 1949
Mather, Frank Jewett, "Rivera's American Murals," *Saturday Review of Literature,* New York, May 19, 1934
Monroe, Harriet, "Mexico: Murals at Chapingo," *Poetry,* Chicago, May 1933
"The New Rivera Frescoes in San Francisco," *London Studio,* Apr 1932
"Notice Biographique et Bibliographique" *L'Amour de l'Art,* Paris, Nov 1934
"On the Mexican Question: Concerning the Case of Comrade Diego Rivera," *Socialist Appeal,* New York, Oct 22, 1932
Pach, Walter, "The Evolution of Diego Rivera," *Creative Art,* New York, Jan 1920, 19 pp 9 il
"A Passionate Artist," *Manchester Guardian,* Mar 27, 1935
Poore, Charles G. "The American Murals and Battles of Diego Rivera," *New York Times,* May 13, 1934
———Rivera's Pageant of Mexico," *New York Times,* Apr 11, 1937
Richardson, Edgar P. "Diego Rivera, *Bulletin of the Detroit Institute of Arts,* March 1931

"Rivera's Detroit Murals," *Fortune,* New York, 9 il, 6 color
"Rivera Builds Secret Temple for Ancient Mexican Art," *Look,* New York, Mar 1, 1949, 8 il
Rohl, John, "Guadalupe Marín en la Obra de Diego Rivera," *El Nacional,* Caracas, Sep 14, 1947
Rosenfeld, Paul, "Rivera Exhibition," *New Republic,* New York, Jan 6, 1932
Southhall, Joseph, "An Artist of Revolt," *The Friend,* London, Jun 7, 1935
"Sunday in the Park: Murals of the Hotel del Prado," *Time,* New York, Oct 6, 1947
Ugarte, Juan Manuel, "Diego Rivera y su Expresión del Arte," *Claridad,* Buenos Aires, Dec 1937
Villaurrutia, Xavier, "Historia de Diego Rivera," *Forma,* Mexico, Vol. 1, No. 5, 29 il
———"Los Niños en la Pintura de Diego Rivera," *Hoy,* Mexico, Nov 16, 1940
"Walls and Ethics: Has the Owner of a Work of Art the Right to Destroy It?" *Art Digest,* New York, Mar 1, 1934
Werbik, Adolf, "Diego Rivera," *Thieme-Becker Künstlerlexikon,* Leipzig, 1934.
Wiegand, Charmion von, "Portrait of an Artist," *New Masses,* New York, Apr 27, 1937
"Will Detroit Whitewash Its Rivera Murals?" *Art Digest,* New York, Apr 1, 1933
Wilson, Edmund, "Detroit Paradoxes," *New Republic,* New York, Jul 12, 1933
Wolfe, Bertram D. "Art and Revolution in Mexico," *Nation,* New York, Aug 27, 1924, 4 il
———"Diego Rivera on Trial," *Modern Monthly,* New York, Jul 1934
———"Rise of a New Rivera" (Frida Kahlo), *Vogue,* New York, Oct 1938
———"The Strange Case of Diego Rivera," *Arts,* New York, Jan 1, 1955
Youtz, Philip N., "Diego Rivera," *Bulletin of the Pennsylvania Museum of Art,* Philadelphia, Feb 1932
Smith, Robert C. and Wilder, Elizabeth, *A Guide to the Art of Latin America,* Bibliography, Washington, D.C. Library of Congress, 1948

INDEX

About the Author

Bertram D. Wolfe's last major work of biography and history was *Three Who Made a Revolution,* which Edmund Wilson called "the best book in its field in any language." Born in Brooklyn in 1896, Wolfe lived in Rivera's Mexico for many years and knew the painter well from 1922 until Rivera's death in 1957. He co-authored two books with Diego Rivera, *Portrait of Mexico* and *Portrait of America,* and in 1939 published an earlier biography of Rivera which he discusses in the introduction to the present work. Wolfe is the author of *Communist Totalitarianism* and *Khrushchev and Stalin's Ghost.* For four years he served as Chief of the Ideological Advisory Staff of the State Department and the Voice of America. He has lectured, among other places, at Harvard, Columbia, Johns Hopkins, the Universities of Carolina (North and South), Oxford, and Geneva. He was Visiting Lecturer in Spanish Culture at Stanford and Distinguished Visiting Professor of Russian History at the University of California, from which he received an honorary doctorate. Mr. Wolfe received three Guggenheim Fellowships. His shorter writings appeared in *Harper's, Foreign Affairs, American Heritage, Life, The New Leader,* and dozens of scholarly journals. Bertram Wolfe's books have been translated into sixteen languages. Mr. Wolfe died in 1977.